Letters of Sir George Etherege

LETTERS OF
SIR GEORGE ETHEREGE

Edited by

FREDERICK BRACHER

UNIVERSITY OF CALIFORNIA PRESS

BERKELEY, LOS ANGELES, LONDON

University of California Press
Berkeley and Los Angeles, California

University of California Press, Ltd.
London, England

CONTENTS

ACKNOWLEDGMENTS

Professor John Harold Wilson of Ohio State University and Dr. Ludwig Hammermeyer of Munich have been most generous in supplying me with information from their files, and I have profited from Sybil Rosenfeld's *Letterbook* and her direct assistance. Professor David M. Vieth of Southern Illinois University provided invaluable criticism of and additions to the annotation. Godfrey Martin of Wembley, England gave me a copy of an Etherege family tree prepared by his father.

I am obligated also to the Rev. William James Anderson of the Scottish Catholic Archive in Edinburgh; Father Mark Dilworth, OSB, Fort Augustus, Scotland; B. C. Jones, Archivist at Carlisle, England; Dr. Conrad Swan, York Herald of Arms; and Walter Zacharias of Regensburg, West Germany. For assistance of various kinds I am indebted to Professors Stephen B. Baxter of the University of North Carolina; Hans-Dieter Brueckner, Godfrey Evans, and Phyllis Johnson of Pomona College; David F. George of Howard University; Stephen Glass of Pitzer College; Robert Halsband of the University of California; and H. H. R. Love of Monash University, Victoria, Australia.

I am especially grateful to my two research assistants, Julie Anne Byars and Anne Woltmann McCammon, whose aid was made possible by a generous research grant from Pomona College. Travel grants from the American Council of Learned Societies and from Pomona College enabled me to complete the project. Transcripts of Crown copyright records in the Public Record Office appear by permission of the Controller of H.M. Stationery Office. I am indebted to the Trustees of the British Museum, to the Houghton Library of Harvard University, and to Sir Fergus Graham, Bart., KBE, TD, JP, Netherby, Longtown, Cumberland, for permission to print manuscript material.

FREQUENTLY CITED WORKS

BM	British Museum Add. MS. 11513.
Brett-Smith, *Works*	*The Dramatic Works of Sir George Etherege,* ed. H. F. B. Brett-Smith. 2 vols. Oxford, 1927.
CSPD	*Calendar of State Papers, Domestic Series.*
CTB	*Calendar of Treasury Books.*
H-1 and H-2	Houghton Library (Harvard) fMS Thr. 11 and 11.1.
HLB	Frederick Bracher, "Sir George Etherege and His Secretary." *Harvard Library Bulletin,* 15 (1967), 331–344.
HMC *Downshire,* or other short title	Historical Manuscripts Commission. *Calendar of the MSS of the Marquis of Downshire (or other).*
LB	*The Letterbook of Sir George Etherege,* ed. Sybil Rosenfeld. London, 1927.
Luttrell	Narcissus Luttrell. *A Brief Historical Relation of State Affairs* . . . . 6 vols. Oxford, 1857.
M-1 and M-2	The Middleton Papers, BM Add. MSS. 41836, 41837.
Repertorium	F. Hausmann. *Repertorium der Diplomatischen Vertreter aller Länder.* Berlin, 1936. Vol. I.
RES	*Review of English Studies*
Thorpe, *Poems*	*The Poems of Sir George Etherege,* ed. James Thorpe. Princeton, 1963.
Urkunden	*Urkunden und Actenstücke zur Geschichte des Kurfürsten Friedrich Wilhelm von Brandenburg.* 23 vols. Berlin, 1864–1930.
V&A Dyce MS 43	Odes, Songs and Satyrs in the Reign of Charles II. Victoria and Albert Museum Library, Dyce MS #43.

Vieth, *Attribution*

David M. Vieth. *Attribution in Restoration Poetry.* Yale Studies in English, Vol. 153, New Haven, 1963.

Wilson, *Court Wits*

John Harold Wilson. *The Court Wits of the Restoration.* Princeton, 1948.

INTRODUCTION

The surviving letters of Sir George Etherege are the only considerable body of personal correspondence by a Restoration dramatist, courtier, and wit. Though the other Restoration playwrights may have written as frequently and as frankly as Etherege, little of their correspondence has been preserved. Dryden is best represented, with seventy-five surviving letters, but there are only a handful from Wycherley, Congreve, and Shadwell, and Vanbrugh's more numerous letters are mainly about the building of Blenheim Palace. From Etherege we have more than 400 letters, and fewer than half of these have up until now been printed.

From November 1685 to January 1689, Etherege was the British "Resident" [1] at the Diet of the Holy Roman Empire at Ratisbon (now Regensburg, Bavaria). As a diplomat he was required to write regularly to Whitehall, and much of his official correspondence and a number of personal letters have been preserved. The latter are continually harking back to the great days of Etherege's career in the theater—that halcyon period when the King attended the opening performance of *The Man of Mode* and there seemed to be no end to the stream of ambitious actresses and amiable court ladies who visited his Bow Street lodgings. Etherege's nostalgic picture of his past and candid account of his life in Ratisbon provide a vivid and authentic self-portrait of a writer on the fringes of the Restoration court.

A manuscript letterbook in the British Museum (Add. MS. 11513) contains copies of about 180 letters written from Ratisbon. These were edited in 1927 by Sybil Rosenfeld as *The Letterbook of Sir George Etherege*. In addition, two volumes of holograph letters form part of the Middleton Papers in the British Museum (Add. MSS. 41836 and 41837, referred to hereafter as M-1 and M-2). Catalogued too late for inclusion in Miss Rosenfeld's edition, the volumes have been briefly described by her in *Review of English Studies*, 10 (1934), 177–189.

---

[1] This was the lowest rank in the diplomatic hierarchy. Etherege was, as he frequently complained, "without a Character"—that is, an observer only, ineligible to treat officially with the other envoys at the Diet.

They include 55 letters earlier or later than the period covered in the British Museum (BM) letterbook—November 29, 1685, to March 11, 1688—and 134 letters written during that period but not copied into the letterbook. The holograph letters are addressed mainly to the Earl of Middleton[2] or his secretary, and they are of course the most reliable of the sources. None of the personal letters appears in this collection, though many official letters contain bits of personal news or comment. The last letter in M-2 is dated "18/28 October, 1688," the time when Middleton succeeded the Earl of Sunderland[3] as Secretary of State for the Southern Department.

Two letterbooks now in the Houghton Library at Harvard (fMS Thr. 11 and fMS Thr. 11.1, hereafter referred to as H-1 and H-2) constitute the only other major source of Etherege letters.[4] H-2 was briefly described by Miss Rosenfeld in 1952 in *Review of English Studies*. In March 1685,[5] Etherege's secretary Hugo Hughes[6] began to copy most of Sir George's diplomatic dispatches and some of his

[2] Charles, 2nd Earl of Middleton (1640–1719), was from 1684 to 1688 Secretary of State for the Northern Department, which included Holland and the Empire. While Resident at Ratisbon, Etherege wrote to him or his secretary two or three times a week. When James II went into exile in France, Middleton remained loyal. He joined James at St. Germain in 1693 and became Secretary of State in exile.

[3] Robert Spencer, 2nd Earl of Sunderland (1640–1702), became Principal Secretary of State in 1684 and President of the Council in 1686. He was dismissed from both offices on October 27, 1688, and fled to Rotterdam, but under William III he once more rose to power. Etherege believed he owed his post as Resident to Sunderland.

[4] In addition to these, three holograph letters to the Earl of Sunderland are in the Public Record Office: State Papers (German States) 81, #86. Thirteen holograph letters to Sir William Trumbull have been deposited in the Berkshire Record Office at Reading, but their owner, Lord Downshire, will not permit them to be copied, though they are available for study. They have been printed, slightly abridged, in HMC *Downshire*, 1, and I have used this as a source. Nothing significant has been omitted by the abridgment. A recently discovered letterbook at the Library of the University of Birmingham is a careless copy, by unknown scribes, of most of the British Museum letterbook. It is valueless as a source. Some Etherege letters are referred to in HMC *First Report*, 1870, p. 56, as part of the "Papers belonging to T.E.P. Lefroy, Esq." This collection, the correspondence of Sir Richard Bulstrode, was broken up and sold to a number of buyers at Sotheby's on May 3 and 4, 1889, and I have been unable to trace the letters.

[5] Except for one earlier letter dated "30 Nov./10 Dec. 85."

[6] For Hughes' character and career, see my "Sir George Etherege and His Secretary," *Harvard Library Bulletin*, 15 (1967), 331–344.

personal letters into H-1 and H-2. These letterbooks were the official record of Etherege's correspondence. Letters which were not copied in full were frequently summarized, and many lost letters were listed by date and addressee. Hughes maintained H-2 until Etherege's departure for France in 1689, and thus included many letters of a later date than those in any other source. The concluding list (by date and addressee) of 29 letters written from Paris between February 20 and September 28, 1689, proves that Etherege took H-1 and H-2 with him to France. Corrections in Etherege's hand are frequent, and the Harvard letterbooks must hence be considered as second in authority only to the holograph letters in M-1 and M-2.

Hughes's errors in transcribing[7] show that the BM letterbook edited by Miss Rosenfeld is a copy of parts of H-1. However, the letterbook contains copies of a number of personal letters not found elsewhere, though many of them are listed in H-1. It also contains unique evidence that Hughes, a fervent Whig and censorious Puritan, hated his master's libertine ethic and royalist sympathies. A scurrilous verse attack on Etherege in wretched Hudibrastic couplets is matched by four long and malicious letters from Hughes to an unidentified "Honoured Sir" in England. These attack both Sir George's private life and his performance as a diplomat. The inclusion of this material shows that BM was not meant for Etherege's eyes, and certain entries added after Sir George's departure for Paris prove that Hughes kept the BM letterbook with him in Ratisbon. I have attempted to show elsewhere[8] that Hughes was in league with the English Whigs who were hoping to displace James II and with those Hollanders who were plotting to put William of Orange on the throne of England. This secret copy of part of the official letterbook was probably a means of revealing Etherege's diplomatic dispatches to the enemies of James II in England and Holland. It also may have been intended to discredit Etherege in London. Though it is only a copy of a copy, the BM letterbook is invaluable as the only source for many of the letters to Etherege's friends, but it is the least reliable of the three main sources.

Although the general outline of Etherege's life is clear, actual records are relatively scanty. For concrete details we are dependent on indirect sources, mainly records of law suits, and on inferences from incidental allusion in satires and letters of the period. Bits and

[7] Frederick Bracher, "The Letterbooks of Sir George Etherege," *Harvard Library Bulletin*, 15 (1967), 240–241.
[8] Ibid., pp. 331–344.

pieces to fill out the admirable sketch in H. F. B. Brett-Smith's edition of the *Works* have appeared in scattered articles over the past forty years. I bring them together here, combined with the results of my research.

The name George Etherege recurs frequently in the genealogy of the family[9] from 1520 on, and particularly in two branches, one centered at Thame and Oxford (which produced the Dr. George Etherege who became Regius Professor of Greek at Oxford in 1553), the other (from which Sir George was descended) at London and Maidenhead. Etherege's grandfather, "George Etherege, gent." (1576–1658), was a prosperous vintner and a shareholder in the Virginia and the Bermuda companies.[10] He moved from the parish of St. Clement Danes, London to Bray parish, Maidenhead sometime after February 1628.[11] His son, known as Captain George Etherege (1607–1650), was sent as a young man to look after his father's shares of land, amounting to 98 acres, in Paget's Tribe, Bermuda.[12]

In 1634 Captain George returned to England and married the daughter of Richard Powney, Gent., of Maidenhead. The parish records of Bray church during this period have been destroyed, but the bishop's transcript, now in the Diocesan Library at Salisbury Cathedral, records that "George Etheredge, gent and Mary Powney were Married on October the 7th day" in 1634. Nine months later, in July 1635, a daughter, Ann Etherege, was christened. The edge of the transcript is torn at this point, so that the actual day of the month is missing, and this entry, unfortunately, is the last in the remaining fragment. But it proves that Sir George, though the oldest son, was not the oldest of the seven children born to George and Mary Etherege[13] and that he could not have been born before the summer of 1636, the year cited by Oldys in *Biographia Britannica*.

In that same year, Captain George was able, by putting together £300 from his father and £300 from his wife's dowry, to purchase a place at Court "worth about two hundred pounds per annum before the troubles"—the office of purveyor to Queen Henrietta Maria.[14]

---

[9] An annotated family tree prepared in 1965 by Geoffrey Martin, a descendant of the family, has been given to the Houghton Library.

[10] Dorothy Foster, "Concerning the Grandfather and Father of Sir George Etherege," *Notes and Queries*, 12th Series, 10 (1922), 341, 343.

[11] Foster, "Sir George Etherege: Collections," *N&Q*, 153 (1927), 417.

[12] Foster, *TLS*, May 31, 1928, p. 412.

[13] Deposition of his mother at a trial quoted in Foster, *N&Q*, 153 (1927), 437.

[14] Eleanore Boswell, "Sir George Etherege," *Review of English Studies*, 7 (1931), 207; Foster, *RES*, 8 (1932), 459.

When the Queen escaped to France in 1644, Captain George probably followed her into exile. The 8th Interrogatory at a trial in 1657 asks, clearly expecting an affirmative answer, "whether George Etherege the elder [Grandfather Etherege] bought, for £300, the office of purveyor to the late Queen for his elder son Captain George, and whether that son enjoyed the office during his life?" [15] If so, he must have followed the Queen to France, since he died there in 1650.[16] His absence from England would explain the testimony of several witnesses that Grandfather Etherege had had to support his son's wife and children, "att greate cost and chardges, ever since their Father's decease and for many years before." [17] Looking back nostalgically from Ratisbon, Sir George remembered Christmas time in his grandfather's household and the drinking of holiday plum broth by an old servant "whose onely grace all the good time was God love me as I love Plum pottage." [18]

The tradition that young George Etherege, along with Anthony à Wood, attended the Lord William's Grammar School at Thame[19] cannot be substantiated. A passage in a letter to Sir William Trumbull (December 18, 1685) suggests that Etherege had had some experience of school life: "The Diet breaks up as formally as a great school before Christmas"; but the early records of the school at Thame have not been preserved, and it seems almost certain that, if Etherege had been there with Anthony à Wood, his name would have been included in Wood's list[20] of members of the school who later became famous. Probably Lee and others were misled by the number of Ethereges from the Thame branch of the family who did attend the school and who carved the family name on the oaken desks.

Wherever he received it, Sir George had a fairly good education. The letters show that he was well read, especially in the English poets, and despite Dennis's flat statement that Etherege "understood neither Greek nor Latin," [21] his letters contain a number of quotations from Horace in the original. Certainly he read and wrote French with ease. If it could be confirmed, Oldys' conjecture that he "travelled into

[15] Boswell, *loc. cit.*

[16] Foster, *N&Q*, 153 (1927), 437, quoting PRO Chancery Depositions: Hamilton 245/38. Miss Foster corrected the date from 1649 to 1650 in *RES*, 8 (1932), 459.

[17] Testimony of Grace Luckins, PRO: C 24/811/33.

[18] See below, p. 163.

[19] F. H. Lee, *History . . . of the Prebendal Church . . . of Thame*, London, 1883, pp. 528–529; John Howard Brown and W. Guest, *History of Thame*, Thame, 1935, p. 112.

[20] Bodleian MS Wood D. 11, f. 172.

[21] Brett-Smith, *Works*, 1, p. xiv.

France, and perhaps Flanders also, in his younger years" would explain Etherege's facility with that language. Sir George's father was certainly in France in, and probably for some years preceding, 1650. He might well have had with him his oldest son, then 12 or 13, especially since many schools, like Lord William's at Thame, had been badly disorganized by the fighting during the Civil Wars.[22] But I can find no real evidence.

In 1654 Etherege was apprenticed to George Gosnold, an attorney at Beaconsfield,[23] and he was still an articled clerk to Gosnold in August 1658.[24] In June 1659, he went to London with his solicitors to hear a Master of the Court of Chancery direct that his uncle should post a bond securing the nephew's right to lands inherited from Grandfather Etherege.[25] Then there is no record until the winter of 1663–64,[26] when Mr. George Etherege in London was carrying on a bawdy verse correspondence with a friend in the country, Lord Buckhurst, to whom he dedicated his first play, *The Comical Revenge*, in 1664. By the time of his second play, *She Wou'd if She Cou'd* (1668), Etherege was a recognized member of the circle of courtiers and wits which included Sir Charles Sedley and the Earl of Rochester. In his account of the opening of *She Wou'd if She Cou'd*, Pepys[27] adds an even more eminent name to the list of Etherege's friends, the Duke of Buckingham; and by 1676 Etherege was in the service of Mary of Modena, Duchess of York,[28] who held him, according to Gildon, "in particular esteem." Etherege's well-deserved reputation for grace and wit may be a sufficient explanation for his advancement, but one wishes there were evidence to explain how the country lawyer's clerk managed his original entrée to the Court circle.

The success of his first two plays enhanced Etherege's standing among the Wits, and his favor at Court is indicated by his being made a Gentleman of the Privy Chamber in Ordinary in 1668.[29] His first experience of diplomacy came in the same year. As secretary to the Ambassador, Sir Daniel Harvey, Etherege went to Constantinople,

[22] John Howard Brown, *History of Thame School*, Thame, 1873, pp. 86–88.
[23] Foster, *N&Q*, 153 (1927) 435, 438; *RES*, 8 (1932), 458.
[24] Boswell, *RES*, 7 (1931), 207.
[25] Foster, *N&Q*, 153 (1927), 439–440.
[26] Thorpe, *Poems*, pp. 109–111.
[27] *Diary*, February 6, 1668.
[28] Dedication of *The Man of Mode*: "To her Royal Highness, the Duchess. . . . I hope the honor I have of belonging to you will excuse my presumption."
[29] Boswell, *RES*, 7 (1931), 209.

from which capital he sent in 1670 the first of his extant letters—a vivid and remarkably astute account of the Turkish court.[30] When he returned to London in the fall of 1671, after a merry stop in Paris,[31] he resumed a life of dissipated idleness. An abortive duel "within the rayles of Covent Garden" [32] which ended when Etherege's opponent fell down and a tavern squabble with Henry Bulkeley[33] in the course of which Fleetwood Shepherd,[34] attempting to separate them, "was runn with a sword under the eye" [35] are recorded. More serious was his part in the notorious scouring of the watch at Epsom, when a Mr. Downs was badly wounded because of the Earl of Rochester's readiness to run away from the violence his ugly temper had brought on. Etherege and the others, who had been tossing a fiddler in a blanket and defying the watch, were in Andrew Marvell's words[36] left "exposed and the Rusticks animadverted so severely upon them that Downs is since dead and the Crowner has found it Murther." [37] This was in 1676, the same year that saw the production of Etherege's last and best play, *The Man of Mode, or Sir Fopling Flutter*.

Between 1677 and 1679 Etherege was knighted [38] and married, presumably in that order, since contemporary gossip had it that Etherege was given the knighthood so that he might marry his "rich old widow," Mary Sheppard Arnold.[39] Just how rich she was is not known, but she was a daughter of a London merchant, John Sheppard, and from him she inherited £100 and half of his goods and household stuffs. From her first husband, Edmund Arnold, she inherited £600 in money, all the plate and household goods, and £240 annually in rents and profits from the Manor of Furthoe in Northamptonshire.[40] On Novem-

[30] Thomas Fujimura, "Etherege at Constantinople," *PMLA*, 62 (1956), 465 f.

[31] Brett-Smith, *Works*, 1, p. xx.

[32] HMC *Bath*, 2, pp. 152–153. E's opponent was Edmund Ashton. See p. 113n.

[33] A bellicose young Guards officer (Wilson, *Court Wits*, p. 208).

[34] Shepherd (1634–1698), a minor poet, was gentleman steward to Lord Buckhurst.

[35] HMC *Bath*, 2, p. 160.

[36] *Letters*, ed. Margoliouth, Oxford, 1967, 2, p. 322.

[37] A fuller account of the affair is in the *Hatton Correspondence*, 1878, 1, pp. 133–134.

[38] Dr. Conrad Swan, York Herald of Arms, has informed me that the College of Arms has no official record of either the knighthood or armorial bearings granted to the family. But records during the reign of Charles II were carelessly kept.

[39] J. W. Nichols, "Dame Mary Etherege," *Modern Language Notes*, 64 (1949), 422.

[40] PRO: Prob 11/352 (1675–76).

ber 9, 1677, Dame Mary, still a widow, was able to lend £300 to one John Rowley, who assigned as security two parcels of land in Westminster worth £230 a year.[41] The recovery of this land, probably much increased in value, was the purpose of the suit against West and Barbone, begun by Sir George and Lady Etherege in 1687 and frequently mentioned in the letters.

In 1683, according to Thomas Wood's *Juvenalis Redivivum* (p. 17), Etherege was squandering "Grannum's old gold" on cards and dice at Locket's, while his "Lowsy Footmen for their wages wait." The early 1680's were probably also the period when Etherege was a regular visitor, and regular loser, at the basset table of the Duchess Mazarin, referred to in the letters.

When in 1685 Etherege gratefully accepted the post of Resident at Ratisbon, his letters suggest that he was escaping from something, probably from heavy gambling debts in London. Upon his arrival in Ratisbon, he felt a great sense of relief. He now had a regular though small income, his injured wife was far away in England, and a new city and court awaited his exploration. Determined to justify the confidence placed in him by Sunderland and the King, Etherege furnished the house inherited from his predecessor, provided himself with carriage and equipage, and set out hopefully to make his official visits.

Almost at once he found himself entangled in the ceremonial red tape which he repeatedly denounced as "the plague of this place." The ministers, Etherege notes, always wore the grave demeanor of office, and they could hardly bring themselves to put it off even when they approached their wives or their mistresses. They were also obsessed with protocol. Who was entitled to be received at the carriage door, at the portal on the street, or at the head of the stairs inside? Who was allowed to walk on the right-hand side of whom? Who, as Lady Mary Wortley Montagu[42] put it a few years later, was entitled to be addressed as "Your Excellency"?—These were the questions that really mattered to the diplomats at the Diet. Of all the diplomats the most ceremonious snob was the Count of Windischgrätz, the Co-commissioner from the Emperor whose pretensions to be considered Principal Commissioner (his nominal superior, the Bishop of Passau, being a muddled old man who wanted only to be left alone) by turns amused and irritated Etherege.

Accustomed to the casual informality of Whitehall, where one could

[41] Foster, *TLS*, Feb. 16, 1922, p. 108; *N&Q*, 153 (1927), 457.
[42] *Letters*, ed. Halsband, Oxford, 1965, 1, p. 257.

say outright whatever one thought—even to the King, so long as he said it wittily—Etherege soon antagonized most of the German ministers. By London standards, the social life they could have offered was severely limited by the meager resources of Ratisbon. In place of such friends as Rochester, Sedley, Buckhurst, and the other wits of King Charles' court, in Ratisbon Etherege could turn for informal relaxation only to the French envoy, the Count de Crécy.[43] An occasional performance by a troupe of strolling players was a poor substitute for the perpetual gaiety of the London theaters; and instead of the splendid basset tables of the Duchess Mazarin, Etherege was reduced to playing six-penny ombre with the Countess de Crécy. Worst of all, for a man who had always preferred the ritual of flirtation and assignation to the rival pleasures of drinking and gambling, the ladies of Ratisbon seemed to be impregnably virtuous. Except for one flamboyant affair with an itinerant actress from Nuremberg, amusingly and maliciously described by his secretary,[44] Etherege, who at 50 had not yet learned to "love the rustling of papers so well as . . . the rustling of Petty-coats," [45] had to content himself with servant girls and women of the town.

Nevertheless, he managed to be, as he put it, "often very hearty." He entertained the English volunteers on their way to fight the Turks in Hungary; his servants were able to give him a little music; he kept up his fencing and played chess and tennis. His favorite recreation was coursing with greyhounds, and one of his last recorded acts before leaving Ratisbon was to turn his dogs over to the Prince of Hohenzollern. The climate of Germany he found harsh and unwholesome and he was often ill, but in spite of everything he maintained in his letters that inextinguishable gaiety of spirit which had made his comedies so popular.

Etherege suffered from the exile's poignant hunger for news from home, and his isolation made him all the more eager to preserve his friendships in London. To lure his friends into reporting the gossip of theater and court, he sent them wry but vivid comments on his life among the pompous German statesmen, who seem to have gone out

---

[43] Louis Verjus, Comte de Crécy (1629–1709), was the French plenipotentiary at the Diet from 1679 to 1688. A member of the French Academy, he thought of himself as a *bel-esprit*. Etherege spent much time with him and his Countess in their apartments at the Scottish Benedictine Monastery. I owe to Dr. Ludwig Hammermeyer references to occasional comments on Etherege, not always flattering, in Crécy's official dispatches to Paris.

[44] See below, p. 299–303.

[45] Below, p. 201.

of their way to snub him. His secretary, writing with deliberate malice, was not above stretching the truth in describing the slights and insults received and repaid by Etherege, but other observers, like the Count de Crécy, confirm that by the end of his first year in Ratisbon Etherege was practically a social outcast. He reacted by becoming all the more arrogant in his official capacity[46] and apparently more dissolute in his private life.

The Puritanical secretary was outraged, and very likely exaggerated the drunken brawls in the course of which, he said, Etherege "tormented the whole town with coaching, fiddling, piping, and dancing till two, three, or four o'clock in the morning." [47] His further charge that Etherege went about breaking windows and beating passersby seems improbable. Etherege was not by nature inclined either to heavy drinking or to violence; and if his frustration had led him to the excesses described by the secretary, it is unlikely that he could have kept the friendship of the prudent Abbot Fleming[48] or the polished Count de Crécy. Still, his letters to friends in England indicate that the staid Germans had grounds for their disapproval.

What brought Etherege to his senses was the discovery, in the spring of 1687, that the Count of Windischgrätz was writing damaging letters about him to important people in Paris, Vienna, and London. Thereafter he began to take his official duties more seriously, and he made a

[46] For an amusing example, see his dealings with Co-Commissioner Seiler, pp. 230–231.

[47] See below, p. 295.

[48] Placid Fleming, Abbot of the Scottish Benedictine Monastery in Ratisbon, had hoped to be made Resident in 1685. The former Secretary of State, Sir Leoline Jenkins, had recommended him, but the death of Charles II had prevented the appointment (Ludwig Hammermeyer, "Restauration von 'Revolution von Oben' in Grossbritannien," *Historisches Jahrbuch*, 87 [1967], 85). In spite of his disappointment, Fleming was generous in aiding Etherege, and they became good friends. When Etherege went to France in 1689, he left his books and papers to the monastery. (Brett-Smith, *Works*, 1, p. lxvi; Foster, *N&Q*, 153 [1927], 477–478.) Some of the books, I was told in 1965, are still in Regensburg, but the papers were moved to the country house of the Benedictines at Strahlfeld in the Upper Palatinate and were destroyed there in a fire early in the 19th Century ("Scottish Religious Houses Abroad," *Edinburgh Review*, 119 [1864], 182). The destruction of the papers, including "all James VII correspondence with Etheridge, his ambassador, . . . and most of the correspondence of Abbot Fleming," is noted in a letter of March 18, 1832, from James McHattie in Regensburg to Bishop James Kyle in Scotland. This letter is now in the Scottish Catholic Archive in Edinburgh. I owe the reference to Dr. Hammermeyer and a transcription of the letter to the Rev. William James Anderson, the former archivist.

pleasant discovery: once one takes the trouble to learn what is going on, diplomacy can be genuinely interesting, and "it is a great pleasure not to be deceiv'd by the wrong reasoning of fools." By May 19, 1687, he confessed to "such a relish of business that I should be more vain of making a good dispatch, than of writing a witty letter." Fortunately, he was able to do both.

Dryden was being conventionally hyperbolic when he called Etherege "the undoubted best author of [prose] which our nation has produced," [49] but the letters certainly prove Etherege to be a master of the informal style. Although his witty speech and nonchalant grace of manner were wasted on the German envoys, the letters show that Sir George retained good title to his old nickname, Easy Etherege. The same talents that had made him a successful playwright appear in his characterization of Count Windischgrätz or in his thumbnail sketch of the Turkish Sultana. As a whole the letters provide a self-portrait that is both vividly individualized and yet typical of the mob of gentlemen who wrote with ease.

Etherege's service in Ratisbon covered approximately the period of uneasy truce preceding the War of the League of Augsburg. The Diet of the Holy Roman Empire had been meeting at Ratisbon since 1663, but by 1685 it had lost much of its importance. Etherege's continual complaint that the Diet never *did* anything is understandable though exaggerated. Legally the Diet was the official legislative body of the Empire, but practically its composition almost guaranteed that action would be slow and infrequent. By the 1680's, the electors and princes who had once gathered in Ratisbon had been replaced in most cases by envoys, who referred all important matters to their masters for decision. While they waited for instructions, they spent their time arguing over points of law, ceremony, or protocol and exchanging rumor and gossip.

The chief duty of the British resident was to keep his eyes and ears open and to send reports to Whitehall. During Etherege's term of office, the main topics reported on were the alleged violations of the truce by the French, who were fortifying the territory temporarily allotted them along the Rhine; the conference at Altona, at which the Emperor tried to mediate the territorial dispute between the King of Denmark and the Duke of Holstein-Gottorp; the imperial army's campaign to drive the Turks out of Hungary, culminating in the capture of Buda in the summer of 1686 and the victory at Mohács in

[49] See below, p. 276.

xxi

1687; and the preparations, political and military, for the Prince of Orange's invasion of England.

The first two of these topics seem to have had little interest for Etherege, though he reported them dutifully. But the progress of the imperial army with its complement of English gentlemen-volunteers fascinated him, and he sent back long and vivid accounts of the siege of Buda and its eventual capture. The growing threat of a move against James II by William of Orange and his Whig supporters in England obsessed Etherege from midsummer of 1688 to the actual invasion in November. He tried to prohibit or refute the propaganda pouring into the Empire from Holland; he urged his friend Lord Carlingford, envoy at Vienna, to inform the Emperor of William's plot against a Catholic monarch; and he wrote repeatedly to both Middleton and Sunderland urging them to warn the king of the danger that threatened.

These letters are particularly interesting for their evidence of Etherege's deep and unshakable loyalty to King James II. What may have begun in 1685 as a mixture of esteem for his sovereign and gratitude for past and present favors had become, by 1688, a fanatical devotion that blinded Etherege to political realities and led him to exchange his post in Ratisbon for the uncertainties of exile in France, "being resolved to live and dy in serving His Majesty faithfully." "I hope," he added, "you will think it a Lawfull ambition to desire to be where I may venture my Life in performing my Duty. My allegiance and my gratitude tell me it is base to be unactive when my King and my Master's Crown and person are in danger." [50]

On January 18, 1689, Etherege received word that the King had arrived safely in Paris, and the next day Sir George wrote Carlingford of his intent "very suddainly to be with his Majesty." In 1685 it had taken him fifteen days, on the winter roads, to go from Cologne to Ratisbon. The longer winter journey from Ratisbon to Paris must have taken about three weeks, so that if Etherege had left during the last week of January, he should have been in Paris by mid-February. Actually, the first of the letters from Paris listed in H-2 is dated February 20. The last in the list was written on September 28, 1689. What Etherege was doing in the seven-month interim is unknown, but his financial troubles seem to have continued: eleven of the twenty-nine Paris letters were sent to Treasury officials in London.

Etherege may well have arrived at St. Germain too late either to aid the Jacobite cause or to find a patron. King James had left on

[50] See below, p. 264.

February 15 for Brest to begin his invasion of Ireland [51] and did not return to St. Germain until after the Battle of the Boyne in 1690. The Queen had been Etherege's patron in 1676, when he had dedicated his best comedy to her, but Etherege is not mentioned in the surviving lists of the court in exile, and no record of his last years in France has been found.

The monks of the Benedictine Cloister in Ratisbon claimed that Etherege converted to Catholicism before his death: in their syllabus of Benefactors to the monastery they list Sir George and add "Obiit Parisiis factus Catholicus." [52] Abbot Fleming, a close friend to whom Etherege continued to write from Paris, would certainly have known of a conversion and it seems unlikely that he would have permitted a false statement in the Syllabus. Considering the number of Jacobites who became Roman Catholics, Etherege's conversion would not be surprising or out of character; increasing evidences of religious interest, if not actual piety, are found in later letters. But no supporting evidence exists.

Sir George's death is variously reported. On February 3, 1691, Etherege's former attorney, George Bradbury, writing to a Mr. Wharton at the Hague, said, "I am sure I should have been Dead, as I heare Sr Geo. Etherege is at Paris." [53] The Benedictine monks at Ratisbon in their Syllabus of Benefactors noted the day of death as July 28, 1699, but at some later time the year was changed, in pencil, to 1691. [54] Narcissus Luttrell, [55] summarizing news from abroad, noted in February 1691 a report of Sir George's death. But Etherege's nephew George, testifying at a trial on December 4, 1697, said, "on or about the Tenth day of May in the year of our Lord one thousand six hundred and ninety two the said Sr George Etherege dyed without Issue. . . ." [56] Both Bradbury and Luttrell are quoting a report from Paris, quite possibly the same newsletter. The Benedictines also probably used a continental source when they corrected their Syllabus. Poor health, which had increasingly plagued Etherege during his stay at Ratisbon, might have given rise to premature rumors of his death in 1691. All

[51] F. C. Turner, *James II*, London, 1948, p. 463.

[52] MS Syllabus Benefactorum Monasterii S. Jacobi Scotorum Ratisbonae, at St. Benedict's Abbey, Fort Augustus, Scotland.

[53] Carte MS 79, p. 339.

[54] Father Mark Dilworth, who verified this for me, suggests this emended date was misread by the printer and hence appears, in the printed *Records of the Scots Colleges* (Aberdeen, 1906, 1, p. 273), as "1699 (1694)."

[55] *Brief Historical Relation*, 2, p. 171.

[56] Foster, *N&Q*, 153 (1927), 472.

things considered, the nephew's May 1692 date is probably the most reliable, though this would mean that Etherege outlived his wife, whose estate was administered in February 1692.[57]

As H. F. B. Brett-Smith noted in 1929, "Etherege's correspondence is of very variable importance." [58] The majority of the extant letters are official dispatches on the politics of the Empire, shrewd and cogent but of minor interest today. Though I have listed all of the letters known to me, I have included in this edition only those letters and parts of letters which seem to me to be, in Brett-Smith's words, "of most interest to the student of Etherege and of English literature." But I have interpreted this principle broadly for letters not included in Miss Rosenfeld's edition, especially the very early and the very last letters from Ratisbon. I have omitted approximately 150 letters which throw no light on Etherege or his life in Ratisbon. Letters which combine personal detail with diplomatic news are printed in part, with omissions indicated. A little more than half of the letters in this edition appear in print for the first time.

The letters have been transcribed from M-1 and M-2 whenever possible, from H-1 or H-2 when this is the earliest available source, and from BM when it is the only source. The entries in H-1 and H-2 listing by date and addressee letters not copied into the letterbook are included to suggest the scope and size of Etherege's correspondence. In indicating sources, I list first the manuscript from which the transcription was made, followed by references to other copies of the letter. However, instead of giving references to BM, I have given page references to Sybil Rosenfeld's edition (*LB*), to help readers find the text of some of the letters I have omitted.

Etherege's punctuation was very inconsistent. In order to make the text intelligible, I have added punctuation where modern convention requires it and omitted many of Etherege's interior commas. I preserve the original spelling, except that I have expanded abbreviations (retaining Mr., Mrs., Dr.) and have written *th* for *y* in words like *ye* and *v* for *u* in words like *fauour*. Letters in French also preserve Etherege's spelling, which has fewer diacritical marks than would be found in modern French. I have silently corrected some obvious slips of the pen—e.g., "begingings" for *beginnings*, "magristrates" for *magistrates*, etc. All of Etherege's paragraphing has been retained, but I have

[57] Wills and Administrations, 1692, Fane 1, at the Public Record Office. See also George Baker, *The History . . . of Northampton, Part II*, London, 1822, p. 158.

[58] *RES*, 5 (1929), 77.

marked additional paragraphs here and there to break up large blocks of type and lighten the page.

Etherege was inconsistent in writing dates, sometimes using the form "30 Nov./ 10 Dec., 1685," but sometimes writing "30 Nov., O.S. (or St. V.)" or "10 Dec., N.S. (or St. N.)" for Old and New Style. In the text I have transcribed Etherege's dates exactly as he or his secretary wrote them, but when I am myself citing a date (as at the beginning of each letter), I use New Style, following standard practice for letters written on the Continent, where the Gregorian calendar was in general use.

THE LETTERS

To Joseph Williamson[1]

[Constantinople,[2] 1670[3]]

Sir.

Were you acquainted with this place you wou'd not condemne mee much for not giving you before this time any account of the affaires of Turky. During the Warr of Candia, the News we had from thence was sent us from Smyrna, where you hold a correspondence with Consul Ricaut,[4] so that the advices which I shou'd have given you wou'd have bin stale and insignificant. Besides, the remoteness of the Court (which has bin ever since our arrivall in Thessaly and Macedon) has made this citty as barren of intelligence as a village. Here seldome happens any thing worthy remarke, and when there does, it is so uncertainly reported to us by our Druggermen,[5] who are our only Intelligencers, that experience makes us very incredulous; what Wee heare one day is commonly contradicted the next, and shou'd I give you a dayly account of things according to your desire, my busines wou'd bee almost every other Letter to disabuse you in what I had writt to you before.

My Lord is lately return'd from Salonica, where hee has had Audience. Hee arriv'd there some days before the Court and had notice given him that hee shou'd expect the Grand Signior's coming from Larissa. The Grand Signor arriv'd upon Thursday, 25 November, in the evening, came in incognito to Visit his Hasachi, or Sultana, and the next morning went out againe to make a publique entry. His traine consisted of Footemen and Pages, Faulconers and Huntsmen, who were in all about two thousand. Hee was attended by no men of note but the Mufti, the Kaimakam[6] of the Port, and his favorite, commonly called Culogli. His Footmen were all clothed in cloth of gold and silver, and his Pages who are his Guard were clad in coates of Male with Olive colour'd Sattin Vests over them, all Young men pick'd out for their strength and beauty. Severall Doggs were lead cover'd with Vests of cloth of gold and silver. Doubtless this Entry wanted much of that magnificence hee appeares in when hee enters Adrianople or Constantinople, Yet it made a very handsome showe, and was a very splendid hunting equipage, for such it was accounted.

The Munday following My Lord visited the Chimacam, and the next day had audience of the Grand Signor, who treated him with extraordinary markes of respect and civility. The Grand Signor is about thirty yeares of age, of a middle stature, leane and long visag'd. He has lately let the haire grow on his chin. His complexion is a darke browne. His aspect is not disagreeable; however hee is generally accounted very ugly. Hee is a Bigot in his Religion and a most extravagant lover of hunting. The fatigue hee undergoes in it is almost incredible. Great numbers of poore people are summon'd in to attend him, and many of them perish in the Feild through hunger and cold. This has cheifly got him the hatred of his Subjects. In all other recreations hee is moderate.

Hee is very constant to his Hasachi and not given to that unnaturall vice with which he has bin slander'd. The Sultana is a Candiot, and though women here are not so polite and refin'd as in Christendome, yet shee wants not her little arts to secure her Sultan's affections. Shee can dissemble fondnes and jealousy and can swoone at pleasure. The Grand Signor has had two children by her, a son and a daughter. The son is called Sultan Mustapha. Hee is about six yeares old and design'd by his father to bee circumciz'd when hee comes to Constantinople to make the allaigresse[7] the greater. The Daughter is not much more than a yeare old, and is already married to the Favorite, Culogli, a man of seaven and twenty yeares, well featur'd, modest and wise. Hee avoids busines and by that meanes makes himselfe less lyable to the envy of the Ministers of State. His equipage is not much inferior to his Masters. His footmen and pages weare the same Livery. Hee is allow'd six hundred thousand Dollers a yeare besides all necessaries for his retinue, and yet this vast income is not able to keepe him out of debt, but whether that bee an effect of his generosity or prudence is uncertaine, for there is nothing here more dangerous than to be rich.

The Grand Signors Privy Councell consisted here but of five persons, the favorite, the Chimacam of the Port,[8] the Mufti Vani Effendi, a famous Arab preacher, and one of the Pasha's of the Bench, most of the great men being with the Vizir who is employ'd in Candia in fortefying and setling the affaires of that Kingdome. Hee is to come to Court in the Spring as it is reported, and then the Grand Signor intends to begin his journey hither. This Chimacam's name is Mustapha Pasha. Hee was formerly Captain Pasha or Admirall of the Gallies and has married the Vizier's sister, yet this allyance keeps them not from secret emulations and hatreds, and it is thought the Chimacam will dispute the Grand Signor's favour with him at his returne. The Vizier they say exceeds not the age of two and thirty yeares. Hee is of a middle stature and has a good Mine.[9] Hee is prudent and just, not to bee corrupted by money, the generall vice of this country, nor inclin'd to cruelty as his father was. The Chimacam is about the age of forty five, well spoken, subtill, corrupt and a great dissembler. Hee flatters the Grand Signor in his inclinations, and ever accompanies him in his hunting, a toyle which nothing but excessive ambition and interest cou'd make him undergoe. All conclude the Vizier will commence another Warr, but who will fall under the [pai]ne of it is unknowne.

The Chimacam of this place, Ibrahim Pasha,[10] has a particular respect for my Lord, and is exceeding courteous and obliging whensoever hee treats with him about any busines; hee is a man of great resolution, wisdome and honesty. Hee is neere sixty yeares old but very vigorous of his age. Hee was bred a souldier and by his courage and other merits has rais'd himselfe to this eminent degree. Hee was Kiabeigh or Lieuetennant of the Janizaries at the battel of Rab, where hee was shot through the shoulder, and upon the death of his Captaine was there made Aga. Hee serv'd in that charge at Candia till hee was this yeare sent hither to bee Chimacam in the stead of Useph Pasha, a timorous doting old man who was remoov'd for multiplying the danger and giving a dreadfull account to the Court of some little stirs that hapned here some months since upon a report that the Grand Signor had sent to cutt off his brothers, Sultan Soliman and Sultan Achmet. 'Tis thought these princes will bee in great danger when the Grand Signor arrives here. My business was at the beginning to excuse my not writing to you, and now I ought to begg your pardon for having writt soe much, but I hope you will let mee know you have forgiven mee the impertinencies of this Letter, and that will incourage mee to give you notice of whatsoever I shall bee inform'd of here worthy your knowledge. I am, Sir, Your very humble Servant

Geo: Etherege

Source: PRO State Papers 97/19, f. 150.

[1] Joseph Williamson (1633–1701), at the time a secretary in the Secretary of State's Office, was knighted in 1672 and became Secretary of State in 1674.

[2] In August 1668, Etherege went to Constantinople as secretary to Sir Daniel Harvey, English Ambassador to Turkey. Cf. Thomas Fujimura, "Etherege at Constantinople," *PMLA*, 62 (1956), 465–481.

[3] The letter is undated, but a notation on the back indicates that it was received on May 8, 1670. Because the letter notes the Ambassador "is lately return'd from Salonica," where he had had an audience with the Grand Signor on November 30, 1669, Etherege's letter was probably written early in 1670.

⁴ The historian, Paul Rycaut, British consul at Smyrna.

⁵ *Dragoman,* an interpreter.

⁶ *Kaimakam,* a deputy or deputy-governor (OED). Cf. the spelling "Chimacam" in the next paragraph.

⁷ Mn. French *allégresse,* "mirth, gaiety."

⁸ Mustapha Pasha, the Grand Vizier's deputy. "Porte" in the late seventeenth century meant the central government of the Ottoman Empire, not the city of Constantinople.

⁹ The English equivalent of the French *mine* is *mien,* "appearance."

¹⁰ The deputy-governor of Constantinople.

To The Earl of Middleton[1]   October 5, 1685

Hague

My Lord.

Since my arrival in Holland, which was Yesterday was Seaventh-night, I went to Amsterdam about a bill of Exchange I had to receive there, where I grew acquainted by accident with a Gentleman[2] whome I have brought to Mr. Skelton[3] in order to do the King a considerable service. You will have a full account of the wholle busines by Mr. Skeltons Letters. I shall stay here two or three dayes longer to expect a good Success of what is propos'd to be don and then go forward on my Journey. I am with all the Duty imaginable, My Lord, Your most faithfull and most obedient Servant

Geo: Etherege

Source: M-1, f. 1.

¹ Middleton's name does not appear in the MS, but is verified by a letter from him to Bevil Skelton (BM Add. Mss. 41823, f. 29).

² A secret agent named Douglas, who subsequently proved unreliable (BM Add. Mss. 41812, f. 220).

³ Bevil Skelton, English envoy to the States General at the Hague. He was transferred to Versailles in January 1687.

To Bevil Skelton[1]   November 5, 1685

Cologne

Sir.

When I came to Arnhem I was inform'd the Court was remov'd from Deiren to Loe, and not having perfectly recover'd the indisposition I had at Utrich, I durst not venture so far out of my way, to a place where I cou'd have no accomodation. As I past by Cleve, remembring what you had told me of a Consultation there, tho our Waggon went not into the Towne, I did, where I was credibly inform'd there had been Fower Englishmen[2] who went a way but the day before, who had stayd there 3 or 4 dayes and lay at the same howse my Lord Gray[3] had Lodged at. I cou'd not learn their names. I am verry sorry I had not an oportunity to serve you in what you desir'd of me. I shall never forgett the Civillities I receav'd from you in Holland, and you may be confident no man is more sincerely then myselfe, Sir, Your most humble and most obedient Servant

Geo: Etherege

Source: M-1, f. 3.

[1] In his holograph letters, Etherege usually wrote the name of the person addressed in the lower left margin of the first page. In the letterbooks, Etherege's secretary usually put the name of the addressee in parentheses after the salutation.

[2] These were probably fugitive followers of the Duke of Monmouth.

[3] Forde, Lord Grey of Wark, fled to Holland after the Rye House Plot and accompanied the Duke of Monmouth on his abortive invasion of England.

To THE EARL OF MIDDLETON   November 5, 1685
                                                          Cologne

My Lord.

I came hither yesterday and entend to go forward to morrow. I have left Mr. Ds[1] busines wholly to Mr. Skelton, with directions where to heare off him; I feare he promis'd to do what was not in his power. I took my Leave of Mr. Skelton at Utrich, who told me he was inform'd some people were to meet and consult at Cleve. As I past by that place two dayes ago, I went into the Towne and enquir'd what English were there. I was told there had been Fower English Gentlemen who lay at the same howse my Lord Gray lay at formerly, but cou'd not learne their names, that they had stayd 3 or 4 dayes and were newly gon. I shall not give your Lordship any more trouble without anything happens worth your knowledge till I gett to Ratisbonne. I am, My Lord, Your most faithfull and most humble Servant

Geo: Etherege

Source: M-1, f. 5.

[1] The Mr. Douglas referred to in the letter of October 5, 1685.

To THE EARL OF MIDDLETON[1]   November 26, 1685
                                                          Ratisbon

My Lord.

I ariv'd at this place on Wednesday last,[2] very much tir'd, having rid post about 8 or 9 stages in very ill wayes and on worse Horses; the rest of my Company came on Fryday following. I entend as soone as

I can possiblie to make my Visits that I may be able to send you the best intelligence can be had of affaires from hence. Yesterday I saw Monsieur du Crecy privately in the Abotts owne apartement. He sent Father Eliot, who Governes in Mr. Flemings absence, to desire it, and I thought I ought not to refuse it, having no Character to oblige me to any Ceremonie, It being my busines to informe myselfe of matters here as soone as I cou'd.

After many Complements I learn'd from him that the Emperor had sent 2 Commissions Decrees to the Diette the last weeke. In the first he finds fault with the ministers that nothing of moment has been debated in the Diette this halfe yeare and more but the time trifl'd away in unprofitable disputes and wranglings about Ceremonies, admonishing them for the future to abstaine from the like and carefully to consult about what may be usefull to the Empire.

The Count de Windichgratz,[3] who has occasion'd most of these disputes by pretending to be treated equally with the Bishop of Passau,[4] has been some time at Vienna and is now uppon his Journy back. There he has excus'd himselfe to the Emperor and layd the fault on those who have opos'd him in his pretentions, which has been the occasion of this Commission. He has so incens'd the Emperor against the Colledge of the Ellectors that he has sent them a Letter in which he treats them with such severe and harsh Language about these matters that they are now in Consultation what answere is fit to be made to it. Every Deputy is order'd to project something apart, that when they compare them they may choose what shall be judg'd most proper. This is yet a great Secret, and the Letter came so lately that they send their severall Maisters copies of it this day. This, Monsieur du Crecy is of opinion, is like to make more unnecessary disputes rather then put an end to them and that the Emperor may have occasion to repent the credit he has given to Count Windichgratz, but I find by his discourse he has allwayes been ill with the Count and is very well with most of the Electorall Colledge.

The second Commissions Decree is to facillitate some difficultis which have occasion'd former disputes and seemes to have been projected by the Count to make his proceedings more plausible to the Emperor. It is That, whereas many disputes have been whither or no the said Count being absent when a Reichsguttachten[5] passes in the Diette ought to have his name mention'd, his Emperial Majestie condescends it shall not, since his Character seems to be suspended while he is with his Emperiall Majestie whome he represents, with

8

this Condition that he shall loose none of his Rights when he is present.

[News of Imperial military successes in Hungary.][6]

By that time this weeke is over, I hope to have made most of my visits. It has cost me all the time I have been here to fitt myselfe in Order to it, and I have allready got a Coach and horses. Then I shall be able to give your Lordship a better account of things, not omitting any thing that may be for his Majesties service. I am with all the Duty imaginable, My Lord, Your Lordships most faithfull and most obedient servant

Geo: Etherege

Source: M-1, ff. 7–8.

[1] Name omitted in the holograph, but verified by the first sentence of the following letter, dated November 27.

[2] This was November 21, New Style.

[3] Gottlieb Amadeus, Count von Windischgrätz (1630–1695), was Imperial Co-Commissioner with the Bishop of Passau to the Diet.

[4] Sebastian von Pötting, Bishop of Passau, was Principal Commissioner of the Emperor at Ratisbon (Urkunden, 21, p. 457).

[5] Literally, "Imperial Judgement," but Etherege uses it interchangeably with "Act of the Diet."

[6] News of no immediate relevance to Etherege is omitted, as here, with a brief indication of the contents in brackets.

To The Earl of Middleton   November 27, 1685
                                                      Ratisbon
My Lord.

I writ to your Lordship Yesterday by the way of Cologne and was straightn'd in time, the Post goeing a way 2 howers sooner then I expected. I send this by Bruxells and in it a paper of Newes which came last Night from Vienna. Pray, my Lord, let my Lord Mulgrave[1] know I have just now receiv'd the Newes of his being Lord Chamberlain and that I have my share of satisfaction in all the good Fortune that befalls him. I intend as soon as I am setled to find out a way to get the best intelligence and carefully comunicate it to your Lordship, the continuance of who's favour I beg to, My Lord, Your most faithfull and most obedient servant

Geo: Etherege

Source: M-1, f.9.

[1] John Sheffield, Earl of Mulgrave (1648–1721), who became Duke of Buckinghamshire in 1703.

To The Earl of Middleton   November 29, 1685
                                                          Ratisbon

My Lord.

Yesterday the Diette pass'd two Acts which have been delayd above
these two Monthes on the dispute wheither the Count de Windichgratz ought to have his name inserted in his absence. Uppon the
Emperors Commission, which I acquainted you with before, his Faction gave upp the game, and this day or to morrow the Director of
the Diette is to waite uppon the Bishop of Passau and present him
with these Reichsguttachtens. One is to Congratulate the Emperor
uppon his Victories in Hungarie, the other uppon the birth of the
Duke of Austria.

I have seen incognito a Deputy[1] of the Elector of Brandenbourg,
who receiv'd me with many Complements. At parting he assur'd me
he wou'd constantly acquaint me with what pass'd in the Diette and
send me Coppies of what Newes he receiv'd from other parts. I have,
uppon his information of the methods us'd here, agreed uppon the
manner of making my visits, and he tells me (to my great comfort)
that himselfe and the cheife of their Colledge have agreed to receive
me with the same formalities and honors as if I had a Character. He
desir'd I wou'd give him leave to acquaint his Maister with the favour
he had receiv'd, and made me promise not to mention his name in
my Letters into England. Men are politick as well as Civill in this
place.

This Day the newes comes from Vienna, but very late by reason
of the illness of the Road this Winter time. As soon as it arives, I
am promis'd a Coppy which I shall inclose in this for your Lordship.
Pray, my Lord, believe I am extreame sensible of your favours and
that none of your Dependents can be more humbly nor more sincerely then myselfe, My Lord, Your Lordships most faithfull and
most obedient Servant

                                                    Geo: Etherege

Source: M-1, ff. 11–12.

[1] Godfrey de Jena (1620–1703). He was recalled in February 1687 for
allegedly favoring the French (*LB*, pp. 36–37, 153 fn., 265–266). There are
many references to de Jena throughout *Urkunden*.

A Ratisbon

Monsieur.

Je ne fai que d'arriver ici, et j'ay esté si embarrassé pour m'establir, que Je n'ay pas eu le Loisir de vaguer ni pour moy même ny pour mes amis. J'ay fait tout ce que je pouvois pour m'informer sur le sujet dont nous avons parlé. Et je trouve que toute l'Empire est épuisée, et la Boheme plus que toutes les autres Païs hormis l'Autriche. Je eu beaucoup de deplaisir de ces nouvelles que vous aviez receues lors que nous nous *disions*. Adieu. J'espere que c'estoit plustôt la crainte que vos veritables Amis avoient pour vous, qu' aucune chose reelle. J'ay deja une fort jollie maison, une Carosse, et des bons cheveaux, des valets, et un Cuisinier, mais Je ne *me* puis pas venter d'estre bien servi dans ma cuisine. Tout le reste est passable. Je ne manqueray pas de vous donner les nouvelles que Je vous ay promises quand le temps servira. Si les Choses ne vont pas à vostre gré, et que vous avez envie de changer de Climats vous pourrez vivre tout doucement et serez toujours le mieux venu du monde chez un homme qui est sincerement Monsieur v.t.h.e.t.o.s.

G.E.

à Monsieur Germain a la Haye.

Source: BM, f. 2; *LB*, p. 53.

[1] Probably John Germain, "of the parish of St. Margaret, Westminster" (H. K. S. Causton, *The Howard Papers*, 1862, p. 259), or his brother Philip, who lived at the Hague. Etherege would have been more likely to know John, who was famous enough as a gambler to have been included in Theophilus Lucas' *Memoirs of the Lives . . . of the Most Famous Gamesters*, London, 1714. In the summer of 1685 his affair with the Duchess of Norfolk became generally known (Luttrell, 1, p. 359), and in September the Duke and Duchess went separately to Paris, where in November she was left, as she said, locked up in a monastery (*Howard Papers*, p. 236). Germain may have followed the Duchess to the Continent. In any case, he returned with William of Orange in 1688 and subsequently was knighted. I owe these references to Professor John Harold Wilson. See also footnote 1 on p. 269, below.

To The Earl of Sunderland[1]   December 3, 1685

Ratisbon

My Lord.

I have taken the Howse Mr. Pooley[2] liv'd in, and am very well setl'd allready considering the shortnes of the time and how hard it is to find Conveniencies here. I am just now goeing to make my first

11

Visit to the Prince of Passau. I will dispatch all the rest as fast as I can, that I may have more Liberty to informe myselfe about affaires. I have inclos'd a paper of what newes is currant here. This day the post comes from Vienna, and if I can get intelligence of what it brings time enough, I will inclose it in this likewise.

I am not well enough acquainted with this Towne yet to give you an account how people spend there idle howres here, and whither it is like to make any amends for what I have lost in London; but I can assure your Lordship that I find I can live without play, a thing my best Freinds will hardly beleive. I have really no more concerne for Basset[3] then I us'd to have for an old Mistris in her absence, nor am I troubl'd at the losse of any thing but the oportunitys I had of being neare your Lordship and the rest of my Freinds. This touches me so nearly that nothing but now and then an assurance of the continuance of your Lordships favour is able to bring any confort to, My Lord, Your Lordships most faithfull and most obedient servant

Geo: Etherege

Source: PRO State Papers (German States) 81, #86, f. 271; *LB*, pp. 408–409.

[1] The addressee is not named, but the holograph is bound in the State Papers with two other letters addressed to Sunderland.

[2] Edmund Poley, Etherege's predecessor at Ratisbon, had been transferred to Sweden. The location of his house is unknown. Etherege lived in it till May 10, 1688, when he moved to the house on the Jakobsplatz. See below, p. 196.

[3] A card game recently introduced from France, to which Etherege had been addicted. See Thorpe, *Poems*, pp. 85–87.

Omitted: December 3, 1685. To Middleton with miscellaneous diplomatic news.

Source: M-1, ff. 13–14.

To The Earl of Middleton   December 6, 1685
Ratisbon

My Lord.

[News of squabbling at the Diet.]

Pray my Lord give order to one of your Secretaries to revenge this long letter and lett me know what is doeing in England. I have visited the Bishop of Passau, the French Plenipotentiarie, and the Deputy of Mayance [Mainz] and have been receiv'd with the same Ceremonis as if I had a Character. I have a great many more to make before I am a freeman of the Towne. The Deputy of Mayance has promiss'd me to informe me still of what he knows in matters of importance, that the king my Maister may the better know the truth of things. I am, My Lord, Your most faithfull and most obedient servant

Geo: Etherege

Source: M-1, ff. 15–18.

My Lord.

I find the Prince of Passau is a quiet good man and medles little in affaires saving onely in the formes his Commission obliges him too. He is, as I judge by his person, neare Threescore yeares of Age. The Count de Windichgratz is betweene 40 and 50, as I am told, hot and of a busy insulting temper which has lost him the goodwill of most of the members of the Diette, especially of the wholle Electorall Colledge, who still opose him in all his designes and pretentions.

The clashing of these Two Factions has been the reason why matters of moment have been deliberated on with so much delay. The Directors of the Princes Colledge are of the Count de Windichgratz Faction and will never propose any thing to their Colledge which comes to them from the Colledge off Electors if they judge their party is not strong enough to carry it as they wou'd. This made them keep the Acts lately passd for congratulating the Emperor on his victories etc. from the 1st of September, which date the Reichsgotachten beares and was then pass'd in the Electoral Colledge, till the Emperor sent lately a Comissions decree not to name the Count de Windichgratz in such Acts of the Diette as pass'd in his absence and never read them in the Colledge till the point was yealded. The Deputys of the Towns serve only for forme sake and have never any busines transmitted to them till the other two Colledges have agreed. I have inclos'd with this all the news we have here and am, My Lord, Your Lordships most faithfull and most humble servant

G Etherege

Source: M-1, ff. 19–20. This is the first letter copied into the Harvard Letterbook (H-1, pp. 1–2). It was copied with an incorrect date in BM and hence is dated incorrectly in *LB*.

Omitted: December 13, 1685. To Middleton with news of the Diet, Speyer, and Berlin.

Source: M-1, ff. 21–23.

To The Earl of Middleton   December 17, 1685
                                                              Ratisbon
My Lord.

[Inaction at the Diet]

The Count of Windichgratz is expected here within this Day or two from Vienna, and then you will heare what is occasion'd by the letters which were sent at his instance to the Electors and their Deputys here. I was misinform'd about the Count's Age. He is neare Five and Fifty, and very much troubl'd with the Gout and Stone.

I have had since my last a little fever, which made me keep my bed till yesterday. I am now fallen on my legs again and in a state of convalescence. I shall be glad if I pay no dearer for my entrance into this rough Climate.

If the news from Vienna comes in time, I will enclose it. I have begun to write to all his Majesties Ministers abroad and have been so exact in the observance of my Duty that I have not been wanting to Sir Peter[1] nor Sir Richard.[2] Tho I do not doubt but I am sometimes in your Lordships memorie, yet if Mr. Wynne[3] had order from you to let me know it, it wou'd be a good help to my philosophy and ad more to my cheirefulnes then the divertions of Ratisbonne. I am, My Lord, Your Lordships most faithfull and most obedient servant

                                                          Geo: Etherege

Source: M-1, ff. 25-26.

Omitted: December 18, 1685. A brief note to Middleton with news from Vienna.

Source: M-1, f. 27.

[1] Sir Peter Wyche, resident at Hamburg, was envoy to the Hanse towns.
[2] Sir Richard Bulstrode, envoy at Brussels.
[3] Dr. Owen Wynne, by seniority the second ranking clerk in the Secretary of State's office. He received and filed all papers and letters, made copies of the Secretary's letters, and corresponded with several of the King's ministers abroad, including Etherege. He knew Latin, French, Spanish, Italian, and German (F. M. G. Evans, *The Principal Secretary of State,* Manchester, 1923, p. 192).

To Sir William Trumbull[1]   December 18, 1685
                                                              Ratisbon

I was going about making of legs and muttering of compliments and had wished a merry Christmas to half the Ministers here when I was stopped by a small fever. . . . The Diet never does anything

14

in holidays, and breaks up as formally as a great school before Christmas. I doubt not but my Lady Trumbull likes Paris as well as London with . . . your good company, and I should like Ratisbon as well as Knightrider Street, were not the chief charm wanting, for here silence, solitude, and good hours are in as great perfection as there, and keeping at home is the greatest pastime, for no visits can be made without sending a herald before to agree upon the entertaine.

Source: HMC *Downshire*, 1, p. 71. See Introduction, p. xii, fn. 4; *LB*, p. 423.

[1] Trumbull was envoy to France from 1685 to October 1686, when he was replaced by Bevil Skelton and sent as Ambassador to Turkey.

To The Earl of Middleton

December 20, 1685
Ratisbon

My Lord.

The Diette have met once since my last, but it was onely to wish one an other a merry Christmas, a ceremonie it seems that is usuall. It will be a good while before they meet again, for they keep the Hollydaies according to both accounts, the members being mixt Catholicks and Lutherains.

The Day before yesterday the Count de Windichgratz arriv'd here. He pretends a new Commission from the Emperor to be in equall power as to the matter of the Diette with the Prince of Passau and cheife Commissioner for all forraigne affaires here and all over the Empire.

> [Windischgrätz' efforts to have himself accepted as the chief Imperial Commissioner at the Diet and the consequent dissension among the Ministers.]

I hear this from the French Ambassador and others of the Electorall Faction. I have not yet any intimacy with any of the other party.

Our letters go from hence now 4 howers sooner than usuall because of the illnes of the ways this winter, so that I cannot send you any news from Vienna but on Tuesdays. Here is a copy of a letter in Towne, but I cannot yet get to see it, from the Princess of Ragotzi to Caprara[1] in which she declines the Conditions the Emperor offers her and seems to be assur'd her Husband is not kept as a prisoner but is honorably treated by the Turks. I have pretty well recover'd my health again and hope I shall enjoy it to give your Lordship many

Testimonies of the gratitude of, My Lord, Your Lordships most humble and most obedient servant

Geo: Etherege

Source: M-1, ff. 29–31. Parts of this letter are printed without date in *LB,* pp. 59–61.

1 Helen Zrinyi Rákóczy, widow of Prince Francis Rákóczy. In 1682 she married General Imre Tököly, a Hungarian rebel who later fought on the side of the Turks. When she refused to surrender her fortress of Munkács to the Emperor, it was besieged by Aenius Sylvius, Count of Caprara (1631–1701), a Field Marshal in the Austrian army. It surrendered January 14, 1688. See Etherege's letter of April 1, 1686.

To The Earl of Middleton   December 24, 1685
Ratisbon

My Lord.

Nothing of moment has been debated in the Diette since my last, and they meet no more till after the Holydays. The Emperor does all he can to make him selfe able to carry on the war vigorously against the Turk next spring. In order to refill his Coffers he dos intend by Letters to demand subsidies of all the Etates of the Empire which they call here (Römer Monat),[1] and I have seen a Coppy of a Letter sent to the Magistrates of this Town to that purpose.

[The Circle of Franconia has agreed to treat with the Emperor about a defensive alliance against the French.]

I have been to visit the Count de Windischgratz, who has receiv'd me very courteously. The Plenipotentiarie of France and the Electoral Colledge will not visit him, he receiving them at the staires head onely and taking the Right hand in his owne house, which they will allow to no Commissioner of the Emperors that is not a Prince of the Empire. The Emperor, besides his being in equal Comission with the Prince of Passau, has made him his Extraordinarie Ambassador for all forreigne affaires here and all over the Empire. By vertue of this Comission he esteems him selfe a Minister of the first Order, and will allow Monsieur de Crecy to be onely of the Second, wanting the word represantaunt in his Credentialls.

I wish your Lordship a happy new yeare, a daily encrease and a long enjoyment of all your honors. Pray, my Lord, let me now and then by Mr. Wynne receave some marks of your favour in this drooping place to cheere up the Spirits of, My Lord, Your most faithfull and most humble servant

G Etherege

Source: M-1, ff. 33–34.

[1] The Roman Months was a war tax payable monthly from the States of the Empire to the Emperor. According to Etherege, "one Roman month throughout the Empire" amounted to 27,300 florins, or about £4,000. See his letter of January 24, 1686.

TO THE EARL OF SUNDERLAND

December 24, 1685
Ratisbon

My Lord.

Since my coming hither I have had a little Fever, which has been the reason I have not payd my Duty so regularly as I ought to do to your Lordship. I am now pretty well recover'd, and hope I am quit at a reasonable price for what I was to pay on the change of Climate and a greater change in my manner of Living. Is it not enough to breed an ill habit of body in a man who was us'd to sit up till morning to be forc'd for want of knowing what to do with himselfe to go to bed in the Evening; one who has been us'd to live with all freedom, never to aproach any body but with Ceremonie; one who has been us'd to run up and down to find out variety of Company, to sit at home, and entertaine himselfe in Solitude?

Play and women are not so much as talk'd of, and one wou'd think the Diett had made a Reichsguttachten to banish those passtimes the Citty. Here was the Countess of Nostitz,[1] but malice wou'd not let her live in quiet, and she is lately remov'd to Prague. Good Company met at her howse, and she had a little Ombre[2] to entertaine 'em. A more comode Lady, by what I heare, never kept a Bassett in London. If I do well after all this you must allow me to be a great Philosopher, and I dare afirme Cato left not the world with more firmenes of Soule then I did England.

The Disputes that happen about Ceremonials in the Diett I shall onely torment my Lord Middleton with, being properly appartenances of his Province. When anything of moment is debated I shall acquaint you with it, but that which I shall be most carefull to informe you of is what is done when the Campagne opens, knowing the king loves to heare of those matters.

The best acknowledgement I can make to your Lordship for all I owe you, which is Indeed all I have, is to be industrious in my station.

You prefer'd me to his Majesties Service, and in gratitude I shall daily studdy to acquit myselfe well in it. I know no better way here to make your Lordship see how truly sensible I am of your favour. Where ever I am hereafter, all the actions of my life shall still show with how much sinserity and humility I am, My Lord, Your Lordships most faithfull and most obedient servant

G Etherege

Source: PRO State Papers 81, #86, ff. 273–274. This letter was copied with some slight changes and an incorrect date in BM, ff. 3–4 and appears in *LB*, p. 58.

[1] Probably the wife of Anton Johann, Graf von Nostitz, who went to Sweden as Imperial envoy in December 1685 (*Urkunden*, 22, p. 601; *Repertorium*, 1, p. 165).
[2] A popular card game of the time.

To Monsieur Barillon[1]   December 24, 1685[2]
Ratisbon

Monsieur.

Je vous dois tout ce qui m'est agreable ici. La faveur, et la bonne opinion de Monsieur de Crecy, et le privilege d'estre chez luy sans Ceremonie, est un meuble qui ne se trouve pas dans aucune autre maison de la Ville. Car les messieurs de la Diète sont toujours vêtus de leur Caractere, et à peine s'en dêpouillent-ils à ce que je crois quand ils s'approchent de leurs femmes, ou de leurs maistresses. On ne rend jamais des visites qu'a une heure *assignée,* et si vous manquez un peu de vostre temps vous courez risque de morfondre un pauvre Ministre qui se tient en sentinelle, pour vous recevoir à la portiere de vostre Carrosse.

Il est vray que la Bassette nous manquent, mais nous nous consolons d'un peu de l'Hombre, et la Comette commence à s'établir. Le divertissement le plus galant du Païs cet hyver c'est le traineau, ou l'on se met en croupe de quelque belle Alemande, en manier que vous ne pouvez ni la voir ni luy parler à cause d'un Diable de tintamarre des sonnets dont les harnois sont tous garnis. Le Droit neantmoins du Traineau[3] est quelque chose de considerable. Vous pouvez pretendre un baiser dans tous les Carrefours de la belle que vous menez. Et la faveur n'est pas meprisable, puisque le baiser ne se donne pas en ceremonie comme chez nous. Si par bonheur vous renversez la belle, vous luy pouvez faire present d'une nouvelle jupe, et Elle ne la peut refuser. Je ne veux pas plus dire sur cet Chapitre de peur de ne vous degoûter des plaisirs de Londres. Quoy que Je ne merite pas ce que vous avez écrit en ma faveur, Je tacheray de m'aquiter en sorte qu'on vous excusera la bonté que vous avez eu pour moy, et je ne manqueray jamais en toute occasion de reconnoistre les obligations que J'ay à vostre Excellence d'estre, Monsieur, V. T. h. e. t. o. s.

G.E.

A Monsieur Barrillion
Ambassadeur de France en Angleterre.
    Source: BM, ff. 2–3; *LB*, pp. 54–55.

[1] Paul Barillon d'Amoncourt, Marquis de Branges (1639–1691), was Ambassador to England from 1677 to 1688.

[2] The date given in *LB*, p. 54, is incorrect. In copying this letter into BM, Hughes first wrote 19/29 December but then corrected it to 14/24. A letter written to Sunderland on the same day (*LB*, pp. 58–59) is clearly dated 14/24 December in the PRO holograph.

[3] *Le droit du traineau* is explained in the next sentence.

To The Earl of Rochester[1]   December 24, 1685
                                                           Dito

My Lord.

I have onely ventur'd to trouble you with one letter since my being here, the Season of the Year affording nothing worth the interrupting you one moment from the great business you are perpetually employ'd in. Your Lordship knows this Countrey and this place. They are not apt to change; women keep their own longest who are not over handsome. I dare say noe more of them. 'Tis hard to be pleasant, when we are affraid of being impertinent.

The Imperial Army has some time since taken up their Winter quarters in Transylvania, and I expect noe news from Hungary worth your knowledge 'till the Campagne begins to open. The Princesse of Ragotzi keeps her Fortress of Mongatz still and the Imperialists have been soe civil to draw from the Town at her request. Caprara nevertheless has block'd up the Avenues with three Regiments. The Count de Windisgratz is return'd hither from Vienna, and there is like to be more disputes about ceremonials, but I reserve them to entertain my Lord Middleton, as my duty obliges me.

I shall be very dilligent to serve his Majestie as well as I am able in what can be expected from me here. If in doing that your goodness will afford me any marke of your favour, I shall not regrett whatever I have lost in London. I wish your Lordship a long enjoyment and dayly encrease of your happiness, and my self the good fortune to have an opportunity to shew how warmly I am, My Lord, Your Lordships m. f. a. m. h. s.

Source: BM, f. 3; *LB,* pp. 56–57 (misdated).

[1] Laurence Hyde, Earl of Rochester (1641–1711), second son of the Earl of Clarendon, had been reappointed Lord of the Treasury on the accession of James II.

Omitted: December 27, 1685. To Middleton with diplomatic news from Rome.

Source: M-1, ff. 35–36.

Omitted: December 31, 1685. To Sir Richard Bulstrode, acknowledging with thanks his letter of December 14th.

Source: Historical Society of Pennsylvania, Gratz Collection, pp. 11–15.

To The Earl of Middleton   December 31, 1685
                                                                        Ratisbon
My Lord.

Since my last of the 27th instant the Diet open'd shop one day and agreed uppon a Complement to be made this Christmas time, as the custome is here, to the Imperial Commission, which was to be deliver'd at the Prince of Passau's, whither the Count de Windischgratz came to take his share of it. All we have from Vienna is that great preparations are made to follow their blow and push the Turks very vigorously in the Spring.

The Count de Crecy has endeavourd some time to be recalled from hence. He pretends he has onely desir'd leave to make a Journy into France to regulate something about his private concerns. It is thought he will suddainly obtaine his request, and that the young Marquis de Torcy,[1] Monsieur Colberts sonne who is now here, will succeed him. The Count de Thunne[2] since his arrival at Vienna has had a Commanderie fallen to him by seignioritie. He had one before of grace, which is worth to him Fourscore thousand Crownes. This the Count de Windischgratz told me in a visit I made him, and that it helps well towards the making upp of his losses in England.

If your Lordship dos not constantly receave Letters from me they must miscarry or be retarded by some accident, for I have not mis'd writing by every post since my coming hither, resolving not to be

20

wanting in my Duty, nor in the sense I ought to have of your favour to, My Lord, Your Lordships most faithfull and most humble servant

Geo: Etherege

Source: M-1, ff. 37–38.

[1] Jean-Baptiste Colbert, Marquis de Torcy (1665–1746), was the son of Charles Colbert, Marquis de Croissy, a former Ambassador to England and French Secretary of State for Foreign Affairs.

[2] Franz Sigmund, Count von Thun, was the representative of the Empire in London from 1680 to September 1685 (*Repertorium*, 1, p. 139). He had suffered heavy gambling losses in London, according to Etherege's letter of January 12, 1688.

To The Earl of Middleton   January 9, 1686
                                                          Ratisbon

My Lord.

The Duke of Lorrain,[1] having heard that his Majestie had been pleas'd to send me hither, sent inclos'd in a letter to the Count de Windischgratz a Memorial of his Rights and pretentions to be deliver'd to me, for my better information in his affairs, on the Succes of which he depends on the protection of his Majestie and his powerfull mediation with the King of France. This was sent me yesterday by the Count, with the Duks Letter; I do not send you a Coppy since I know you need no farther knowledge in this matter. He desires the Count likewise that he wou'd be a meanes to make the Diet to consider of his interests in this conjuncture. I told the Gentleman who brought me the paper that I was sent by his Majestie only to informe him by your Lordship of what shou'd be transacted here, and of other matters of concernment which shou'd occurre in any other parts of the Empire, and that in case the Diet did do any thing in the Dukes affaires, I shou'd not faile to give a particular account of it. I am invited to Day to Dinner by the Count of Windischgratz, and am very glad I have nothing more at present worth troubling you with least I shou'd make a man of compleat Ceremony stay. I am, My Lord, Your Lordships most Dutiful, and most faithfull servant

Geo: Etherege

Source: M-1, ff. 39–40.

[1] Charles, Duke of Lorraine and Bar (1643–1690), the most distinguished of the Imperial generals, who commanded at the siege of Buda. His efforts to recover the Duchy of Lorraine (referred to here) were unsuccessful.

Omitted: January 15, 1686. To Sir William Trumbull, summarizing news of the Diet.

Source: HMC *Downshire*, 1, p. 94. Printed in *LB*, p. 423.

Omitted: January 15, 1686. To Sir William Trumbull reporting military news from Hungary.

Source: HMC *Downshire*, 1, p. 95. Printed in *LB*, pp. 423–424.

To The Earl of Middleton   January 19, 1686
                                                  Ratisbon

To my Lord Middleton with the following Copie of Verses.

> From hunting Whores and hanting play ⎫
> And minding nothing else all day   ⎬
> And all the night too you will say— ⎭
> To make grave legs in formal fetters,
> Converse with Fops and write dull Letters,
> To goe to bed 'twixt eight and nine
> And sleep away my precious time
> In such an idle sneaking place
> Where vice and folly hide their face,
> And in a troublesome disguise
> The wife seems modest, husband wise.
> For pleasure here has the same fate
> Which does attend affaires of State.
> The Plague of Ceremony infects
> Ev'n in Love the softer Sex:
> Who an essential will neglect
> Rather than loose the least respect.
> With regular approach we storm
> And never visit but in form:
> That is, sending to know before
> At what a Clock they'll play the Whore.
> The nymphs are constant, Gallants private;
> One scarce can guesse who 'tis they drive at.
> This seems to me a scurvy fashion ⎫
> Who have been bred in a free nation ⎬
> With Liberty of speech and passion. ⎭
> Yet I cannot forbear to spark it
> And make the best of a bad market.
> Meeting with one by chance kind hearted,
> Who noe preliminaries started,

22

I enter'd beyond expectation ⎤
Into a close negotiation ⎬
Of which hereafter a Relation. ⎦
Humble to fortune, not her slave,
I still was pleas'd with what she gave
And with a firm and cheerfull minde ⎤
I steer my cours with every wind ⎬
To all the Ports she has design'd. ⎦

Source: BM, ff. 5–6; *LB,* pp. 62–63.

Omitted: January 21, 1686. A letter to Middleton reporting diplomatic news from Ratisbon and Vienna.

Source: M-1, ff. 41–42.

To The Earl of Middleton   January 24, 1686
                                                               Ratisbon

My Lord.

From Vienna we heare that the Prince of Newberg[1] having begun his Journy homeward, the Princess his wife, the Emperors Sister, found herselfe ill, which made them go back again to Vienna. She is with child and has hurt herselfe, and besides has had a Hectick fevor some time. Tis said this will put off their Journy for some weeks, but I was told yesterday by one of the Emperors Ministers she is in great danger and will hardly escape it. The news continues of the Serasquier Bassa's being strangl'd at Belgrade, and the Bassa of Buda's having his command. We have also a confirmation of the Ratification of the Treaty betweene the Emperor and the Elector of Brandenburg. Yesterday the Commissions Decree by which the Emperor demands Fifty Roman Months was dictated in the Diet. One Roman Month throughout the whole Empire comes to 27,300 Florins, which in our mony is so many three shillings.

> [Dispute over revenues taken by the King of France from the
> Teutonic Order, contrary to the Armistice.]

Pray my Lord continue your favours to a poor man who is so very sensible of them, and when you think it needfull, now I am so far out of Sight, put his Majestie in mind of Your Lordships most faithfull and most Obedient Servant

                                                               G. Etherege

Source: M-1, ff. 43–44.

[1] Prince Philip William of Neuburg had become Elector Palatine in 1685.

23

To THE EARL OF MIDDLETON   February 4, 1686
                                                  Ratisbon
My Lord.

The business of Segedin[1] is contradicted in our last Letters from
Vienna. General Caprara was first deceiv'd, he deceiv'd the Emperor
and the Court, and we follow'd the Dance. The particulars were very
exact, and the wholle so well design'd that he seemes to be as able a
workeman, who made this lye, as most you have of that Trade in
London.

> [Efforts to check the spread of bad money. Military news
> from Hungary.]

Our winter has been mild till within this weeke, but now it is a
little severe, and we expect to heare of something done against
Mongatz, General Caprara onely waiting till the Frost makes it capable to be attack'd. The pleasure I had when I receiv'd your Lordships Letter is yet fresh, and I find the least marke of your favour is
able to make Ratisbonne agreable. I received yesterday, inclos'd in a
Letter from Mr. Wynne, One from his Majestie to the Elector of
Saxonie, which I deliver'd in the afternoone to his Minister here. I
am, My Lord, Your Lordships most faithfull, and most humble Servant
                                                  Geo: Etherege
Source: M-1, ff. 45–46.

[1] The modern Szeged in Hungary on the banks of the river Tisza. Fortified
by the Turks, the town resisted the Imperial forces until April 1686.

To THE EARL OF MIDDLETON   February 7, 1686
                                                  Ratisbon
My Lord.

Here has been no action lately, and I think the Diet as well as the
Army have taken up their winter quarters. They say there are many
among them who have not yet receiv'd instructions from their Prin-
cipals, which is the reason they proceed not to deliberate on what has
been propos'd. We have nothing from Vienna but what is in the
Gazets, and that so insignificant and so uncertaine it is not worth
troubling your Lordship with.

Mr. Jacob Richards,[1] a young Ingenire (whom his Majestie has
sent to make the next Campagne in Hungarie), arriv'd here the latter
end of last week. He is very ingenious; I have caried him to the Count
of Windisgratz who has promis'd him all the favour his Recommenda-
tions can do him at Court, and I will omit nothing that may help

24

him to follow his instructions. This place is allways as barren of pleasure as it is now of News; wherefore instead of giving you an account of my private affaires, I recommend my selfe to your pittie, and remain, My Lord, Your Lordships most faithfull, and most Obedient Servant

Geo: Etherege

Source: M-1, ff. 47–48.

[1] Richards published a *Journal of the Siege and Taking of Buda*, London, 1687.

Omitted: February 11, 1686. To Middleton reporting military rumors from Poland.

Source: M-1, ff. 49–50.

Omitted: February 12, 1686. To Sir William Trumbull, with news from Poland and Ratisbon.

Source: HMC *Downshire*, 1, p. 114. Printed in *LB*, p. 424.

To The Earl of Middleton   February 14, 1686
Ratisbon

My Lord.

There has nothing pass'd in the Diet since the dictating the Memorials and the Comission for 50 Roman Months, which I have mention'd in my former Letters. Nevertheless they meet every day and Complement one an other till it be time to eate their Sauer Craut.

[News of Prince Tököloy's unsuccessful attempt to persuade the Hungarians to revolt against the Emperor.]

They write from Buda that there is an Embassie on the way from the Grand Seignor to the Emperor with instructions to offer all manner of Satisfaction to the Emperor and his Confederats in Order to procure a peace. The news is confirm'd that the Persian designes a war against the Turk, which makes this be the rather beleiv'd.

Tis now the time of our Carnaval here. They talk of great doeings at Munick, but Mistress Meggs[1] Maskarade, I feare, is beyond what is expected here by, My Lord, Your Lordships most faithfull and most humble servant

Geo: Etherege

Source: M-1, ff. 51–52.

[1] Mrs. Mary Meggs in 1663 was granted a concession to sell oranges and other confectioner's wares in the new Covent Garden Theater of the King's Company. Among those employed by "Orange Moll" was the thirteen-year-old Nell Gwyn (J. H. Wilson, *Nell Gwyn*, 1952, pp. 27–29).

Omitted: February 21, 1686. To Middleton reporting news from Hungary and Hamburg.

Source: M-1, ff. 53–54.

Omitted: February 25, 1686. To Middleton—a miscellany of diplomatic news.

Source: M-1, ff. 55–57.

To Monsieur Purpurat[1]   February 27, 1686
                                                              Ratisbon

Monsieur.

Nous avons esté employez ici plus que d'ordinaire le temps de ce Carnaval. Autrement je n'aurais pas manqué *devant*[2] de vous faire mes reconnoissances. Vous m'accablez d'une telle maniere de Compliments, et de Tabac, que Je manque des paroles et de moyens en ce miserable Endroit pour faire le retour que vostre generosité merite, et pour tout ce que Je vous dois. Je vous puis seulement asseurer que Je suis avec beaucoup de Sincerité, Monsieur etc.

A Monsieur Purpurat à Vienne.

Source: BM, f. 6; *LB,* p. 63.

[1] According to Hughes, a gambler from Vienna who went by the name of Count Purpurat won 1500 florins from Sir George. See p. 293.

[2] Underlined in the MS.

To The Earl of Middleton   March 4, 1686
                                                              Ratisbon

My Lord.

We are still becalm'd here, not the least breese of busines stirring. Ease and quiet, the breeders of discord and mutiny, has renew'd the quarrell which was made up betweene the Count de Windisgratz and the Electorall Colledge; and a Civill war of ceremony is afresh broke out. The Emperors concommissarie is recall'd for not behaving himselfe to the liking of his Superior Officers. Severall things that happen on this occasion make part of our divertion here, but they wou'd be very unpleasant shou'd I give the detail of them to your Lordship.

[Dispute over the right of the Duke of Zell to winter-quarter his troops in Hamburg.]

The Elector of Brandenburg offer'd the Hamburgers Two thousand Foote, but they have refus'd them. They are Jealous (not without cause) all their Neighbours have a mind to 'em, and it is happy for 'em so many have a longing. The number of the Rivalls onely hinder the Rape. To morrow our post comes in from those parts. It is generally thought here the Luneburgers will draw off as soon as honorably they can. Pray, my Lord, continue me in your favour, and when you are in any of those Leisur-places where Idle Fellows are admitted, let me intrude sometimes into your memory. I am, My Lord, Your Lordships most faithfull and most obedient servant

Geo: Etherege

Source: M-1, ff. 59–60. This letter differs considerably from a version printed in *LB*, pp. 63–67. Presumably Hughes was copying from a first draft, which Etherege had revised before sending.

Omitted: March 5, 1686. To Sir William Trumbull, reporting news as in the preceding letter.

Source: HMC *Downshire*, 1, p. 124; *LB*, p. 425.

Omitted: March 11, 1686. A letter to Middleton describing events at Hamburg and preparations for the General Assembly at Augsburg.

Source: M-1, ff. 61–62.

Ratisbon March 11, 1686

A letter to my Lord Middleton with an other to My Lord Sunderland.

Ratisbon March 12, 1686

A letter to Sir William Trumball. [This letter is printed in *LB*, p. 426.]

Source: H-1, p. 2.

To The Earl of Middleton   March 14, 1686
Ratisbon

My Lord.

I send you inclos'd a Coppy of the Memorial Monsieur de Crecy deliver'd to the Diet yesterday. By that you will Judge what his Christian Majestie designes against the Elector Palatin. It seemes to me a protestation that what he undertakes in that business is not against the Armistitia.

[The King of France's terms for accepting the mediation of the Pope in the Palatinate, and the legal reasons for them.]

27

This evening the post comes in from Vienna, and if I have time enough after I receive the news, I will transcribe it and send it to Mr. Wynn for your Lordship. Mr. John Cook[1] in a Letter I lately had the favour to receave from him gave me a plesant account of the adventures of a marriage, which I hope is happely consumated by this time and Numps[2] is now in the Stocks in earnest. I am My Lord Your most faithfull and most obedient Servant

Geo: Etherege

Source: M-1, ff. 63–64; H-1, pp. 2–4; *LB*, pp. 67–69.

[1] John Cooke, by seniority the chief clerk in Middleton's office and Latin Secretary. See F. M. G. Evans, *The Principal Secretary of State*, Manchester, 1923, pp. 172, 192.

[2] The Earl of Mulgrave was married to the widow of the Earl of Conway on March 18, 1686 (Wilson, *Court Wits*, p. 212). Etherege here alludes to a couplet in Mulgrave's "An Essay on Satire" (Brett-Smith, *Works*, 1, p. 121):

Beauty and Wit had seiz'd his Heart so fast,
That Numps himself seem'd in the Stocks at last.

Omitted: March 18, 1686. To Middleton with a revised legal opinion on the Duchess of Orleans' claim and news of the Roman months.

Source: M-1, ff. 65–66; H-1, pp. 4–7; *LB*, pp. 69–71, with incorrect date.

Omitted: March 19, 1686. A letter to Sir William Trumbull about the Duchess of Orleans' claim.

Source: HMC *Downshire*, 1, pp. 131–133; *LB*, pp. 426–428.

To The Earl of Middleton   March 21, 1686
                                                        Ratisbon

My Lord.

Yesterday the conclusion about 50 Roman Months was agreed uppon by the 3 Colledges, and the Townes carried the two points they insisted on: an abatement for the Troops they have furnish'd and a consideration for the Winter-quarters; and this day it passes in forme.

[Diplomatic reports from France and Hamburg.]

I heare there is a marriage towards
And Cuckolds smile in hope of sweet revenge[1]
(as an author has it). As soon as I am assur'd of it's being compleated, I entend to felicitate the Lusty Bridegrome, having more then ordinarie

28

obligations to do that, as well as to be, My Lord, Your Lordships most faithfull and most obedient Servant

Geo: Etherege

Source: M-1, ff. 67–68.

1 Etherege here combines a line from Mulgrave's "An Essay on Satire" (Brett-Smith, *Works,* 1, p. 121) and a similar line from "An Essay Upon Satyre," Bodleian MS Don. b. 8., p. 638.

To my Lord Middleton   March 21, 1686
Mr. Cooke and
Brother Wynne about Extraordinaries.
  Source: H-1, p. 7.

Omitted: March 25, 1686. To Middleton about two Commission Decrees dictated in the Diet.
  Source: M-1, ff. 69–71; H-1, pp. 8–9; *LB,* pp. 72–73.

Omitted: March 28, 1686. To Middleton reporting on complaints about the Roman months and the affairs of Hamburg.
  Source: M-1, ff. 72–73.

To my Lord Middleton about Mecklenburg[1]   March 28, 1686
To Mr. Bradbury.[2]
  Source: H-1, p. 10.

1 Complaints from the Duke of Mecklenburg are discussed in the following letter, not in this one.
2 George Bradbury, a barrister engaged by Sir George and Lady Etherege to prosecute their suit against John West and Dr. Nicholas Barbone (Dorothy Foster, "Sir George Etherege," *TLS,* Feb. 16, 1922, p. 108).

To The Earl of Middleton   April 1, 1686
Ratisbon

My Lord.

[Complaints in the Diet from Mecklenburg.]

The Conclusion the Diett has past for the Römer monath is not yet deliver'd to the Imperial Commission, by reason of the difference betweene the Commission and the Electorall Colledge about the Ceremonial. I intend very suddainly to trouble your Lordship once for all with the detaille of this misunderstanding because it has been, and is like to be, the delay of all affaires that tend to the good of the Empire.

29

The Prince of Passau, it is said, goes on Wednesday next from hence to Passau about his privat busines; and it is thought by some he will excuse himselfe from returning again, being a quiet man and not able to endure the wrangling he finds daylie among the Ministers. It is certain that Caprara lay down before Mongatz on the Ninth of this instant, and that some time since he had finish'd all his batteries and other works necessary for the Seige. The answer the Princess of Ragatzi made to the last message he sent her was that she wou'd not come out of that place till she was drawn out by the hair of the head.

[News of General Tököloy.]

If I have not writ to my Lord Treasurer so often as I ought to have don, it is my Modestie and not my negligence has made me commit the fault. Pray make a Complement for me there, when it lights in your way, and beleive I am with the greatest sense of gratitude, My Lord, Your Lordships most faithfull and most Obedient Servant

G Etherege

Source: M-1, ff. 74–75.

To my Lord Middleton   April 1, 1686
my Lady and Mr. Negus[1]

To my Lord Geo: Savile[2]   April 3, 1686
Comte Leslie[3] and Monsieur Purpurat.

April 4, 1686
To my Lord Middleton about the Conclusion (touching the 50 Roman Month) which the Electorall College refus'd to send to the Emperors Commissioners by a generall deputation as was wont: pretending they were deny'd the Honour of Punctillios due to them. Therefore the Minister of Mayance carry'd it alone.

Source: H-1, p. 10.

[1] Probably Francis Negus, secretary to the Duke of Norfolk (HMC *11th Report*, App. 7, pp. 105, 107).
[2] Son of the Earl of Halifax and nephew of Etherege's friend Henry Savile. Lord George was wounded at the siege of Buda.
[3] Jacob, Count Leslie, a field marshal in the Austrian army (Wurzbach, *Biographische Lexicon*). His secretary, William Leslie, later Bishop of Laibach, wrote regularly to Etherege's secretary (BM Add. Mss. 41842, ff. 3–23).

Omitted: April 4, 1686. The letter summarized above, including a plan of the Alliance to be proposed at Augsburg. It is unaddressed and unsigned, though in Etherege's hand.
Source: M-1, ff. 76–77.

Omitted: April 8, 1686. To Middleton with news of a duel in Vienna.
Source: H-1, pp. 11–12; *LB*, pp. 74–75.

To The Earl of Middleton   April 18, 1686
                                                                Ratisbon
My Lord.

I have had a little fit of Sickness which has held me this week, but I begin to recover and hope within these two or three days to be perfectly well again. By reason of the Holidays, here is little news stirring. The report is that the Seidge of Mongatz is given over by reason of the difficultys that were found in it, tho' our News from Vienna this day says it continues, but is likely to be very painefull by reason of the obstinacy of the beseidged. I cannot yet acquaint you what is agreed concerning the next Campagne at Vienna since the Duke of Lorrains arrivall there. Here are severall discourses but all is but conjecture. On the 18th of May next, tis said, the generall Rendevouz is to be neare Presburg. The Elector of Bavaria[1] (who the latter end of this Month has a Randevouz of all his Troops at Stroben some 6 Leagues from this place) will command a body of 25000. Whither the Emperor will make them up out of his own Troops wholly or joyne some of the other auxillaries is not yet known. Will Herbert,[2] Thomas Cheeks[3] brother in Law, with one or two more young Sparks, pass'd by this place last Week, and are design'd for the Campagne in Hungarie. This Cutting Morecraft[4] promises to make as good an Officer as Falstaff. I am, My Lord, Your Lordships most humble and most obedient faithfull Servant

                                                        Geo: Etherege
        Source: M-1, ff. 78–79.

[1] Maximilian Emanuel II, Elector of Bavaria (1662–1726), fought at Buda under the Duke of Lorraine.
[2] William Herbert (1667–1745), who later became the 2nd Marquis of Powis.
[3] Captain Thomas Cheke, Lieutenant of the Tower in London, and William Herbert both married daughters of Sir Thomas Preston.
[4] The usurer Morecraft in Beaumont and Fletcher's *The Scornful Lady* (V, iv, 131) is tricked of his money and decides to lead a dissipated, gallant

31

life. Thereafter he is called "Cutting (i.e., swaggering) Morecraft." Dryden refers, in the Prologue to *Marriage-a-la-Mode,* to "Cutting Moorcraft," apparently meaning a cit dressed in foppish clothes and impersonating a gallant. I owe these references to David M. Vieth.

Omitted: April 21, 1686. To Middleton, reporting diplomatic news from the Diet.
Source: M-1, ff. 80–81.

Omitted: April 25, 1686. To Middleton, enclosing the Elector Palatine's memorial.
Source: M-1, ff. 82–83. Summarized in *LB,* p. 76, and followed by the text of the memorial.

Ratisbon April 29, 1686

To my Lord Middleton, with the Duke of Zells letter to the Emperor, a Copie of Verses, and about two little places on the other side of the Elb taken by the said Duke from the Hamburgers and fortify'd.

Dito

The Verses

Since Love and verse as well as Wine
Are brisker where the sun doth shine,
'Tis something to loose two degrees
Now age itself begins to freez;
Yet This I patiently cou'd bear ⎫
If the Rough Danube's Beauties were ⎬
But onely two degrees less faire ⎭
Than the Kind Nymphs of gentle Thames,
Who warme me hither with their beames.
Such power they have they can dispense
Five hundred Miles their Influence.
But hunger forces men to eat
Tho' no temptation's in the meat.
How wou'd the ogling Sparks dispise
The Darling Damsel of my eyes
Did they behold her at a Play
As she's trick'd up on holiday,
When the whole family combine
For publick pride to make her shine.
Her Hair which long befor lay matted
Are on this day comb'd out and pleated,

A Diamond bodkin in each tress
The badges of her nobleness;
For every Stone as well as she
Can boast an ancient Pedegree.[1]
These form'd the Jewell erst did grace
The Cap o' th' first Graff o'th' Race,
Now preferr'd by Graffin Marian
T'adorne the handle of her fan,
And as by old Records appears
Worn since in Kunigunda's ears,
Now sparkling in the Frawleins hair. ⎫
No Serpent breaking in the Air   ⎬
Can with her starry head compare. ⎭
Such Ropes of Pearls her hands incumber
She Scarce can deal the Cards at Ombre.
Soe many Rings each finger fraight
They tremble with the mighty weight.
The like in England nere was seen
Since Holbin drew Hall and his Queen.
But after these fantastick fights
The lustre's meaner than the lights,
For she that bears this glitt'ring Pomp
Is but a Tawdry ill bred Rampe,
Whose brawny Limbs & marsiall face
Proclaime her of the Gothick Race
More than the painted Pagentrie
Of all her father's Heraldry.
But there's an other sorte of Creatures
Whose ruddy Look and grotesq features
Are soe much out of nature's way
You'd think them stamp'd on other clay,
No lawfull Daughters of old Adam.
From these behold a Citty madam
With Arms in mittins, head in muff,
A dapper cloack and rev'rend ruff;
No farse so pleasant as this Maukin, ⎫
The pretty jett she has in walking   ⎬
And the soft sound of high Dutch talking. ⎭
Here unattended by the Graces
The Queen of Love in a sad Case is.
Nature, her Active Minister,
Neglects affairs and will not stir,

Thinks it not worth her while to please
But when she does it for her ease.
Evn I her most Devout Adorer
With wandering thoughts appear before her,
And when I'm making an oblation ⎤
Am fain to spurr Imagination   ⎬
With some old London inclination. ⎦
The bow is bent at German Dame;
The Arrow flys at English Game.
Kindness that can indifference warm
And blow that calm into a storm
Has in the very tendrest hour
Over my gentleness noe pow'r,
True to my Country womens charms
Whilst Kiss'd & press'd in forraigne Arms.

Fragments Left Out[2]

With thousand Diamonds whose prices
You must not guess at by their Seizes
Their antick cut, and want of lustre
Which in a shop will not pass muster
But by the Laws of Herauldry
Th' ear's the Judge and not the Eye.
Let them who live in plenty flowtt
I must make shift with sauer Kraut.
What matter is't what this stone cost
Or what t'will yield since it can boast
These are the charmes of this great Nation
No Coquetrie nor no belle passion
To force the lock of Natur's Door
And make her lavish out her Store
Diffring in faith in birth and dress
When I ingeniously confess
They all agree in ugliness
The Virgins of the Church of Rome
The Daughters wrought on Luther's loom
Have in this world the same sad doom.

Source: BM, ff. 14–16; *LB*, pp. 80–82.

[1] This couplet is written in the margin of the MS but starred for insertion here.

[2] These couplets are deleted in the MS.

Omitted: April 30, 1686. To Sir William Trumbull, reporting news from Vienna.
Source: HMC *Downshire,* 1, p. 155; *LB,* p. 428.

Omitted: May 6, 1686. To Middleton, reporting actions at the Diet.
Source: M-1, ff. 84–85; *LB,* pp. 83–84.

TO THE EARL OF MIDDLETON   May 9, 1686
                                                                        Ratisbon
My Lord.

Here is ariv'd lately Count Lamberg,[1] who has been long expected in quallity of first Commissioner for Austria. This occasions new disputes about Ceremonialls; the Electoral Colledge has refus'd to visit him, saying the Ministers of the Colledge of Princes (tho they are the last comers) ought to make them the first visit. The Emperor (who wou'd gaine this point) has made it be contested formerly; the Colledge of Princes will not see him without he will promise to returne their visit, which is contrary to his instructions, he being to imitate the Count de Windizgrats in an inferior post. He has given me notice of his arrival in a long Complement he sent me by his Secretarie, and I intend to go and see him to morrow.

[News of the Diet and of troop movements through Ratisbon.]

I receiv'd this day a Letter from Gratz, which tells me General Leslie has sent word to the Court that the preparations they have made are not corespondent to their project. We heare this day from Vienna that General Mercy[2] (who has long watch'd the Motions of Tekelie[3] in the Upper Hungarie), having notice that he was advancing in hast with 5 thousand Turks towards Mongatz, met him uppon the Bancks of the Theÿs (not far from Sedgedin) and fell uppon him, routed him, kill'd a thousand on the place, with a Bassa, besides severall who threw themselves into the river in hope of escaping and were drown'd. Tekelie sav'd himselfe by flight. I am, My Lord, Your Lordships most faithfull and most humble Servant

                                                                Geo: Etherege

The Bassa which was kill'd is said by some to be the Serasquire Bassa who had joyn'd himselfe with Tekelie. Mercy had but 4,000 men with him.

Source: M-1, ff. 86–87; H-1, p. 15; *LB,* pp. 84–85 (in part).

[1] Johann Phillip, Count von Lamberg, was Austrian envoy to the Diet, 1686–1689 (*Urkunden,* 22, p. 600). Etherege had "great esteem" for him:

"he is a gentleman who (besides his other merits) knows how to live." See letter of February 12, 1687.

[2] Peter, Count Mercy, a Lieutenant Fieldmarshal in the Austrian army, died a few months later at the siege of Buda.

[3] Tököly was attempting to relieve Munkács, where his wife was besieged.

May 13, 1686

To my Lady and to Brother Wynne with the Circular Letter.

May 16, 1686

To my Lord Middleton about the King's letter to the Emperor and the Dyet.
Source: H-1, p. 16.

Omitted: May 16, 1686. The letter to Middleton calendared above, with news of preparations for forming the League of Augsburg.
Source: M-1, ff. 88–89.

May 20, 1686

To my Lord Middleton about the meeting of the Ministers of the Elector of Brandenburg, Elector of Saxony, the Houses of Brunswick and Hesse and Cassell at the faire of Leipswig. With an account of the designe of those Princes, and also of the Elector of Saxony to meet the Prince of Orange at Cleve in order to conferre about securing the Protestant Religion.
Source: H-1, p. 16; *LB*, p. 85.

Omitted: May 20, 1686. The letter to Middleton calendared above.
Source: M-1, ff. 90–91.

To Owen Wynne   May 23, 1686
                                                  Ratisbon

Sir.

Here has been nothing done in the Diet of late, and we have so little news by this post from Vienna that I did not think it necessarie to trouble my Lord now. I have enclos'd part of a letter which I had from Mr. Jacob Richards this day. It is of the 19th instant New Style. I can hardly beleive the Emperor's Armie will be of the Number he mentions, the Auxillaries this yeare consisting not of above 27 thousand men. After the generall Randevouz, I shall be able to give you a true account by the correspondence I have with some considerable Officers.

Here is my Lord Montjoy[1] and severall other Vollunteers arriv'd, and we are endeavoring to get them conveniencies to carry them to Vienna. I shall allways be sensible of your favours, and put Mr. Robson[2] in mind that the wellcomest News we can receive must come from him. I am, Sir, Your most humble and obedient Servant

Geo: Etherege

Source: M-1, f. 92.

[1] William Stewart, 1st Viscount Mountjoy (1653–1692), volunteered for service with the Imperial army and was wounded at Buda.
[2] Thomas Robson, a Treasury Office clerk.

To The Earl of Middleton   May 27, 1686
                                             Ratisbon
My Lord.

The Deputys who are to assist at Augsburg for the renuing the Alliance so much talk'd of are making what hast thither they can. The Count de Leill is to preside at that conference for the Emperor. He is now on his way from Ulm, where he has been to endeavor to dispose the Circle of Swabe to comply with the Emperor's desires. Here is great briguing to hinder this Alliance. We shall suddainly see the succes of it.

[Negotiations between Hamburg and the Duke of Zell. Illness of the Elector of Bavaria and the Duke of Lorrain.]

There are many reports of what is to be done this Campagne, but the great designe is kept secret (as I am inform'd by the Count de Windisgratz). The Army is to be devided: the Duke of Lorrain is to command 40 thousand men, and the Elector of Bavaria 16 thousand Foot and 5 thousand Horse. General Leislie is nam'd to Command the first under the Elector, and the Prince Lewis of Baden[1] the second, but Leislie is now at the Baths, and not fit by reason of his gout to be in the Feild; so that Prince Lewis will in effect have the first Command under the Elector, which was so ordered by Prince Herman[2] in favour of his Nephew. I am, My Lord, Your Lordships most dutifull and most humble servant

G Etherege

Source: M-1, ff. 94–95.

[1] Louis William, Margrave of Baden (1655–1707), distinguished himself in the Imperial Army at Buda, Fünfkirchen, Esseck, and Mohács. His crush-

ing defeat of the Turks at Slankamen in 1691 drove the Turks from Hungary.

2 Prince Hermann of Baden (1628–1691) was the younger brother of Louis William's father, and hence uncle to the Margrave. He was President of the Imperial Council of War and Principal Commissioner at Ratisbon following the Count of Windischgrätz' departure.

May 27, 1686

To my Lord Middleton about the meeting at Augsburg, and about the businesse of Hamburg.

To Mr. Robson

May 30, 1686

To my Lord Middleton and Mr. Montstephens.[1]

Source: H-1, p. 16.

1 John Mountsteven, a secretary to the Earl of Sunderland (HMC *Downshire*, 1, pp. 52, 105).

Omitted: May 30, 1686. To Middleton about new members of the Diet, German losses in Hungary, and plans for the campaign against the Turks.

Source: M-1, ff. 96–97; H-1, p. 17; *LB*, pp. 85–86 (in part).

June 3, 1686

To my Lord Middleton and Mrs. Merry.[1]

Source: H-1, p. 17.

1 Twenty-four letters to Mrs. Merry are recorded in the Harvard letter-books between June 3, 1686 and September 28, 1689. None has been found, and I have not been able to make a positive identification of Etherege's correspondent. It seems likely that she was his sister Elizabeth, who is mentioned in the will of a sister, Anne Etherege. The will reveals, incidentally, that Elizabeth was alive and married on March 13, 1680, the date of the signing, and that Sir George was a residuary legatee. The estate of an Elizabeth Merry, widow, of Maidenhead, Berkshire, who died in poverty, was administered in 1700. That this Elizabeth Merry was Etherege's sister Elizabeth is suggested by the subject matter of one letter to Mrs. Merry: "Bateman's business." The phrase refers to an attempt by Sir George to recover part of the estate of a distant cousin from which his sister Elizabeth could also have benefited.

To THE EARL OF MIDDLETON   June 3, 1686
                                             Ratisbon

My Lord.

[News of meetings at Ulm and Nuremberg to instruct the deputies at the Augsburg conference.]

That which has retarded the Campagne is a dispute which has been about the Road the Auxilliary Forces shou'd march into Hungarie. Generall Schoninck[1] refus'd to march his Troops the way which was set down by the Emperors Comissaries till he had receiv'd new orders from his Master, the Elector of Brandenburg, it being contrarie to what was first stipulated, and besides the way is so very bad and mountainous that it is impossible for the Carriages to pass, nor can the Horse without great fatigue and loss: but the busines is accommodated, the Carriages are permitted to goe through Moravia, and the Troops keep the road prescrib'd through Silesia by Jabluncka, a way far about and very incommodious.

The stayeing of the Electors Forces some time on this occasion in this Countrie gave some Jealosie at Court, and rais'd a talk as if instead of goeing into Hungarie according to the agreement, he had given his Generall order to seise on some principalities he pretends a title to in Silesia. The true reason of the changing of the Road which occasion'd this delay and these rumors is that some of the cheife ministers at Court were unwilling the Armie shou'd march through a Country where their Estates lay, which wou'd have run the hazard of receiving a considerable damage by it.

The report of the Imperialists having receiv'd some loss in the Upper Hungarie is in some sort confirm'd, and it is said the heat of the busines fell on the Bavarian Troops, who remain'd there all the winter. I am, my Lord, Your Lordships most faithfull and most humble Servant

Geo: Etherege

Source: M-1, ff. 98–99.

[1] Hans Adam von Schöning (1641–1696) commanded the troops sent by the Elector of Brandenburg to fight the Turks.

To The Earl of Middleton   June 6, 1686
                                                        Ratisbon
My Lord.

I send you enclos'd an account of what pass'd at Newrenberg and Ulm, in order to instruct their Deputys for the Conference at Augsburg.

[Obstinacy of the Circle of Swabia. Plans for formally admitting the Prince of Waldeck to the College of Princes.]

The Ministers who occasion'd the changing of the Road for the March of those Troops were Serini[1] and Kaunitz,[2] whose estates lye in

Moravia; and having no more news to send you I will venture being impertinent in telling you a Storie of a Case of conscience, which happen'd uppon the Elector of Bavaria's marriage to the Arch-dutches. Kaunitz being the Emperor's Envoyé at Munick, the Elector made Love (and scandal says not unsuccesfully) to his wife, who is very agreable and very Gallante (for a Dutch Lady). The Emperor, knowing the matter, after the marriage made it be debated in his Council whither he ought not to recall Kaunitz; but it was urg'd the Elector being young and of a constitution that wou'd incline him now and then to wrong his faire Princess, it was better to continue Kaunitz and his wife in that Court, she having an ascendant over the Elector's Spirit and being like to keep it by her Subtilty and wit, then by removing her to let him fall into worse hands, who may incline him to an other interest, she and her Husband being firmely bound to the Emperor's. Whereuppon Kaunitz was, and is, continu'd, and his wife has great power in that Court. I hope your Lordship will excuse this by-play since I but seldom take the Libertie. I am, My Lord, Your Lordships most faithfull and most humble servant

Geo: Etherege

Source: M-1, ff. 100–101.

[1] Johann Karl, Count Sereni, an artillery general and later a field marshal, was the Bavarian envoy to the Empire (*Repertorium*, 1, p. 14).
[2] Domenic Andrew, Count von Kaunitz (1642–1705), Imperial envoy at Ratisbon, carried out various diplomatic missions for the Emperor. In January 1687, he replaced Count von Thun as Imperial envoy to England (George H. Jones, *Charles Middleton*, 1967, pp. 148–149).

June 9, 1686

To my Lord Montjoy.

June 10, 1686

To my Lord Middleton and Sir Peter Wyche
To Mr. Malle[1] and
To Brother Wynne.
  Source: H-1, p. 18.

[1] Thomas Maule, Etherege's friend and correspondent, obtained, among other sinecures, the office of King's Remembrancer in the Court of Exchequer in Ireland (*CSPD, 1677–78*, p. 131). On January 1, 1688, Etherege congratulated him on being made "Gentleman of the Prince's Bedchamber."

Omitted: June 10, 1686. To Middleton, reporting rumors of a league between Poland and Russia and plans for the campaign.

Source: M-1, ff. 102–103.

Omitted: June 11, 1686. To Sir William Trumbull with news from the Diet and from Hungary.

Source: HMC *Downshire,* 1, pp. 176–177; *LB,* p. 428.

Wednesday June 12, 1686

To Mr. Herbert[1] Att Raab.[2]
    Source: H-1, p. 18.

[1] Probably William Harbord, because other evidence shows that Etherege was corresponding with him about this time. See *Savile Correspondence,* p. 297.
  [2] The modern Györ, Hungary.

To The Earl of Middleton   June 17, 1686
                                                Ratisbon
My Lord.

The Brandenbourg Troops were so ill satisfied with the changing of their Route that they have not march'd since above a League or a League and an halfe a day, and have done much mischief in their passage thro' Silesia, which occasions complaints; they were expected at Râb the last week, but we have no advise of their arrival yet. The designe of having two Armys and the besieging of Alba Regalis[1] is chang'd, and the whole power, under the command of the Duke of Lorrain, is to besiege Buda. Monsieur Stratsman[2] is sent by the Emperor (who came last week from Neustadt to Vienna) to the Camp to use his skill to dispose the Elector of Bavaria to comply, and to be content to make this Campagne under the Duke of Lorrain. What success his negotiation will have with a Young Prince who has been long ambitious to be at the head of an Army, who has the Emperor's promise for it, and the reputation of being in a manner in possession of it thro' all Christendom, is not yet knowne.

[Reasons for not attacking Alba Regalis. Debates in the Diet.]

I am with all the Duty imaginable, My Lord, Your Lordships most faithfull, and most humble servant.

                                       Geo: Etherege

Source: M-1, ff. 104–105. Summarized in H-1, p. 18; *LB,* pp. 86–87.

[1] The modern Hungarian town of Szekesfehérvár (German "Stuhlweissenburg"). Captured by the Turks in 1543, the town was a patriotic shrine because the ancient Hungarian kings had been crowned and buried there.
[2] Theodore Henry Strattmann, Court Chancellor of the Empire.

Dito [June 17, 1686]
To Sir Peter Wyche and Sir Gabriel Sylvius[1] about the King's letters, et ut supra. [These letters are summarized in *LB,* pp. 88–89.]
Inclos'd to my Brother[2] a letter from Mr. Negus, Mr. Moore, Mr. Vadrey[3] and Mr. St. John (als. Captain St. John.)
Source: H-1, p. 19.

[1] Envoy Extraordinary to Denmark.
[2] Owen Wynne and Hughes were related by marriage.
[3] Edward Vaudrey, James Fitzjames's tutor.

To Owen Wynne   June 17, 1686

Sir.
I have not this weeke received any letters from England, which is a thing that touches me here as near as ever a disappointment did in London with the woman I lov'd most tenderly, but I flatter my self in this case, as I us'd to doe in the other, that it is some misfortune and not your want of Kindness has been the occasion. I have writ my Lord all the news we have, which you have constantly the perusall of. That which makes me break off this letter soe abruptly is the news I just now receiv'd of Mr. Fitzjames's[1] being arriv'd in This Town, which I hope you will take for an excuse for my Silence 'till next Post. I am etc.
Source: BM, f. 18; *LB,* pp. 87–88.

[1] James Fitzjames, the illegitimate son of James II by Arabella Churchill. He was created Duke of Berwick in 1687.

Omitted: June 20, 1686. To Middleton with news of the Diet and of military movements toward Buda.
Source: M-1, ff. 106–107; *LB,* pp. 89–91.

Omitted: June 24, 1686. To Middleton inclosing the French answer to the Imperial Commission.
Source: M-1, ff. 108–109.

To Brother Wynne about dues out of the Treasury
To Mr. Lengenberg about Post Letters.
 Source: H-1, p. 21.

Omitted: July 1, 1686. To Middleton about the efforts to create the
League of Augsburg.
 Source: M-1, ff. 110–111.

July 1, 1686
To my Lord Middleton with the Complaints of the Empire against
France. About the Conference at Augsbourg, and Mr. Fitzjames.
To my Lady.
Bradbury and Manlove.[1]
 Source: H-1, p. 21.

[1] An associate of Bradbury's who later took over the prosecution of the
suit against West and Barbone.

TO THE EARL OF MIDDLETON   July 4, 1686

My Lord.

[Reports of French and Danish aggression.]

It is thought the conference at Augsburg will end suddainly without any effect, the Duke of Wirttenberg and the Circle of Swabe remaining possitive not to admitt any Strangers into the Alliance,
though a Letter which came this day from Munick saies they are
come to an agreement there and that they are now at work about the
recess, which is kept so close that even the Secretaries are not trusted.
It saies further that a Minister from the Prince of Orange is expected
at that conference. Monsieur Valquenir[1] (the Holland Minister) is
gone from hence to Augsburg, and here the report is now that it is
to consult with him who is to come hither from the said prince. Some
say there will be two Alliances made there: One betweene the three
Circles of Franconia, Swabe, and Bavaria and the other betweene the
Forraigne Princes and those who will joyne with them. You may
beleive what you please of all these rumors; I acquaint you with
them onely because they make a Noise here.

I send you enclos'd the News we have from Buda. The Bavarian
Troops, not withstanding Pest was disserted, did not possess them-

selves of it without some Loss. There happen'd to be a wolfe in the Towne (whether he was left there by some body who was fled, and allmost starv'd, or whether it was one who had far'd well the last Siege and came to look for pray is uncertaine). As they enter'd the place he fell on a Souldier and tore him in pieces. Severall Cavaliers came in vaine to his rescue, among the rest Monsieur Belque, General of the Elector's Horse, who fir'd a pistol but did not kill the beast, who in revenge flew at him and carried away a great peece of his Jack-boote. A Captain of Horse drew out a pistoll, which miss'd fire, and it cost him a great peece of his Sholder which was torne a way, after which a luckie shot layd the wolfe sprauling.

I had a letter of the 24th instant New Style from Vienna from Mr. Vaudrey, who is with Mr. Fitzjames, which tells me he is well and was taking post for Buda.

Since the begining of the Campagne our letters from Vienna find a Rub in their way, which I took notice of in talking with the Count de Lamberg. He smil'd, and told me we shou'd receive the good News time enough, so that I find great care is taken by the Court there to Cross the proverbe. Pray my Lord continue your goodnes to me, and keep me alive in his Majestie's memorie. The hope of this onely makes me cherefull in this place. I am, My Lord, Your Lordships most faithfull, and most humble Servant

Geo: Etherege

Source: M-1, ff. 112–113.

---

[1] Pierre Valkenier, resident at Ratisbon from the States General and a fervent supporter of the Prince of Orange, was Etherege's chief enemy at the Diet. He seems to have conspired with Hugo Hughes, Etherege's secretary, to obtain information for the Dutch from Etherege's letterbook (*HLB*, pp. 331–344).

Omitted: July 8, 1686. To Middleton, with details of the negotiations at Augsburg.

Source: M-1, ff. 114–115.

Munday July 8, 1686

To my Lord Middleton, about the Complaints against Contraventions. With the news-paper or journall of the Siege of Buda to the 29 inclusive.

To Sir Peter Wyche and Sir Gabriel Sylvius.

To Mr. Vaudrey

A Copie of his Majesties Letter to the Emperor deliver'd the same day to the Bishop of Pasau.

Source: H-1, p. 22.

Omitted: July 11, 1686. To Middleton, reporting the conclusion of the Augsburg Alliance.

Source: M-1, ff. 116–117; H-1, pp. 22–24; *LB*, pp. 91–93.

Dito [July 11, 1686]

To Mr. Webster.

Source: H-1, p. 24.

Omitted: July 15, 1686. To Middleton, reporting on disputes between Brandenburg and Saxony over the principality of Querfurt.

Source: M-1, ff. 118–119; H-1, pp. 24–26; *LB*, pp. 93–95.

Dito [July 15, 1686]

To Mr. Guy.[1]

Source: H-1, p. 26.

[1] Henry Guy of Tring (1631–1710), an attorney educated at Christ Church and the Inner Temple, was an old friend of Etherege's. He appears to have begun his career at court as a Gentleman Usher to the Queen (*CSPD, 1661–1662,* p. 388), and through a series of lucrative posts became very wealthy (Stephen Baxter, *The Development of the Treasury,* London, 1957, pp. 190, 192). Through Sunderland's influence, he became Secretary to the Lords of the Treasury in 1679 (J. P. Kenyon, *Robert Spencer, Earl of Sunderland,* London, 1958, p. 25). He served till 1689 and was replaced by William Jephson.

To THE EARL OF MIDDLETON
July 18, 1686
Ratisbon

My Lord.

[Alliances made at Augsburg still kept secret.]

Our Voluntairs at Buda are very sparing in writing what passes there; nevertheless I shall tell your Lordship what is come to my knowledge. I was shown a letter by the Count de Windisgratz, which was sent him by the Count de Starenberg and came to his hands yesterday, in which it is said that uppon the coming of the Brandenbourg Troops they were taken by the Turks for a Succor which was come to them, and were not undeceiv'd till they had taken their post and began to entrench themselves; and then to hinder their entrenching and to fall them, they made a Salley in which the Brandenbourgers receiv'd some loss, and the Young Durffling,[1] the eldest son of the Elector's General (of the same name) was kill'd.

[Plans for the siege.]

The Letters which are come to this Towne to day say that on the 8th instant at night the Turks made a great sally in which the Imperialists and the Brandenbourgers suffer'd, after which towards the morning they sprung a mine which had like to have buried a young prince of Neubourg, which caus'd a little confusion. The Imperialists blame the Brandenbourgers for this loss, and they lay the fault on the others. The Turks tried the next night if they cou'd make an other sally with the like success, but they were beaten back in time. On the Tenth at Night it is said they prepar'd to make the Turks a fine fire, by which I suppose is meant that they intended to Bombard the place more vigorously then they had done yet. I am, My Lord, Your Lordships most faithfull and most humble servant

G Etherege

The Count de Windisgratz told me on Teusday last he heard the Duke of Holstein Gottorp had Five and Fifty Thousand Crowns at Hambourg with which he design'd to take up the Prince of Denmarks Mortgage.[2]

Source: M-1, ff. 120–122.

[1] Georg von Derfflinger, a Field Marshal from Brandenburg (*Urkunden*, 22, p. 596).

[2] Prince George of Denmark (James II's son-in-law) had loaned 50,000 dollars to the Duke of Holstein-Gottorp and, when the interest was not paid, seized the districts of Tremsbüttel and Steinhorst as security (Carl Brinkmann, "Relations between England and Germany, 1660–1688," *English Historical Review*, 24 [1909], 468).

Omitted: July 22, 1686. To Middleton describing legal and semantic haggling at the Diet.

Source: M-1, ff. 124–125; H-1, pp. 26–28; *LB*, pp. 95–97.

Dito [July 22, 1686]

To my Lord Treasurer with Monsieur Carossio's List of the slaine and wounded in the assault made the 13 July New Style 86 at Buda.

To Mr. Bridgeman[1] and Mr. Fourcade[2]

July 23, 1686

July 24, 1686

To my Lord Mountjoy.
Source: H-1, p. 29.

[1] William Bridgeman was undersecretary to the Earl of Sunderland in the office of Secretary of State (Evans, *The Principal Secretary of State*, p. 164).

[2] Florent Fourcade was named "one of his Majesties Chyrurgeons in ordinary" on December 20, 1672 (PRO, LC 5/140, p. 155). A Mrs. Fourcard ran "a bathing establishment or 'Pockage' in London." She was famous for treating venereal disease by "sweating in lanthorn" (J. Prinz, *John Wilmot, Earl of Rochester*, 1927, p. 253). Etherege refers to the treatment in an early poem (Thorpe, *Poems*, p. 43): "Were I still in lantern sweating." Hugo Hughes first met Etherege at the house of Fucadius, a French surgeon. See below, p. 308.

Omitted: July 25, 1686. To Middleton giving details of the Alliance made at Augsburg on July 6.
Source: M-1, ff. 126–127; H-1, pp. 29–30; *LB,* pp. 97–98.

To The Earl of Middleton

July 29, 1686
Ratisbon

My Lord.

Nothing has been done in the Diet since my last. I receiv'd a Note this day in which I am promis'd some time this week a Copy of the great Recess (as it is call'd) made at Augsburg. It is 12 sides of paper, of which I will send what is material to your Lordship.

[Memorial from the Swedish Minister.]

I have not had a Letter from any of our volunteers before Buda since the 14th instant, the Day after the fatal assault. The Count de Windisgratz sent for the Austrian Minister to day and bad him acquaint the Diet that the Emperor had receiv'd a Letter from the Elector of Bavaria, which informes that the Turks made a great sally of his side, kill'd about 100 of his men, and Nail'd 3 peices of his Cannon, but were at length beat back very vigorously, during which action the great Magazin in the Towne (by what accident is unknown) was blown up, and occaison'd so great a trembling of the Earth that many howses, part of the Castle, and of the walls of the place are fallen down: which has mightily encourag'd the Christians, in so much that they doe not doubt to be suddainly masters of it.

47

I saw just now a letter from a French Gentleman,[1] who is a Volunteere in the Bavarian Troops, who gives an account of this sally in the same manner, but makes no mention of the blowing up of the Magazin. He saies the Turks are very resolute and do the Christians daily a great deale of mischiffe, that the Visier is now certainly in the Feild and marching with a considerable Army to raise the siege, which makes the succes doutfull. Most of the letters that are come this post contradict one an other, so that we must not expect to know the truth of things. It is likewise talk'd of that General Major Palffi[2] has defeated the succor which was coming from Erla, and that Shaffenberg[3] has routed a party in Transilvania. I am, My Lord, Your Lordships most humble and most faithfull servant

Geo: Etherege

Source: M-1, ff. 128–129.

1 Etherege later describes Charles-François de Caradas, Marquis Du Héron (1667–1703), as "fort de mes amis." Details of his diplomatic career are given in *Repertorium*, 1, pp. 220, 242.
2 Johann Karl Pálffy (1645–1694) was an Austrian cavalry general.
3 Friederich Sigmund, Graf von Schärffenberg, led the troops from Transylvania.

July 29, 1686[1]

To Brother Wynne about Mr. Robson
To Sir P. Wyche and Sir G. Sylvius
Source: H-1, p. 31.

1 Between July 29 and August 29 no letters are copied into the official Letterbook (H-1), though 28 are calendared, two in Sir George's hand. A letter from Vaudrey (*LB*, p. 364) implies that Hughes had left Etherege's service, but he was back on the job by August 29 (H-1, p. 32).

Omitted: July 30, 1686. To Sir William Trumbull with news from Buda.
Source: HMC *Downshire*, 1, p. 200; *LB*, p. 429.

Wednesday July 31, 1686

To Mr. Fitzjames, Mr. Vaudry, and Mr. Harbert.[1]
Source: H-1, p. 31.

1 William Harbord, a fanatical Whig and enemy of Roman Catholicism, was a volunteer in the Imperial forces at Buda. Upon the accession of James II he had taken refuge on the continent, where he continued to work for William of Orange. Returning to England with the invasion fleet in 1688, he became Commissary-General of the Army, Paymaster-General, and

48

eventually a member of the Privy Council. In 1687 he was probably in league with Etherege's secretary and Pierre Valkenier, the Dutch envoy, working to overthrow the government of James II (*HLB*, pp. 334–341).

To The Earl of Middleton   August 1, 1686
                                                          Ratisbon

My Lord.

[Nothing done in the Diet.]

I have not had a letter from any of our Countrymen who are left before Buda since those of the unfortunate assault (tho' I write to them constantly) except one which I had this day from Mr. Clark of the 14/24 instant. He tells me the 11/21 the Duke of Lorrain sprang two Mines under the breach on the Southwest part of the Town, which had a contrarie effect and kill'd about 20 of their own men. On the 14/24 in the morning he sprung an other with worse success, for it kill'd about 100 of their own, so that no good is expected from that way of working.

Mr. Burch, my Lord Clanrickards son, is dead of the Flux which begins to be in the Army.

Mr. Carre was shot thro' the head in the Trenches, and fower English servants were kill'd at the same time. Will Harbert, whose nom de guerre is Monsieur Hatchet, left the Camp on the 24 with my Lord George Savile, who is pretty well recover'd of his shot thro' the Belly, and Mr. Bellamy, apprehending the sicknes which begins, and is retreating to Vienna.

This same night my Lord Mountjoy and Mr. Forbes[1] (who is yet very ill of his wounds) were Rob'd by the Hussars of the worth of 500 £ in mony and cloathes. I suppose these afflictions hinders them from writing regularly to their Friends.

By a letter I receiv'd this day of the same date with the other from a Gentleman of good judgement who is a volunteere in the Bavarian Troops. His name is Du heron, a norman. I sought his acquaintance being inform'd that the last campagne he drew out of the Duke of Zells Troops, where he was then a Volunteere, and fought with and wounded an Officer of that Duks before the wholle Army, for extolling the Duke of Monmoth uppon the false newse of his succes and speaking reflectingly of his Majestie.

He confirmes the sally the Turks made against the Bavarians of which I gave you an account in my last, the blowing upp of the Magazin which happen'd by the lucky falling of a carcass shot out

49

of a mortar they had endeavour'd to Naile. There was so great a quantity of powder in the place that it shook the earth at 4000 paces distance. The damage it has done is considerable, but the ill luck is: it has happend in a place they can make no advantage of the breach it has made in the wall, which is of about 60 paces, for besides a little precipice which is before it, there are two walls and a pallissado behind. The Duke of Lorrain intended to give an assault on the 24th instant and for that reason sprung the Mines mention'd before, which instead of blowing up the wall of the midle Rondelle, it threw the ruines on them who were design'd in case it had succeeded to have given the assault. The ruines which he saies kill'd 200 men has put the Imperialists so much backwarder that it will require 3 dayes to repaire the harme it has done in the Trenches. The Turks have made a Sally on the Saxons in which they kill'd a Collonel of those Troops and 200 men.

The Governor of Buda has seis'd a Country fellow who had letters for the Camp from the Treasurer of the place, who promis'd on conditions to deliver the Towne. The Countryman is hang'd and the Treasurer strangl'd.

Uppon the blowing up the Magazin the Duke of Lorrain summon'd the place and sent a letter to the Governor, which they took, and 3 howers after they sent this answer: That they put a great trust in god tho' he chastis'd their bretheren at Newheusel last yeare, That the Imperialists might remember how god has punish'd them before this place, That they hope from his goodnes he will as certainly chastise them now for their Temerity in offering, against his will, to restraine the bounds of an Empire he has given to the true beleivers. This answer is very devoute but not very humble. As to the Besiegers, There is no thing said in any Letters which are come this post of any succor. The manner of the Turks, as some have observ'd, is not to appeare with their Army when the raising of a Seige is design'd till the enemy has been fatigu'd and weaken'd, which the Imperialists will be if the Seige continue much longer, especially if the Flux encrease among them. Seiges are often unsuccesfull when they draw out in length. I hope this will have a happy and a speedy end. I am, My Lord, Your Lordships most faithfull and most humble Servant

Geo: Etherege

Source: M-1, ff. 130–132.

[1] Brother of Lord Mountjoy. See letter of September 2, 1686.

To Monsieur du Heron

Munday August 5, 1686
To my Lord Middleton about the good news from Buda and to Mr.
Mountstephens about the same thing.
Source: H-1, p. 31.

To The Earl of Middleton   August 5, 1686
                                                        Ratisbon

My Lord.

Having just now receiv'd good news from Buda, I will not trouble
you with what has pass'd in the Diet this post. You will easely beleive
me, it will keep cold till the next. On Saturday the 27th of this
instant New Style the general assault was given, in which the Turks
did all that either dispair or zeal cou'd inspire in their defence. The
verie women assisted, and behaved themselves as well as the boldest
Janisaries; the musket shot, arrowes, Bombes, stones, and granados
made a great slauter on the assailants, but that which did most mischiffe in the attack on the Duke of Lorrains side was nine mines which
the Turks sprung successively. The souldiers nevertheless went on
with Courage, made themselves masters of the breach and of the
two Rondels on the sides of it, and posted themselves there. The 28th
in the morning the besiegers sprung two mines under the second wall
with good success; and that night built a batterie on the breach, which
they hope will dislodge the Turks from a Retrenchment they have
made within the Towne.

On the Bavarians side the Turks did not behave themselves so
vigorously, for after they had sprung a mine and kill'd about 20 or
30 souldiers, they left the Bavarians masters of the Rondell under
which they were before posted. The souldiers advanc'd 300 paces
farther, where a wall forc'd them to retreat after they had taken
6 or 7 peices of cannon and fower Mortars, which the Turks had
wisely nail'd before hand. The Grand Vizier is certainly marching
with a verie considerable Army to the releif of the place, which will
make the besiegers press it more vigorously.

This short account of what pass'd in the attack on the Duke of
Lorrains side I had in a Letter from Mr. Vaudrey, who sends me the
good news likewise of Mr. Fitzjames his being verie well. That of what
pass'd on the Duke of Bavarias side I had in an other from Monsieur

Du'heron. Every body here expects daylie to heare of the Town's being taken. The Count de Dona[1] (brother to him who was lately killd before Buda) came from the siege thro' this Towne last night post, and is gon for Cleve to the Elector of Brandenbourg, in who's Troops he serves. He wou'd not give any account of the Siege, tho' some of the Ministers desir'd it of him: which confirmes what was beleiv'd, that the Brandenbourgers are ill satisfied, and endeed they have not been nam'd in any Action since the first unlucky assault in which they refus'd to joyne. I am, My Lord, Your Lordships most faithfull and most humble servant

Geo: Etherege.

Source: M-1, ff. 133–134.

[1] Alexander, Count de Dohna (1661–1728), a lieutenant-colonel in the army of Brandenburg (*Urkunden*, 22, 596). His father, Christoph Delphicus, Count de Dohna, had been the Swedish ambassador in London, where he died in 1668 (*Repertorium*, 1, p. 490). Count Alexander was later the Swedish envoy at Vienna (H-2, p. 124).

Tuesday August 6, 1686

To Sir William Trumbull and Mr. Show.[1]

Source: H-1, p. 31.

[1] Probably William Shaw, a senior clerk in the Treasury Office.

Omitted: August 8, 1686. To Middleton inclosing a digest of the Alliance of Augsburg, with comments.

Source: M-1, f. 135.

Thursday August 8, 1686

To my Lord Middleton, Mr. Bridgeman and Mr. Robson. Inclos'd in my Lord's the Ausburg Recesse.

Munday August 12, 1686

To Brother Wynne with the News paper.

Source: H-1, p. 31.

Omitted: August 12, 1686. An unsigned, unaddressed letter and a paper of news from Vienna about the fighting at Buda.

Source: M-1, ff. 137–138.

To Mr. Mountstephens. News.
Source: H-1, p. 32.

Omitted: August 15, 1686. To Middleton reporting difficulties of protocol in signing the Alliance.
Source: M-1, ff. 139–140. Summarized in H-1, p. 32.

August 15, 1686

To Mr. Bridgeman with the news.
Source: H-1, p. 32.

To THE EARL OF MIDDLETON   August 19, 1686
                                                                 Ratisbon

My Lord.

I might in this correct some mistakes in my former Letters, which give an account of what has pass'd at the Seige of Buda, but they are not very materiall; a little time made me see I was misinform'd in some particulars, and a little more will show you the truth of all things. As for example, the blowing up of the great Magazin was not occasion'd by the falling of a Bombe shot out of the Morterpeece (on the Bavarian Batterie), but as it is since said by the intelligence of 2 Armenians (brothers), the one living in Vienna, the other in Buda (gain'd by the Prince Herman von Baden.) I will trouble you with no more, they being of little consequence, especially as matters now stand.

The Batterie the Imperialists had rais'd on the breach, where they are posted, is ruind by the falling of a Bombe into some powder, which gave fire to a thousand Granados (which were there ready for service.) There are now but two attacks: that of the Bavarians and that of the Imperialists, the Brandenburgers being all cut off but sixteene or seventeene hundred, which are taken in to the Duke of Lorrain's Body.

I receiv'd this day a Letter from my Lord Montjoy's Steward of the 10th instant, New Style, who onely tells me Mr. Forbes (who has long languis'd of his wound) is got to Vienna, where there is hopes of his recovery; that the misfortunes and afflictions my Lord has had has made him an ill correspondent, and the wound he receiv'd on the 3ᵈ instant (tho' it be not dangerous) makes him not in a condition to write. You may judge by the enclos'd paper you will not expect long before you know how things will go. Prayers are order'd here too, and begun yesterday, for the good Success of the Army. I am, My Lord, Your Lordships most faithfull and most humble Servant

Geo: Etherege

Source: M-1, ff. 141–142.

Omitted: August 20, 1686. A note to Middleton inclosing additional war news.

Source: M-1, f. 143.

August 22, 1686

To my Lord Middleton and Mr. Wynne

August 26, 1686

To my Lord Middleton Mr. Wynne and Mr. Petit.[1]

Source: H-1, p. 32. This entry and the one preceding are in Etherege's hand.

[1] Daniel Petit was English consul at The Hague and later secretary to the Marquis d'Albeville, British envoy to Holland.

To The Earl of Middleton   August 26, 1686

Ratisbon

My Lord.

The Diet has done nothing this good while, and I beleive wee shall be quiet here till the event of the Seige of Buda is knowne.

[A conference at Nuremberg to consider matters not settled by the Augsburg Alliance.]

I have been these two Months little better than broke, and if my Lord Treasurer dos not consider me suddainly, I shall be declar'd a Banquerout.[1] It will be, by that time you receive this, a yeare since I left England. I have formerly told your Lordship the stock I had, by which you will be able to judge of my condition. Pray do what you can to support the credit of, My Lord, Your Lordships poore, but most faithfull and most humble servant,

Geo: Etherege

Source: M-1, ff. 145–146.

[1] I.e., bankrupt.

To Mr. Mountstephens, with the news from Buda.

    Source: H-1, p. 32.

Omitted: August 29, 1686. To Middleton with diplomatic news from the Diet.

    Source: M-1, ff. 149–150; H-1, pp. 32–34; *LB*, pp. 98–100.

Omitted: August 29, 1686. To Middleton reporting rumors of inconclusive fighting at Buda.

    Source: M-1, ff. 147–148.

Dito [August 29, 1686]

To Mr. Mountstephens, and Brother Wynne.

    Source: H-1, p. 34.

To The Earl of Middleton   September 2, 1686
                                            Ratisbon

My Lord.

I have a paper by me of what has been done at Neurenberg, but cannot send it you translated till the next post. You will find by it, here is a great crie, but not much wool (as the proverbe goes.) For the Caisse[1] (which is the maine point in these Alliances) is agreed to remain emptie, it not being convenient to fill it yet. The Swedish Minister is not instructed yet what Troops the King his Master will allow, and the Articles (which were at Ausburg concluded to be ratified in six weeks) have been taken all in peices again. The Ministers who have made the most bustle and noise in this busines seem like men who wou'd set others togeather by the eares with out engaging themselves.

I know not what jugement to make of the Siege of Buda;[2] our hopes and our feares change daily. The Elector of Bavaria is not Master of all the Castle (which was formerly the King's Palace), and if he were, here are some (who have been in the Towne) who say it cannot command the place by reason of an eminence on the other side of the Ditch and the Wall, which are yet to be gain'd. The Governor has sent letters by severall to the Grand Vizier, some of which have been taken, and it is found, he tells him, that of the 150 Janisaries which enter'd, there were not above 50 who were not wounded. He presses him for more succors, with out which he cannot hold out long. The Grand Vizier by his motions seemes to be resolv'd at any prise to releive the place; the Imperialists are verie watchfull to prevent his designe.

Great care is taken at Vienna to send provisions to the Camp both for Horse and man, they having been for some time scarce there. Scharfenberg did not arrive (as was expected), and there is a generall complaint of the slownes of his march, it being imposible to undertake any thing of consequence till he is come. I send your Lordship the Copies of 2 letters from the Camp, one of the 21th instant (which I was oblig'd not to communicate to any body here), an other of the 25 in which you will see how the Bavarians got into the Castle. Mr. Fitzjames is in good health, but Mr. Forbes (my Lord Mountjoys brother, after having languish'd a great while) is dead lately at Vienna of his wounds. I am, My Lord, Your Lordships most faithfull and most humble servant

Geo: Etherege

Source: M-1, ff. 151–152.

[1] Cash box.
[2] Buda was taken on this day, September 2, 1686.

September 2, 1686

To my Lord Middleton with 2 French letters from the Camp, 1 of the 21th, the other of the 25. Aug.
To Sir Peter Wyche
To Mr. Show
Mr. Mountstephens and Mr. Skelton (upon his being nam'd Minister for France.)
Source: H-1, p. 34.

Omitted: September 3, 1686. To Sir William Trumbull reporting the siege at Buda.
Source: HMC *Downshire,* 1, p. 213; *LB,* pp. 429–430.

To The Earl of Middleton   September 5, 1686
Ratisbon

My Lord.

The Newes we have by the post this day from Buda is that on the 29th instant New Style the Grand Vizier endeavor'd to put a farther succor into the place: he attack'd the besiegers Lynes in severall places, and at length the party was routed and beat back by the Imperialists with great slaughter. General Mercy was wounded in this action. While this was doeing, 25 squadrons of Scharfenbergs Troops arriv'd and pass'd the bridge to joyne the Camp. This strook such a Terror in the Turks that they durst not advance to support those they had detach'd. The next day Scharfenberg came himselfe with the rest of his little Army, which with a body of Hungarians he gather'd up by the way amount to 12 thousand men.

Just now arriv'd here a Currier sent by Mr. De Vauguyon to the King his Master, who brought a letter to Monsieur de Crecy desiring him to forward him all he can. It is dated the 3 of September and onely says that the Prince of Commercy had brought the good News of the taking Buda to the Emperor: that he was taking horse for Inspruch to carry it to the Queene of Poland and had not time to acquaint him with any particulars. The Courrier says he heard it was taken by assault, but knows not on what day. By my next I shall endeavor to satisfie you of the manner. We expect this will be follow'd by some action of consequence, and that this Campagne, whose success has been long doubtfull, will now have a glorious end. I am with all Duty, My Lord, Your Lordships most faithfull and most humble servant

Geo: Etherege

Source: M-1, f. 153.

September 5, 1686

To my Lord Middleton of the taking of Buda
To my Lord Sunderland. of the same.
Mr. Show.

September 8, 1686

To my Lord Mountjoy
and Mr. Vaudrey.
Source: H-1, pp. 34–35.

To The Earl of Middleton September 9, 1686
Ratisbon

My Lord.

On Friday last the 28th instant the Imperial Commission, by a Decree dictated, acquainted the Diet in the Emperor's name with the taking of Buda, and the next day the Diet return'd the Complement to the Commission: the same Friday betweene 3 and 4 in the afternoone pass'd thro' this place a Courrier dispatch'd by Mr. Fitzjames to his Majestie. I sent you the news the day before by the Ordinary.

All the particulers we know yet are that the assault began on this day seaventh night at 4 in the evening, that the Imperialists were beaten back twice, but the 3rd time carried the place and enter'd it betweene 7 and 8 at Night. There were about 500 Janisaries left in the Towne, which were put to the Sword. The Governor had entrench'd and pallisado'd his howse in which he defended himselfe with 50 Janisaries, but was soon forc'd and kill'd in the throng. He was Intended to be sav'd, and his Lieutenant had the good luck to be sav'd in his stead. They talke of a great booty. They have been more mercifull then they were at Newhasell; they have spar'd the sex and all who did not bear armes.

The Grand Vizier, who stood on a hill and saw this don à sa barbe, is march'd away, and has left some part of his Artillerie. Yesterday pass'd by here a Courrier from the Camp who is sent to the Elector of Cologne: he saies Tenn Regiments are left to guard the ruines of the Town, or rather the ground where it stood, the disparing Turcks having fir'd their howses, and that the rest of the Army is march'd after the Vizier, having sent a body of Horse who are with all dilligence to stop his passage by getting betweene him and the bridge of Esseck.

[French contraventions of the Truce, and inconclusive action at Nuremberg.]

I am with all Duty, My Lord, Your Lordships most faithfull and most humble servant

Geo: Etherege

Source: M-1, ff. 155–156.

Monday September 9, 1686

To my Lord Middleton about Buda etc. and a Copie of the Resultat of Nurnberg.
To Mr. Corbet.[1]
Sir Peter Wyche and ⎤
              ⎬ the news of Buda.
Sir Gabriel Sylvius ⎦
Source: H-1, p. 35.

[1] Judging from Etherege's letters, his good friend "Mr. Corbet" was a gentleman-gambler, who operated in London and Tunbridge Wells. In a letter to Barillon (November 21, 1686) Etherege speaks of "mon correspondant sur les affaires de la bassette, Monsieur Corbet." He was not the "Miles Corbet, a cheat," described by Theophilus Lucas in his *Lives . . . of the Most Famous Gamesters*, p. 166. He was probably the "Robert Corbet, Esq." who is named, along with such good friends of Etherege as Thomas Maule,

Charles Boyle, John Cooke, and Henry Guy, at the Church of King Charles the Martyr at Tunbridge Wells in a MS list of contributors to the chapel enlarging fund from 1688 to 1696.

Omitted: September 10, 1686. To Sir William Trumbull with news from Buda and advice about the Embassy at Constantinople.
Source: HMC *Downshire*, 1, p. 214. Printed in *LB*, pp. 430–431.

Omitted: September 12, 1686. To Middleton summarizing recent diplomatic activity at the Diet, mainly about Hamburg and Denmark.
Source: M-1, ff. 157–158; H-1, pp. 35–36; *LB*, pp. 102–103.

Dito [September 12, 1686]

To Mr. Manlove
Mrs. Merry
Mr. Robson

September 16, 1686

To my Lord Middleton, and
Mr. Shaw.
Source: H-1, p. 36.

To The Earl of Middleton   September 16, 1686
Ratisbon

My Lord.

It is now a time of rejoyceing here; the Diet have done nothing since my last but sung te deum and eate and drunk their acknowledgements for the taking of Buda. Since the Army has been in pursuite of the Vizier, neither myselfe nor any of my acquaintance have receiv'd any private Letters from our Freinds who are among them. The publique news saies that the Grand Vizier makes hast to pass the bridge of Esseck, that many of his Souldiers dissert for feare, that in passing by Alba Regalis he put in 2000 men to strengthen that Garrison, that the Duke of Lorrain has detatch'd a considerable body of Horse who are to go as far as the bridge of Esseck and to endeavor to ruine it, that he has made a bridge over the Danube and pass'd part of his Army who are to march to Segedin and try if they can carry it. How the differences stand betweene the Elector of Bavaria and the Duke of Lorrain is not knowne, for as Chancelor Straitsman came to the Camp to compose them, Buda was luckely taken. The arrival of Scharfenberg and the Death of the Governor of Buda, which happen'd some few days before the last assault was given, made this Campagne very

59

successfull at a time when every body had reason to apprehend the issue. I am, My Lord, Your Lordships most faithfull and most humble servant

G. Etherege

The Volunteers are all leaving the Army, and the Count de Kaunitz who was at Munick is nam'd for Envoyé Extraordinary for England.
    Source: M-1, ff. 159–160.

To THE EARL OF SUNDERLAND   September 19, 1686

To my Lord Middleton about the Baron of Hernsch [?]
To my Lord Sunderland about the Businesse of Zimeren and Lauteren,[1] and of the Differences between the Count de Windisgratz and the Electorall College. Of Monsieur de Crecy's improving them. It follow'd. . . .

The Count de Windisgratz is about 56 years of age, tormented often with the Gout and gravel, which adds to his naturall ill humor. He has Children by a former Wife which he neglects, being fond of some he has by a Lady to whom he has bin married some few years. She was Maid of Honor to the Empress Dowager, and esteem'd a great ornament to that Court. She is very like and full as handsome as Mrs. Betty Mackerell,[2] but more affected than Mrs. Middleton.[3] The Count is of a temper soe jealouse that he tormented her before her time, when he was her Lover; if he observ'd her speaking to any man in the Drawing room, he would get her into a Corner and pinch her black and blew; and she was resolv'd not to have him, had not his tears to the Empress softned her to impose her Comands to marry him.

He is hott and Imperious, and uses those of the Dyet who have some dependance of him as scurvily as he does his Domesticks. He has had experience in affaires and understands his Masters interest, but will sacrifice any thing to his pride and Ambition; and indeed all his passions are soe violent that he does him little service for want of conduct. These qualities (some of his Countrymen say) got him this Employment, the Ministers at Vienna for their own quiet favouring him in this Honourable occasion of his absence.

He has been formerly employd in the French Court and has twenty times told me how he was received there, with as much heat as an old Lady tells some pleasant passage of her Youth which warms her. His conversation is soe loud, he is vehement even in trifles; and he speaks french as well as my Lord Peterborough.[4] If you flatter him, the Lion becomes a Lamb, and without examining any thing you advance will (like the Lord Chamberlain in Hamlet) cry Oh very like a Weasel.

The Bishop of Passau is a good old man, who loves his quiet, without either genius or Experience; defers generally in all things to the Count; and looks as meekly as the chief of your Commission Ecclesiastic. . . .

Of Contraventions and allyances.

Source: H-1, pp. 36–37; *LB*, pp. 103–104.

1 The Duchies of Simmern and Lautern were part of the territory claimed by Louis XIV on behalf of his sister-in-law the Duchess of Orleans, a sister of the Elector Palatine. In 1688 Louis used this claim as a pretext for invading the Palatinate and thus precipitating the War of the League of Augsburg.

2 Betty Mackarel, an orange girl at the Theatre Royal, famous for her height, impudence, and promiscuity (J. H. Wilson, *All the King's Ladies*, p. 167).

3 Jane Middleton, daughter of Sir Robert Needham, was married to Charles Middleton of Morton Hall, county Denbigh, in North Wales. Her beauty was noted by both Pepys and Evelyn, but she is described in the *Memoirs of Count Grammont* as being languishing and affected. St. Evrémond saw her at the gambling tables of the Duchess Mazarin in Chelsea. Cf. G. Steinman Steinman, *Memoir of Mrs. Myddleton*, Oxford, 1864, and Lewis Melville, *The Windsor Beauties*, Boston, 1928, p. 146 f.

4 Henry Mordaunt, 2nd Earl of Peterborough, had lived in France during the Civil War.

To Monsieur Le Febure[1]
September 20, 1686
Ratisbon

Monsieur.

Bude fut prise lundy le second de ce mois. On commença à donner l'assaut à 4 heures apres midy, et l'on entra la Ville sur le 7 heures du soir. Le gouverneur c'estoit retrenché dans sa maison avec 50 Janizaires, ou il fut tué, mais son Lieutenant fut pris prisonnier. On fit passer tous par le fil de l'Epée hormis la sexe, dont nos amis selon toute apparence ont fait un beau butin. Si ce n'estoit pour la maison de Monsieur le Comte de Crecy, Ratisbonne seroit un triste sejour. Je n'ay pas veu la Dindonelle depuis vostre depart, et je suis plus sensiblement touché de la perte de vous, que vous ne le devez estre pour tous les beautez d'ici. Je suis, Monsieur, Vôtre tres affectionné et obeissant serviteur, G.E.

Source: BM, p. 28; *LB*, p. 105.

1 According to Etherege's secretary, Le Febure was a disreputable refugee from Vienna who lived with Etherege during the summer of 1686. See below, p. 295.

To Mrs. Newstead.[1]
Mr. Geo: Etherege.[2]
My Lady Etherege
Mr. Boyle[3]
Brother Wynne and
To my Lord Middleton. prout Sequitur
    Source: H-1, p. 38.

[1] Sir George's mother, born Mary Powney (c. 1616–1690), married Christopher Newstead after the death of her first husband, Captain George Etherege.
[2] Sir George's nephew, the son of Richard Etherege. In the 1681 will of his aunt, Anne Etherege, he is mentioned as being under 23 years of age.
[3] Charles Boyle was the second son of the Earl of Burlington. He later became the Earl of Clifford.

Omitted: September 23, 1686. To Middleton reporting diplomatic news from the Diet.
    Source: H-1, pp. 38–39; *LB,* pp. 105–106.

September 26, 1686
To my Lord Middleton, with the Holstein Letter.
Mr. Dreyden[1]
My Lord Mountjoy and Mr. Parenzie
    Source: H-1, p. 39.

[1] John Dryden wrote Etherege on February 16, 1687, acknowledging a letter received "three weeks . . . since." Etherege replied on March 20, 1687.

Omitted: September 30, 1686. To Middleton reporting on activities at the Diet.
    Source: M-1, ff. 161–162; H-1, pp. 39–40; *LB,* pp. 106–107.

Dito [September 30, 1686]
To Mr. Guy.
    Source: H-1, p. 40.

Omitted: October 3, 1686. To Middleton reporting diplomatic news from Hamburg and the Diet.
    Source: M-1, ff. 163–164.

Omitted: October 7, 1686. To Middleton with military news from Venice and Hungary.
    Source: M-1, ff. 165–166.

October 7, 1686

To my Lord Middleton
Mr. Mountstephens

October 10, 1686

To Mr. Cooke.
    Source: H-1, pp. 40–41.

To THE EARL OF MIDDLETON   October 14, 1686
Ratisbon

My Lord.

Mr. Wynne in his Letter of the 17th of September complaines that you have receiv'd none from me since mine of the 26th of August. Where the fault lyes I know not; I have not been wanting in my duty, having writ twice a week constantly to your Lordship. It is now a dead time; the Campagne is in a manner ended, and the Diet has not yet enter'd into matter about the French Contraventions.

> [Speculations on Imperial motives toward France and on French intentions.]

If I had the honor now and then to receive some assurances of your Lordship's favour in this Dull place it wou'd keep up the spirits of, My Lord, Your Lordships most faithfull and most obedient Servant
Geo: Etherege

Mr. Fitzjames was expected at Vienna on the 11th instant New Style.
    Source: M-1, ff. 167–169; H-1, pp. 41–42; *LB*, pp. 107–109.

Dito [October 14, 1686]

To Sir Peter Wyche and
Dr. Wynne. about the Feasts.
    Source: H-1, p. 42.

Dito [October 14, 1686]

To Mr. Wynne, telling him that he had his visits constantly return'd (tho' nothing can have less of Truth in it).[1] That one of the Dyet, having lent money to an other, was offer'd to be pay'd back in French

63

money, which the person refusd to accept of, calling it the money of Corruption. That grave Fops abound here; That nature, who is the best Poet and in all her works shews the inclination she has for a Comedy, wou'd be thought degenerated into a Farce to give a true description of them. That the fowls at the Bishop of Passau's Feast for the taking of Buda were brought from his Bishoprick to save charges; that they stunk; and that he had given some 3 Oams of Birish[2] wine amongst the People, which might cost him about 40 shillings English.

That the Count de Windisgratz at his feast had (as it was computed) thrown out at the windows about 10 Crowns to outdoe the Bishop in magneficence, etc.

Source: BM, f. 31; *LB,* p. 109.

[1] The Secretary's own comment, in parentheses.
[2] Probably "Bayerisch" is intended—a cheap local wine.

Omitted: October 17, 1686. To Middleton reporting on French moves in Flanders and the Palatinate.
Source: M-1, ff. 171–172; H-1, pp. 43–44; *LB,* pp. 109–110.

Omitted: October 21, 1686. To Middleton commenting on the fort built by the French at Hüningen on the Rhine.
Source: M-1, ff. 173–174.

Omitted: October 24, 1686. To Middleton reporting diplomatic maneuvering at the Diet.
Source: M-1, ff. 175–176.

October 28 [1686]

To Segnor Parenzie.
To my Lord Middleton about the Conclusion
To Mr. William Richards[1]
To Mr. Robson and Mrs. Merry
Source: H-1, p. 44.

[1] Etherege could have known at least three men named William Richards. One is "an old servant" of Etherege's friend the Earl of Dorset, who used to drink heavily with Dorset and Shadwell (Brice Harris, *Charles Sackville, Sixth Earl of Dorset,* 1940, pp. 75–76). David Vieth (*Attributions,* p. 60) notes that a publisher named Will Richards resided in "Bowe-Strete, Covent-Garden," which is Etherege territory. (Cf. also Philip Gray, "Rochester's *Poems on Several Occasions," The Library,* 4th series, 19 [1938–39], 185–197.) The most likely candidate in my opinion is the William Richards, gent., who in 1668 was an attorney in the King's Remembrancer's Office (*CTB,* III,

Pt. 1, p. 263), and who handled large amounts of Treasury funds from 1675 (*CTB*, IV, pp. 732, 745) to July 1687 (*CTB*, VIII, Pt. 3, p. 1457). Hughes states that Richards was Sir George's agent, who received his pension money and sent Etherege letters of exchange from the Treasury. According to the satires of the time, Richards was a regular patron of the Rose, one of Etherege's favorite taverns.

Omitted: October 28, 1686. To Middleton with further news of "the Conclusion . . . touching the execution of the Truce" and military news from Hungary.
    Source: M-1, ff. 177–178.

October 31, 1686
To Brother Wynne with a Bill of Extraordinaries till the 30ᵗʰ of August, 86.
    Source: H-1, p. 44.

Omitted: October 31, 1686. To Middleton describing Count Windisch-grätz's dissatisfaction with the Conclusion.
    Source: M-1, 179–180; H-1, p. 45; *LB*, p. 111.

Omitted: October 31, 1686. A paper of military news from Vienna, in Etherege's hand but unaddressed and unsigned.
    Source: M-1, ff. 181–182.

Omitted: November 4, 1686. To Middleton, confirming the surrender of Szeged, with other military news.
    Source: M-1, f. 183.

Munday November 4, 1686
To my Lord Middleton. News of Segedin and Fünfkirchen.
To Mr. Guy.
    Source: H-1, p. 46.

Omitted: November 7, 1686. To Middleton reporting complaints about the winter-quartering of troops.
    Source: M-1, ff. 185–186.

November 7, 1686
To my Lord Middleton, and
My Lord Sunderland about the Designs in the Empire.
    Source: H-1, p. 46.

65

Omitted: November 11, 1686. To Middleton: further talk about winter-quartering.

Source: M-1, ff. 187–188.

November 11, 1686

To my Lord Middleton Mr. Etherege[1]
Brother Wynne and Sir Peter Wyche.
Source: H-1, p. 46.

[1] Sir George's brother, Richard Etherege.

To The Duke of Buckingham[1]

November 12, 1686
Ratisbon

My Lord.

I Received the News of your Grace's retiring into Yorkshire, and leading a sedate contemplative Life there, with no less Astonishment than I should hear of his Christian Majesty's turning Benedictine Monk, or the Pope's wearing a long Perriwig, and setting up for a flaming Beau in the seventy-fourth Year of his Age. We have a Picture here in our Town-Hall, which I never look upon but it makes me think on your Grace; and I dare swear you'll say there is no Dishonour done you, when you hear whose it is: In short, 'tis that of the famous CHARLES the V, Who (amidst all the Magnificence that this foolish World affords, amidst all his African Lawrels and Gallic Triumphs) freely divested himself of the Empire of Europe, and his hereditary Kingdoms, to pass the Remainder of his Life in Solitude and Retirement.

Is it possible that your Grace (who has seen ten times more Luxury than that Emperor ever knew, convers'd with finer Women, kept politer Company, possess'd as much too of the true real Greatness of the World as ever he enjoyed) should in age still capable of Pleasure, and under a Fortune whose very Ruins would make up a comfortable Electorate here in Germany, Is it possible, I say, that your Grace should leave the Play at the Beginning of the fourth Act, when all the Spectators are in Pain to know what will become of the Hero, and what mighty Matters he is reserv'd for, that set out so advantageously in the first? That a Person of your exquisite Taste, that has breathed the Air of Courts ever from your Infancy, should be content, in that Part of your Life which is most difficult to be pleased and most easie to be disgusted, to take up with the Conversation of country Parsons; a sort of People, whom to my Knowledge, your Grace never much

66

admir'd; and do penance in the nauseous Company of Lawyers, whom I am certain you abominate.

To raise our Astonishment higher, Who coud ever have prophecy'd (though he had a double Gift of Nostradamus's Spirit) that the Duke of Buckingham who never vouchsafed his Embraces to any ordinary Beauty, wou'd ever condescend to sigh and languish for the Heiress apparent of a thatch'd Cottage, in a straw Hat, flannen Petticoat, Stockings of as gross a thrum as the Blew-Coat Boy's Caps at the Hospital,[2] and a Smock (the Lord defend me from the wicked Idea of it!) of as course a Canvas as ever serv'd an Apprenticeship to a Mackarel Boat? Who could have believed, till Matter of Fact had confirmed the Belief of it, (and your Grace knows that Matter of Fact is not to be disputed) that the most polished, refined Epicure of his Age, that had regaled himself in the most exquisite Wines of Italy, Greece, and Spain, would, in the last Scene of his Life, debauch his Constitution in execrable Yorkshire Ale? And that He, who all his Life Time had either seen Princes his Play-fellows or Companions, would submit to the nonsensical Chat, and barbarous Language of Farmers and Higlers?

This, I confess, so much shocks me that I cannot tell what to make on't; and unless the news came to me confirmed from so many Authentic Hands, that I have no room left to suspect the Veracity of it, I should still look upon it to be Apocryphal. Is your Grace then in earnest, and really pleased with so prodigious an Alteration of Persons and Things? For my Part, I believe it; for I am certain that your Grace can act any Person better than that of a Hypocrite.

But I humbly beg your Graces pardon for this Familiarity I have taken with you: Give me leave therefore, if you please, to tell you something of my self. I presume that an Account of what passes in this busie Part of the World, will not come unacceptable to you, since all my Correspondents from England assure me, your Grace does me the Honour to enquire often after me, and has express'd some sort of a Desire to know how my new Character sits upon me.

Ten Years agoe I as little thought that my Stars designed to make a Politician of me, and that it would come to my share to debate in public Assemblies, and regulate the Affairs of Christendom, as the grand Signior dream'd of losing Hungary. But my royal Master having the Charity to believe me Master of some Qualities, of which I never suspected my self, I find that the Zeal and Alacrity I discover in my self, to support a Dignity which he has thought fit to confer upon me, has supply'd all other Defects, and given me a Talent, for which (till now) I justly fancied myself uncapable.

I live in one of the finest, and best manner'd Cities in Germany, where tis true we have not Pleasure in that Perfection as we see it in London and Paris, yet to make us amends, we enjoy a noble serene Air, that makes us hungry as Hawks; and though Business, and even the worst Sort of Business, wicked Politics, is the distinguishing Commodity of the Place, yet I will say that for the Germans, that they manage it the best of any People in the World; they cut off and retrench all those idle Preliminaries and useless Ceremonies that clog the Wheels of it everywhere else: And I find, that, to this Day, they make good the Observation that Tacitus[3] made of their Ancestors; I mean, That their Affairs (let them be never so serious and pressing) never put a stop to good Eating and Drinking, and that they debate their weightiest Negotiations over their Cups.

'Tis true, they carry this Humor by much too far for one of my Complexion, for which Reason I decline appearing among them, but when my Master's Concerns make it necessary for me to come to their Assemblies. They are, indeed, a free hearted open sort of Gentlemen that compose the Diet, without Reserve, Affectation, and Artifice; but they are such unmerciful Plyers of the Bottle, so wholy given up to what our Sots call Good-fellowship, that 'tis as great a Constraint upon my Nature to sit out a Night's Entertainment with them, as it would be to hear half a score long-winded Presbyterian Divines Cant successively one after another.

To unbosome my self frankly and freely to your Grace, I always looked upon Drunkenness to be an unpardonable Crime in a young fellow, who without any of these foreign Helps, has Fire enough in his Veins to enable him to do Justice to Caelia whenever she demands a Tribute from him. In a middle aged Man, I consider the Bottle only as subservient to the nobler Pleasure of Love; and he that would suffer himself to be so far infatuated by it, as to neglect the Pursuit of a more agreeable Game, I think deserves no Quarter from the Ladies: In old Age, indeed, when tis convenient very often to forget and steal from our selves, I am of Opinion, that a little Drunkenness, discreetly used, may as well contribute to our Health of Body as Tranquillity of Soul.

Thus I have given your Grace a short System of my Morals and Belief in these Affairs. But the Gentlemen of this Country go upon a quite different Scheme of Pleasure; the best Furniture of their Parlours (instead of innocent China) are tall overgrown Rummers, and they take more care to enlarge their Cellars than their patrimonial Estates: In short, Drinking is the Hereditary Sin of this Country, and that Heroe of a Deputy here, that can demolish (at one Sitting) the rest of his Brother Envoys, is mention'd with as much Applause as the Duke of Lorain for his noble Exploits against the Turks, and may claim a Statue erected at the public Expence in any Town in Germany.

Judge then, my Lord, whether a Person of my sober Principles, and one that only uses Wine (as the wiser sort of Roman Catholics do Images) to raise up my Imagination to something more exalted, and not to terminate my Worship upon it, must not be reduced to very mortifying Circumstances in this Place; where I cannot pretend to enjoy Conversation, without practicing that Vice that directly ruines it.

And as I have just Reason to complain of the Men for laying so unreasonable a Tax upon Pleasure, so I have no less Occasion to complain of the Women for wholy denying it.

Could a Man find out the Secret to take as long a Lease for his Life as Methuselah and the rest of the Anti diluvian Gentlemen, who were three hundred Years in growing up to the Perfection of Vigour, enjoy'd it the same Number of Years, and were as long a decaying, something might be said for the two crying Sins of both Sexes here; I mean Drunkenness in the Men, and Reservedness in the Ladies.

What would it signify to throw away a Week's, nay, a Month's Enjoyment upon one Night's Debauch, if a Man could promise himself the Age of a Patriarch?

Or where wou'd be the mighty Penance in dancing a dozen Years Attendance after a coy Female, watching her most favourable Moments, and most accessible Intervals, at last to enjoy her, if Infirmities and old Age were to come so late upon us?

But since Fate has given us so short a Period to tast Pleasure with Satisfaction, three or four Days Sickness is too great a Rent-charge upon humane Nature, and Drunkenness cannot pretend (out of its own Fund) to acquit the Debt.

And, my Lord, since our Gayety and Vigour leaves us so soon in the lurch, since Feebleness attacks us without giving us fair Warning, and we no sooner pass the Meridian of Life but begin to decline, its hardly worth a Lover's while to stay as long for compassing a Mistress, as Jacob[4] did for obtaining a Wife; and without this tedious Drudgery and Application, I can assure your Grace that an Amour is not to be managed here.

But, my Lord, I forget that while I take upon me to play the Moralist, and to enlarge so Rhetorically upon the Preciousness of Time, I

69

have already made bold with too much of your Graces: For which reason I here put a stop to my Discourse, and will endeavour the next Pacquet that goes from this Place, to entertain your Grace with something more agreeable. I am, My Lord, Your Grace's most obedient Servant

G. Etherege.

Source: George Villiers, Duke of Buckingham, *Miscellaneous Works,* 1 (1704), pp. 124–131.

1 George Villiers, 2nd Duke of Buckingham (1628–1687). By 1686 the Duke had retired from an active career at the court of Charles II and was living at his manor of Helmsley in Yorkshire. He died near there April 16, 1687.

2 Chelsea Royal Hospital, founded by Charles II for old and invalid soldiers.

3 *Germania,* 22. The Germans, according to Tacitus, debate such matters as war and peace or the appointment of chiefs at their feasts, "conceiving that at no time is the soul more opened to sincerity" than when drinking. However, they postpone voting to the following day.

4 Jacob served Laban for seven years to win Rachel's hand. *Genesis* 30: 18–20.

Omitted: November 14, 1686. To Middleton with diplomatic news and the first reference to the strolling players from Nuremberg: "The Imperial Comission entend to celebrat St. Leopols Day with a Dutch Feast and a Dutch comedie."

Source: M-1, ff. 189–191; H-1, pp. 46–47; *LB,* pp. 111–113.

Dito [November 14, 1686]

To Mr. Fr. Rooth at Rotterdam
Source: H-1, p. 47.

Omitted: November 18, 1686. To Middleton summarizing legal arguments in the Diet.

Source: M-1, ff. 192–193; H-1, pp. 48–49; *LB,* pp. 113–115.

Dito [November 18, 1686]

To Sir William Trumbull and my Lady
Source: H-1, p. 49.

To Sir William Trumbull[1]   November 18, 1686
Dito

Sir.

By this time you know that the Secretary of that Embassy is allow'd six hundred Lyon Dollers a year, which is payd by the Merchants, that the Company esteem him their servant and pretend a right to choose

70

him. If you think fit to have a private Secretary, you must pay him yourself, but you may endeavour to get the Company to approve one whom you shall recommend. The man who enjoys the place at present is one Mr. Cooke, who has been long in Turky and their ancient servant. I know not whether you will like his Countenance and his Principles. They are both very odd. He has had much experience in the Country and is of an humor that agrees with that people, is a man of good acquir'd and naturall parts, but I fear you will not find them turn'd to your liking. He is reserv'd and subtil. If he is not disaffected to the Government, he is beholding to his being at soe great a distance.

As for other matters I recommend you to Sir Dudley North,[2] who is the best able of any I know to inform you; he is a kinsman of my dead friend, Sir William Soames,[3] and can tell you what agreement he made. He has been Treasurer to the Company at Constantinople, and knows what things you will find there and what will be necessary for you to carry with you; . . . . he is very much a gentleman, and will not be wanting to oblige one who has deserved his Majesty's favour.

Source: BM, ff. 34–35. The last paragraph is from HMC *Downshire*, 1, p. 224.

[1] Trumbull, who was preparing to go as Ambassador to Turkey, had written Etherege on August 16, asking for information about the post (Letterbooks of Sir William Trumbull, Trumbull Additional MSS #87, Vol. III. Berkshire County Record Office, Reading).

[2] Sir Dudley North (1641–1691), a leading merchant in the Turkey Company, had returned to England in 1680.

[3] Sir William Soame, or Soames (1645–1686), of Thurlow, Suffolk, was knighted in 1674 and created Baronet in 1685 (Cockayne, *Complete Baronetage*, 4, p. 136). In 1680 he translated Boileau's *Art of Poetry* with aid from and (according to Jacob Tonson) "very considerable alterations by" Dryden (Hugh Macdonald, *John Dryden: A Bibliography*, Oxford, 1939, p. 36).

Ratisbon November 21, 1686

To my Lord Middleton about the Comedie.
To Monsieur Barrillon
Mr. Robson and
Brother Wynne.
  Source: H-1, p. 50.

To The Earl of Middleton   November 21, 1686
                                                          Ratisbon

My Lord.

On Tuesday last the ninth Instant (in matters of consequence a man cannot be too exact) the three Colleges met in the *neben Stube* (the

71

room where the generall Conferences are always held) and after a grave debate which took up some time, by reason of unhappy difficulties which I shall acquaint you with annon, a conclusion was unanimously made that they shou'd goe and see a Farce that afternoon, to which they were invited by a Deputy from a Company of Strolers, who are lately come from Nurenberg to divert us here.

The Minister who was sent on this Embassy (either thro' ignorance of the Customes of this nice place, or thro' an excess of Civility, A common Error in their Politicks) when he made his Compliment to the severall members of the Dyet, without distinguishing between the Colleges layd them all on promiscuously with *Illustrious* and *Excellence.* This had spoyl'd his business had not some good natur'd husbands, who consider'd the inclinations of their wives, bestirr'd themselves and becalm'd the most tempestuous Spirits. Then it was consider'd whether they shou'd be distinguish'd by their Seats. The Theatre being noe better than a Barn and improper for so great a Ceremony, they resolv'd to meet *Pell mell.* There was a Quota collected, and they tax'd themselves at 4 shillings a head, reserving the Libertie to bring their families. The Deputies of the Towns wou'd have modestly declin'd the being on the same foot with the other Colleges, but the Excellence which had been advanced to them made their Excellencies *make them* advance the money.

There is a Comedian in the Troop as handsom at least as the faire made of the West,[1] which you have seen at Newmarket, and makes as much noise in this little Town and gives as much jealousies to the Ladys as ever Mrs. Wright[2] or Mrs. Johnson[3] did in London. The Importance of this letter will lett you see his Majestie does not misemploy the money he allows me, and I hope perswade my Lord Treasurer to remember me when the good time comes.

This is all has been done in the Dyett since my last, and it is but reasonable they shou'd breath a while. I just now received a letter from Mr. Vaudrey, which makes me expect Mr. Fitzjames here to morrow or next day. I am, etc.

Source: BM, pp. 35–36.

[1] Evidently the actress who had played the title role in Heywood's play at Newmarket.

[2] In 1670 Mrs. Wright had been an actress in the Duke's Company at Drury Lane (J. H. Wilson, *All the King's Ladies,* p. 191).

[3] With the Duke's Company from 1669 to 1673, Mrs. Johnson was famous for her dancing. In 1677 she became the mistress of the Earl of Peterborough (*Ibid.,* pp. 152–153). Etherege refers to her in a letter of February 26, 1688, as kind as well as handsome.

Monsieur.

Ne vous attendez pas a une excuse que Je doit faire de n'avoir pas repondu à une lettre que vous m'avez fait l'honneur de m'écrire. Vous savez les obligations que je vous ay des honnestetez que J'ay receves de Monsieur de Crecy, mais vous ne savez pas le mal que vous m'avez causé. Je paye bien cher les plaisirs que J'ay en me divertissant quelque fois avec Madame la Comtesse à l'Hombre. Les Deputez Subalternez d'Austriche n'osent pas me donner pratique, et moy Je ne me puis pas resoudre à faire une Quarantaine pour entrer chez eux. Il est vray que leur maistre Lieutenant le Comte de Windisgratz aprez luy avoir fait une requeste en forme me permettoit quand il n'estoit point incommodé de la pierre, de la Goutte, ou de la jalousie de me venir planter a sa gauche dans sa salle d'Audience, et aprez y avoir esté bien ennuié de luy en faire des Compliments. Pour me consoler de ce malheur, vous devriez faire en sorte qu'on ne s'oublie pas tout à fait de moy dans les bonnes Compagnies ou vous allez.

Mon Correspondant sur les affaires de la Bassette, Monsieur Corbet, ne m'en a pas envoyé des nouvelles il y a long temps; asseurement que J'en suis en peine; la Bassette a ses charmes en certains endroits, et j'aimerois mieux y perdre mon Argent en voyant Madame Mazarine,[1] que de gagner les bonnes graces de toutes les Dames et méme de Demoiselles d'ici. Si j'osois m'etendre sur ce Chaptre-la, je ne vous dirois pas si tost que Je suis, etc.

Source: BM, f. 36; *LB,* p. 118.

[1] Hortense Mancini, Duchess Mazarin, was notorious for her gambling. Her lodgings in Chelsea, according to Theophilus Lucas, "were more frequented than the Groom Porters."

To Owen Wynne   November 25, 1686
Ratisbon

Sir.

I must desire you to excuse me to my Lord for not writing to him by this ordinary. I have gott soe great a Cold that I was forc'd to be lett blood this day. Nothing has bin done lately in the Diette, and we have little news now from Vienna. Pray lett my lord know that Mr. Fitzjames arriv'd here by Post from thence on fryday last and continu'd his journey towards Ulm on the next morning by six a clock.

The Winter has been here already very severe, and it has frozen very hard, but on Saturday morning some Snow fell, and itt began to thaw. This has made the aire milder, but the wayes are much worse.

I hope you will have suddenly an account of Mr. Fitzjames being safely arriv'd at Paris. He is in very good health, and very much grown. The Emperor presented him with a Turkish Horse and Furniture. The horse is Strong but not finely Shaped, as he was pleas'd to tell me, for I saw him not, the Horse being with his baggage which goes through Bohemia. The Furniture is very fine. When he arrives in England you will know from himself how much he has been made of, both in the Army and at the Court. I am, Sir, Your very humble and obedient servant.

Geo: Etherege

Source: M-1, f. 194. In Hughes' handwriting, but signed by Etherege.

To Baron Sensheim[1] November 26, 1686
Ratisbon

J' estois surpris d'apprendre que ce joly Gentil-homme travesty en Italien hier au Soir estoit le Baron de Sensheim. Je ne Savois pas que les honnestes gens se méloient avec des Laquais ramassez pour faire le Fanfarons et les Batteurs de Pavéz. Si vous avez quelque chose à me dire, faites le moy Savoir comme vous devez, et ne vous amusez plus à venir insulter mes Domestiques ni ma maison. Soyez content que vous l'avez echápé belle et ne retournez plus chercher les recompences de telles follies. Pour vos beau Compagnons J'ay des autres mesures a prendre avec eux.

Dito.

Monsieur Sensheims answer to the Stadtkammerer Wielden. Er war ein Reichs Cavalier, und hatte ebenmassig ein Session im Reichstag. Er war auch nicht sein Kammerdiener der den Englischen Herren Abgesanten offendiret hatte sondern erselbst. Also dass wenn er wolte Satisfaction haben, solte er ihm solches durch einen Cavalier berichten lassen. Er wollte für ihm geben auff was orth und weise er sie verlanget.

Source: BM, f. 37; *LB*, p. 119.

[1] Baron Sensheim's attack on Etherege's house is described by Etherege's secretary in his letter to "Honoured Sir," pp. 300–302, below.

Omitted: November 28, 1686. To Middleton reporting "a very dead time for news here."

Source: M-1, f. 196; H-1, p. 50; *LB*, p. 119.

Omitted: December 2, 1686. To Middleton with routine diplomatic news.
Source: M-1, ff. 198–199; H-1, pp. 50–51; *LB*, pp. 120–121 in part.

December 4, 1686
To my Lord Taaffe[1]
Source: H-1, p. 51.

[1] Francis, Viscount Taafe, later the 3rd Earl of Carlingford (1639–1704), served the Imperial army from 1673 on and commanded a regiment in 1687. His older brother, Nicholas, 2nd Earl of Carlingford, was envoy to Vienna in 1688.

Omitted: December 5, 1686. To Middleton reporting diplomatic maneuvering over the proposed truce with France.
Source: M-1, ff. 200–202; H-1, pp. 51–52; *LB*, pp. 121–122.

Dito [December 5, 1686]
To Brother Wynne—about Extraordinaries.
Source: H-1, p. 52.

Omitted: December 9, 1686. To Middleton, commenting on an enclosed copy of an Imperial decree and reporting on French fortifications and the problem of winter quarters.
Source: M-1, ff. 204–205; H-1, p. 53; *LB*, pp. 122–123.

Dito [December 9, 1686]
To Mr. Corbet

Ratisbon December 12, 1686
To Brother Wynne about Verses etc. About Entertainment.[1] With Clarkes note for 150 Florins.
Source: H-1, p. 53.

[1] Etherege was allowed to claim expenses for official entertainment.

To THE EARL OF MIDDLETON   December 23, 1686
                                              Ratisbon
My Lord.
I have had lately a little fitt of Sickness, of which I am not yet perfectly recover'd. This, and there being no busines on the board at present, is the reason I have not given you the trouble of a Letter these two or three posts. I have receiv'd the directions from Mr. Wynne

of the method you wou'd have me use in writing, which I shall carefully observe, since it will be for your ease.[1]

The Elector of Bavaria intends to pass the Carnaval at Venice, and begins his journey (as it is said) on the 15th of the next Month, new Stile.

Monsieur de Caunitz is on his way for England. If his Majestie after his arrival shou'd think of making any Complement to the Emperor,[2] I leave it to your Lordships Goodnes to be mindfull of, My Lord, Your Lordships most faithfull and most humble Servant

Geo: Etherege

Source: M-1, f. 206.

[1] The next letter is unusually dense and dull, and subsequent letters show no trace of a new method.

[2] A hint that Etherege would have liked a mission to Vienna.

December 23, 1686

To my Lord Middleton. Of the method in writing. Of the Elector of Bavaria's Progress and of being sent to Compliment the Emperor.

To Mr. Graham[1] of his Honour's Pension.

To Mr. Wynne, of making a Complement to the Emperor with an Inclosed to Mr. Graham.

To Mrs. Merry, about Mr. Smithsbys[2] neglect and about Batemans[3] business.

Source: H-1, p. 54.

[1] Probably James Graham, Keeper of the Privy Purse.

[2] James Smithsby, Gent., (CTB, 7, p. 3) was authorized to receive Etherege's pension from the Keeper of the Privy Purse and to distribute parts of it to Mrs. Merry and possibly to Lady Etherege. On December 15, 1687, Etherege cancelled this authorization and sent Robson an order to pay Mrs. Merry £15 from his Extraordinaries. A "Cuckold Smithsby" is included in a list of members of the Green Ribbon Club in 1679, along with two friends of Etherege—William Jephson and George Bradbury—and a "Squire Thomas Merry" (Sir George Sitwell, The First Whig, 1894, p. 202).

[3] Etherege had a claim, through the will of his distant cousin, Elizabeth Middleton Bateman, to a two-thirds interest in the manor of Hartford in Huntingdonshire (Foster, N&Q, 153 (1927), 472).

Omitted: December 26, 1686. To Middleton about winter quarters, French forts on the Rhine, and the Alliance of Augsburg.

Source: M-1, ff. 208–209; H-1, pp. 54–55; LB, pp. 124–125.

My Lord.

The onely busines of the Diet has been for some time to wish one an other a merry Christmas: so that your Lordship is not to expect any news from hence.

Mony has been given out some time since at Vienna to make the recruits. The Horse will be easely made up, but it will be a hard matter to recruite the Foot, who were very much ruin'd the last Campagne: the Hereditarie Countries being depopulated, and the other parts of the Empire goeing but unwillingly to serve in Hungarie. Nevertheless my Lord Taffe writes me word the Officers doubt not but to have their Regiments compleat by the Spring.

I have had a little fevor which was occasion'd by a Cold. I am pretty well recover'd but shall not be strong enough to venture abroad till next week. I am, My Lord, Your Lordships most humble and most faithfull Servant

                                                    Geo: Etherege

Source: M-1, f. 210.

Omitted: January 6, 1687. A letter to Middleton reporting delay in the Truce negotiations and a blunt statement from Louis XIV.

Source: M-1, ff. 212–213; H-1, p. 55; *LB*, p. 436.

                                                    January 6, 1687

To Mr. Robson about 20 £ to buy his wife a pl[ate].
To Brother Wynne about the same.
To Sir Peter Wyche.

Source: H-1, p. 55.

To The Earl of Middleton   January 9, 1687
                                                    Ratisbon

My Lord.

I have made bold to enclose a Letter in your Lordship's for my Lord Treasurer, in which I have inserted what I thought was fit to give advise of from hence. I hope you will excuse me the repeating of the same things, since you may have the perusal of it, if it be worth the while.

The Count de Thun is arriv'd at the Court of Bavaria, and one of his instructions is to disswade the Elector from his intended Journy into Italie. The Emperor is jealous it is entended a Journy of debauche, that Prince being something that way inclin'd; and many have said he design'd it partly in spight, a Lady[1] being remov'd for whom he had some consideration. You might (if her good man had thought fit) have seene her in England. The States of his Country use likewise their endeavour to divert him from this resolution, it being their interest since he askes of them one hundred thousand Crownes to defray his expences.

I entended, now I have recover'd my health againe, to have writ to my Lord Sunderland and my Lord Chamberlaine, and a letter of an other nature to your Lordship, but I am so shortn'd in time that I am forc'd to put it off till next post. Tho' Germany be not very fertill in Beauty, I have seen a Lady[2] so very handsome as wou'd puzle most Countrys to match her. The Scarsety makes them very cruelle, as you will perceive by the Song I send you, the first and onely one I ever made in french. It is a venture, for tho' the Dutch have not abounded in wits, they have had their share of Criticks. I am, My Lord, Your Lordships most faithfull, and most Obedient Servant.

Geo: Etherege.

Source: M-1, ff. 214–215. Summarized in H-1, pp. 58–59 and in *LB*, pp. 128–129.

[1] The Countess of Kaunitz, according to Etherege's letter of June 6, 1688, was the mistress of the Elector of Bavaria. Despite the complaints of the Electrice, who was a daughter of the Emperor, Kaunitz was kept at Munich so that his wife might promote Imperial interests. In January 1687, however, Kaunitz was sent to England.

[2] The comedienne from Nuremberg.

Inclos'd this French song following.

> Garde le secret de ton Ame,
> Et ne te laisse pas flatter
> Qu'Iris espargnera ta flamme
> Si tu luy permets d'eclatter;
> Son humeur, à l'amour rebelle,
> Exile tous ses doux desirs,
> Et la tendresse est criminelle
> Que veut luy parler en Soupirs.
>
> Puis que tu vis sous son Empire,
> Il faut luy cacher ton destin
> Si tu ne veut le rendre pire,

Percé du trait de son dedain.
D'une rigeur si delicate
Ton coeur ne peut rien esperer:
Derobe donc à cette ingrate
La vanité d'en trionfer.

Source: BM, f. 43; *LB,* p. 129.

Omitted: January 9, 1687. To the Earl of Rochester containing a long summary of affairs at the Diet.
Source: H-1, pp. 56–58; *LB,* pp. 125–128.

January 10, 1687

To Mr. Maule.
To Mr. Corbet.

January 11 [1687]

To my Lord Sunderland, on the new Year.
Source: H-1, p. 59.

To The Earl of Sunderland   January 11, 1687
                                                                   Ratisbon
My Lord.

I doubt not but your Lordship knows all I am able to say of matters in agitation here. Within few dayes the Diet will open again, and then there may happen something which may excuse my troubling you with it. All that I have to doe now, according to the good breeding of this place, is to wish your Lordship a happy new yeare: this piece of formallity is far from satisfieing me, who have allways your benefits in my mind and can never enough acknowledge them, tho' my wholle life were employd in your Lordships service. You may think this a time of Leisure, but I assure you I never had so much busines since I left England.

The Countess of Zinzendorffe[1] and two of her Daughters are come from Neurenberg to pass the Holydaies here. I cannot think you have a good Opinion enough of my Judgement in beauty to beleive me when I say: these two young Ladys have in full perfection all that three or fower of our Countrywomen (which I need not name) have in a manner lost. Germanie has no good name in this matter, I confess; but it is no new thing for Countrys who have no reputation in the general to produce something very extraordinary in particular. All the

79

false Catos of this place lay by their Sower looks and put on smiling faces, neglect their Ceremonies, forget their Excellencies, and vie in making of their Court. I leave your Lordship to think whether I am idle. I know nothing can make this letter be pardon'd but your considering it has taken up some minutes of that time which shou'd be wholly employd in so important a business by, my Lord, Your Lordships most faithfull and most humble servant

Geo: Etherege

Source: PRO State Papers (German States) 81, #86, ff. 281–282; *LB,* pp. 410–411.

1 Probably the widow of Albrecht, Count von Zinzendorf (1618–1683).

[January 11, 1687]

To Mr. Guy. with a Copie of French Verses.
Source: H-1, p. 59.

To Henry Guy

January 11, 1687 1
Ratisbon

Sir.

The date of this letter is enough to make you expect a complement, but I have given and receiv'd soe many in this formall place that I cannot think of one to my minde. Be satisfy'd that every day I wish you encrease of happiness in what is possible. For lett me tell you, however we may flatter ourselves, the least addition of days, and much more of years, to the number we have already cannot doe us much good. I have troubl'd my Lord Treasurer with a tedious account of the news of this place. I hope his goodness will forgive me, and you must forgive me the not having writ to you oftner, since it has been occasion'd by a fitt of sickness I have had this winter. I am now soe well recover'd that my heart begins to be sensible again. I dare not boast of what is more to the purpose.

Here is at present a Lady who lives commonly near Nurenberg; she is soe very handsom that it may be sayd she has robb'd the whole Countrey, for the rest of the women look as if nature had spar'd from them what she has bestow'd on this. She is as fière as she is fair, which may be allow'd to a beauty that has noe Rivall. I send you a french song which she has been the occasion of. Mr. Vice-Chamberlain² is soe able a frenchman that I fear his Critisismes, but pray tell him I am not the onely man who have engag'd myself in a love-business without considering whether I was able to go thro' with it. I beg the continuance of your favour and doe not doubt but you will help Mr. Robson to succeed in what nearly concerns, Sir, etc.

Source: BM, ff. 43–44; *LB,* pp. 129–130.

[1] The date in the manuscript is "1. Jan. 86/7. S.V. [that is, Old Style]." The abbreviation is erroneously transcribed as New Style in *LB,* p. 129.

[2] The Vice-Chamberlain in 1687 was Henry Savile, who had lived long in Paris.

Twelveth Day. 86/7 [January 6, 1687]

To Mr. Robson, about solliciting.

To Mr. Wynne about Williams and Clarke.

9 Dito [January 9, 1687]

To Monsieur Purpurat

Source: H-1, p. 59.

Omitted: January 13, 1687. A letter of news to Middleton summarized, with the incorrect date of December 31, in BM, f. 43, and *LB,* p. 129. In H-1, p. 59, the summary is correctly, though inconspicuously, dated in the margin. In copying into BM, the secretary evidently overlooked the marginal date.

Source: M-1, ff. 216–217.

Omitted: January 20, 1687. To Middleton reporting French dissatisfaction with the delays in the Diet.

Source: M-1, ff. 218–219; H-1, pp. 59–60; *LB,* pp. 131–132.

Omitted: January 23, 1687. To Middleton summarizing a letter from the Emperor on French plans.

Source: M-1, ff. 220–221; H-1, pp. 60–61; *LB,* pp. 132–133.

[January 23, 1687]

To Mr. Wynne of change in the Treasury and about Entertainment.

Source: H-1, p. 61.

Omitted: January 27, 1687. To Middleton explaining delays in the Diet.

Source: M-1, ff. 222–223; H-1, pp. 61–62; *LB,* pp. 133–134.

Omitted: January 27, 1687. Part of a letter to Sunderland reporting news of the Diet.

Source: H-1, p. 63; *LB*, pp. 134–135.

[January 27, 1687]

To Sir Peter Wyche
and Mr. Wynne

January 30, 1687

To Mr. Dryden
My Lady
Mr. Manlove and
Dr. Wynne.
Source: H-1, p. 63.

Omitted: February 3, 1687. A letter to Middleton enclosing a copy of a medal struck at Nuremberg.

Source: M-1, ff. 224–225; H-1, p. 64; *LB*, pp. 135–136.

To The Earl of Middleton

February 6, 1687
Ratisbon

My Lord.

Here has been nothing yet done in the Diet. They continue consulting at Vienna what they shall doe concerning the Treaty for the execution of the Truce. The time drawes near which the French have fix'd to be satisfied in this business. They are resolv'd not to loose the advantage of being before hand this Spring, in case the Empire will not secure them by a peace from what they apprehend when the war with the Turk is ended. The French complaine the Emperor is very slow in his deliberations. Nevertheless they think he will be forc'd at last to comply with what they desire.

Two days since, the Courrier the French Plenipotentiarie sent to his Master return'd hither, and this morning he has dispatch'd him back again. He tells me the King his Master has order'd him, while this matter depends, constantly to informe him whether any thing be done in it or no by way of express and that the substance of this is that the Emperors Council have not yet determin'd any thing in it. I beleive his Christian Majesty is impatient to know what the Emperor resolves and thinks he may guess at it by what he may Learne from hence before he can receave the certaintie from Rome.

By the many Visits Monsieur de Crecy has lately made I imagin he has endeavour'd to find out what Electors and Princes of the Empire are well dispos'd for the Treaty and has inform'd his master of them, for on my discoursing with him on this Subject he told me that severall Ministers were allready instructed in the matter.

The Count de Windisgratz has been tax'd with the discovering of a Secret which has made the French more earnest in the pressing of this affaire. He was pleas'd after having examin'd himselfe to doe me the honor to say he never spoke of it to any body but to me and that he did not tell it me directly but onely by seeming to consent to several things I discours'd off and that if ever he recover'd the use of his hands again, which were then very goutie, he wou'd be reveng'd (but he was pleas'd to be so favourable as to explaine himselfe) by writing.

This Secret has hardly been one to any Shopkeeper in this Towne this halfe yeare, and a child by their proceedings ever since I have been here might have guest at it. It is that *they never intended to keep the Truce any longer then they shou'd think it convenient, it being made so much to the prejudice of the Empire.* This has been own'd to me out of vanitie by some Ministers who were violent for the Alliance of Ausburg when they put no confidence in me, esteeming his Majestie to have too strickt an Alliance with France uppon my first acquaintance with them.

The morning Mr. Fitzjames went from hence towards Hungary, having waited uppon him to his boate, I return'd in Company of a French Gentleman, and seeing the Swedish Ministers[1] Coach at his doore, who was then setting forward for the assemblie at Ausburg, I went to him and wish'd him a good Journy, but the French man told him *he wish'd him all prosperity as to himselfe but he cou'd not wish him good success in his business.* Seeing some other Ministers afterwards who came to take their leave of him, he told them he had had a very fine complement just then made him on his journy and told them what the Frenchman had said, malisciously not distinguishing who had made it. I was surpris'd two days afterwards to hear that the Secretary of Austria maintain'd publiquely that it was I that had said these words.[2] I complain'd to the Count de Windishgratz but cou'd have no satisfaction against his creature, but uppon Monsieur Schnolski's returne from Ausburg I oblig'd him to clear the business and in the next visit he shou'd make to the Emperors Ministers to declare to them that it was a lye, which they own'd to me he did accordingly.

On the taking of Buda the Imperial Comission in their rejoycings, tho' they invited not onely all the Ministers here except the Count de Crecy but many Cavaliers who were strangers, they took no notice of me, notwithstanding I had made them my Complement on the occasion. This was very much wonder'd at and blam'd by most of the ministers, who knew how zealous his Majestie and our Nation had been for the prosperity of that Seige. I beleive their reason was they wou'd have no body there who might check the Liberty they had a mind to take of talking what was in their power to do after so great a Victorie.

When it came to the Count de Lambergs turne to treat, he invited me and us'd me with more then ordinary Civillity. Since that time I have apply'd myselfe to him and have neglected the Count de Windisgratz, who never made me the least returne for all the Civillitys I advanc'd him. The change may be advantagious since the Count de Lamberg is likely to be first Comissioner here, which is a dignity the Empire will never suffer the other to rise too. These things I suppose made the Count de Windishgratz jealous. I might have talk'd of matters he trusted me with when I us'd constantly to visit him, but finding by my behavior in this busines that I have better principles then he expected a man shou'd have, he now says he was mistaken and that he never trusted me with any thing. But he thought of this so late that all the Ministers take his first word and not a man will beleive me, what ever I say to the Contrarie. I am, My Lord, Your Lordships most faithfull and most humble Servant

Geo: Etherege

Source: M-1, ff. 226–230. In part in H-1, pp. 65–66, and in *LB*, pp. 136–138.

1 Georg Fredrik von Snoilsky was the Swedish emissary at the Diet (*Repertorium*, 1, p. 487).

2 This story is summarized innocuously in the official Letterbook (H-1, p. 66), but in his own copy (BM, f. 48) Etherege's secretary maliciously added in parentheses the story going round in Ratisbon: that Sir George had wished Snoilsky's "Coach might break on the way because he went with a design of making an Alliance against France." Hughes repeated the charge in his first letter to "Honoured Sir." See below, p. 296.

To BARON GODOLPHIN[1]   February 10, 1687
Ratisbon

My Lord.

I noe sooner received the news of the change Which was to be in the Treasury, but I straight fix'd my thoughts on your Lordship to be my Patron. The vertues which you enjoy proper for such a trust, your great experience in those affairs, the confidence which his Majestie has in you, and the particular esteem he has for you, made me not doubt but you would be one of the Commissioners. Cou'd I shew as much judgement in the performance of my duty, as I have done in this choice, I should not dispair of meriting your Lordship's favour; and your Justice would allow me what I must wholely expect from your goodness. Instead of congratulating your Lordship I should congratulate his Majestie and the Kingdom on this occasion, for you will have the trouble wholly, and they will have the greatest share of the profitt of your honorable Employment.

I have long wish'd for a pretense to write to your Lordship, and I hope you will think this soe Lawfull a one that you will forgive my presumption. I shall be modest at first and not importune you with a long letter. If I could by any way learn that your Lordship desires I should acquaint you immediately with what is done here, you would find me very diligent to gain your good Opinion. I am too Lazy and too careless to be ambitious, but it is soe pleasing an advantage to have the reputation of your favour that the hope of it is enough to change the natural inclination of, My Lord, Your Lordship's most faithfull and most obedient Servant

Source: H-1, pp. 66–67; *LB*, pp. 138–139.

[1] Sidney, Baron Godolphin of Rialton (c. 1645–1712), formerly a member of the Privy Council and a Secretary of State, had just been named a Commissioner of the Treasury.

To The Earl of Dover[1]   February 10, 1687
                                                        Dito

My Lord.

I have been long an admirer of your vertues without suspecting your loving of businesse was one of them. Did I not know the perfect resignation you have to his Majestie's Pleasure, I should wonder at your courrage in loading yourself at first setting forth with the most weighty charge in the Kingdome. Sir Jo. E. and Sir S. F.,[2] who began with carrying a Calf, may bear this Ox without staggering; but what a fine thing will it be to you (who have never scarce sullied your fingers with telling of Silver) to cast up a monstrous Exchequer-account, whose head is as big as a million while the tayl dwindles into a halfe penny farthing. However honorable your title is, you are noe other than one of the first Cash-Keepers in the Nation. But what is a man of honor not capable of undertaking when he is call'd to serve soe gracious a Master. I doubt not but you will governe the Treasury with as much address and aplause as Lucullus[3] did of old the Roman Legions, and were I to be an Eye-wittnesse, I shou'd see you loose your

Ease with the same temper I have seen you loose your money. I know not whether I ought to rejoyce or condole with you, since I think you sacrifice yourself in this matter; but you must give me leave to congratulate my own good fortune, now you are plac'd in a Post from whence you may more powerfully continue the dispensing of your favour to, My Lord, Your Lordships most humble and most obedient Servant

Geo: Etherege

Source: H-1, pp. 67–68; *LB*, pp. 139–140.

1 Henry Jermyn, Earl of Dover (c. 1636–1708), had just been appointed a Commissioner of the Treasury.
2 Sir John Ernle and Sir Stephen Fox were also Commissioners of the Treasury.
3 Lucius Licinius Lucullus was famous as a general and an administrator, and in his later years as a wealthy sybarite.

Dito [February 10, 1687]

To Mr. Guy.
Source: H-1, p. 68.

TO THE EARL OF MIDDLETON   February 10, 1687
Ratisbon

My Lord.

I din'd yesterday with the wholle Electoral Colledge, and his Majesties health was the first which was begun at the Table. In the morning I receiv'd two pacquets From Mr. Wynne, the last being of the 14th instant, and had an oportunity by this meanes of undeceaving them of several infamous Lys which came in a hand Gazet from the Hague uppon what has been lately done in England.

All the news I have to send you by this post is that there is none.

> [Report from Lord Taaffe in Vienna of the unfavorable reaction to the proposition made by the King of France to the Pope.]

I hope your Lordship will take a little care of me and speak in my favour to the Comissioners of the Treasurie. You know my owne Rents¹ come but slowly out of England. There will be near a Thousand pounds due to me for entertainment and Extraordinaries by the end of February. But my comfort is, tho' I have but little mony left, I owe nothing in the Empire. I was tax'd by a Friend of being guilty of an indiscretion at play, but the storie is false, and I find the follies I have committed in that kind were only the effects of my Idleness,² having thought of nothing since my being here but how I might fit myselfe to serve his Majestie. I am, My Lord, Your Lordships most humble and most faithfull Servant

Geo: Etherege

Source: M-1, ff. 232–233. A brief summary in H-1, p. 68 and *LB*, pp. 140–141.

1 The old sense of the word is income or revenue of any sort.
2 MS: "Idles."

[February 10, 1687]

To Mrs. Merry.
To Dr. Wynne.
    Source: H-1, p. 68.

To Viscount Taafe   February 12, 1687
                                                        Ratisbon

My Lord.

I believe the report of my going into Sweden is grounded on a mistake. I should be sorry to leave the Empire before I have had the honor of being personally known to your Lordship and, in the happiness of your conversation, forget the chagrin which the dulness of this place occasions. I need not trouble you with discoursing of the reasons which have made the French King make the propositions at Rome in this conjuncture. You are soe clear-sighted that you doe not want any illuminations I can give. The French urge the Treating of a peace is part of the Execution of the Armistice. Your Lordship will best judge of that by reading the 11th Article.

Some ministers here are soe passionate that it makes them unfitt to serve their Masters as they might doe. I am confident the King our master will doe all he can that these differences may be happyly compos'd for the benefit of all Christendome, and will never contribute to the unlawfull oppressing of the Empire. Judge you how gratefull it is to me to hear his Majestie call'd *bon françois,* and to have it sayd that the Empire is too poore to purchace soe good a friend?

I have a great esteem for the Count de Lamberg. He is a gentleman who (besides his other merits) knows how to live, which is a thing most of our Doctors are to learn. I have apply'd myself wholely to him and endeavour'd to cultivate a friendship with him, since I had reason to think the Count de Windisgratz slighted our nation.

Your Lordship is not ignorant of the zeal his Majestie and all his good subjects shew'd for the prosperity of the Siege of Buda. I made

87

my compliments to the Imperiall Comission for the taking of the place, and yet when severall Cavalliers were invited among the ministers, I was thôt unworthy to partake in the publick rejoycings. This was blam'd by all the Ministers, and the reflexion I made upon it has been the cause I have not since made my Court (for I can give it noe less a name, he never making any return of Civilities) to the Count de Windisgratz. Upon his being lately tax'd with having discover'd a secret upon which some say the proposition at Rome is founded, he was pleas'd to say if he spoke ever anything of it, it must be to me. I doe not doubt but he has discours'd of this business to severall, and did not soe much think to whom he had trusted the secret as to whom he had given occasion to disclose it.

As for me, I protest upon my honor I know of noe secret he trusted me with, and in case he should have trusted me with any, I am too honest and too reasonable a man upon a private pique to revenge myself on the whole Empire, whose prosperity I sincerely wish. I have received noe certain news of what his Majestie intends to doe for Mr. Fitzjames. I send your Lordship all the news the last Post brought me out of England and shall be overjoy'd to have a good opportunity to shew you how faithfully I am, etc.

Source: H-1, pp. 69–70; *LB*, pp. 141–143.

To Bevil Skelton[1]

February 13, 1687
Ratisbon

Sir.

I had the good fortune, by reason of the distance I am at, not to know of the danger you were in in your passage from England before I knew you were safely arriv'd at Paris. I take it very kindly that you ordered Captain Slater to make me the offer of doing me what curtesies you cou'd in your station. I am sorry to find by the other part of his letter that you have had an occasion to apprehend I have been wanting in what is due to your merrit. In mine he will shew you the answer I made him as to those matters, and had I not the testimony of all that are honest here to vindicate me, I doubt not but my own word wou'd be taken against whatever malicious reports have been in Holland to the prejudice of, Sir, Your most humble and most obedient servant

Geo: Etherege

Source: H-1, pp. 70–71; *LB*, p. 143.

[1] Skelton, former envoy to Holland, had just been transferred to Paris to replace Sir William Trumbull.

Sir.

I received yesterday a letter[2] from you dated at Paris the 28th of December last. I know not by what fate it was sent to Roterdam where it lay in the Post-house 'till an English Merchant was soe kind as to redeem it and send it to me. The truth is, the businesse you write to me about might better be clear'd in Holland than here. Judge you how much I was surpris'd with what (you tell me) the reports in Holland accuse me withall; I whose conduct ever since I have been in the Empire has been quite contrary. I have had often occasion to Speak of Mr. Skelton, but I have always done it in such a manner that I have not onely done justice to his merit, but according to my poor Ability payd some part of the obligation I owe him. How could a man who is soe zealous for all that concerns his Majestie (as I am) censure the negotiations of a gentleman who has soe eminently signaliz'd himself in his service?

As for Sir Robert Peyton[3] I am not to be inform'd of his Crimes. I have told the whole history of his behaviour since the begining of the Plot and satisfy'd all honest and reasonable men that the States onely take it ill that their Countrey cannot be an unviolable Sancturary for all Rebells. I knew nothing of any letters Peyton had sent to Mr. Skelton, but was told by some ministers here (who hold a correspondence with Valkenier, who has been some time since recall'd from hence by his high and mighty Masters) of the breach of faith you mention, to which I answer'd: I did not believe Mr. Skelton ever made him any promise, that Peyton might write to him, but that I cou'd not imagin any use was made of his letters but to communicate the contents of them to his Majestie. This is not the first trick has been playd me since my being here, and is not the last. Mr. Skelton knows by experience the temper of the Dutch, how little they value a lye to doe a man a good turn, especially those his Majestie Employs, now they esteem him to have a strict Allyance with France.

Valkeneer was here long after my arrival, and us'd all the means possible to perswade me to visit him; but upon the certain knowledge I had that he receiving the false news (of a victorie the late Duke of Monmouth was sayd to have in the west) had made it be printed here and sent it with great joy to severall of his friends, I never could be prevail'd with. He is a true Burgeois of Amsterdam and since his departure has supply'd our Gazeteers here with lys from his own Country, among which there have been some dangerously reflecting on his

Majestie. But upon my Complaint they are commanded not to doe the like for the future. Whether the reports you talk of come from this source, or any other, they are wholly false upon my honor. I take your good intentions very kindly, but pray rectify your mistake hereafter and doe not let any idle Reports make you have an ill opinion of, Sir, Your humble servant

Geo: Etherege

If Mr. Skelton desires to know what passes here, he may freely command me, who have ever had an inclination to serve him.

Source: H-1, pp. 71–73; *LB*, pp. 143–146.

[1] After his unsuccessful attempt to kidnap Sir Robert Peyton (see note 3, below), Captain Solomon Slater, an English officer in the service of the Dutch, fled to Paris, where he became secretary to Bevil Skelton.

[2] This letter is printed on pp. 273–274, below.

[3] Sir Robert Peyton, indicted by a Grand Jury for sedition in 1685, had fled to Holland. In October 1686, when Skelton was about to leave Holland, he authorized an attempt by Slater to seize Peyton and transport him to England on Skelton's yacht. Peyton, who had become a citizen of Amsterdam, was rescued by a mob, and the Dutch magistrates complained to James II about this violation of political asylum (James Walker, "The English Exiles in Holland," *Transactions of the Royal Historical Society*, 4th series, 30 [1948], 118; George H. Jones, *Charles Middleton*, Chicago, 1967, pp. 183 f.).

Dito [February 13, 1687]

To Mr. Bradbury
Mr. Richards and
Mr. Wynne of minding Mr. Robson.

Source: H-1, p. 73.

Omitted: February 17, 1687. To Middleton reporting "How matters stand" at the Diet.

Source: M-1, ff. 234–235; H-1, pp. 73–74; *LB*, pp. 146–147.

Dito [February 17, 1687]

To Sir Peter Wyche
and Mr. Vincent Neering.

Source: H-1, p. 74.

Omitted: February 20, 1687. To Middleton reporting the Emperor's response to a French proposal made at Rome.

Source: M-1, ff. 236–237; H-1, pp. 74–75; *LB*, pp. 147–148.

To Mr. George Etherege about the French Bookes
To Dr. Wynne.
 Source: H-1, p. 75.

To OWEN WYNNE   February 24, 1687
                                              Ratisbon

Sir.

I received yours of the 28th of January and thank you very kindly for the pains you have taken in sending me soe much of the news of the Town.

[Diplomatic maneuvering between France and the Empire.]

I must entreat you to lett Mr. Robson know I am in great want of his assistance, and I hope before this reaches you, he will lett me know I may draw a Bill upon him. I am.

P.S. The Marquis d'Albeville[1] has not yet, I suppose, had leasure to give me notice of his being in Holland. Pray send me word what delays Mr. Poley so long.
 Source: H-1, pp. 75–76; *LB*, pp. 148–149.

[1] Ignatius White, an Irish adventurer who had received the title of Marquis d'Albeville in the Holy Roman Empire, succeeded Bevil Skelton as envoy to Holland (F. C. Turner, *James II*, p. 347). Dalrymple (*Memoirs,* 1, p. 139) describes him as "a man who received one pension from France, and probably another from Holland, and whose talents were as mean as his mind."

Omitted: February 27, 1687. To Middleton summarizing the French proposals at Rome and the Emperor's answer.
 Source: M-1, ff. 238–239; H-1, pp. 76–78; *LB*, pp. 149–152.

Omitted: March 3, 1687. To Middleton reporting on three decrees dictated in the Diet, concerning the truce, Denmark, and winter quartering.
 Source: M-1, f. 240; H-1, p. 79; *LB*, p. 152.

                                              March 3, 1687

To Mr. Robson. About a Bill drawn upon him
To Dr. Wynne.
 Source: H-1, p. 79.

Omitted: March 6, 1687. To Middleton enclosing the three decrees and commenting on them.

Source: M-1, ff. 242–243; H-1, pp. 79–81; *LB,* pp. 152–155.

To The Duke of Buckingham   [March, 1687?] [1]

My Lord,

I never enjoy my self so much as when I can steal a few Moments, from the Hurry of public Business, to write to my Friends in England; and as there is none there to whom I pay a profounder Respect than to your Grace, wonder not if I afford my self the Satisfaction of conversing with you by way of Letters, (the only Relief I have left me to support your Absence at this distance) as often as I can find an opportunity.

You may guess by my last, whether I don't pass my Time very comfortably here; forc'd as I am by my Character, to spend the better part of my time in Squabling and Deliberating with Persons of Beard and Gravity, how to preserve the Ballance of Christendome, which would go well enough of its self, if the Divines and Ministers of Princes would let it alone: And when I come home spent and weary from the Diet, I have no Lord D[orse]t's, or Sir Charles S[edle]y's to sport away the Evening with; no Madam I——, or my Lady A——'s; in short, none of those kind charming Creatures London affords, in whose Embraces I might make my self amends for so many Hours murdered in impertinent Debates; so that not to magnifie my sufferings to your Grace, they really want a greater stock of Christian Patience to support them, than I can pretend to be Master of.

I have been long enough in this Town (one would think) to have made Acquaintance enough with Persons of both Sexes, so as never to be at a loss how to pass the few vacant Hours I can allow my self: But the terrible Drinking that accompanies all our Visits, hinders me from Conversing with the Men so often as I would otherwise doe; and the German Ladies are so intollerably reserv'd and virtuous, (with Tears in my eyes I speak it to your Grace) that 'tis next to an impossibility to carry on an Intrigue with them: A Man has so many Scruples to conquer, and so many Difficulties to surmount, before he can promise himself the least Success, that for my part I have given over all Pursuits of this Nature: Besides, there is so universal a Spirit of Censoriousness reigns in this Town, that a Man and a Woman cannot be seen at Ombre or Picquet together, but 'tis immediately concluded some other Game has been played between them; and as

92

this renders all manner of Access to the Ladies almost impracticable, for fear of exposing their Reputation to the Mercy of their ill-natur'd Neighbours, so it makes an innocent Piece of Gallantry often pass for a criminal Correspondence.

So that to deal freely with your Grace among so many noble and wealthy Families as we have in this Town, I can only pretend to be truly acquainted but with one: The Gentleman's Name was Monsieur Hoffman, a frank, hearty, jolly Companion; his Father, one of the most eminent Wine-Merchants of the City, left him a considerable Fortune, which he improved by marrying a French Jeweller's Daughter of Lyons: To give you his Character in short, he was a sensible ingenious Man, and had none of his Country Vices, which I impute to his having travelled abroad and seen Italy, France, and England. His Lady is a most accomplish'd ingenious Person, and notwithstanding she is come in to a Place where so much Formality and Stiffness are practiced, keeps up all the Vivacity, and Air, and good Humor of France.

I had been happy in my Acquaintance with this Family for some Months, when an ill favour'd Accident rob'd me of the greatest Happiness I had hitherto enjoy'd in Germany the loss of which I can never sufficiently regret. Monsieur Hoffman, about three Weeks ago, going to make merry with some Friends (at a Village some three Leagues from this Place) upon the Danube, by the Unskillfulness or Negligence of the Watermen, the Boat, wherin he was, unfortunately chanced to over-set, and of some twenty Persons, not one escaped to bring home the News but a Boy that miraculously saved himself by holding fast to the Rudder, and so by the Rapidity of the Current was cast upon the other Shore.

I was sensibly afflicted at the Destiny of my worthy Friend, and so indeed were all that had the Honour of knowing him; but his Wife took on so extravagantly, that she (in a short Time) was the only talk both of City and Country; she refus'd to admit any Visits from her nearest Relations, her Chamber, her Antichamber, and Pro-antichamber were hung with Black, nay the very Candles, her Fans, and Tea-table wore the Livery of Grief; she refus'd all manner of Sustenance, and was so averse to the Thoughts of Living, that she talk'd of nothing but Death; in short, you may tell your injenious Friend Monsieur de Saint Evremont, that Petronius's Ephesian Matron, to whose Story he has done so much Justice in his noble Translation, was only a Type of our more obstinate, as well as unhappy German Widow.

About a Fortnight after this cruel Loss (for I thought it would be Labour lost to attack her Grief in its first Vehemence) I thought my self obliged, in Point of Honour and Gratitude to the Memory of my deceased Friend, to make her a small Visit, and condole her Ladyship upon this unhappy Occasion: And tho' I had been told that she had refused to see several Persons who had gon to wait on her with the same Errand, yet I presumed so much upon the Friendship her late Husband had always express'd for me, (not to mention the particular Civilities I had received from her self) as to think I wou'd be admitted to have a sight of her: Accordingly I came to her House, sent up my Name, and word was immediately brought me, that if I pleas'd I might go up to her.

When I came into the Room, I fancy'd my self in the Territories of Death, every thing looked so gloomy, so dismal, and so melancholly. There was a grave Lutheran Minister with her, that omitted no Arguments to bring her to a more composed and more Christian Disposition of Mind. Madam (says he) you don't consider that by abandoning your self thus to Despair, you actually rebel against Providence; I cann't help it, (says she) Providence may e'en thank it self, for laying so insupportable a Load upon me: O fye, Madam, (cries the other) this is down right impiety; What would you say now, if Heaven should punish it by some more exemplary Visitation? That is impossible, replies the Lady sighing, and since it has rob'd me of the onely Delight I had in this World, the only Favour it can do me is to level a Thunderbolt at my Head, and put an end to all my Sufferings. The Parson finding her in this extravagant Strain, and seeing no likelihood of Perswading her to come to a better Temper, got up from his Seat and took his leave of her.

It came to my turn now to try whether I was not capable of comforting her, and being convinced by so late an Instance that Arguments brought from Religion were not like to work any extraordinary Effects upon her, I resolved to attack her Ladiship in a more sensible part, and represent to her the great inconveniences (not which her Soul, but) her Body received from this inordinate Sorrow.

Madam, saies I to her, next to my Concern for your worthy Husband's untimely Death, I am griev'd to see what an Alteration the Bemoaning of his Loss has occasion'd in you: These Words raising her Curiosity to know what this Alteration was, I thus continu'd my Discourse; In endeavouring, Madam, to extinguish, or at least to alleviate your Grief, than which nothing can be more prejudicial to a

94

beautiful Woman, I intend a publick Benefit, for if the Public is interested, as most certainly it is, in the preserving of a beautiful Face, that Man does the Public no little Service who contributes most to its Preservation.

This odd Beginning operated so wonderfully upon her, that she desired me to leave this general Road of Complements, and explain my self more particularly to her. Upon this (delivering my self with an unusual Air of Gravity, which your Grace knows I seldom carry about me in the Company of Ladies) I told her, that Grief ruines the finest Faces sooner than any thing whatever; and that as envy it self could not deny her Face to be the most charming in the Universe, so if she did not suffer her self to be comforted, she must soon expect to take her Farewel of it. I confirm'd this Assertion, by telling her of one of the finest Women we ever had in England who did her self more injury in a Fortnight's time by lamenting her only Brother's Death, than ten Years could possibly have done; that I had heard an eminent Physician at Leyden say, That Tears (having abundance of saline Particles in them) not only spoild the Complexion, but hastned Wrinkles: But, Madam, concluded I, why should I give my self the trouble to confirm this by foreign instances, and by the Testimonies of our most knowing Doctors, when alas! your own Face so fully justifies the Truth of what I have said to you.

How! reply'd our disconsolate Widow, with a Sigh that came from the Bottom of her Heart, And is it possible that my just concern for my dear Husband, has wrought so cruel an Effect upon me in so short a Time? With that she order'd her Gentlewoman to bring the Lookinglass to her, and having survey'd her self a few Minutes in it, she told me she was perfectly convinced that my Notions were true; but, cries she, what would you have us poor Women do in these Cases? For something, continues she, we owe to the Memory of the Deceased, and something too to the World, which expects at least the common Appearances of Grief from us.

By your leave, Madam, saies I, all this is a Mistake, and no better; you owe nothing to your Husband, since he is dead, and knows nothing of your Lamentation; besides, cou'd you shed an Ocean of Tears upon his Hearse, it would not do him the least Service; much less do you lye under any such Obligations to the World, as to spoil a good Face only to comply with its tyrannic Customs: No, Madam, take care to preserve your Beauty, and then let the World say what it pleases, your Ladyship may be revenged upon the World whene'er you see fit. I am resolved, answers she, to be intirely govern'd by you, there-fore tell me frankly what sort of a Course you'd have me steer? Why, Madam, saies I, in the first place forget the Defunct; and in order to bring that about, relieve Nature, to which you have been so long unmerciful, with the most exquisit Meats and the most generous Wines. Upon Condition you'll sup with me, cries our afflicted Lady, I will submit to your prescription. But why should I trouble your Grace with a Narration of every Particular? In short, we had a noble Regale that Evening in her Bed-chamber, and our good Widow push'd the Glass so strenuously about, that her Comforter (meaning my self) could hardly find the way to his Coach. To conclude this Farce (which I am afraid begins now to be too tedious to your Grace) this Phoenix of her Sex, this Pattern of Conjugal Fidelity, two Mornings ago was marry'd to a smooth-chind Ensign of Count Trautmandorf's Regiment, that had not a farthing in the World but his Pay to depend upon: I assisted at the Ceremony, tho' I little imagin'd the Lady wou'd take the Matrimonial Receit so soon.

I was the easier perswaded to give your Grace a large Account of this Tragi-comedy, not only because I wanted better Matter to enter-tain you with at this Lazy Conjuncture, but also to show your Grace, that not only Ephesus in ancient, and England in later Times, have afforded such fantastical Widows, but even Germany it self; where, if the Ladies have not more Virtue than those of their Sex in other Countries, yet they pretend at least a greater Management of the outside of it.

By my last Pacquet from England, among a heap of nauseous Trash, I received the Three Dukes of Dunstable, which is really so mon-strous and insipid, that I am sorry Lapland or Livonia had not the Honour of producing it; but if I did Pennance in reading it, I re-joyced to hear that it was so solemnly interr'd to the Tune of Catcalls. The 'Squire of Alsatia, however, which came by the following Post, made me some amends for the cursed impertinence of the Three Dukes; and my witty Friend Sir C[harles] S[edle]y's Bella mira gave me that intire Satisfaction that I cannot read it over too often.

They tell me my old Acquaintance Mr. Dryden has left off the Theatre, and wholly applies him self to the Study of the Controversies between the two Churches. Pray Heaven! this strange alteration in him portends nothing disastrous to the State; but I have all along observed, That Poets do Religion as little Service by drawing their Pens for it, as the Divines do Poetry by pretending to Versification.

But I forget how troublesome I have been to your Grace, I shall therefore conclude with assuring you that I am, and to the last Moment of my Life shall be ambitious of being, My LORD, Your Grace's most obedient, and most obliged Servant,

G. ETHEREGE.

Source: Buckingham's *Miscellaneous Works*, 1 (1704), 131–141.

1 The date for this letter given in the printed source (October 21, 1689) is certainly wrong: by that time Etherege was in France and Buckingham had been dead two and a half years. Although the third paragraph from the end, with its references to Durfey's *Three Dukes of Dunstable* and Shadwell's *Squire of Alsatia*, must be dated not earlier than the spring of 1688, the main part of the letter must have been written before May 19, 1687, when Etherege mentions the death of the Duke of Buckingham (April 18, 1687). I conclude that the paragraph which must be dated 1688 is part of a lost letter interpolated here by the printer of the 1704 edition of Buckingham's *Miscellaneous Works*. All the rest of the letter fits neatly into the context of March 1687, when the Diet was trying "to preserve the balance of Christendom" by negotiating about the Truce between France and the Empire, and when Dryden was working on his "Study of the controversies between the two Churches," *The Hind and the Panther*. The story of the Widow Hoffman looks like the fulfillment of Etherege's promise, at the end of the first letter to Buckingham (November 12, 1686), "to entertain your Grace with something more agreeable" in his next letter from Ratisbon.

To The Earl of Middleton   March 10, 1687
                                                   Ratisbon

My Lord.

I receiv'd yesterday your Lordship's circular letter[1] about regulating of Extraordinaries. I have been so modest in that point that I cannot think I have contributed any thing towards the making of that Order.

My being in your Lordships province recommends me to your care, but I have a better title to it: the many precedents I have of your favour. It is natural to think we are a little hardly dealt with when we are retrench'd a bounty we have been us'd to, tho' we are conscious of our owne want of merit, and I doe not doubt but you will represent my condition to the Lords of the Treasurie. You know it is very much for me to be three quarters of a yeare in arreares in a Towne where there is no Credit.

Nothing has been done in the Diet since my last. The Emperor's Ministers have had a privat conference, but it is not yet knowne what is resolv'd among them.

The Count de Lamberg is not return'd from Saltzburg. The Bishop still continues ill, and tho' the Emperor's phisician (who attends him) says he will reestablish him in his health, it is not beleiv'd he will

97

recover. I am with all Duty, My Lord, Your Lordships most faithfull, and most humble Servant

Geo: Etherege

Source: M-1, ff. 244–245; H-1, p. 82; *LB*, pp. 155–156.

¹ The order limiting Etherege's Extraordinaries to £50 a quarter is copied into H-2, f. 115, numbered from the back of the book.

To OWEN WYNNE   March 10, 1687

Dito

To Mr. Maule and Mr. Wynne. about Williams, and the Saddles to be sent by Mr. Crafts. About the business of the Treasury. . . . I have not yet been acquainted with Monsieur D'Albeville's arrivall in Holland. Tho' he has writ to Abbot Flemin about regulating his Chappel, I suspect his Secretary (Consul Petit) may have done me some ill office, for he has broke off long since the Intelligence he held with us in Mr. Skelton's time: upon my refusing to allow 60¹ Dollars per annum to a friend of his (as he pretended) who was to furnish me with a written Gazette from those parts. I did not think I was to be so ill a husband of his Majestie's money.

The Marquis d'Albevilles Harangue to the States is printed here in french. Some ministers here who are of the Reform'd Religion report that my Lord Castlemain,² at the magnificent Treat he gave to the Prelates at Rome, drew a Curtain behind which was his Majestie's Picture with John Calvin under his feet, drawn soe like that he was to be known. I am, Sir etc.

Source: H-1, pp. 82–83; *LB*, pp. 156–157.

¹ In BM (and hence in *LB*) the amount is given as 80 dollars.
² Roger Palmer, Earl of Castlemaine, had been sent in 1686 as ambassador to the Pope.

Omitted: March 13, 1687. To Middleton reporting news of the Diet.
Source: M-1, ff. 246–247; H-1, pp. 83–85; *LB*, pp. 157–159.

To OWEN WYNNE   March 13, 1687

Dito

Sir.

I must desire the favour of you to acquaint my Lord that Monsieur Valkeneer (who was not long since here from the States of Holland) is coming back with the Character of Envoyé. I formerly acquainted his Lordship with the reasons why I did not visit him, which was chiefly because he had shewn great Demonstrations of Joy upon the report of a Victory which the late Duke of Monmouth had got against his Majestie in the West, causing the lye to be printed here and dispersing it among such as he thought it would be wellcome to. It goes against my Stomach to have any Commerce with such as I know to be noe wellwishers to his Majestie's prosperity. Wherefore I desire to have orders in this case, that I may know better how to behave myself when he arrives.

I let my Lord know by a letter I sent him not long since, that there was a misunderstanding between the Count de Windisgratz and me, and how it happen'd. The malice which has been us'd to ruin some Ministers of the Diet who live civilly with the Count de Crecy, by forging of many lies against them, makes me think I ought to be soe cautious as to desire nothing may be believ'd at Court to my prejudice 'till my answer be heard. Tho' there is a Truce between the Empire and France, some of the Emperor's Ministers cannot forgive a man who does not live in open hostility with the French; such is the good breeding of this place. My conduct has been to live well with all who have a due regard to his Majesties Dignity. My conversation has been impartiall, and I have given (according as I have been able) an account of matters without any inclination or favour to either party. I am etc.

Source: H-1, pp. 85–86; *LB*, pp. 159–160.

Dito [March 13, 1687]

To my Lady. and
Mr. Corbet
    Source: H-1, p. 86.

To Thomas Maule   March 13, 1687
Dito to Mr. Maule
The Substance of the letter was: That no pleasure but the seeing of him in England cou'd be greater than the receiving of a letter from him. That it is no new thing to be his Debtor, seeing he had neglected one Post since he had receiv'd his letter. But that it was no lesse troublesome to write upon duty, and neglect writing to him, than it is to a wife with whom her husband impertinently employs the kind hour in which she had a Rendezvous with her Lover. That his letter made him (Sir George) of good humor, and the like favour now and then wou'd render him less sensible of the loss of Countrey and friends. That every line of his letter was full of Entertainment, but

99

that which charmes the most is the assurance of his kindness. That Sir George is fond of being a man of business, that there is a greater reformation in him than he can imagin, and that he is no more guilty of those errors which he has known him committ, when necessity had got the better of his judgement. That upon receiving a letter from his Lady and being call'd Rogue at 800 miles distance, it makes him cry, in consideration of my Lord Mulgrave, Solamen miseris[1] etc.

Source: BM, ff. 61–62; *LB*, pp. 160–161.

[1] The full quotation, from Marlowe's *Doctor Faustus*, is "Solamen miseris socios habuisse doloris" (The consolation of the miserable is to have companions in suffering). Etherege is referring to Mulgrave's unhappy marriage to Lady Conway.

To LADY ETHEREGE   March 13, 1687
                                                          Dito

To my Lady thus:
I beg your pardon for undertaking to advise you. I am so well satisfy'd by your last letter of your prudence and Judgement that I shall never more comitt the same Error. I wish there were Copies of it in London. It might serve for a pattern for modest wives to write to their husbands. You shall find me so carefull hereafter how I offend you that I will no more subscribe myself your loving, since you take it ill, but, Madame, Your most dutyfull husband

                                                          G. E.

Source: BM, f. 62; *LB*, pp. 161–162.

To ROBERT CORBET   March 13, 1687
                                                          Dito

Sir.
I am much oblig'd to you for the favour you did me in delivering a letter I enclos'd to you for Mr. Maule. He has sent me one in return, and I leave you to imagin how wellcome it was from one whom I so very much esteem, being both extream pleasant and kind. I have answer'd his by the last Post, but had not time then to satisfy my inclinations in writing to you and cherishing your friendship, which I reckon among those things which are most dear to me.

Besides your other merits the opinion I have of your Sincerity makes all that comes from you have more charmes than I know in Ratisbonne or Nurenberg, and I shou'd have known few solid pleasures since I left England had not your kindness been bountifull to me. I find a convenience now and then in this Countrey, but can boast as little success in the pursuit of what I have lov'd as Captain Pack[1] himself, but I have more passive love and endure the torment without making so much noise. In a word les badinages is all the freedome has been allow'd me by these sorte of Mistresses. I have good Greyhounds and coursing is one of my greatest recreations. We have such plenty of game that now and then I start 6 brace of hares in a day.

When I was in Holland I won near two hundred pounds and lost near the same summe at my first coming hither, which has given an occasion for an idle report, as I am inform'd from London. I have not playd at any thing but 6 penny ombre these 13 months, and am rather a winner than a looser since I saw you. I am in a post where I have more business than people believe, and the desire I have to discharge myself as well as I can of my duty makes me apply my head to it, and has in a manner quite allay'd the passion I had for play.

I was very sorry, tho' I did not wonder, to hear of Dr. Conquest's[2] indiscretion in the Coffee-house. I should be glad if Charles Boyle wou'd play the brave and come this Campagne into Hungary that I might shew him, tho' he has forgott me, I am still the same man on his score. If Whitaker[3] would bear him company he should stay and pass the time at Chess with me 'till the Warriours return'd again; but nothing can be more gratefull to me as an occasion to shew you how faithfully I am etc.

Source: BM, ff. 62–63; *LB,* pp. 162–163.

[1] Apparently a traditionally unsuccessful lover. See Maule's letter to Etherege, p. 275, below.

[2] A Catholic physician who, according to Luttrell, spoke against the Prince and Princess of Orange.

[3] Charles Whittaker, Gent., enjoyed a sinecure of £40 a year as Foreign Opposer in the Exchequer (*CTB,* 1, p. 716 f). A contemporary satire lists him, among other fops of the time, as "soft Whitaker" (Danvers Miscellany, BM Add. MS. 34362, f. 154).

TO THE EARL OF SUNDERLAND   March 17, 1687
                                             Ratisbon

My Lord.

I have given my Lord Middleton constantly the best account I have been able of what has been done or discours'd of here and am confident, when there has been any thing worth your knowing, it has been imparted to you, wherefore I shall not trouble your Lordship with any idle repetitions.

[Monsieur de Crécy's reports of the French attitude toward a treaty.]

By this time you know the full contents of Monsieur Deykvelt's[1] Errand. It has been long reported here that one part of it was to know the reason of his Majestie's Arming, which to mee seems as saucy and impertinent as if a Yeoman should send to a Gentleman (his neighbour) to ask him why he wears a good Sword.

I have writ to my Lord Godolphin and my Lord Dover to beg their favour in the Treasury, but I have but little confidence in my letters, and therefore must once more beg your Lordship to speak to them in my behalf. I know the consideration they have for your word; and when they look upon me as your Creature, it will supply my want of merit. I am etc.

Source: H-1, pp. 87–88; *LB,* pp. 163–165.

[1] Everard van Veede van Dykvelt was sent to England to discover James's real attitude toward the Prince of Orange and to assure English Protestants of William's support.

To Mr. Mountstephens.
To Dr. Wynne desiring to know Count Caunitz business and about Mr. Robsons neglect.[1]
Source: H-1, p. 88.

[1] In BM, f. 64, Hughes omitted the reference to Mr. Robson's neglect and wrote "N.B. a Fr. Quest" instead.

Omitted: March 20, 1687. To Middleton reporting prospects of peace in Europe and among the ministers at the Diet.
Source: M-1, ff. 248–249; H-1, p. 89; *LB,* p. 166.

To JOHN DRYDEN[1]   March 20, 1687
                                                          Ratisbon
Sir.

You know I am noe Flatterer, and therefore will excuse me when I tell you I cannot endure you should arrogate a thing to your self you have not the least pretence to. Is it not enough that you excell in soe many eminent vertues, but you must be putting in for a vice which all the world knows is properly my Province. If you persist in your claim to Laziness, you will be thought as affected in it as Montaigne is, when he complaines of want of memory. What soul has ever been more active than your own? What Country, nay what corner of the earth, has it not travell'd into? Whose bosom has it not div'd into, and inform'd itself there soe perfectly of all the Secrets of man's heart that onely the great being (whose Image it bears) knows them better? I (whose every action of my life is a witness of my Idlenesse) little thought that you, who have rais'd so many Immortall monuments of your Industrie, durst have set up to be my Rival; but to punish you, I will distinguish. You have noe share in that noble Lazinesse of the minde, which all I write make out my just title to. But as for that of the body, I can let you come in for a Snack without any Jealousy. I am apt to think you have 'bated something of your mettle since you and I were Rivalls in other matters, tho' I hope you have not yet attain'd the perfection I have heard Sir Charles Sydlie brag of, which is that when a short youth runs quick through every veine and puts him in minde of his ancient prowesse, he thinks it not worth while to bestow motion on his *et cetera muscle.*

Tho' I have not been able formerly to forbear playing the Fool in verse and prose, I have now Judgement enough to know how much I ventur'd, and am rather amaz'd at my good fortune than vain upon a little Success, and did I not see my own error, the commendation you give me would be enough to perswade me of it. A woman who has luckily been thought agreeable has not reason to be proud when she hears herself extravagantly prais'd by an undoubted beauty. It wou'd be a pretty thing for a man who has learn'd of his own head to scrape on the Fiddle to enter the lists with the greatest Master in the Science of music. It is not to contend with you in writing but to vie[2] with you in kindness that makes me fond of your Correspondence; and I hope my want of Art in friendship will make you forgett the faults it makes me commit in writing.

I have not time now to acquaint you how I like my Employment. Nature noe more intended me for a Politician than she did you for a Courtier; but since I am embark'd I will endeavour not to be wanting in my duty. It concerns me nearly, for shou'd I be shipwreck'd, the season is too far gone to expect an other adventure. The conversation I have with the ministers here improves me daily more in Phylosophie than in Policy and shews me that the most necessary part of it is better to be learn'd in the wide World than in the Gardens of Epicurus. I am glad to hear your son is in the office,[3] hoping now and then by your favour to have the benefit of a letter from him. Pray tell Sir Henry Shere[4] his honesty and good understanding have made me love him ever since I knew him. If we meet in England again, he may finde the gravity of this place has fitted me for his Spanish humor.

I was so pleas'd with reading your letter that I was vex'd at the last proof you gave me of your Lazinesse, the not finding in your heart to turn over the paper.[5] In that you have had the better of me, but I will allways renounce that darling Sin, rather than omit any thing which may give you an assurance of my being faithfully, etc.

Source: H-1, pp. 89–91; *LB*, pp. 167–169.

[1] This is in answer to Dryden's letter of February 16, 1687, pp. 276–277, below.

[2] MS: *view*.

[3] Charles Dryden left Trinity College, Cambridge, without a degree and entered the Secretary of State's office.

[4] A close friend of Pepys, Sir Henry Shere, the engineer who had completed the Mole at Tangier, went with Lord Dartmouth's expedition to destroy it in 1683. In 1688 he commanded the King's artillery in London.

[5] "Turn over the paper" and continue writing on the other side.

Omitted: March 24, 1687. To Middleton, reporting his speculations on Austrian reactions to a letter from the French King.

Source: M-1, ff. 250–251; H-1, p. 92; *LB*, p. 169.

To Bevil Skelton   March 24, 1687
                                                              Dito

Sir.

I received the favour of yours of the 7 Instant yesterday and am very glad to find you open your heart soe freely to me. I protest to you upon my honor I am so sure of the Innocence of mine as to those matters which have been maliciously reported of me that there is not one thought which ever pass'd in it concerning you which I can wish you should be ignorant of. I have been soe far from being guilty of what you have heard of me either in Holland or at Paris that all honest people here can witnesse that when you or any of your actions have been talk'd of, I have spoaken in your behalf with noe less heat than I cou'd have done had my own life or reputation been in question. In this I did not onely an act of Justice but gratified my own inclination, which has been, ever since I had the good fortune to be more particularly acquainted with you at the Hague, to endeavour to deserve your friendship. I have allways liv'd without art and dissimulation, and shou'd not have the Confidence were I the least in the wrong to say soe much in my vindication. I have say'd more to satisfie you than I shou'd have done to satisfy one who is indifferent to me. The Esteem and kindness I have for you make me Impatient you should have any Jealousie of me, and the greatest favour you can doe me will be to examine this thing to the bottom.

with the news as in the Foregoing letter.

Source: H-1, p. 93; *LB*, p. 170.

Dito

To Captain Slater.

Source: H-1, p. 93.

To EDWARD VAUDREY   March 24, 1687
Dito

Sir.

Tho' I naturally love writing as little as you do, yet you had not been so long without being importun'd by me did I not know a letter from hence wou'd be much about as acceptable as Madamoiselle Regal in London. The fugitive Protestants of Austria and the Pillage you saw at Buda are very fine booty indeed compar'd with what you get by riffling in the richest Citty in the world (setting other matters aside) for beauty.

I am told from the Secretaries office that you come this year again into Hungary. I recomend (if it be so) to your care the onely happy hour I expect in this Countrey, the seeing you in your journey that way. In obedience to Mr. Fitzjames I writ to my Lord Taaffe. I wish I cou'd often give him proof of the pleasure I have in obeying him *himself,* and the favours he did me here have so Charm'd me that I have vow'd myself wholely to his Service.

[Report of plans for the next campaign against the Turks.]

Source: BM, f. 67; *LB*, pp. 170–171.

To THE EARL OF ROCHESTER[1]   March 27, 1687[2]
Ratisbon

My Lord.

Tho' it has pleas'd his Majestie (after having given yourself and the world all the Honorable marks possible of his being highly satisfy'd with your prudence and good services) to ease you of the many cares the most painefull charge in the Kingdome made you hourly labour under and give you more time to enjoy yourself, in the management of which Treasurie you will find a more reall Satisfaction, yet your Lordship can never recover a perfect Liberty. You must expect ever to be follow'd and persecuted by the Impertinent

105

acknowledgements of those poore gratefull men who have been oblig'd by your bounty. The share I have had of your favour and the
generous assurance you gave me of it when I left England have made
such an impression in me that I cannot forbear troubling you without thinking I neglect my duty. I hope your Lordship will lett me
see you forgive me this presumption by continuing on all occasions
your goodness to me.

Since the arrival of Monsieur de Caunitz your Lordship knows better than I doe what has pass'd concerning the execution of the Truce,
which has been the onely business of moment here.

[Etherege's guesses as to the intentions of the French and of
the Empire.]

Source: H-1, pp. 94–95; *LB*, pp. 172–173.

[1] The Earl of Rochester had been dismissed from the office of Treasury
Commissioner on January 4, 1687, for refusing to convert to Roman Catholicism.

[2] The date in *LB* is incorrect; both H-1 and BM date the letter March
17/27.

Dito

To Mr. Guy.
To Mr. Robson and
Mr. Wynne about Williams and Clark
Source: H-1, p. 95.

To HENRY GUY   March 27, 1687
                                                Dito
Sir.

I have enclos'd a letter for my Lord Rochester, knowing I cou'd
not put it into better hands to be deliver'd for my advantage. The
experience I have of your favour to me gives me more confidence to
trouble you and gives me at the same time an assurance that you will
forgive me. While all the great and happy seek your friendship, you
are generously industrious to find out occasions to oblige the unfortunate. All the return you are like to have from me is onely poor
acknowledgments while I live, and when I dye such an other Legacie
as was left you by our friend Thom. Nailer.[1] Mr. Robson has lett me
know what you have done for me in the Treasury. Considering the
little leisure you have, and that ceremony is as unsufferable to me as

noise was to Morose[2] . . . you have answer'd me the best way with your money.

Pray make my complements to my Lord Godolphin and my Lord Dover. I intend to do it suddainly myself, for it is as great a pleasure to me to discharge my duty to the men whom I am oblig'd to honor as it is to a Lover to discharge the impatience he has in his veines on his Mistress. Pardon the Laciviousness of my thoughts; my body is become almost as modest as your own, and I know not a woman whose favours I so passionately desire as I do the opportunity to shew you how faithfully I am etc.

Source: BM, f. 69; *LB,* pp. 173–174.

1 Thomas Naylor made Guy his residuary legatee (*LB,* p. 174).
2 A character in Ben Jonson's *Epicoene.*

Ratisbon March 31, 1687

To Sir Peter Wyche.
Source: H-1, p. 95.

Omitted: April 3, 1687. To Middleton with news of the Elector of Bavaria and recruiting for the Imperial army.
Source: M-1, ff. 252–253; H-1, pp. 95–96; *LB,* pp. 174–175.

To James Fitzjames   April 3, 1687
                                                       Dito
Sir.

It is a little confident for a poor man at this distance to put in to make his Court to you with the throng of great ones who encompass you at London. Cou'd I have found out a way to have contributed from hence any thing towards the Advancing of your pleasures, I shou'd sooner have congratulated with you all you have enjoy'd since your return to England. You have yet but tasted the weak beginings of that happiness which will dayly grow stronger and attend you all your life long. I wonder, in an Age and in a place where you have soe much businesse for your Love, to hear your ambition is so active to bring you back again to Hungary. Sure some Cruell Nymph will not let you snatch a Sprig of Mirtle 'till she can in Revenge take her Arms full of Laurell. If this resolution hold, I hope you will not skip Ratisbonne in your journey nor make any difficulty of coming to an eclaircissement with me about the Secret of it. There are bright

107

English Eyes more fatall than the glittering Cimeterres of the Turks. If I have leave now and then to come into your memorie, it will be a favour much above the merit of Sir, etc.

Source: H-1, pp. 96–97; *LB*, pp. 175–176.

Dito

To Mr. Vaudry and
Mr. Wynne
    Source: H-1, p. 97.

Omitted: April 7, 1687. To Middleton commenting on relations between France and the Empire.
    Source: M-1, ff. 254–255; H-1, pp. 97–99; *LB*, pp. 176–177.

To VISCOUNT TAAFE   April 9, 1687
                                                        Ratisbon
My Lord.

The favour I have receiv'd of your Lordship of the 3rd Instant is noe less wellcome to me here than an advantage got against the Turks is to you at Vienna. I know there are idle people all the world over who take too much liberty in talking, which made me never take any notice in my Letters into England of what I mention'd to your Lordship, especially since it came out of the mouths of Protestants, some of which in this Countrey are as true blew as many of ours. As for the fierté of the Count de Windisgratz (not to trouble myself to give it a more proper name), The Civilities I receive from the Count de Lamberg make over and above up what I loose by it.

Mr. Fitzjames is speedily to be made Duke of Cumberland (some say of Barwick). The Earl of Powis[1] is to be made a Marquis. Arthur Herbert[2] is fallen into his Majestie's Displeasure, upon what account I am not inform'd. He is a man of a violent temper, open and obstinate to the last degree, and has still been a declar'd enemy of my Lord Dartmouths.[3] His place of Master of the Robes is sayd to be given to my Lord Thomas Howard,[4] his Regiment of foot to my Lord Hunsdon.[5] That of Rear Admiral the King keeps in his own hands.

Since the Diet has been adjourn'd by reason of the holy days, the Imperiall Commission have given a Decree which was dictated in the Dictature by which his Imperiall Majesty has communicated to them all that has pass'd in the business of the Truce between him and the French King. I believe it is in order to prepare them for the granting

108

the 100 Roman moneths which are desir'd. I wish it were in my power to give you daily proofs how faithfully I am.

Source: H-1, pp. 99–100; *LB*, pp. 177–179.

1 William Herbert, 1st Marquis of Powys (1617–1696), a prominent Roman Catholic peer who followed James to St. Germain after the Revolution.

2 Arthur Herbert, later Earl of Torrington (1647–1716), Rear-admiral of the Navy, was dismissed from all offices by James II in March 1687, for refusing to vote for the repeal of the Test Act. He commanded William of Orange's invasion fleet in 1688.

3 George Legge, Baron Dartmouth (1647–1691), was given command of the British fleet in 1688.

4 Lord Thomas Howard, the second son of Henry Howard, 6th Duke of Norfolk. His older brother, the 7th Duke, married Lady Mary Mordaunt. See footnote on John Germain, p. 11, above.

5 Robert Carey, 6th Baron Hunsdon, followed James II to France in 1688.

To The Earl of Middleton   April 10, 1687
                                            Ratisbon

My Lord.

Having at present no businesse of the Diet to trouble you with, I have made choice of this time to acquit myselfe of a promise I made some time since to the Abbot[1] of the Scots Benedictins here. Your Lordship knows by experience how impossible it is for any of our Country to be in this place without being very much oblig'd to him, his greatest care (next to that which he has for his Cloister, and matters of Religion) being to doe good Offices to strangers. I am confident I tell your Lordship no news when I acquaint you that his pietie, his Courtisie, his industrie, and his good husbandrie are the wonder of all who know him and the poor Condition of his Monasterie, and I do not doubt but your Lordship will be very glad to have an occasion to give him a proofe of your favour.

The Monasterie, you know, beares his Majestie's name and was founded by Prince William, brother to Achaius, king of Scots in the time of Charlemaigne. It has been ritchly endow'd, but was so ruin'd in the long war in which the Swedes made such hovock in the Empire that it has not now above one hundred pounds a yeare left to maintaine the Abbot and the Religious men, which nevertheless are kept up to the number of Twelve.

A little after my arrivall here, the Bishop of this place and of Fryzing[2] died; and Prince Clement,[3] brother to the Elector of Bavaria (who is now about Fifteene yeares of Age), was made Bishop of the two Bishopricks. The Temporalls (which are Threescore and Tenn thousand Crowns a yeare, that of Ratisbon being 20 and that of Fryzing 50) are put into the hands of Comissioners, and will remaine so for Tenn yeares to be dispos'd of by his Holyness to pious uses. The most considerable part of this revenue is given to the Elector towards the maintenance of his Troops during the War against the Turk. But there is yet so much undispos'd of as will over and above answer the modest desires of the Abbot, which are onely to have a smale pention order'd him by his Holynesse during those Ten yeares towards the repairing of his Monasterie, which is much ruin'd, and the putting him and his Religious men out of that misserable wanting condition they are now allways in.

The Cardinal of Norfolk[4] is his Friend, and will favour him in all he can and dos not doubt, if his Majestie wou'd by a gracious Letter appoint him to make use of his name to his Holyness, but the thing wou'd be graunted. The Abbot as well as myselfe referre this wholly to your Lordship to judge whither it be convenient to move his Majestie in it and beg the favour that you will order Mr. Wynne to acquaint us with your Lordships opinion. I am, My Lord, Your Lordships most faithfull and most humble Servant

Geo: Etherege

Source: M-1, ff. 256–257; H-1, pp. 100–102; *LB,* pp. 179–181.

1 Placid Fleming. See above, p. xx.
2 Freising, near Munich.
3 Prince Joseph Clement (1671–1723). His much-disputed appointment as Elector of Cologne in 1688 precipitated the French invasion of the Palatinate and the War of the League of Augsburg.
4 Philip Howard, chief adviser to the Holy See in matters relating to Great Britain (*LB,* p. 181).

Omitted: April 10, 1687. To Owen Wynne, asking his aid for Abbot Fleming.
Source: H-1, p. 102; *LB,* pp. 181–182.

To The Earl of Mulgrave   April 10, 1687
                                                                Ratisbon

My Lord.

Never Lover was more agreeably surpris'd with the favours of his Mistress than I have been with the letter[1] you have done me the honor to send me. I am yet soe overjoy'd (tho' it is three days since I received it) that my mind has not regain'd the temper which is necessary to make you a reasonable answer. You must excuse therefore the Impertinencies of what I write, as women doe the imperfect Speeches of those who love too well to express themselves handsomely.

The pleasure you have given me makes me forgive the malice you have shew'd in putting me in minde of my being old. I have always by my way of Living taken care to banish age from my thoughts, and what have I done to provoak your envy, who are young and vigorous, to remember me that I bear a burthen my humor makes me insensible of. It is but seldom I have had occasion in this grave place to draw my Bow, and when I have, I did not perceive my Nerves were slacken'd. You should quietly have let me alone 'till age had surpris'd me, and not have wounded my imagination with your raillery.

You are more cruell than the Murderers of Caesar. They gave him the Death he wish'd, but you have attempted to make me old against my will. Nevertheless since my time cannot be long, I will prepare myself for taking my Leave of the pleasures of this world by being in charity with you and wishing the happiness you enjoy may be dayly increas'd, tho' none besides yourself can think it uncompleat. When the Ladys know me to be good for nothing, it will be a Comfort to me if I can find opportunitys to assure you that I am etc.

Source: H-1, pp. 103–104; *LB,* pp. 182–183.

1 This letter is printed on p. 278, below.

Ratisbon April 14, 1687

To Mr. Wynne.
To Mrs. Merry and to
My Lord (Middleton)
Source: H-1, p. 104.

Omitted: April 14, 1687. To Middleton, about a dispute between the Elector of Brandenburg and the Duke of Zell over the commandery of Gartow.
Source: M-1, ff. 258–259; H-1, pp. 104–105; *LB,* pp. 183–184.

Omitted: April 17, 1687. To Middleton reporting news from Brandenburg and Bavaria.
Source: M-1, ff. 260–261; H-1, pp. 106–107; *LB,* pp. 184–186.

Omitted: April 21, 1687. A letter of miscellaneous diplomatic news to Middleton.

Source: H-1, pp. 107–108; *LB*, pp. 186–187.

To JAMES FITZJAMES   April 21, 1687
                                                                           Dito

My Lord.

I have receiv'd with much joy the news of his Majesties creating you Duke of Barwick. You had noe need of a title to make you great. The care nature has taken in forming of your minde and body has made you eminently so, and you alone can make yourself greater by the way you take to improve your virtue. Nevertheless the glittering favours of fortune are necessary to entertain those who, without examining any deeper, worship appearances. Besides she is a Mistress you are resolv'd to court, and it is a pleasure to have her kind. May she allways lead you by the hand and never let you make a false step to disoblige her.

The same letters confirm to me your coming into Hungary again. Tho' you are cruel to the Ladys in England in depriving them of the onely delight of their Eyes, I hope you will be good natur'd to a poor man who reckons on the happiness of seeing you. Let the convenience of the Danube move you in my behalf. It will be as sensible an affliction as can touch me to loose the least opportunity of giving you a proof how faithfully I am, My Lord, Your Graces most etc.

Source: H-1, pp. 108–109; *LB*, p. 187.

                                                                           Dito

To Mr. Wynne.

Source: H-1, p. 109.

Omitted: April 24, 1687. To Middleton, about the Roman months, French contraventions, and the death of Prince Louis of Brandenburg.

Source: M-1, ff. 262–263; H-1, pp. 109–110; *LB*, pp. 187–189.

                                                         Dito [April 24, 1687]

To Mr. Richards.

                                                   Ratisbon April 28, 1687

To Mr. Robson

To Mrs. Merry with order for 20£.

Source: H-1, p. 110.

Dito

Sir.

Yesterday your letter of the 30th of March came to my hands and gave me a pleasure which nothing but the like proof of your kindness can give me here. If my Ghost be as restless when I am in the other world as my minde is now I am in an other Countrey, my friends must expect to be much haunted. It will cost them some frights and it may be some money to lay me. There is not a day but my thoughts dog you from the Coffee-house to the Play, from thence to Marribone,[1] allways concern'd for your good luck and in paine I cannot make one with you in the Sports you follow. Some of the ancients have imagin'd that the greatest torment of the dead was an Impatient longing after what they delighted most in while they were living, and I can swear by my damnation in Germany this Hell is no jesting matter.

Now Mr. B—— is promoted, I hope Mr. Swan will be mounted. I am sorry on so good an occasion I have not a quibble in my head which wou'd pass muster. I pitty Mrs. Debora's loss in Mr. Whitakers being gone to board in an other quarter. If he happens into a house with Mr. Crowne,[2] John's songs and Josephs voice will charme the whole family. I find the Collonel[3] is resolv'd to blaze to the last as well as my self. Methinks I see in a Triumph of our present loves a Cupid, for fear of burning his fingers, with a little piece of a Torch on a Save-all. He has beauty, the strongest cordiall, to keep up his Spirits. I have onely a plain Bavarian with her sandy coulor'd locks, brawny limbs and a brick complection, and yet I find myself often very hearty.

Pray remember me kindly to all my friends and particularly to Tom Maule. I am very sensible of the Trouble the Correspondence you have with me gives you. I shall not tire you with any tedious acknowl-edgements but onely assure you, you oblige one who cannot be un-gratefull and is extreamly, Sir etc.

Source: H-1, pp. 110–111; *LB*, pp. 189–190.

[1] Marylebone Gardens, a pleasure resort just south of the present site of Regent's Park.

[2] John Crowne, the dramatist.

[3] Probably Edmund Ashton, Lieutenant-colonel in the Life Guards, who was famous for his small size. A biographical sketch is given in Vieth, *Attributions*, pp. 254–270.

Omitted: April 28, 1687. To Middleton about the Roman months, monetary abuses, and military plans.

Source: M-2, ff. 1–2; H-1, pp. 111–113; *LB*, pp. 190–191.

Dito [April 28, 1687]

To Mr. Wynne about Marquis d'Albeville and saddles.
    Source: H-1, p. 113.

Omitted: May 5, 1687. A letter of diplomatic news and rumor to Middleton.
    Source: M-2, ff. 3–4; H-1, pp. 113–114; *LB,* pp. 191–193.

Dito [May 5, 1687]

To my Lady
Mr. George Etherege and
Mr. Wynne.
    Source: H-1, p. 114.

Omitted: May 8, 1687. To Middleton reporting on the Roman months and military movements.
    Source: M-2, ff. 5–6; H-1, pp. 114–115; *LB,* pp. 193–195.

To Owen Wynne   May 8, 1687
                                                                    Dito

Sir.

On tuesday last the Count de Lamberg came to see me and shew'd me a letter which he had receiv'd that day from the Count de Caunitz, his Cousin, three days fresher than yours of the 8th of this instant which came to my hands on Sunday. He tells us the Duke of Berwick comes again into Hungary. If he dos, pray let me know when he leaves you that I may the better judge at what time he may pass by here, in case he comes this way.

The Count de Lamberg wou'd fain have a good English Gelding of about 50 or 60 £ price and has desir'd me to write to some body who has an interest to lett one be bought and brought with the Dukes Equippage. He as well as my self believes this letter will come too late. If it dos not, pray beg the favour of Mr. Vaudrey and tell him besides the obliging the Count and me, the Gelding will be a good letter of Exchange at Ratisbon and that as it is but reasonable we will stand to all accidents.

An other part of Monsieur de Caunitz' letter says some of the Spightfull people of this place have written some thing to doe me ill offices. I know it is not unlikely, being well acquainted with the Count de Wyndisgratz's nature. Pray endeavour to find out what this is. His

114

Majestie did not send me hither to make my Court to the proud and fantastic humor of any man, but to live well with all and to give an Impartiall account of affaires, and I have carried myself with that Civility and moderation that nothing but a malicious lye can doe me any harme. I am etc.

Source: H-1, p. 116; *LB*, p. 195.

Omitted: May 12, 1687. To Middleton, speculating on plans for the summer campaign, with a report on the Roman months.

Source: M-2, ff. 7–8; H-1, pp. 117–118; *LB*, pp. 196–197.

Ratisbon May 13, 1687

To Captain Slater.
Source: H-1, p. 118.

Omitted: May 15, 1687. Military and diplomatic news to Middleton.

Source: M-2, ff. 9–10; H-1, pp. 118–119; *LB*, pp. 197–198.

To OWEN WYNNE   May 15, 1687
Dito

Sir.

I was last night with the Abbot Fleming, with whom I drank your health. We hope you will not neglect soliciting my Lord about obteining his Majesties letter to the Cardinall of Norfolk and will take care to lett us know what is resolv'd in the businesse.

The Count de Lamberg, who went from hence yesterday for Saltzburg to the Election which is now briguing there, shew'd me a letter from Monsieur de Caunitz to him in which he owns the Count de Windisgratz had writ to him concerning me. No body can imagin the Pride and malice of that man, who esteems himself the Emperor of this place and cannot suffer any one who will not neglect all besides to cringe to him. This I do not think becoming a person his Majesty employs. The onely pique he has to me is because I wou'd not play the fool to please him.

He has endeavourd to play me many mean tricks, as to hinder me from the Liberty of Coursing, to make my footmen be enroll'd by officers who have made Levies here, but I have had the good luck to get the better of him in all, and now we live on the foot of a cold Civility. I onely mention this to you that you may give me notice in

115

case any thing shou'd be spoken to do me a prejudice, not that I have reason to fear any ill office from Monsieur de Caunitz, who seems to believe the Character his Kinsman the Count de Lamberg gives of me rather than that he had from the Count de Windisgratz.

I have not yet had an account of my pension from those I employ to receive it. Pray present my service to the privy purse and tell him I am very sensible of his favour. I am sorry I am in a Post where I can onely return him a Complement for it. I am. etc.

Source: H-1, pp. 119–120; *LB*, pp. 198–199.

To The Earl of Sunderland   May 19, 1687
                                                              Ratisbon

To Sir Peter Wyche
To the Earl of Sunderland as follows
My Lord.

Tho' the Dyet and I cannot agree in all things, in one thing we are very well met. They are as Idle and it may be as negligent as I can wish to be. They seldom have much business and have the best art of spinning out a little to all the advantage of loss of time. No school-boy is more fond of a Holy-day, and they have the pleasure of keeping them double by reason of the two Religions profess'd.

This was a fine place for your Lordship to choose to send me to, to correct the laziness of my nature, but yet you have not quite lost your aime. The sense I have of your benefits has so spurr'd me up that I have twice a week given the best account I have been able to do of what has pass'd in the Empire, which begins to beget in me such a relish of business that I shou'd be more vain of making a good dispatch than of writing a witty letter. I shall endeavour by fitting myself for this to shew my gratitude to your Lordship. I know it will be more acceptable than any dull acknowledgements I can make.

I find in the news I receiv'd yesterday from England that His Majestie, upon the Death of the Duke of Bucks,[1] intends to give your Lordship the Garter. I have never known you ambitious of any thing but of serving him well, which assures me this is a voluntary marke of his favour. Honors of this kind cannot make any great impressions of joy in you, but since they are not the unhappiest nor it may be the unwisest who can please themselves with Toys, I wish you may be as fond of it as some I have known, and that you may wear it with as much pleasure as I have done in my younger days the favours of a Mistress. Your goodness makes me so Much belong to you that I share in all the good fortune that befalls you, and there is always self interest in the case when your prosperity is wish'd for by etc.

Source: H-1, pp. 120–121; *LB*, pp. 199–200.

[1] George Villiers, the Duke of Buckingham, died on April 15, 1687.

Omitted: May 19, 1687. To Middleton with military news and about the Bishop of Passau's incapacity and Windischgrätz's pretensions to be Principal Commissioner.

Source: M-2, ff. 11–12; H-1, pp. 121–123; *LB*, pp. 200–202.

Omitted: May 19, 1687. A note to the Marquis d'Albeville, welcoming him to the Hague.

Source: H-1, p. 123; *LB*, p. 202.

Dito [May 19, 1687]

To Mr. Wynne about Mr. Petit's Prints.
Source: H-1, p. 123.

To Owen Wynne   May 19, 1687
Dito

Sir.

If any thing had offer'd itself which had been necessary for His Majestie's Service to have been communicated to the Marquis d'Albyville, I shou'd not have omitted the doing it. I consider that above all things and can never neglect it for a foolish punctillo. I have writ to him to offer him my service and to let him know I am ready to receive his commands in what may be for his Majestie's.

I wonder at the Article you send me word is in his Extraordinaries, having never heard from him or his Secretary. If he has sent those prints to any body else at the Dyet, I humbly conceive they had been better sent to me, who am employ'd by his Majestie. I cou'd have made use of them to return the obligations I have to some Ministers who impart their prints and papers to me.

But to be plaine with you I believe his Secretary Petit the cause of this misunderstanding, who upon my refusing to allow him fourscore crowns a year for a manuscrit which I did not think fit to fling away his Majestie's money upon, broke off an intelligence he held with your Brother,[1] as I have mention'd in a letter I writ formerly to you. We had in Mr. Skeltons time some Gazets from him, but Mr. Petit sent

117

them generally the day after the faire, that is the next weeke after he had made use of them. But since Mr. d'Albyville arriv'd we have had none, so that I believe Mr. Petit has put in that Article for Prints in the Marquis's Extraordinaries for some former pretensions of his own. I am etc.

Source: BM, ff. 87–88; *LB,* pp. 202–203.

[1] Hugo Hughes, Etherege's secretary.

Omitted: May 22, 1687. To Middleton reporting Windischgrätz's efforts to be recognized as Principal Commissioner and other diplomatic news.

Source: M-2, ff. 13–14; H-1, pp. 124–126; *LB,* pp. 203–205.

Omitted: May 22, 1687. An enclosure of military news to Middleton.

Source: M-2, f. 15; H-1, pp. 126–127; *LB,* pp. 205–206.

To Charles Boyle   May 22, 1687
                                                                              Dito

Sir.

Did I not know you to be one of the most careless men in the world, I shou'd imagin you were the most ungratefull so wholely to forget me who lov'd you so entirely. It is long since I writ to you, and having receiv'd no answer, I am grown Spitefull enough to wish you had so just an excuse for yourself as having been a year in Ireland. I need not tell you I am good natur'd. I who have forgiven so many Mistresses who have been false to me can well forgive a friend who has onely been negligent. My heart was never touch'd for any for whom there remains not still some impression of kindness.

Pray if you can spare one quarter of an hour from the pleasures of London to please an absent friend send me some news of all my friends, particularly of my Lord Dunbar[1] and of Ned Lee,[2] whose prosperity I have allways wish'd. Let me know how Mrs. Hughes[3] has dispos'd of her self. Mrs. Davis has given a proof of the great passion she always had for musick, and Monsieur Peasible[4] has an other (guess) Bass to thrum than that he playd so well uppon. Make the Kindest compliment you can for me to Mrs. Willis[5] and lett me know how she and her little family does. That you may know I am not alltogether Idle here and to oblige you to do the like for me, I must tell you I have stolne this little time to write to you while no less than twenty Chanoinesses are expecting me in a wood by a fountain with

118

musick and a Collation. Notwithstanding the resentment I ought to have against you, I am very faithfully.

Source: H-1, p. 127–128; *LB,* pp. 206–207.

[1] Robert Constable, Viscount Dunbar.

[2] Edward Henry Lee, Earl of Lichfield, was a nephew of John Wilmot, Earl of Rochester.

[3] Margaret Hughes, a minor actress, was mistress to Prince Rupert, who left her a notable collection of jewels. See below, p. 162, n. 2.

[4] James Paisible, a French musician who came to England in 1680. In 1686 he married the actress Mary Davis.

[5] Sue Willis, a minor actress and "a prostitute who operated on the fringe of the Court circle" (Rochester's *Complete Poems,* ed. David M. Vieth, 1968, p. 137). She is frequently mentioned in the satires of the time.

Omitted: May 26, 1687. To Middleton, reporting a dispute over imposts received from vessels entering Rostock.

Source: H-1, pp. 128–129; *LB,* pp. 207–208.

Dito [May 26, 1687]

To Mr. Batterton. and
Mr. Wynne about Compositions.

Source: H-1, p. 129.

To Thomas Betterton   May 26, 1687
                                                          Dito

Sir. (Batterton the Player)[1]

A poor man who has lost the enjoyment of his friends and the pleasures of London ought to use all the means he can to divert his Chagrin and pass away the time as easy as is possible. In order to this I am often forc'd to trouble my acquaintance in England, and I do not doubt but you will forgive me my making bold with you among the rest.

I have three in my little family who now and then give me a little musick. They play very well and at Sight. We have all the Operas, and I have a Correspondent at Paris who sends me what is new there. If you wou'd do me the favour to procure me some of the best composition with the Several parts and let them be given to Dr. Wynne, at my Lord Middleton's Office, he will take care to send them to me.

I shall esteem my self much oblig'd to you for this Courtesie, and your kindness will be greater if now and then you give me an account of the Stage and of other matters which (you shall judge) I will be glad to hear of. You will not mistak if you have the same opinion of me you had formerly, for I assure you I am not chang'd in my inclinations and can never be otherwise than.

My humble Service to Mrs. Batterton.

Source: BM, f. 92; *LB*, pp. 208–209.

[1] Thomas Betterton (c. 1635–1710), the famous actor-manager of the Duke's Company, was married to the acrtess Mary Saunderson. Betterton had played Dorimant in the first production of *The Man of Mode*.

To Henry Guy   May 29, 1687
                                                             Ratisbon

Sir.

The assurance you are pleas'd to give me of your kindness comforts me almost for all I have lost in England. You are so generous you do not onely assist me in what is necessary, but you contribute towards my pleasure. You do not onely take care to make me be supply'd with money, but you give yourself the trouble to write to me, and were I in a better condition, I know so well how to value things I shou'd prefer this favour to the other. I know you have but little time to spare from publique affaires and that little in Charity (which begins at home) you shou'd employ in pleasing of yourself, but you are so prodigall you throw away part of it in delighting so poor a man as I am, who can make you no return but in kind wishes. May the women love you for what you have done, and may the men you oblige be all as sensible and as gratefull as I am.

As soon as the Campagne is begun I intend to write to my Lord Godolphin. The business of the Diet for the most part is onely fit to entertain those insects in politiques which crawl under the trees in St. James's Park, and I am not so vain as to think my dull imaginations capable of making his good nature receive them well. Make my Court for me to him and to my Lord Dover, and tell them I think it is more for their ease to take your word for my Receipt of their benefits than to exact a tedious acquittance under my own hand. If it be possible for them to think I merit their favour, it must be by your means, and I shall ascribe to you what Horace dos to the Muses, Quod Spiro et placeo, si placeo, tuum est.[1] I am Sir

[1] *Odes*, IV, 3. "My inspiration and my power to please, if I do please, are due to you."

                                                    Dito [May 29, 1687]
To Mr. Wynne about entertainment and Extraordinaries

Source: H-1, pp. 129–130; *LB*, p. 210.

Sir.

I have nothing this post worth the informing my Lord of. We are like to have a long vacation here, since it has pleas'd his Imperial Majestie to give the Prince of Passau (the head of his Comission) leave to retire for some time to his Bisshoprick to endeavor to recover his understanding, which has allways been infirme and is now in a deep consumption. When the news comes in from Vienna, I will enclose it for my Lord. The letter I send you for Mr. Guy may help Mr. Robson in his soliciting my business in the Treasurie. It is not good to be much in arrear, and the 30th of this Month I have halfe a yeare's Entertainement due, besides all my extraordinaries ever since I have been abroad. I am, Sir, Your most humble, and Obedient Servant

Geo: Etherege

Source: M-2, f. 16; H-1, p. 130; *LB*, pp. 209–210.

Omitted: May 29, 1687. An unsigned paper of news from Vienna, in Etherege's hand.

Source: M-2, f. 18.

Omitted: June 2, 1687. To Middleton, reporting troop movements.

Source: M-2, ff. 20–21; H-1, pp. 130–131; *LB*, p. 211.

Dito [June 2, 1687]

Mr. Wynne
Mr. Robson. and
Mr. Will. Richards

Source: H-1, p. 131.

To William Richards   June 2, 1687
                                                  Dito

Sir.

. . . . pray remember my humble Service to my Lord Lumley.[1] I am very sensible of the obligations I have to him and tell him I had taken care to have payd a little debt of tenn Guyneas before now if those I employ in my affaires in England had not been negligent.

I have heard of the Success of the Eunuch[2] and am very glad the Town has so good a tast to give the Same just applause to Sir Charles Sidley's writing which his friends have always done to his conversation. Few of our plays can boast of more wit than I have heard him speak at a Supper. Some baren Sparks have found fault with what he has formerly done on this occasion, onely because the fatness of the Soile has produc'd to big a Crop. I dayly drink his health, my Lord Dorsets,[3] Mr. Jepsons,[4] Charles Godfrys,[5] your own, and all our friends, but this is not much you will say for one who lives in this drinking Countrey. That you may then take it more kindly, I wish it as heartily as I do my own, and tho' I have no very good memory for other things, I never forget the least favor which has been done me, and therefor you may be confident I am: (D. Will)

Source: BM, f. 94; *LB*, pp. 211–213.

[1] Richard, Baron Lumley, later the 1st Earl of Scarborough. A Roman Catholic favorite of Charles II, he gave up his army commission and became a Protestant in 1687 because of dissatisfaction with James's policies.

[2] Sedley's *Bellamira,* an adaptation of Terence's *Eunuchus,* was produced at the King's Theatre in Drury Lane in May 1687.

[3] Charles Sackville, Earl of Dorset (1638–1706), to whom Etherege dedicated his first play, *The Comical Revenge,* in 1664.

[4] William Jephson, a long-time Whig and member of the Green Ribbon Club (Sitwell, *The First Whig,* p. 203), became Secretary for English Affairs to the Prince of Orange in December 1688 (Luttrell, 1, p. 492), and was made Secretary of the Treasury in 1689. According to Constantin Huygens (*Register op de Journalen,* II, 268) Jephson rose, through a wealthy marriage, from a lawyer's clerk to a high office. A letter from John Verney (HMC, *7th Report,* p. 467) names Jephson as one of the participants, along with Etherege and Rochester, in the notorious skirmishing of the watch at Epsom in June 1675. He died June 7, 1691 (Luttrell, 2, p. 242).

[5] Captain Charles Godfrey, "a rank and file Whig" who married Arabella Churchill, former mistress of the Duke of York, was a famous duellist. He became a colonel after the Revolution (John Carswell, *The Old Cause,* London, 1954, p. 188).

Ratisbon June 5, 1687

To Mr. Wynne with a Copie of a letter from my Lord Taaffe.

Source: H-1, p. 131. The letter from Taafe is in M-2, ff. 24–25.

Omitted: June 9, 1687. To Middleton reporting troop movements through Ratisbon and the Count de Crécy's visit to France.

Source: M-2, ff. 22–23; H-1, pp. 131–132; *LB*, pp. 213–214.

Omitted: June 12, 1687. To Middleton reporting military and diplomatic news.

Source: M-2, ff. 26–27; H-1, pp. 132–133; *LB*, pp. 214–215.

To Mr. Wynne.
   Source: H-1, p. 132.

Omitted: June 16, 1687. A short note to Owen Wynne reminding him of "Abbot Fleming's business." Cf. letter of April 10, 1687.
   Source: H-1, p. 134; *LB,* pp. 215–216.

Omitted: June 16, 1687. An unaddressed "paper of news" probably for Middleton, mainly about troop movements down the Danube.
   Source: M-2, ff. 28–29.

Omitted: June 19, 1687. To Middleton with news of the Duke of Berwick and of troop movements.
   Source: M-2, ff. 30–31; H-1, pp. 134–135; *LB,* p. 216.

Omitted: June 19, 1687. To Sunderland reporting news and asking for the continuance of his favor.
   Source: H-1, p. 135; *LB,* pp. 216–217.

Ratisbon June 22, 1687

To my Lord Taafe.
   Source: H-1, p. 136.

To The Marquis d'Albeville   June 23, 1687
                                                 Ratisbon

Sir.
   I am asham'd I have been so long without acknowledging the favour of yours of the 2ᵈ Instant, but I doubt not but you will forgive me, considering the hurry I have been in in providing boats and other necessaries for the transporting the Equipages belonging to our Volunteers who are gone into Hungary and the making of our Country men wellcome in this place.
   The Duke of Berwick arriv'd here on Wednesday last and the next morning embarqu'd on the Danube with my Lord Charles Hamilton,[1] my Lord Dongan,[2] and Sir Edward Vaudrey to make what diligence he cou'd (according to his Majestie's order) to joine the Duke of Lorraine, who with a good body of the Army (all the Troops being not yet arriv'd at Barkan, particularly those of the Circle of Swabe and

123

what are this year sent by the Circle of Franconia) is already pass'd the Sarwitz and marches towards the Drave to hinder the Turks from repairing the Bridge of Esseck, but I fear he will come too late, we having a report that that work is already perfected and that the enemy have a body of men on this side the River. The Elector of Bavaria, who has been a little indispos'd, had not yet left Vienna. When our Post comes in, I will inclose what news it brings today.

Monsieur Valkenir, who came hither some time since from the States of Holland, has given me notice of his arrival. When he was here before, I made him no visit, being credibly inform'd that he, receiving the false report that the late Duke of Monmouth had routed his Majestie's Forces at Philips Norton, sent the news to many Ministers to whom he thought it wou'd be welcome, and was the occasion of the printing of the lye here, it being sent him by some Brother Cittizen of Amsterdam, but meeting of him lately by accident and protesting upon his honor he did it not with any malicious design to disserve his Majestie but onely dispers'd it as he us'd to do the other news which comes from his Countrie, the Secretary of State has left it to my choice whether I will see him or no, and I intend to give him a visit this week. I write this to you because I know the Prince of Orange has been told I have neglected him, that you may tell his Highness (if you find it convenient) the reason of it.

There has happen'd a thing which has made me omit the visiting the Count de Windisgratz, who is join'd in Commission with the Prince of Passau, but by reason of the Prince's infirmity he in a manner does all, and the other is but a Cypher. It wou'd be too tedious to give you a Character of the man and to let you know how he is embroil'd with most of the Diet, particularly with the Electorall college. We liv'd some time very well together, and I made him a hundred visits, all which time he never so much as sent a man to make me a Complement. Uppon the taking of Buda I sent to congratulate the Imperiall Commission, but they, when they made their publique rejoicing and invited the Ministers and many Cavaliers of this Town, to the wonder of every body never took any notice of me. I considering the Zeal his Majesty had shewn for the success of that Siege and how many English Gentlemen had perish'd at it, thought I cou'd not but resent it for the honor of our nation. This has made the Count tax me for being of the French Faction, but all the account I have given of affaires into England before the business of the Truce was settled shew that I have behav'd myself according to my instructions with all the impartiallity imaginable. If I have visited the Count de Crecy more than the Emperors Ministers it is because I was admitted without ceremony, which is the plague of this place, there being scarce an other house here where I cou'd enjoy my freedome and find any divertion, and his Majestie did not send me hither to live in Sollitude.

The Count is so revengefull he will not stick at any thing to do a man a mischief he has a pique to. Valkenir (whom I suspected) to justify himself to me told me the Count has own'd to him that he has writ against me into Holland, and I believe has been the occasion by the falshoods he suggested of a difference between Mr. Skelton and me. He has writ likewise into France, to Vienna, and into England, but I have not had much difficulty to get the better of him, truth being on my side.

I lett you know this least any indirect means shou'd be us'd to do me any ill offices with you. Those whom his Majesty imploys, in my opinion, shou'd omitt nothing to have a good understanding, and I shall be very carefull to do you all the service in my power, especially in letting you know what is done here and in Hungary, to help you a little to pay such as communicate things to you in kind. You will very much oblige me when you have leisure if you do the like for me. This day the 100 Roman Moneths which the Emperor has desir'd and have lain dormant for some time are waken and put in deliberation, with what success you will know hereafter. I am with much esteem and sincerity, Sir, etc.

Source: H-1, pp. 136–139; *LB*, pp. 217–220.

1 Lord Charles Hamilton, son of the 5th Earl of Abercorn, took part in the battle of Mohács (*LB*, p. 217).

2 Walter Dungan, only son of the Earl of Limerick, was given the courtesy title of Lord Dungan. Born in Spain about 1664, he was naturalized, became an M.P. for Naas, County Kildare, and was made a Gentleman of the Bedchamber to James II. He fought for James at the Battle of the Boyne and was killed there.

Dito [June 23, 1687]

To Mr. Petit [A letter from Hugo Hughes, printed in *LB*, pp. 220–221.]

Mr. Wynne

Source: H-1, p. 139.

To Owen Wynne   June 23, 1687

$$\text{Ratisbon } \frac{13}{23} \text{ June. 1686 }^{1}$$

Sir.

Yesterday I received yours of the 27th of May together with the part of the Hind and Panther[2] enclos'd in an other Paquet. Pray let me know how this Poem is approv'd by the Court.

Mr. Petit has writ to your Brother to excuse his breaking off his correspondence. This is one part of his letter. "I know I have omitted writting to you since the Marquis's arrivall, which I did by order to save needless Postage," but I have writ to the Marquis this day, and I believe their minds will change, wherefore I wou'd desire you to keep it to yourself.

I had some reason to be jealouse of Mr. Petit, but I am of opinion it was groundless, for meeting Mr. Valkeneer by accident and taxing him with the divulging and occasioning to be printed the false report about the skirmish at Philips Norton, he protested he onely did as he us'd to do with news sent him out of his Countrey and that upon his Honor he had no intention to do his Majesty any ill Service. He likewise protested he had done me no ill offices in Holland, but that the Count de Windisgratz has own'd to him privately since his return hither he had writ into Holland, to Paris, Vienna and into England against me, and I am perswaded from this Source had Sprung those lyes which made a Misunderstanding between Mr. Skelton and me, and that Petit is innocent. Upon this eclaircissement, this confidence, and the liberty which is left me to do what I think fit, I intend to see Monsieur Valkenier. I wish you all happiness, and am, Dear Sir.

Pray press Mr. Robson to sollicite for 6 Moneths entertainment and not to let my extraordinaries run on farther. I wonder at their not being payd, they being so very reasonable.

Source: BM, ff. 101–102; *LB*, pp. 221–222.

[1] So in BM, but the year should be 1687. Cf. calendaring in H-1, p. 139.
[2] The first part of Dryden's *The Hind and the Panther* was published on May 27, 1687 (Hugh MacDonald, *John Dryden: a Bibliography*, p. 46).

Omitted: June 23, 1687. To Middleton with diplomatic news from the Diet.

Source: M-2, ff. 32–33; H-1, p. 139; *LB*, pp. 222–223.

Omitted: June 26, 1687. To Middleton about Windischgrätz' pretensions to be Principal Commissioner.

Source: M-2, ff. 34–36; H-1, pp. 140–141; *LB,* pp. 223–224.

TO WILLIAM BRIDGEMAN   June 26, 1687
         Dito

Sir.

Tho I have been negligent in writing to you, I have not forgot how much I have been oblig'd to you, and particularly the debt I owe you, and to convince you of it, I have enclos'd a note and a letter to Mr. Robson for the payment of it. My Lord Dongan when he pass'd by here told me you wou'd do him the favour to send his letters to him and I have promis'd him to forward them in case they are directed to me. I pray give the paper of news to my Lord, and give me some proof of your kindness by doing me what friendly offices you can with him. You may be confident where ever I am I shall allways be. etc.

Source: BM, f. 104; *LB,* p. 225.

TO MR. ROBSON   June 26, 1687
         Dito

Sir (Mr. Robson)

I pray do me the favour to pay to William Bridgeman Esquire the sum of 12 guineas, being a debt I have long ow'd him, and you oblige etc.

TO MR. ROBSON   June 26, 1687
         Dito

Sir (Mr. Robson)

I must desire you to move my friends in the Treasury for me. There was six moneths entertainment due to me in May last. I pray press my Extraordinaries very earnestly, for they are very reasonable and will begin to grow stale. It is a very troublesom thing to be in debt, and particularly here. I have known so much the inconvenience of it that I hope you will endeavour to prevent it. I have sent Mr. Bridgeman, who will deliver you this, a note for twelve guineas on you. Pray lett him receive it. I hope you will suddainly send me some good news, that I may be in a Condition to make a Complement to Mrs. Robson without making of you Jealous of etc.

Source: BM, f. 104; *LB,* pp. 224–225.

To Owen Wynne   June 30, 1687
                                                           Ratisbon
Sir.

I receiv'd yesterday your favour with the 2d and 3d part of the Hind and panther, which I have not yet read quite over. Nothing is done here, the Count de Windisgratz being gon to Etteing to pay a vow he made to the holy Virgin in the last fit of the Stone he was tormented with, wherefore I have not writ to my Lord, onely enclosing for him what news is come to us from Vienna this day. On Fryday last my Lord Konoull [1] with Captain Brown went from this place towards Hungarie. I have not yet heard from any of our Volunteers in those parts, but I learn in a Letter from Vienna of the 26th instant New Style that the Duke of Berwick is arriv'd in that Towne in good health. You will see by the paper I send you for my Lord in what condition things are in Hungarie and that wee cannot be long without hearing of some considerable action. I am, Deare Sir, Your most humble and obedient Servant

                                                           Geo: Etherege.

Source: M-2, f. 36; H-1, p. 141; *LB*, pp. 225–226.

[1] George Hay, 5th Earl of Kinnoul. He died at Mohács in August 1687 (*LB*, p. 226).

                                                           Dito [June 30, 1687]

To Sir Peter Wyche. and
Mr. Montstephen's. with the news paper.

Source: H-1, p. 142.

Omitted: July 3, 1687. A short note to Wynne.

Source: M-2, f. 37.

To The Earl of Middleton   July 3, 1687
                                                           Ratisbon

My Lord.

Having no business to acquaint Mr. Secretary with at present, I hope you will excuse me to him and by your interest prevail with him to forgive me the liberty I take of writing onely to My Lord Middleton. I have had the honor to know your Lordship long, and when you were not so great I lov'd you no less then I do now. The favours which fortune bestows move the weak to admire and the false to Flatter. I look on them as fine Cloathes which are Ornaments to such as nature has been kind to and never fail to make them more loathesome who have no merrit. Such as are imediatly distinguish'd from other men by heaven will be ever prefer'd by me to such who onely ware the marks of a Prince's Kindness.

You see what a fine Courtier I am like to make if ever I come back to England. I do not doubt but you have done me many benifits in my absence, and I must thank you for choosing the most generous way of doeing them, which is without letting me know any thing of it. I dare not mention any thing of London to you. The aire of the Towne may be so alter'd that I shall be thought to talk like an Indian. Some of my Country men who have pass'd this way have given me faint discriptions by which I guess a little at the Countenance of things. Mr. Wynne has sent me the Hind and Panther, by which I find John Dryden has a noble Ambition to restaur Poetry to it's auncient dignitie in wrapping up the Misteries of Religion in verse. What a shame it is to me to see him a Saint and remain still the same Divil. I must blame the goodness of my Constitution, which cannot be much alter'd, since my mind is not much chang'd from what it was at the Gravil pits.

I saw a play about Tenn yeares ago call'd the Eunuch, so heavy a lump the Players durst not charge themselves with the dead weight, but it seemes Sir Charles Sydlie has animated the mightie mass and now it treads the Stage lightly. He had allways more wit then was enough for one man and therefore dos well to continue his Charity to one who wants it. Dryden finds his Mac-flecknoe dos no good. I wish him better success with his Hind and Panther.

I am apt to think your good Nature makes you steal some nights from your business to enjoy your Friends. I will not desire you now to speak about any thing which may concerne me at Court, but in retorn I hope you will put some of my old acquaintance in mind of me. I can never forget those who have oblig'd me and have drunk many a gratefull Cup to their memorie. How much Rhenish have you made me swallow for your share? You? who have given me so much cause to be ever, My Lord, Your Lordships most faithfull and most Obedient Servant

Geo: Etherege

Source: M-2, ff. 38–39; H-1, pp. 142–143; *LB*, pp. 226–228.

To Monsieur de Gennes   July 3, 1687[1]
                                                                                    Dito

Monsieur.

Vous m'avez tant roué d'Excellence que J'ay envie de vous bien donner du Marquis si je ne faisois pas conscience d'ôter les armes de la main de nostre ami le Norman,[2] a cette heure qu'il se batte contre l'ennemi commun de la Chrestienté. Je n'ay pas le temps de barbouiller beaucoup de papier à present. C'est pourquoy Je vous diray seulement, que Mr. L'Evéque continue à estre bien exact dans toutes ses fonctions. Il donna hier un grand feste à Madame la Countesse de Stubenberg, et à toutes les plus jollies Fräwlins d'icy. Mr. de Stocken et moy fusmes ses Coadjuteurs. Tout se passa de sa part avec beaucoup de ceremonie et de Magnificence, et de la nostre avec beaucoup de rejouissance. La petit Stubenberg devient tous les jours plus jollie et plus meure, et je crois que les doux Zephyres que soufflent les amants feront bientost épanouir ce petit bouton de rose.

Monsieur le Comte et Madame la Countesse de Windisgratz surprirent Monsieur Stocken et moy l'autre jour dans le bois auprez de la fontaine, ou nous fesions bonne chere avec Mademoiselle dé Vernerin. La Countesse se jetta presque hors de son carosse pour voir ce qui s'y passoit, et alongea le Coû jusqu'à ce que nous fusmes a perte de veuë. Pour me venger un peu aprez j'estoit dans une assemblée ou Mr. le Comte vint luyméme pour rapeller sa femme à la maison. Le Crasseux Ecuyer ayant negligé son devoir ce jour là, je la pris par la main, et Elles fit beaucoup d'effort pour me l'arracher; j'ay tenu ferme, et luy dit en françois Je ne pouvois pas me dispenser de conduire une personne de sa qualité et de son merite dans son Carosse. Elle me dit beaucoup de chose en aleman, que je ne pouvois, ou que Je ne voulois pas entendre, la plus grand part de la Compagnie se mit à rire, et Elle fut obligé d'appeller à l'aide pour me faire dire que cela ne se pouvoit faire.

Nous n'avons pas encore fait le voyage de Nuremberg, quoy que Je sais que les belles Zinzendorffs y sont de retour, mais nous esperons de les voir bientost. Mademoiselle de Windizgratz est bien plus amoureuse de Monsieur de Stocken, que Je n'estois jamais d'elle. Toutes les belles luy en veulent; et il est chassé par une meute de Fräwlins. Cela qui fait que Je le plains, est, qu'il y a si peu de gibiers dans cette Ville qu'elles ne peuvent pas prendre le change. Il court risque d'estre mis en pieces, et Dieu scait que le tout n'est qu un petit morceau et à peine peut rassassier une. Adieu, mon cher. Vous m'avez tant rebuté de la Ceremonie, que Je ne veux pas vous faire d'autre compliment que l'ordinaire. Je suis etc.

Source: BM, ff. 108–109; *LB*, pp. 231–233.

[1] In BM this letter, headed "Ditto," follows a letter of 7/17 July, 87. The calendaring in H-1 (p. 143) indicates that the correct date is "23 June/3 July, 1687."

[2] The Marquis du Héron. See the letter of July 29, 1686.

Omitted: July 7, 1687. To Mr. Wynne with miscellaneous news of the Diet.
Source: M-2, ff. 40–41; H-1, pp. 144–145; *LB*, pp. 228–229.

Omitted: July 10, 1687. To Middleton reporting the dissension in the Diet over Count Windischgrätz' pretensions.
Source: M-2, ff. 42–43; H-1, pp. 145–146; *LB*, pp. 229–230.

Ratisbon July 14, 1687

To Sir Rowland Gwynne
To Sir Peter Wyche. and to
Dr. Wynne.
Source: H-1, p. 146.

Omitted: July 15, 1687. To Middleton, assuring him that dispatches are sent "constantly twice a week."
Source: M-2, ff. 44–45; H-1, pp. 146–147; *LB*, pp. 230–231.

Ratisbon July 16, 1687

To My Lord Dongan. with an inclosed for my Lord Charles Hamilton
Source: H-1, p. 147.

Omitted: July 17, 1687. To Middleton: a short letter of news from the Diet.
Source: M-2, ff. 46–47; H-1, p. 148; *LB*, p. 231.

[July 17, 1687]

To the Marquis D'Albyville
Mr. Mountstevens.
Mr. Smithsby
My Lady

July 21, 1687

To Dr. Wynne with the news.
Source: H-1, p. 148.

Omitted: July 24, 1687. To the Earl of Sunderland with news of the campaign in Hungary.
Source: H-1, pp. 149–150; *LB*, pp. 233–234.

Omitted: July 24, 1687. To Middleton about Windischgrätz' pretensions and the infirmity of the Bishop of Passau.
Source: M-2, ff. 48–49; H-1, p. 150; *LB*, pp. 234–235.

To Mr. Robson.
    Source: H-1, p. 150.

To The Earl of Middleton   July 28, 1687
                                                            Ratisbon
My Lord.

The Electorall Colledge on Saturday last made a conclusion about the Dictating of the Decree of Comission left by the Prince of Passau, a Copy of which I send you. The same day the Princes Colledge made a Conclusion uppon this Conclusion which was not communicated, the Electorall Colledge being rissen before they had done, so that the Decree is not yet dictated.

It is true this Decree can have no effect as to the main business (the naming of a Deputation to Complement the Prince on his departure). Nevertheless the Director, I think, made a fault which has given the Count de Windisgratz's Faction the advantage of engaging the wholle Colledge of Princes in their interest. He ought not to have suppress'd the Decree but with the consent of all the Diett, whom first he ought to have acquainted with his reasons for doeing it, for tho' this be not of much moment, they pretend to be jealous the Director may assume a right of suppressing on his owne head at some time or other a Comissions Decree which may be of consequence to the Empire.

This great affair has taken upp the wholle care of the Diet these two months, by which your Lordship may see how hardly the Deputys are put to't to find out work to make their Principalls beleive they earn their pentions.

Here has been a report the French had given over the designe of making the Fort at Trarebach, but the Agent here in the Count de Crecys absence tells me the work still goes on tho' the ground is not proper.

[War news from Hungary]

I am, My Lord, Your Lordships most faithfull and most humble servant
                                                            G: Etherege
    Source: M-2, ff. 50–51; H-1, pp. 151–152; *LB*, pp. 235–236.

To Mr. Corbet and
To Mr. Wynne.
    Source: H-1, p. 152.

To ROBERT CORBET   July 28, 1687
                                                       Dito

Sir.

I begin to think I wear out of the memory of my acquaintance in England since I have not had a letter from any particular friend these 3 moneths. To comfort me for this, I make the best of this place, and do not ommitt any company, or indeed any thing, which can give me any sorte of pleasure. In a former letter to you, I desir'd you to lett me know what my Lady Soames[1] dos since her return, but I hear honest Sir Henry Shere can give me a better account of that than you can.

It may be this may come to your hands at Tunbridge. If it does, let my friends know I wou'd willingly loos a hundred or two Hundred pounds to enjoy them there this Season, but since I cannot immediately have that happyness, be so kind to lett me have it at second hand. You are able to make the relation of what has pass'd there almost as pleasant to me as if I had been a partaker. When you are with Tom Maul, make him drink my health. It is the least he can do for a man who loves him so well. I am. etc.

Source: BM, ff. 111–112; *LB,* pp. 236–237.

[1] The widow of Sir William Soames, who had died in 1686 on his way to the post of Ambassador at Constantinople. See above, p. 71.

Omitted: July 31, 1687. To Middleton, reporting on dissension in the Diet and war news from Hungary.
Source: M-2, ff. 52–53; H-1, pp. 152–153; *LB,* pp. 237–238.

To THE COMTE DE CRÉCY[1]   July 31, 1687
                                                       Dito

Monsieur.

Le Comte de Windisgratz est devenu beaucoup plus considerable depuis vostre depart d'ici, et à cette heure non pas un petit nombre mais tout le College de Princes courent risque d'estre convier à un beau festin aprez la prise d'Essek.

Le Dernieres nouvelles de Vienne disent que l'Empereur n'est pas satisfait de la reponse de sa Majesté Chrestienne au memoire qui luy a esté presenté par Monsieur Skelton, et qu'il espere d'obtenir des meilleurs conditions par la Mediation de sa Majesté Britannique. Pour moy, Je n'ay point changé de sentiment depuis que J'ay seu que Monsieur de Caunitz a desiré la Garantie, et cela qui m'a plus confirmé dans mes pensées est que Monsieur de Caunitz a refusé de donner en écrit ce qu'il a dit en angleterre sur cette reponse. Toute la conduite de ces affaires a une telle liaison, qu'il n'est pas difficile de diviner de ce dont il s'agit à cette heure par cela qui s'est passé.

J'estois bien Surpris d'apprendre que vous vous est souvenu d'une bagatelle qui me touche dans un temps que mile affaires vous occupent, qui vous sont de grande consequence. C'est une obligation dont je seráy toujours reconnoissant. Vous m'avez accablé avec beaucoup d'autres, et je serois l'homme le plus ingrate du monde si je ne vous donnois pas en toutes occasions des bonnes raison de croire, que Je suis, Monsieur, Vostre humble et tres obeissant Serviteur Geo: Etherege

Faites, je vous prie Monsieur, mes tres humble baisemens à Madame la Comtesse, et dites luy que J'espere en peu de temps de baiser les Cartes en les luy donnant à l'Hombre.

Source: BM, ff. 112–113; *LB*, pp. 238–239.

¹ Crécy was in Paris, on leave.

Ratisbon August 4, 1687
To my Lord Middleton all news about the retreat from Esseck
To my Lord Dorset.
Mr. William Richards.
Mr. Mountstevens.
Mr. Wynne.
Sir Peter Wyche.
Source: H-1, p. 154.

To The Earl of Middleton   August 4, 1687
                                             Ratisbon

My Lord.

I send you the News we have receiv'd from the Army by which you will find there is no farther hope of the designe against Esseck.¹ The Imperialists were so perswaded the Turks wou'd uppon sight of them leave their Post and fly that when they had pass'd the wood they enlarg'd their front and march'd boldly towards the Enemy, who stood firme in their retrenchments, and the Imperialists a great while receiv'd the Cannon of Esseck and that of the bulwarks on the retrenchements besides continuall vollees of smale shot but at length were forc'd to retreat. In this engagement Palfi was kill'd and the Elector run great hassar'd. It is beleiv'd the loss is more considerable then is own'd. The next post may cleare it. On Saturday the 23 a French Courier pass'd thro' this place and onely told the Master of the post he wou'd suddainly hear from Esseck. This (no Courier arriving to give any account of matters to the Diet or the Emperors Ministers here) made us beleive the French man a foreruner of ill News. The begining of this Campagne has been unlucky. God send it may end more successfully. I am, My Lord, Your Lordships most faithfull and most humble Servant

Geo: Etherege

Source: M-2, ff. 54–55.

[1] The Hungarian city of Osijek (now in Jugoslavia), near the confluence of the Drava and the Danube, had been in Turkish hands since 1526 but was surrendered to the Imperial troops on September 30, 1687 (M-2, f. 93).

To The Earl of Dorset   August 4, 1687
                                        Ratisbon 25. July 87[1]

My Lord.

When you consider I have been two years from England without letting you know I am sensible you are the person in the world I am most oblig'd to, you will have reason to think me very ungratefull, but I know your humor so well you had rather forgive a debt than be troubl'd with acknowledgement. I hope therefore you will look upon this neglect as the mere effect of laziness, and will easily excuse that vice in me who am in a Countrey from whence I can send you nothing to contribute to your pleasure.

All my business in this dull place is to give a bare account of what is done, which requires onely a little playn sense. I have lost for want of exerccise the use of fancy and imagination, and am grown so very stupid that when I read a new Poem methinks the author should be invited to one of those reverend Cells the Hermite Lee[2] has quitted. Lovers have been Metamorphos'd by the ancient Poets, tho' Churches have not. Yet you and I were n'ere so bold to turn the faire Cuffle,[3] when she fled us, into a tree, not dreaming she wou'd grow as big as one of Evelins Oaks,[4] nor our selves into Bulls when we carried the two dragle'd tayl'd Nymphs one bitter frosty night over the Thames to Lambeth. Sertorius[5] aim'd to make a milke-white hind an Immortal Dame, but his hint's improv'd by the Lady of the Spotted muff's ungracious son.[6] I cannot guesse on whom the Duke of Bucks mantle is fallen, but it is Mac Flecknoe with doubl'd portion of that Prophets art.[7] [There are many lucky hits, and Bishop Martin is a Master

135

Stroak.] [8] I am so glad of an occasion of laughing here, it is no wonder the ridicule gets the better of the Heroick. A letter from Sheppard might get the better of both, if he had as great an alacritie in writing as he has in talking. There wou'd be many congratulations if he had liberty granted him in this point. I wish it him heartily, since I never knew he had any further malice in it than making the Company splitt themselves with laughter. I wou'd gladly be a witness of the Content you enjoy at Copt-Hall [9] now, and I hope to surprise you there one day (your gravity lay'd aside) teaching my Lord Buckhurst how to manage his Hoby-horse. I am etc.

Source: BM, ff. 113–114; *LB,* 239–241.

[1] In H-1, p. 154, this letter is calendared as "25 Jul./4 Aug. 87."

[2] Nathaniel Lee, the dramatist, was periodically confined to Bethlehem Hospital for insanity.

[3] A Mrs. Cuffley is described as a notorious whore in the verse letters exchanged, probably in the winter of 1663–64, between Dorset (then Lord Buckhurst) and Etherege. (Cf. Thorpe, *Poems,* pp. 39, 43–54; Vieth, *Attributions,* pp. 245–248.) The meaning, following the context of *Metamorphoses,* seems to be that Buckhurst and Etherege were not so bold as to change the fleeing Mrs. Cuffley, like Daphne, into a tree, nor to metamorphose themselves into bulls to carry "two dragle'd tayl'd nymphs" across the Thames on another occasion. For the name "Cuffle," see H.F.B. Brett-Smith, *RES* 5 (1929), 227.

[4] John Evelyn, the diarist, was a notable gardener and horticulturist, who urged in his *Sylva, or a Discourse of Forest Trees* (1664), that landowners plant trees to replace those being cut down for fuel.

[5] To impress the superstitious Lusitanians, Quintus Sertorius pretended that his pet white fawn was a gift from Artemis, had supernatural powers, and foretold the future for him. See Plutarch, *Life of Sertorius,* Ch. 11.

[6] An allusion to Dryden, whose *Hind and the Panther* Etherege had been reading. The lady of the spotted muff (see the last line of Part I) is the Panther, representing the Church of England, which Dryden had left to become a Roman Catholic.

[7] See the last two lines of "MacFlecknoe": "The mantle fell to the young prophet's part/With double portion of his father's art."

[8] Deleted in BM. Martin represents Father Petre, King James's Jesuit confessor. See *The Hind and the Panther,* 1865–2076.

[9] Copt Hall and Knole were the Earl of Dorset's two country houses. At the former he entertained needy writers like Shadwell and old friends like Fleetwood Shepherd, who died there in 1698.

Omitted: August 4, 1687. To Wynne, reporting on affairs in Denmark.
Source: BM, f. 114; *LB,* pp. 241–242.

To Mr. Robson ordering him to return the 260£ and to sollicite for more.

To Mr. Poley.

To the Earl of Sunderland as follows

Source: H-1, p. 154.

Omitted: August 7, 1687. To Sunderland, reporting military news from Hungary.

Source: H-1, pp. 154–155; *LB*, pp. 242–243.

Omitted: August 7, 1687. To Middleton with news of the Diet and of the campaign in Hungary.

Source: M-2, ff. 56–57; H-1, p. 156; *LB*, p. 243 in part.

August 11, 1687

To Mrs. Merry.

Mrs. Newstead.

Mr. George Etherege

Mr. Mountstevens. with an Extract of my Lord Dongn's

Mr. Wynne.

Dito

To my Lord Middleton about the Duke of Berwick's ilness and of Stratman's not being gone to the Army.

Source: H-1, p. 156.

To OWEN WYNNE   August 11, 1687
                                                  Ratisbon

Sir.

The Revolter[1] dos not pleas me so well as the first answer[2] to the Hind and Panther. It seemes to be writ by an Angrie Clergieman, and the other I am confident by some stroks I find in it was writ by a Gentleman who has dipt his hands in Satyr e're now. The Author of the Trage-Comedie, while he endeavours to show our Friend an ill man, shows himselfe a very ill Poet.

I am sorry I send you so bad news from Hungarie, but that which afflicts me beyond all comfort is the sickness of the Duke of Berwick in a place where there is so little help. Nevertheless I hope well from his Youth and the goodness of his Constitution. I cannot be in quiet till I am able to let you know he is in a state of Convalescence.

On Friday last a very sad accident happen'd here. A Daughter of the Baron de Regale, one of the handsomest young Gentlewomen in this Towne, was struck dead with the Thunder in a terrible Storme which happen'd that Day. An other Lady was sitting on the same stole with her and was untouch'd. All that appears is a black streak downe her Chin and a spot on the side of her nose. She is lamented by every body, and her death has put an end to all the Divertions of this place for this Summer. I am, Sir, Your most humble and Obedient Servant

Geo: Etherege

Source: M-2, f. 58.

1 *The Revolter, a Trage-Comedy acted between the Hind and the Panther and Religio Laici*, etc., 1687, is a verse satire with prose commentary accusing Dryden of changing his religion for political ends.

2 Probably *The Hind and the Panther Transversed to the Story of the City and Country Mouse*, by Charles Montague and Matthew Prior, 1687.

Omitted: August 11, 1687. A short letter to Middleton reporting military news from Hungary.

Source: M-2, ff. 60–61.

To HENRY GUY   August 14, 1687
                                                  Ratisbon

Sir.

. . . . The Germans call it a very fine and difficult retreat.1 It is a good thing when a man is fallen into a bog to have address and strength enough to get out again, but it is better to take such wise measures as not to make the false step. . . . . News . . . . I wish our friend Mr. Saville2 as good Success in what he is gone into France about as the Christian King3 has had, and the Marquis d'Angeau.

You have a war in England between the Hind and the Panther. Generall Dryden is an Expert Captain, but I allways thought him fitter for execution than for Counsill. Who commands the Panthers forces I know not. The Author of the Revolter, while he endeavours to expose the moralls of his enemy, exposes more his own dulness by his Poetry. The gentleman who has transvers'd the Poem shews that the genius of the Rehersall is not dead with the Duke of Bucks. There are severall stroaks which shew that hand is skilfull in the turn of Satyr, and one line which makes me think he has been acquainted with Sir Benjamin, the Hero in an Essay of Comedy you have heard of. Lett them go on and turn the churches into what beasts they please. I shall never turn my Religion, which teaches me to be always obedient and faithfull to the King my master.

You are always so forward in doing me favours that it is superfluous to beg them of you, and I do not doubt but you will help Mr. Robson in getting my Extraordinaries, now they begin to grow stale, without saying more than that they will come very seasonably to.

Source: BM, f. 116; *LB,* pp. 244–245.

[1] The retreat of the Imperial forces after their defeat at Esseck.

[2] Henry Savile, formerly envoy to France, returned to Paris for surgery in July. He died on October 6, 1687.

[3] In 1686 Louis XIV was given "la grande opération" for an anal fistula by his surgeon Félix, who was rewarded with £15,000, a country estate, and a patent of nobility. (Vincent Cronin, *Louis XIV,* 1965, p. 292.)

Omitted: August 14, 1687. To Middleton: haggling in the Diet and military rumors from Hungary.
Source: H-1, pp. 157–158; *LB,* pp. 245–246.

To William Bridgeman   August 18, 1687
                                               Ratisbon
Sir.

I had yesterday the few lines you were pleas'd to favour me with, and to shew you how gratefull I am to those who are willing to remember me, I cou'd not omitt the thanking of you for them this day. Considering the little time you have to spare from your many painfull Employments, the obligation is more to me than if I shou'd receive a long letter from an Idle fellow, but neither the idle nor the busie are much given to think of a friend so far off as I am. If I have an answer to one letter in three I esteem myself well payd, and if I have none it is not so vexatious, I fancy, as it wou'd be to have two or three answers to a poem, had I the skill and Genius to write one. I send you what news I have from Hungarie, which I desire you to shew my Lord. The Kindest thing you can doe for me in my absence is to preserve me in his memory. I am etc. News of the two Armies being encamp'd at Mohatz and Darda.

Source: H-1, p. 158; *LB,* pp. 246–247.

Omitted: August 18, 1687. To Middleton, reporting the lack of military news from Hungary.
Source: M-2, ff. 62–63; H-1, p. 159; *LB,* p. 247.

To Mr. Wynne.

Dito

To My Lord Middleton. about the Victory against the Turks.
To Mr. Skelton about the same.[1]
    Source: H-1, p. 159.

[1] This letter is copied into BM Add. MS. 41841, f. 60.

To The Earl of Middleton[1]   August 18, 1687
                                                        Ratisbon

My Lord.
    Late this evening an Expresse arrived here by which We Learne
that the 10th instant the armys Engaged. The Turks were drawne
insensibly to a Battle. The Imperialists remaine Victorious. The Turks
had 9000 killed on the Place. 9000 threw themselves into the River
Drave, and the Imperialists endeavour to cutt off the passage of the
rest of the Army. The Christians have lost but 500 men. The Elector of
Bavaria is wounded in the hand, and the Prince of Commercy is shot
thro the Body.
    I have to acquaint you with no more particulars. I am, My Lord,
Your etc.

                                                    G. Etherege
    Source: M-2, f. 64.

[1] This unaddressed letter in an unknown hand is calendared in H-1, p. 159,
as addressed to Middleton. It is probably the message "writ . . . in hast"
referred to in the following letter.

To The Earl of Sunderland   August 21, 1687
                                                        Ratisbon

My Lord.
    I receiv'd yesterday your letter of the 26th of July concerning
mourning for the Dutchesse of Modena[1] and forthwith took care to
performe what you commanded.
    On Munday last the 8th Instant late in the Evening here arriv'd
a Staffeta[2] from Vienna dispatch'd by a friend to the Count de Windisgratz to let him know the Emperor had received the news of a Victory
obtain'd against the Turks the Tenth Instant New Style.[3] The Prince
of Savoy[4] brought this wellcome message, who was dispatch'd as soon
as the Christians were masters of the Turkish Camp. The Same night

I writ a letter in hast to my Lord Middleton to acquaint him with this action, which I sent by Holland, and an Express parting hence for Paris, I writ at the same time to Mr. Skelton, thinking by the diligence of the Express the news might be in England sooner that way.

All the particulars I have yet learn'd are these: the Imperialists drew up in battel, and the Turks drew a very considerable body out of their Trenches, intending onely to skirmish. The Elector of Bavaria comanded the left wing, in which were many of the young Nobility who were impatient of signalizing themselves, and it is sayd the Turks were engag'd by their forwardness to attack them. The Elector himself has a contusion by a blow on the left hand, and the Prince de Comercy, who is reported to have done things beyond belief, is shot thro' both the shoulders, and has lost the greatest part of his Regiment. Nevertheless the Germans reckon but 500 men of theirs kill'd, and we hear of no other person of quality wounded, which makes me hope well of our Countreymen.

It is affirm'd the Turks have lost eight or nine thousand who remain'd dead on the place. The like number is reckon'd to be drown'd in the Drave. The Christians enter'd their Camp with them, where their great body of Reserve took the fright and dispers'd themselves, leaving their artillerie and bagage. The Artillery is said to be one hundred pieces of Canon great and small, and the riches which was found in their Tents incredible. Many here reason on the consequences of this great Victory, but I shall not trouble your Lordship with imaginations. It is likely this ordinary will onely confirme what we have already heard. If it bring any other particulars I will enclose them for your Lordship.

Yesterday was dictated a Decree of Comission deliver'd by the Count de Windisgratz to acquaint the Dyet in forme with this Victory, which will occasion a Conclusion to congratulate the Emperor upon it, who no doubt is infintly pleas'd with his unexpected good fortune, but he cannot be more pleas'd than I was with what your Lordship so kindly added to your Circular letter. I am, My Lord, Your Lordships most faithfull and most obedient Servant.

G.E.

Duplicate to Lord Middleton

Source: H-1, pp. 159–161; *LB*, pp. 247–249. The duplicate is in M-2, ff. 68–70.

1 Queen Mary's mother had died on July 19, and mourning was ordered abroad as well as in London.

[2] A mounted courier.

[3] This is usually called the Battle of Mohács, in which the Grand Vizier was decisively defeated by Imperial troops under the Duke of Lorraine.

[4] Prince Eugene of Savoy (1663–1736) began his long military career fighting for the Emperor against the Turks.

Omitted: August 21, 1687. To Wynne, enclosing a copy of the preceding letter to Sunderland.
Source: M-2, f. 66.

TO THE EARL OF DOVER   August 21, 1687
                                                                  Dito
My Lord.

It is so long since I presum'd to trouble you with one letter that I imagin you begin to think yourself secure from the like persecution, but men in your post lye so open they must expect to be shot at, and I cannot forbear aiming at you, bearing you an Inclination of an older date than I will mention both for your sake and my own. You are not onely a Courtier but a souldier, not onely a fine gentleman but a good Christian, and these things help to embolden me to give you a short account of the Victory the Christians have gain'd against the Turks . . . the news as in the foregoing letter. (it ended) I know so generous a man as you are will help an old acquaintance with a good word when you think it convenient in the Treasury, and excuse me the time I make you loose in shewing you how faithfully I am, &c.

Source: H-1, pp. 161–162; *LB*, pp. 249–250.

                                                Dito [August 21, 1687]
To my Lord Godolphin all news as in the preceding
To my Lady
To Mr. Wynne
To Sir Peter Wyche.
To Mr. Maule

                                                Ratisbon August 25, 1687
To Mr. Bradbury about the petition
To Mr. de Paz[1]
To Mr. Robson about Extraordinaries and Entertainment
To Mrs. Merry.
To my Lord Middleton. all news and repetition.

Source: H-1, p. 162.

[1] Samuel De Paz, a clerk in the Secretary of State's office, substituted for Dr. Owen Wynne while the latter was on vacation. See below, p. 223, n.

142

Omitted: August 25, 1687. To Middleton, speculating on the consequences of the victory at Mohács.
Source: M-2, ff. 71–72.

Omitted: August 28, 1687. A long letter to Middleton summarizing diplomatic activity at the Diet.
Source: M-2, ff. 73–74; H-1, pp. 162–165; *LB,* pp. 250–252.

To THE EARL OF SUNDERLAND   September 1, 1687
                                                                              Ratisbon
My Lord.

I sent my Lord Middleton by the last post the best account I then had of the battel given near Siklos.[1] I now enclos for your Lordship a copie of a letter on the same purpose, order'd by the Gentleman[2] who writ it to be communicated to me. I made an acquaintance with him on my first comming hither. This is the third Campagne he has made in Hungary, a Voluntier in the Elector of Bavarias Troopes. He is very curious in his observations, and his quality and reputation give him occasion to satisfy himself and his friends. The latter part of this letter is wanting (the time being too short to transcribe it). It was sent with what was Copie'd to Monsieur de Croissy.

It gives a description of the Turkish Camp and how it was fortify'd, with a few other particulars, and ends with an other article touching the Duke of Mantova, much more plesant than what is in the part I send you. He had sav'd himself behinde the baggage during the Engagement and cou'd not without much difficulty after the victory be perswaded to enter the enemies Camp to joine the Duke of Lorrain. Nothing cou'd prevaile till they had assur'd him *che tutti gli Turcki stavano amazzati.*[3] Then he let himself be conducted, but with much precaution, finding fault that no more Troops were left to guarde the baggage during the Combate. He has no equipage, the Duke of Lorrain furnishing him by the Emperors order with all things necessary for himself and his retinue, Monsieur de Gombo not excepted, the Most Christian Kings Minister, who is always at his Elbow. I am.

Source: H-1, pp. 165–166; *LB,* pp. 252–253.

[1] The Battle of Mohács.
[2] The Marquis du Héron.
[3] "That all the Turks had been killed."

Omitted: September 1, 1687. To Middleton, enclosing diplomatic documents about Hungary.
Source: M-2, ff. 75–76; H-1, pp. 166–167; *LB,* p. 253.

143

Omitted: September 4, 1687. To Middleton, a long account of politics at the Diet.
Source: M-2, ff. 77–78; H-1, pp. 167–169; *LB,* pp. 254–256.

Omitted: September 8, 1687. To Middleton, reporting growing hostility between the French and the Empire.
Source: M-2, ff. 79–80; H-1, pp. 170–171; *LB,* pp. 256–258.

Omitted: September 8, 1687. An unaddressed note, apparently sent with the preceding letter, reporting the Duke of Berwick's recovery.
Source: M-2, f. 81.

To Sir Edward Vaudrey   September 11, 1687
                                               Ratisbon 1. Sept. 87[1]
Sir.

Notwithstanding the lucky success of the Christians against the Turks, I have receiv'd no news from your army which was so wellcome to me as your letter of the 6 of this moneth New Stile. It has almost restor'd me to that quiet of mind which I lost on the first account I had of the Duke of Barwicks distemper. I hope you have taken care to put all who have the happiness to know him in England as much at ease as you have done me, especially his Majestie, who I am confident has been in very great paine for him. I cannot but tremble yet when I reflect on the malignity of the disease and the little relief he cou'd have in those barbarous parts to help him to overcome it. Nothing can give me an entire satisfaction but the seeing him in his return perfectly recover'd.

Your haste made you forget to let me know where you are, but the freshness of the date of what you write me makes me think you are at Vienna, where you may find all things necessary to assist nature to accomplish speedily what she herself has been long labouring to effect. The Duke must be carefull of himself too, not onely for his own sake, but for the wellfare of all those whom his charmes have equally engag'd with him in whatsoever shall concern him.

If our sex be not worth his thoughts, let him think on the other and how severely he has been reveng'd on them for all the sighs they have cost him. Howsoever *fiere* some of them may have appear'd, their hearts have been tender on this occasion and will scarce leave asking till they see him in London again with that vigour and beauty which has never fail'd secretely to warme them.

I have nothing of consequence from our own Countrey. His Majestie

144

is now in his progress and will join the Queen at the Bath on the 6 Instant, in order to bring her back. I am Very faithfully. Sir &c.

Source: H-1, pp. 171–172; *LB*, pp. 258–259.

[1] Dated "1/11 Sept. 87" in BM, f. 125.

To Samuel de Paz   September 11, 1687
                                                         Ratisbon
Sir.

I am very much beholden to you for the trouble you have given yourself in my businesse in the absence of Mr. Wynne. I shall allways have it in my memory and be willing to serve you in my turne when I have an occasion. Pray give Mr. Wynne the inclosed bill of Extraordinaries, that he may get it allow'd. It compleats the two years I have been out of England. I hope Mr. Robson will sollicite this and those he has already and get them payd alltogether. The heat of this Campagne is over, so that our news is not worth your knowing. I am &c.

Source: H-1, p. 173; *LB*, p. 259.

Omitted: September 11, 1687. To Middleton: arguments in the Diet over the Roman months.

Source: M-2, ff. 82–83; H-1, pp. 173–174; *LB*, pp. 259–260.

Omitted: September 15, 1687. To Middleton: more about the Roman months.

Source: M-2, ff. 84–85; H-1, pp. 174–175; *LB*, pp. 260–261.

To Owen Wynne   September 18, 1687
                                                         Ratisbon
Sir.

I just now receiv'd yours of the 26th of August and hope you have diverted yourself well in the Countrey. The Diet not having yet agreed on the generall Conclusion concerning the Roman moneths, I have nothing to send my Lord to day but the news we receive from Vienna, which I have inclos'd for him in this. The Duke of Barwick is pretty well recover'd of his sickness and is come to Vienna. Most of our Country Voluntiers are at Presbourg, where I hear they intend to stay to see the ceremony of the Arch-Duke Joseph's Coronation,[1] which I am told will be about 3 weeks hence. We have onely lost my poor Lord Kenoul, who dy'd at Mohatz a few days before the battle.

I this day was payd 500 £, which Mr. Robson has taken care to return me. Pray thank him for me, and let him know I will do it Myself the next post. Mr. de Paz has been so kind as to write to me constantly during your absence, of which I am very sensible, and likewise of the trouble which you on all occasions give yourself in what concernes, Sir, etc.

Source: H-1, pp. 175–176; *LB*, 261–262.

[1] The Archduke Joseph (1678–1711), son of Emperor Leopold I, was the first Hapsburg to become hereditary monarch of Hungary when the 700-year-old elective monarchy was renounced in October 1687 by the Hungarian Diet at Pressburg.

Omitted: September 22, 1687. To Middleton, reporting that Wolfgang von Schmettau has been appointed minister from Brandenburg, replacing Godfrey de Jena, who was accused of favoring the French.

Source: M-2, ff. 86–87; H-1, pp. 176–177; *LB*, pp. 262–263.

Dito [September 22, 1687]

To Mr. Poley and
To Sir Peter Wyche.
Source: H-1, p. 177.

Omitted: September 22, 1687. To Edmund Poley, about the Count of Windischgrätz's pretensions and other diplomatic news.
Source: BM, ff. 129–130; *LB*, pp. 265–266.

UNADDRESSED   September 22, 1687
                                                          Ratisbon

Je ne suis pas mort, Monsieur,[1] et le mal que j'ay n'est pas à la main comme vous voyez. C'est à l invincible et Heroique Maximilien que le Ciel reserve des blessures si honorables. Vous n'aurez gueres de peine a diviner ma maladie quand je vous diray maudit soit mon jardin; le louage m'en coûte trop cher. C'est s'expliquer aussi nettement qui si je m'aurois servi du proverbe si connu aux ouvriers en soye: Le Chat echaudé &c.[2] Aprez cette confidence pouvez vous imaginer que c'est une indifference qui a causé un si long Silence? Non, mon ami, c'est le chagrin et la honte d'avoir goûté de ce fruit malsain que vous m'aviez defendu, qui m'ont empeché de paroistre devant vous. Pardonnez une foiblesse qui ne dement point nostre origine.

146

Tout ce que Je say de nos Fräwlins ne vaut pas la peine de vous le mander. Elles sont insensibles à tout hormis le tonnere, qui depuis peu se fait craindre. Vous savez que J'estois toûjours Philosophe, mais vous ne savez pas que je changé de Secte. J'estois peripatetique et j'aimois la promenade, mais tout d'un Coup Je suis devenu disciple d'Epicure, je me tien dans my petite retraite, et je me suis établi pour maxime que la plus grand volupté consiste dans une parfaite santé. Le transport d'une debauche ne paye pas le mal au cœur qu'on sent le lendemain au matin. Ces morales sont admirables, mais je n'ay pas le loisir de m'étendre sur un si digne sujet. Pour ces atomes ils ne me rompent gueres la teste.

Par la grace de Dieu je say ou mon esprit est borné, et je ne me mets gueres en peine de savoir de quelle maniere ce monde icy a esté fait ou comment on se divert dans l'autre. Cette grand humilité vous peut persuader que je suis bien preparé pour reçevoir ces lumieres et ces rayons dont vous faites mention, que la belle Comtesse me vient éclairer. J'admire ses beaux yeux, mais je peur que son ame ne soit aussi aveugle que celles des autres mortelles. Afin que vous ne vous imaginiez pas une étrange affaire de ce qui est arrivé, sachiez que J'en suis deja si bien sorti que je fus avant hier a la chasse et que mes Laquays raporterent trois lievres en croupe à la maison dont Silk en attrapa le plus gros. Cette maniere d'ecrire sans reserve vous doit asseurér que je suis, Monsieur, vostre tres humble et tres obeissant Serviteur. G. E.

Source: BM, 128–129; *LB*, pp. 263–264.

Omitted: September 25, 1687. To Middleton, with the "Generall conclusion about the 100 Roman Months."

Source: M-2, f. 88; H-1, p. 177; *LB*, pp. 266–267.

1 Probably Monsieur de Gennes, to whom Etherege had written frankly on July 17, 1687.

2 "Chat échaudé craint l'eau froide" (a scalded cat fears even cold water).

Ratisbon September 29, 1687

To Mr. Manlove with a note for 10 £ upon Mr. Bradbury.

To Mr. Bradbury about the Interest and the Cancelling of a Bond of a 100.

To Mrs. Merry.

Source: H-1, p. 178.

Sir.

I received yesterday yours of the 2ᵈ Instant. You may imagin I have been much concern'd I have had no better Correspondence with our volunteers this Campagne, that I might oftener give my Lord an account of the Duke of Barwick's health. I did all I cou'd to engage them to it both by making them very wellcome here and writing kindly to them when they were in the Army, but I cou'd never draw more than two letters from them, one from my Lord Dongan after the retreat from the other side of the Drave and one from Sir Edward Vaudry uppon his return to Vienna, the substance of which I sent into England.

I am sorry to hear you were allarm'd with the false news of the Duke of Barwicks death occasion'd by that of my Lord Kenouls at Mohatz. A Secretary at Vienna belonging to the Prince of Mecklenbourg made that impertinent mistake, which I knew not time enough to prevent the Surprise it might occasion, but I hope little Credit was given to it and the apprehension it put the Court into made the news of his recovery be receiv'd more joyfully. The Army drawing towards their Winter quarters and the Disputes the Count de Windisgratz has with the Electoralls about his pretentions to be principall Commissioner here are the reasons I have nothing worth troubling my Lord with at present.

To answer you touching the proposition the Gentleman desir'd you to make me in his behalf, I must tell you I find by your letter you do not well understand the coine of this Countrey. It is very low, and our best guilders are not above half good silver, but this is not to the purpose. I will tell you what I receive here for 500 £ Sterling: by a return by way of Amsterdam I had 2464 dollers, each Dollar being a gulden or a florin (which is all one) and one halfe, the true vallue of a Dollar here currant money being just 4 shillings English, so that I had in that return 36 Dollars of this countrey less than the true value of my money, that being the gain of the merchands. If the gentleman will deal as ingeniously as I do and be willing the merchants shall not have the advantage of your moneys sticking to their fingers, I shall accept of the proposition. I am very much, Sir, &c.

I suppose you mean ducats by what you name Guildiners. Each ducat if in gold and weight comes to 3 florins and one half, the upgelt[1] being counted, which according to 4 shillings a dollar, 150 Guleners amount to 70 pounds sterling, but this dos not reach the sum of 86 or 87 which you mention, so that I must expect 'till the Gentleman explains himself better and whether it is currant mony, or what other sort of money I am to receive.

Source: H-1, pp. 178–179; *LB*, pp. 267–268.

1 German *aufgeld,* the charge for changing money.

Omitted: October 2, 1687. To Middleton: politics at the Diet and news of British volunteers in Hungary.

Source: M-2, ff. 90–91; H-1, pp. 180–181; *LB*, pp. 268–269.

Ratisbon October 6, 1687

To Mr. William Richards.
Mr. Robson (about Extraordinaries) and
Dr. Wynne.

Ratisbon October 9, 1687

To Mr. Cooke
Mr. George Etherege and
My Lord Middleton in his verbis.

Source: H-1, p. 181.

Omitted: October 9, 1687. To Middleton about the continuing disputes over Windischgrätz' pretensions and the surrender of Esseck.

Source: M-2, ff. 92–93; H-1, pp. 181–183; *LB* (with incorrect date), pp. 270–271.

Omitted: October 9, 1687. Military news written in Etherege's hand on a news dispatch from Hungary.

Source: BM Add. MS. 41841, f. 94.

Omitted: October 13, 1687. To Middleton, reporting diplomatic exchanges between the French and the Emperor.

Source: H-1, pp. 183–184; *LB*, pp. 271–272.

Dito October 13, 1687

To Mr. Bradbury
Mr. Manlove and

To The Earl of Mulgrave   October 13, 1687

To my Lord Chamberlain in his verbis.
My Lord.

It cannot be unpleasing to the great to have the most inconsiderable
men enter into their interest, tho' all they can do is to make secret
vows for their happiness. This gives me the boldnesse to tell you I
have been very much concern'd ever since I heard you had left the
Bath on a message sent you by my Lord Dover till yesterday I learnt
you were return'd thither to execute your charge. I am ignorant of
the occasion of this message and imagin it might happen on a mistake,
knowing you too galant to be capable of giving an offense there where
the news mention'd.

The Love and honor I have for you, (and it may be the thoughts
of having a person out of Court who's favor I confidently rely on)
gave me some apprehension, tho' the consequence has been what I
allways expected from your prudence. I know not what your Lordship
thinks of me, or whether you ever think of me or no, but I assure you
I have Allways a gratefull memory of the obligations I have to you
and cou'd not omitt this opportunity of congratulating with you at
least my own good fortune, knowing you will be still ready to forward
what may be propos'd for my advantage. I can pretend but little
merit, but it may be you may think it enough to be faithfully.
Source: H-1, p. 185; *LB*, p. 273.

                                    Dito [October 13, 1687]
To Dr. Wynne with 2 Bills of Extraordinaries
    Source: H-1, p. 185.

Omitted: October 17, 1687. To Middleton, enclosing a copy of a
Commission's decree about the building of a French fortress on the
Moselle.
    Source: M-2, f. 94.

To The Earl of Middleton   October 20, 1687
                                            Ratisbon
My Lord.

On Wednesday the 5th Instant I was taken ill of a fever, which I
suppose was occasion'd by a very odd surfeit of Danube-water. The
day before (it being very fine weather here) the Electorall College
lett me know that they wou'd come and pass away the afternoon in

my gardin, where I forc'd myself to give them the best proofes they cou'd wish of a hearty wellcome, begining myself all the healths which are usuall on the like occasion; and having wisely (as I thought) given order that my glass shou'd allways be three parts water, I behav'd myself boldly and to the Satisfaction of all my guest, who withdrew one after an other according as they felt they had a *rauch*.[1] They went to bed drunk and waked well the next morning. I went to bed with my head undisturb'd but my stomach overcharg'd and wak'd about 5 in the morning with a little shivering, which soon turn'd into a hot fitt. I perceiv'd this was the effect of an indigestion, and tho' I have taken all the care imaginable to relieve my stomack, all I can say is that this morning I awaked without a fever. I yet keep my bed and eat nothing but broth, which I hope (I having nothing extraordinary to communicate to you) will make you excuse my not writing to you with my own hand this Post.

Generally once a weeke, or a fortnight, here uses to blow a tradewind which makes us see the Dyet under sail, tho' she suddenly casts ancor again, but now we have had a dead Calm ever since the instructions of the Electors are come to their Deputies against the Count de Windisgratz's pretentions, and the two conclusions which were made a good while since, the first for congratulating the Emperour on the Victory and the other for the 100 Roman moneths, remain in the Director's hands, and there is no talk how or to whom they will be delivered.

By a letter from Saverne the Count de Crecy lets us know, that he wou'd be at Strasbourg the 13th Instant and sett forwards from thence for this place the 15th, so that we expect him here the latter end of this week.

On fryday last my Lord Charles Hamilton pass'd thro' this Town in compagny with the Marquis de Crequi[2] and a son of the Count de Roy. I cou'd not see him by reason of my illness, but I sent to him to know if I cou'd be serviceable to him in any thing and to inform myself of the Duke of Barwick. He sent me word that the Duke had had a little relapse, but wou'd suddenly be setting forward for England, that he left him on munday last at Vienna, he having reasons to make hast into England, that my Lord Dongan intended to follow him the Thursday after, so that I expect him here dayly.

I send your Lordship an extract of a letter written the 10th Instant New style from Venice by Monsieur de la Haye, the French Ambassador there, which acquaints you with the manner of taking Castel nuovo. Tho' you may have the relation sooner from other parts, yet this coming from so good a hand I thought it not amiss to send it you.

Here has been some time since a rumor as if the Grand Vizir and the Aga of the Janizaries had been strangled in a mutiny of the Spahis and Janizaries at Peterwaradin, but so little credit was given to it that I made no manner of mention of it to your Lordship. But since it is certain there was a mutiny in the Turkish army after their saving themselves on the other side the Drave (which without question was the reason Dunewald[3] had so good a bargain of Esseck and Walpo). The best account of what happen'd on that mutiny is believ'd to be in the printed gazette which I receiv'd this day from Vienna, wherefore I have enclos'd it with the other news.

I hear you have our good Abbot[4] with you in England. I need not desire you to make much of him while he stays with you, but I earnestly beg you to do all you can to send him back in good humour, that Saint Benedict may speake with Reverence of Saint Ignatius and that both their Disciples may live in amity. I am with all Duty, My Lord, Your Lordship's most faithfull and most obedient Servant

Geo: Etherege

Source: M-2, ff. 96–97; H-1, pp. 186–188; *LB*, pp. 273–276. Written in Hughes's hand but signed by Etherege.

[1] German *rausch,* "drunkenness."

[2] François Joseph, Marquis de Créquy (1662–1702), son of Field Marshal François, Chevalier de Créquy.

[3] Johann Heinrich, Count von Dünewalt (1620–1691), was an Austrian General (Halsband, *Letters of Lady Mary Wortley Montagu,* 1, p. 302).

[4] Abbot Fleming, who had gone to England at the end of August. See Ludwig Hammermeyer, *Historisches Jahrbuch,* 87 (1967), 75.

To ROBERT CORBET   October 20, 1687
                                                          Ditto
Sir.

Yours of the 22th of the last moneth found me in a violent fever, which is now over, tho it has left me so weak I dare not yet venture abroad. I hope this will serve to excuse my not making you any return these two last ordinaries. Your letters are always so welcome to me that shou'd I take any neglect of writing unkindly of you, I cou'd not but forget it upon the receiving of two lines from you.

I wish you had not had so just an excuse for not letting me hear from you before as that which you are pleas'd to make. I am yet so sensible how much it puts a man out of humor to be ill treated by fortune at play (tho' I have been long out of her power in that nature) that I cannot blam your omitting a point of friendship on such an occasion. The like has often not onely made me forget my best friends for a time, but even a Mistress in the height of all my passion. I must tell you never the less I am not wholely satisfy'd with you, because you have left me in paine by not acquainting me that that unconstant Lady has been since more favourable to you. I am hearty glad of the account you give me of her smiling on Mr. Maule. I shou'd be in the wrong if I took it ill I have not heard from him, who has so many ways of employing every minute of his time better.

The Emperor's good luck this Campagne (all things well consider'd) is no less wonderfull than that of the Gentlemen you name, who were concern'd in diving for the Treasure of the Gallion.[1] The easy Victory the Turks gave him, their abandoning (the Lord knows wherefore) Esseck, the chief place aim'd at, and their letting Dunewaldt with a small Detatchment of the army and an inconsiderable body of Cravatz[2] make him self Master (to pin up the basket)[3] of almost all that part of Sclavonia which lies between the Save and the Drave. The Venetians have push'd with no less success in the Morea, and we see the vast Ottoman Empire in one ill run, which began from the Siege of Vienna, molder away like Skelton's guneas and its grand Seigneurs in danger to be reduc'd to lead the lives of their ancestors the Succomanni[4] and wander up and down with an army of sheep again.

But these reflections savour too much of the place I live in, and if I shou'd go on farther, you may think the Politicks infectious and believe I may return into England well enough accomplish'd to be admitted to walk with Mr. Spicer and Mr. Vandebendy[5] and the rest of that wise company who never talke of any affaires but such as do not concern them. London is dull by accident, but Ratisbonne by Nature. We have a Theater too, but not onely our plays but our Actors wou'd be hiss'd in a Countrey-faire. St. Barthelmews[6] is too honorable. We have often Lampoons on the Intrigues of State as scurrilous and as witless as yours can be on the Ladys.

Source: BM, ff. 136–137; *LB*, pp. 276–278.

[1] A treasure from a Spanish galleon had recently been salvaged by a group of gentlemen who gained as much as £10,000 from a £100 investment (Evelyn, *Diary*, June 6, 1687).

[2] German dialectal *Krawat*, for *Kroate* (Croatian).

[3] "To conclude the matter" (*OED*).

[4] Richard Knolles (*The Generall Historie of the Turkes*, London, 1638,

p. 2) lists the "Cicimeni" as one of the nations living around the fens of Maeotis in the "bare cold country of Scythia," which he considers to be the original home of the Turks.

5 Mentioned later (p. 201) as would-be politicians. Probably Abraham van den Bende, a naturalized Hollander active at the Court of Charles II, and Richard Spicer of the Treasury Office (*CSPD 1673*, p. 108; *CSPD 1676–77*, p. 574).

6 Bartholomew Fair, named for St. Bartholomew's hospital in Smithfield, had degenerated into a four-day period of license and riot for the lower classes.

To Owen Wynne   October 23, 1687
                                                              Ratisbon

Sir.

I write this to lett you see I am in a fair way of living again. Tho' I was dangerously ill the last weeke, a good constitution, which is the best Physitian every where and almost the onely one here, has soon sett me on my Leggs again. Yesterday was the first I intended to take a little fresh aire, and just as I was stepping into my Coach, word was brought me the Duke of Barwick was arriv'd. I went immediately to see him and saw him look so fresh and so well after his sickness that the joy of it I think has forwarded much the recovering of my health.

We stayd together till tenn at night, and I took my leave of him at five this morning, not being able to prevail with him to stay a day and unweary himself. You will have him before this will come to your hands, for he told me he intended to be in England in ten days, which made me send by him to my Lord what I intended to have writ to his Lordship concerning the Count Caunitz's being made one of the Emperor's secret Council, and that there is a treaty in hand about the furnishing the Emperor with some Troops the next Campagne, but it is not yet perfected tho' some give out as it were. As soon as it is I will send you the conditions agreed on.

All the talke now here is of Dunewald's advancing as far as Belgrade, and no body knows how far he may push the Turks in the consternation they are in, especially if he can, as is endeavour'd, engage the Army, which in the mutiny have revolted from the Grand Vizir, to accept of conditions offer'd them.

I have answer'd your letter long since in which was a proposition for returning my money. I cou'd not guess what you meant by Guldiners, but let me know what the gentleman dos expect in England for 100 Crowns currant money here, and I will suddainly tell you whether it will be for both our advantages or no.

If you cannot send the black lac'd hood and scarlet worsted stockins which I mention'd in a former letter to you in any time by our Abbot, pray venture to enclose them in two packets, and let me have them by the Post. I am, Sir, &c.

I am just now going to meet on the road the Count de Crecy and his Lady, whom we expect this day.

Source: H-1, pp. 188–190; *LB*, pp. 278–279.

TO THE EARL OF MIDDLETON   October 27, 1687
                                                            Ratisbon

My Lord.

I thought I had recover'd my health when I writ my last of the 13th Instant to Mr. Wynne, but I have since found I was deceiv'd, and I have got a double tertian ague, which (tho' it torments me sufficiently) dos not make me apprehend the loosing of any thing but the miserable diversions of this place for a time. On the 14th my Lord Dongan arriv'd here and the next day went easily on in a Coach for Francfort, not being yet well enough recover'd of his Sickness to endure the fatigue of going Post.

The same day the Count de Crecy and his Lady arriv'd from Paris; he was yesterday to see me, and I find he has instructions strongly to defend his Masters right of Building Forts in what part he pleases of the Lands yielded him in Soveraignty. Nothing has pass'd as yet between him and the Ministers but visits of Ceremony. He gave the Con-Commissary, and not the Count de Windisgratz (who looks upon himself as chief of the Imperiall Commission), notice of his arrivall. This Count gives out he has desir'd the Emperor to recall him from this place, but few believe he wou'd seeke of himself to quit an Employment which yields him eighteen thousand florins a year.

The truth is the Emperor can not perswade any Prince of the Empire to accept of being Principall Commissioner while he continues the Count de Windisgratz here with the Power he has given him. But upon his being recalled, he may find enough who will accept of it; and the Emperor may save his Pension of 18,000 florins, which will be a weighty point against the Count (as money-matters stand) without he has better friends than he is reported to have amongst the chief Ministers at Vienna, who admire him for his great learning in the Institutes and Codes, but do not much love his haughty and violent temper.

155

They talk at Vienna and here of two Princes (Saxe Lawenberg and Herman of Baden[1]), one of which is to come hither. All the Duke of Lorrains friends hope it will be the Prince of Baden, and it may be the Emperor is perswaded that the President of his Council of War and his Generall shou'd have a better understanding. I am, My Lord, Your Lordship's most faithfull and most obedient Servant

Geo: Etherege

Source: M-2, ff. 98–100; H-1, pp. 190–191; *LB*, pp. 279–281. Written in Hughes' hand but signed by Etherege.

[1] Hermann, Margrave of Baden (1628–1691), was a Prince of the Empire, a field marshal, and President of the Imperial Council of War. In 1688 he was appointed Principal Commissioner at the Diet.

TO OWEN WYNNE   October 27, 1687

Dito

Sir.

I receiv'd yours of the 30th of September yesterday which found me in a fitt of a double tertian ague, and tho' I hope I may be rid of it before I can have an answer of this letter, yet I must desire you to employ your interest with some friend to inform me of the best way of preparing and taking the Quinquina. I know not whom to direct you to since Dr. Short[1] is dead, who was the Physitian I loved best and chiefly made use of. He has given it me formerly according to Tabors[2] maner. Pray likewise send me the receipt of what we commonly call the Bitter Potion, both of that which purges and of that which dos not. I am pretty confident I shall have no need of them by that time I have your answer, but it will not be amiss to have them lye by one in this Countrey.

We have lately lost the fine weather we had, and now we have nothing but great fogs, high winds, and allmost continuall rains, besides the variety of an Earthquake which rockd the Town so favourably the other day that none but such who by experience knew the thing had any aprehension of the danger. I am, &c.

Source: H-1, pp. 191–192; *LB*, pp. 281–282.

[1] Dr. Thomas Short, a prominent Roman Catholic physician.

[2] Sir Robert Tabor, or Talbor (c. 1642–1681), was thought to have saved the life of Charles II by his improved method of administering quinquina bark. Since Tabor was only an apothecary at the time, Dr. Short got permission for him to administer the drug. Tabor was appointed physician in ordinary to the King and was knighted in 1678.

Omitted: October 30, 1687. To Middleton, reporting relief from his fever, with diplomatic news.

Source M-2, f. 101; H-1, p. 192; *LB,* p. 282.

Dito [October 30, 1687]

To Mr. Corbet. and
To Sir Peter Wyche
Source: H-1, p. 193.

To HENRY GUY   November 3, 1687
                              Ratisbon 23 Oct./ 2 [deleted] Nov. 87 [1]

Sir.

I have spar'd you so long that I begin to fear you may think I grow negligent in paying you the acknowledgements I owe you. It wou'd be a fine thing if I, who am here at school to learn the affaires and Interests of Princes, shou'd be such a blockhead as to forget my own. I wish I were near the Sea or some River which runs your way that, instead of this dull tribute, I might send you some of our good wine to put you in minde of me in your cheerfull houres.

As for our women, they are a Commodity which will turn to no account in England, especially to you who as well as myself have by a long experience of the frailties of the Sex allmost acquir'd a perfect Chastitie. But while we approach this vertue, let us take care our years do not sower us with any of the common vices of age. Let us still preserve our good humor and our good nature to make us wellcome near those young people who possess that plentifull Estat we have pretty well run out of, that we may help them rail at the morose and cry out with fallstaff, "Down with them; they hate us Youth." [2] I have lost the conversation of my friends, but the benefit which I enjoy by your favour of not being so uneasy abroad as I might be in an other matter keeps me from being altogether unhappy. This can never be enough own'd by my being all my life, Sir, etc.

Source: H-1, pp. 193–194; *LB,* pp. 282–283.

[1] The following letter (H-1, p. 194) indicates the correct date: "Dito being the 3 Nov./24 Oct. 87.'
[2] In BM, f. 140, this passage appears as:
                              (youth)
              "They hate us [young men]."

Omitted: November 3, 1687. To Middleton with a brief description of the new Principal Commissioner, Hermann of Baden.

Source: M-2, ff. 103–104; H-1, pp. 194–195; *LB,* pp. 283–284.

157

Dito [November 3, 1687]

To Mrs. Merry.
Source: H-1, p. 195.

To The Earl of Middleton   November 6, 1687
                                                            Ratisbon
My Lord.

His Catholick Majestie has given lately the Golden Fleece to Fowerteene, among which Number are the Count de Caunitz and the Count de Windisgratz. The last has particularly deserv'd it of him, in refusing to Signe the Truce in behalfe of the Spaniards at the time when it was Sign'd betweene the Empire and France, which cost them three millions, besides Luxembourg. He has leave to go to Vienna to receive the Order, so that before his returne and the coming of our New Principal Comissarie it is not expected much will be done here.

The States of Hungarie will struggle at the meeting at Presbourg to preserve their right of Election; but as the case stands, they will be faine to Submit to the Emperor's will.[1]

The Director of the Diette yesterday treated his Bretheren of the Electorall Colledge, and the French Plenipotentiarie sate president of the Feast. I was likewise invited, and notwithstanding my late sickness, I ventur'd to go, but had liberty to drink what I pleas'd.

In the Evening the Duke of Berwick's Equipage arriv'd here. They rest to day and to morrow continue their Journey. I am, My Lord, Your Lordships most faithfull and most humble Servant

                                                    Geo: Etherege
Source: M-2, ff. 105–106; H-1, pp. 195–196; LB, pp. 284–285.

[1] The rump Diet of the Estates of Hungary which met at Pressburg was too weak to refuse the Emperor's demand that the crown of Hungary become hereditary in the Hapsburg family instead of elective.

Dito [November 6, 1687]

To Dr. Wynne with the Italian Gazett.
Source: H-1, p. 196.

Omitted: November 13, 1687. To Middleton, reporting disputes over the French forts in the Rhineland.
Source: M-2, ff. 107–108; H-1, pp. 196–197; LB, pp. 285–286.

Omitted: November 17, 1687. To Middleton, enclosing a copy of the Commission decree on the Moselle fortress.
Source: H-1, p. 198; *LB,* pp. 286–287.

[November 17, 1687]
To Mr. Bridgeman. and
Mr. Wynne.
Source: H-1, p. 198.

Omitted: November 20, 1687. To Wynne, reporting (incorrectly) the coronation of the Archduke of Hungary.
Source: H-1, pp. 198–199; *LB,* p. 287.

[November 20, 1687]
To my Lady Etherege.
Mr. Will. Richard and
Sir Peter Wyche.
Source: H-1, p. 199.

Omitted: November 24, 1687. A news letter, unaddressed and unsigned, but in Etherege's hand.
Source: M-2, ff. 109–110.

To Sir Edward Vaudrey   November 24, 1687
                                                                     Ratisbon
Sir.

Since I have had the Honor to know the Duke of Barwick, I have been so engag'd by his Charming qualities that I cannot but continually wish for his prosperity, and tho' I am too inconsiderable to be able to do him any service myself, I cannot forbear stirring up those who I believe may have it in their power, among which number the opinion I have of your prudence and experience makes me reckon you.

Ambition never wants a Room in the Souls of young men who are born with those advantages his Grace has. Yet there is a certain modesty in Youth which makes them stand in need of a good friend to push them on, or else they run the hazard of loosing the favours of fortune as they often do those of a Mistress for want of being

159

undertaking enough. This is a business most proper for you to minde, and never to lett that croud of pleasures which will be always courting of him make him forget what is more essentiall to make him great and happy.

It is naturall to mankind to love them best whom they have most oblig'd, partly out of fondness for the work which they have brought nearer to perfection and partly because they think they may have more confidence in them. This makes Princes, the more they do for their favourites, still love them better and imagin they can hardly give them sufficient proofs of their kindness. Tho' my Lord Duke has the greatest share in his Majesties favour, it is not impossible this way to improve it, and the fresh marks which he receives of that will encrease the Esteem and reputation which he has already in the world.

The thing I mention'd to you when last I saw you I think almost absolutely necessary for him to get. It is what the favorite has still enjoy'd, as you will find if you reflect in what hands it has usually been. I have been so long absent from Court that I cannot judge as well as you of the measures that are to be taken for the obtaining it. Never the less give me leave to say in generall that as Princes make alliances in order to bring about their designs, so courtiers ought to make freinds which may facilitate what they aime at. It is not amiss to be well with some Lord of the Treassury who is most active and has most opportunities of being near his Majestie. He, in case any recompence be requir'd in lieu, may find out a way to make the Satisfying of it more easy. The Ministers who are most in reputation and can with more freedom speak to his Majesty ought to be sought. They will be always seasonably putting the King in minde of my Lord Duke and of his Merit.

The approbation of other men, especially of the judicious, makes us grow fonder of what we love, and a Prince's inclination by often hearing the object prais'd seldom failes of growing into a violent passion. Thus women in courts have been talk'd into their arms, and when their beauty has been decay'd have kept their posts by the tongues of their faction. The Garter is a feather he must not want in his Cap, and he must leave the Choice of his wife wholely to the King. It is a presumption in me to write on this Subject to you, wherefore I will not tire you with any more Impertinences. I hope my Lord Duke and yourself will look on what I have say'd already as the Extravagance of my Zeal and on that score forgive, Sir, &c.

Source: H-1, pp. 199–201; *LB*, pp. 287–289.

To Mr. Wynne about my concerns. [Last two words deleted.] With a paper of news for my Lord.

Ratisbon November 27, 1687

To Mr. Wynne and
Mr. George Etherege.
   Source: H-1, p. 201.

TO THE EARL OF MIDDLETON   December 1, 1687
                                     Ratisbon

My Lord.

I thought I shou'd have sent you to day a Copy of the Count de Crecys Memorial, which I have so often promis'd in my Letters lately, but the Count, who is not onely an able Minister but a Bel Esprit and of the Academie, is so hard to please that he is faine to take a great deal of pains and after all can scarse please himselfe. I know not whether this is a defect or a virtue in man, but I begin to be sensible it is a signe of growing Old, which is no good thing. The order has been chang'd; the Expressions often polish'd and fil'd. He has read it to me, and impartially speaking I think the French Armes had not more advantage of the Germans when the Truce was sign'd then his arguments have of the Count de Windisgratz's, who drew up the Decree of Comission. Nevertheless, were he not press'd in time, I believe he wou'd be taking of it in peices again. Few have so working and so indefatigable a brain. To morrow it will be Dictated, and on thursday I hope to be able to keep my word with your Lordship.

The Court is still at Presbourg and we have no news of the Coronation. That which makes the Hungarians so stubbornly opose the abolishing the Law which I mention'd in a paper enclos'd in a Letter to Mr. Wynne is the severity which was us'd in the prosecution of those who were in the Conspiracy with Tekely the last yeare, many being put to Death without the usuall formes of Justice, and it is said they are so much insens'd at this that they demand Justice of the Emperor against the Author of those illegall proceedings.

The last week arriv'd here Monsieur Smettau, who comes as principal Minister for the Elector of Brandenbourg. He married Monsieur Fux's daughter, one of the ablest ministers the Elector has and who is now employ'd at the Treaty at Altena.[1] Smettau is well bred and has the reputation of being a man of parts. He liv'd formerly in the Court of Heidelberg and was sent into England by the late Elector Palatin about the Jewells which Prince Rupert left to Mrs. Hughs.[2] I am, My Lord, Your Lordship's most faithfull and most humble servant

Geo: Etherege

The Count de Windisgratz gave yesterday notice to the Dyet of the taking of Erla.[3]

Source: M-2, f. 112; H-1, pp. 202–203; *LB*, pp. 289–290.

---

[1] Altona, near Hamburg, was the site of a conference to settle the controversy over Schleswig between Denmark and the Duke of Holstein-Gottorp.
[2] After the death of Prince Rupert in 1682, his mistress, the actress Margaret Hughes, gambled away the jewels he had left her.
[3] This postscript, written in the margin in Hughes' hand, was contradicted by Etherege in his next letter to Middleton. Actually, Erlau (the German name for the Hungarian town of Eger) was surrendered about a week later.

Dito [December 1, 1687]

To Mr. Bridgeman.
Mr. Manlove and
Mr. Robson with an order for 300 £ for Österlin.[1]
Source: H-1, p. 203.

---

[1] On December 31, 1688, Etherege wrote in French a memo of his indebtedness (108 florins, 45 kreutzers) to a "Monsieur Osterlin," presumably a moneylender. See below, p. 263.

Omitted: December 4, 1687. To Middleton, with the demands made on the Empire by the Elector of Brandenburg.
Source: M-2, ff. 113–114; H-1, pp. 203–204; *LB*, pp. 291–292.

Dito [December 4, 1687]

To Mr. Wynne about the Hoods and stockins.
Source: H-1, p. 204.

Omitted: December 7, 1687. To the Duke of Lorraine, in French, forwarding a letter from James II.
Source: H-1, pp. 204–205; *LB*, p. 292.

Sir (Mr. Cooke)

I shou'd envie the good fortune of the poor Clerk, as you are pleas'd to call him, who has so long satt at the healm in a Secretary of State's warm office, had I not a particular friendship for him, and did I not know his great parts and Industry deserve that profitable and eminent Post. Let him live long in perfect health, that he may the better tast the happiness he enjoys. In return you can do no less than pitty me, who have been forc'd from the shoar of the delightfull Thames to be confin'd to live on the Banks of the unwholesome Danube, where we have been this moneth choak'd with fogs and cannot now sett a foot out of doors without being up to the knee in snow.

The muses when they were banish'd Greece travell'd westward and have establish themselves in other Countreys but cou'd never find in their hearts to dwell here. The Mountains are the abode of wolves and Bears, and the inhabitants of the Towns have something fierce and rugged in their natures. My weak fancy may well suffer here, when the noble Genius of Ovid was dejected at Pontus, and you cannot but forgive the fondness I have for London shou'd I cry out when I shutt this letter: *Hei mihi, quod domino non licet ire tuo.*[1] In the mean time I comfort myself as well as I can, forget Julia,[2] and sute my inclinations to the diversions the Climate affords, the best of which is hunting.

> Manet sub jove frigido
> Venator, tenera Conjugis immemor.[3]

Pray be not so malicious to let the meaning of this come to my wife's ear.

It is not much out of season to wish you a merry Christmas and as good a stomach to the Plumbroth as an old servant of my Grandfather's had, whose onely grace all the good time was "God love me as I love Plum pottage." I will find out a way ere long to engage you and Doctor Wynne to remember me. I hope when I return into England to find your body as vigorous as I find your minde in your favour of the 14th of October last to &c.

Source: H-1, pp. 205–206; *LB*, pp. 293–294.

[1] Ovid, *Tristia*, I, l. 2. With the preceding line, this can be translated "Little book—nor do I begrudge it—you will go to Rome. Alas that your master is not permitted to go."

[2] Miss Rosenfeld and later commentators have assumed that this is the

name of the comedienne from Nuremberg with whom Etherege had an affair. Actually, as J. H. Wilson has shown (*Modern Language Notes*, 62 [1947], 40), the reference is to Ovid's Julia. We do not know the name of the comedienne.

[3] Horace, *Odes*, I, 1, ll. 25–26. "The hunter remains beneath the cold sky, forgetful of his tender wife."

Omitted: December 8, 1687. To Middleton, about negotiations between the Elector of Brandenburg and the Emperor.
Source: M-2, ff. 115–116; H-1, pp. 207–208; *LB,* pp. 294–295.

Omitted: December 11, 1687. To Sunderland, commenting on the arguments over the French fortifications on the Rhine.
Source: H-1, pp. 208–210; *LB,* pp. 295–297.

Omitted: December 11, 1687. To Middleton, enclosing documents and a paper of news from Vienna.
Source: M-2, ff. 117–118; H-1, pp. 210–211; *LB,* pp. 297–298.

Ratisbon December 15, 1687
To Mr. Robson with an order to pay 15 £ to Mrs. Merry out of the Extraordinaries.
To Mr. William Richards with an order annulling that of Mr. Smithsby for receiving the Pension from the Privy Purse.
To Mr. Graham.
To Mrs. Merry with the order for 15 £ on Mr. Robson.
To Mr. Richard Etherege.
To Mr. George Etherege.
Source: H-1, p. 212.

Omitted: December 15, 1687. To Wynne, miscellaneous diplomatic news.
Source: H-1, pp. 212–213; *LB,* pp. 298–299.

Ratisbon December 16, 1687
To Mr. Wynne with the news of the Coronation [of the Archduke Joseph] and of Erla's Capitulating.
Source: H-1, p. 213.

Omitted: December 18, 1687. To Middleton, reporting diplomatic news from Brandenburg, Hungary, and Baden.
Source: M-2, ff. 119–121; H-1, pp. 213–214; *LB,* pp. 299–300.

To The Earl of Middleton   December 22, 1687
                                                    Ratisbon

My Lord.

The Emperor lately goeing a hunting was by a soddain Flood hinder'd from returning to Presbourg. He came to Vienna and lay there one night and the next day went back where the setling the affaires of Hungarie will keep him yet a Month or six weeks.

Prince Herman of Baden is still at Court, and his Famely will not consent he shall come hither till he has Justified himselfe against Caraffa,[1] which cannot be before the Emperor has dispatch'd the publique business with the States.

Here is a report that the Turks have left Gradisca and that Generall Dunwald has not men enough to spare to Garison it. In the mean time we have yet no confirmation of their leaving Erla on the Capitulation which I have sent you.

The Diette has shut up shop and you are to expect no marchandise from hence till after the Holydays, so that I have nothing to do now but to wish your Lordship a Merry Christmas and many happy new Years. Since I am a wishing, I hope you will give me leave to wish a little for myselfe, too: that I may live to enjoy your favour long and be in a Condition to be better able to shew you that I am with all Duty and with a perfect inclination, My Lord, Your Lordship's most faithfull most humble and most Obedient Servant

                                                    Geo: Etherege

Source: M-2, ff. 123–124; H-1, p. 215; *LB,* p. 301.

[1] Antonio, Count Caraffa, an Austrian general infamous for the cruelty with which he punished the Protestant citizens of Eperjes, Hungary. His special court had accused Prince Hermann of secret correspondence with the Hungarian rebel, Tököloy.

                                        Dito [December 22, 1687]

To Sir Peter Wyche
    Source: H-1, p. 215.

To The Earl of Dover   December 28, 1687
                                                    Ratisbon

My Lord.

The advantage I have had by being sent hither was not enough to make me forget what I left in London, but the honor you have been pleas'd to do me makes me now forget the loss of all I enjoy'd there. Your letter has made me more vain than I ever was on a lucky run at Play, or on receiving a kind note from a Mistress, but this vanity is not the effect of the unjust praise you give me in it, but of the assurance I have by it of your favour.

The life I have lead has afforded me little time to turn over bookes, but I have had leisure sufficient while I idly rowl'd about the Town to look into my self and know when I am too highly valu'd. This makes me sensible I can never be out of your debt by writing. One obliging expression of yours is worth more than a thousand of my aery imaginations. All men must be of my mind who preferr le Solide aux badinages. You are naturally gallant, and it has not been the custome of your family to loose that inclination early. This makes me think there may be a beauty who with a few stroaks of her pen is able to convince you that one tender word outweighs all the wit which was ever writ.

The passion which has most power over me is faithfully to serve his Majesty and to endeavour to be well with them who by their merits are particularly prefer'd to his favour. In making my Court to you in this nature, I am sure I cannot committ the fault which may make me forfeit your good Opinion. The price I set on that makes every line you have sent me so dear to me that you may reckon you have already contributed more than I shall be ever able to deserve to the happyness and good fortune of &c.

Source: H-1, pp. 216–217; *LB*, pp. 301–302.

To Henry Guy   December 28, 1687
                                                          Dito
Sir.

You have made me the most agreeable return I ever had since I traded in letters. I never read any thing which has so much of the Sublime in it as your short favour of the 9th of November last. The Transports of pleasure which it gave me are better arguments for that nobleness of Expression (to me at least) than any I find in Longinus, but Sublime apart, the plain way you take to assure me of your friendship has much more force than all the froth of Rhetorick; the Stile you are Master of is the best to perswade the men and the properest to engage the women. When you wou'd play off your rest, you need but choose your Gamester; 'tis your own fault if the partie be refus'd.

While I remember you of your happiness, I cannot but reflect on my Misfortune. I want the onely Charme which so late in the year is capable to warm them. This confirms me the Cardinal was wise

166

who say'd, le belle lettere sono le lettere di cambio.[1] You see I know how to value the proofs I receive of your Kindness. I wish I knew as well how to give you as solid proofs of my gratitude and of that faithfullness with which I am

Source: H-1, pp. 217–218; *LB*, pp. 302–303.

[1] "The beautiful letters are bills of exchange," with a pun on *belles-lettres*.

UNADDRESSED[1]   December 29, 1687
                                                 Ratisbon

I was very much surpris'd, Sir, with your letter. Such a proof of being remember'd by one I love at this distance is what I have been little us'd to. In gratitude I shou'd say much on this subject, but I know you will take it as kindly if I onely think it. You may without jealousy let me keep my complements for those whom I know not how to entertain without them. The women need not rail at our changing; few of us have the gift to be constant to our selves. Sir Charles Sedley sets up for good houres and Sobriety, my Lord [Dorset] has given over variety and shuts himself up within my Ladys arms as you informe me, and late as it is Will Richards begins to pretend to Secrecy, for the devil a word he has ever writ me about my Lady Morland.[2]

Notwithstanding the Ebbing and flowing in the flesh, my mind is a kind of lake and has the same standing pleasures it had in London, Wine and women. But our good fellows are far from being wits, and our whores are yet farther from being beautys. The Town is too little to hid us and the liberty of talking is too great, so that poor lovers like Hares in releifing time are fain to clicket up and down in the Gardins at Midnight. I have a very convenient one belonging to my house. I wish the Rent of it may not cost me too dear some time or other.

I have good horses and often go a hunting. Were I to write to Tom Crud or Roger Wood, this wou'd afford me wherewithall to fill one side of paper. I bungle away now and then a morning at Tennis. Here is a pretty carré Court[3] and players so exactly siz'd for Sir Charles that were he here, he wou'd live in it.

Here are two very handsome young Ladys, but their unconscionable price is marriage. Never the less were I as capable of a belle passion as some at my age are, they wou'd have cost me many a billet and much time in tying my Cravat at 'em, but I cannot think of laying a Siege wanting a stock of things necessary to carry it on and strength sufficient to maintain the place in case I shou'd take it.

Meethinks it is below Bob Woosley's[4] gravity to engage in a war with the Minor Poets. I shou'd pitty him did I not believe the Exercise will do him more good than taking the air at Banstead did. I wear flanel,[5] Sir, wherefore pray talk to me no more of Poetry. If you know any friend of ours in whalebone bodys who has an itch that way give him good advise. Tis time to lay down the Cudgels, before the women lay us on too heavily.

I have ever enjoy'd a liberty of opinion in matters of Religion. 'Tis indifferent to me whether there be an other in the world who thinks as I do. This makes me have no temptation to talk of the business, but quietly following the light within me, I leave that to them who were born with the ambition of becoming Prophets or Legislators. 'Tis not amiss to see an humble Clergy. They are more like the Holymen in the primitive time, but it wou'd be very hard to be excommunicated for fornication, it being a point all the differing Churches agree in. You have done very well to excuse me from giving you an account of foraign affaires. Now I reflect on't it wou'd be as impertinent in me as if a Sollicitor or an Atturny shou'd entertain a man who hates a Law Suite with all the causes depending in his County.

Besides the diversions I have mention'd, there is one thing which makes me more patiently bear with the loss of my friends in England, which no other Country can repair. It is the kindness I find from those who manage the Treasury. Were it possible for me to write any Thing which cou'd be as wellcome to you as your letter is to me, you shoud have twenty for one. Our imaginations are but the effects of Ideas we take in, and having but little to work on in this barren place, I hope you will excuse the dulness of etc.

Source: H-1, pp. 218–220; *LB*, pp. 303–305.

[1] At the bottom of the left margin, where Etherege in his holograph letters usually wrote the name of the addressee, is the single capital letter "H".

[2] Sir Samuel Morland, Pepys' tutor at Cambridge, "being almost distracted for want of monies," was tricked into marrying a supposed heiress who was actually a penniless coachman's daughter turned whore (Arthur Bryant, *Samuel Pepys, the Saviour of the Navy*, London, 1953, p. 149).

[3] The smaller variety of tennis court (V. de S. Pinto, *Sir Charles Sedley*, p. 75) and hence suited to the short stature of Sir Charles.

[4] Robert Wolseley had been engaged in an exchange of verse satire with William Wharton, son of Philip, Baron Wharton. In *The Duel*, Dorset attacked both: "the bloodless rhyming strife" of Will Maevius (Wharton) and Bob Bavius (Wolseley). But the strife did not remain bloodless; on December 9, 1687, Wolseley gave Wharton a mortal wound, for which he was outlawed (Brice Harris, *Charles Sackville*, pp. 110–112).

[5] Since the law required that people be buried in woolen shrouds, the phrase "to wear flannel" referred to old age (*OED*).

168

To Mr. William Richards and
To Mr. Wynne.
  Source: H-1, p. 220.

Omitted: January 1, 1688. To Middleton, reporting the surrender of
Erla and news of the Diet.
  Source: M-2, ff. 125–126; H-1, pp. 221–222; *LB,* pp. 306–307.

Dito [January 1, 1688]

Mr. Corbet

Ratisbon January 5, 1688

To Mr. Manlove
Mr. Wynne
  Source: H-1, pp. 222–223.

To THOMAS MAULE   January 5, 1688 [1]
                                                                              Dito

(Mr. Maul.)
  You are so ingenious, Sir, that I know you need but little time to
make you perfect in whatever you apply yourself to. This makes me
not wonder you are already so arrant a Courtier. A poor friend who
is unable to do you any service is forgot, and the onely thing you
minde is your interest. This is the third letter I send you without
having the favour of one line from you. I shou'd complain did I not
think it wou'd be to as little purpose as for an unfortunate lover to
reproach a faithless Mistress. I know your severall employments take
up so much of your time that so good a husband of it as you are
cannot without regret throw away one minite, but at the same time
I know that they who love well, tho' never so nearly watch'd, will
find an opportunity to satisfy their Inclination.
  If you think it worth while to appease me, for I cou'd not forbear
letting you see I am a little angry, make me an excuse, true or false,
it is all one. It cannot miss of a good effect on a heart which you are
master of. I live in a place of Ceremoney, and according to the rule
I shou'd not congratulate you on your being made Gentleman of the
Prince's Bed-Chamber before you have given me notice of it, but I
think you have not much studie'd those trifles which employ most
of the serious hours of the Ministers here. But to be serious myself,
I assure you the joy I have when I hear of your good fortune is not
at all inferior to that which the greater men at Whitehall give me

when I receive infallible Testimonies of their favour, and it will never be otherwise, I am so unalterably, Sir, etc.

Source: H-1, pp. 223–224; *LB*, pp. 307–308.

1 Misdated in BM and *LB* as January 1.

Dito [January 5, 1688]
To My Lady Etherege and
Mr. Maul

Ratisbon January 8, 1688
To my Lord Abbot.
Source: H-1, p. 224.

To Edmund Poley   January 12, 1688
                                                   Ratisbon
Sir.

You had heard from me sooner but that I was in hope of sending you something from the Countess of Stubenberg, which might have made my letter more wellcome. I was deceiv'd and cou'd get nothing but a Complement in return of your favour; I shall not repeat it, it being the usuall one women make when an old acquaintance makes them sensible he has not forgot them. Comfort yourself; poor Aurelia's growing old and cannot send you any thing acceptable, unless she send you her eldest daughter—

No grape was ere so kindly ripe
so plump, so smooth, so full of Juce.1

Wonder not this shoud be so soon; there is a sort of this fruit which is very early. I know not what Stockholm produces, but all the rest of our fräwlins are but wildings in comparison. Our Souths and Our Swans in England might find fault with her Courtsie, but all our men wou'd like her face, to pin the basket. My Lady Grafton2 never had a better. Yet I must confess I am a Fop in my heart; ill customes influence my very Senses, and I have been so us'd to affectation that without the help of the aer of the Court, what is naturall cannot touch me. You see what we get by being polish'd, as we call it.

Monsieur Schmettau tells me he had the good fortune to see you at Hambourg, and has often mention'd you with much esteem. If the Dyet were compos'd of a few more ministers like him I shou'd spend my time much more to my liking here. Your old friend Monsieur

Schnolsky laughs and talks on, is still the same man. No body can distinguish between his jest and earnest. I had like to have lost him wholely by my being in disgrace with the Count de Windisgratz, but his natural biass inclines him now and then to see me, tho' he ventures a Chiding for it.

I have sent you a paper of what has been lately done here with a little news from other parts. I have onely to add that last night we had advice from Cologne that the Cardinall de Fürstenberg[3] is chosen Coadjutor there. The Count de Caunitz has not had very good Success in his two last negotiations, tho' he has the golden Fleece and is made one of the Emperors secret Council, but the Elector of Bavaria has done enough the last Campagne to merit his friend shou'd be consider'd. Tell the Count de Dona I am overjoy'd to hear he comes to Vienna and do not dispair of an occasion to see him. I have given you good measure and can scarce forbear beginning an other sheet to you, I am so much, sir, etc. You are often obligingly remember'd by the Count de Crecy and his Lady. Her onely quarrell to you and to me is that we are Hereticks. I think she believes you the most obstinate.

Source: H-1, pp. 224–226; *LB,* pp. 308–310.

[1] Etherege remembers, not quite accurately, some lines from Suckling's *A Ballad upon a Wedding:* "No grape, that's kindly ripe, could be/So round, so plump, so soft as she,/Nor half so full of juice."

[2] Isabella Bennet, daughter of the Earl of Arlington, was married at the age of five to Henry Fitzroy, Duke of Grafton, a son of Charles II and Lady Castlemaine. In 1679, at age 12, she was remarried to the Duke. Evelyn describes her as a most beautiful child and woman (*Diary,* November 6, 1679; November 26, 1683).

[3] Cardinal William Egon von Fürstenberg (1629–1704) was supported by the French as candidate for the Electorship of Cologne. The Empire supported the young Prince Clement of Bavaria, whose ratification in 1688 precipitated the War of the League of Augsburg.

[January 12, 1688]
To Mr. Wynne about the Election of Cardinal of Furstenberg Coadjutor at Cologne with a relation of the Grand Seignors being depos'd.
Source: H-1, p. 226.

To Count De Thun   [January 12, 1688][1]

Monsieur.

Depuis que nous nous sommes separé a Amsterdam Je me suis toujours consolé de la perte que je fis alors en me flattant que je

171

pourrois trouver une occasion de vous revoir un peu de temps apres que Je serois établi icy. Il y a long temps que Je scay que vous estes a Munique, et picqué d'impatience de vous voir j'ay tache d'obtenir permission de m'absenter de mon Poste pour quelques jours, pour faire ce petit voyage mais sans y pouvoir reussir. J'ay appris avec beaucoup de plaisir que la fortune s'est repantie de vous avoir un peu mal traitté en Angleterre, et qu'a la fin Elle s'est rangée du Coste du merite, et dans des affaires plus solide que le jeu Elle s'est declarée pour vous et pour vostre illustre famille.

Si je pouvois scavoir que son Altesse Electorale n'iroit point ailleurs chercher des Divertissements dans ce Carnavall, peutestre que je viendrais vous rendre visite, et demeurer un jour ou deux pour voir les galanteries de la Cour, ou il y a maintenant un Gentilhomme que est fort de mes amis, Monsieur le Marquis de Duheron. Je ne scay si vous le connoissez. Ce n'est pas assez de le voir, Il le faut bien observer, car il est adroit a se cacher. Il est homme d'Esprit et de coeur et a toutes les belles qualitez requises pour le faire bien aimer, tant dans les Cours que dans les Camps. Il n'est pas mal fait, et les femmes couroient risque, s'il ne negligeoit pas trop sa barbe. Il a fait plusieurs Compagnes en Hongrie, et il y a quelques trois années passées qu'il fit une action[2] si belle et si genereuse, sur une dispute touchant le Roy Mon Maistre et le feu Duc de Monmouth, que tout ce qu'il y a des honnestes gens de mon pais luy sont redevables. Ne vous laissez pas tromper à son air froid; il est Norman et ne va pas si vite en besoign que les autres francois. Si vous luy pouvez rendre quelque bon office où vous avez du pouvoir, Je vous asseure qu'il n'est pas d'humeur d'estre Ingrat, et Je vous en veux estre si fortement Caution que Je le tiendray comme fait à moy mesme.

J'ay beaucoup à vous dire de mon pais que vous ne seriez pas faché d'entendre, et quelques choses à vous communiquer qui me touchent dans vostre pais. Ce sont des affaires plus propres pour une conversation que pour une lettre. J'espere d'avoir l'occasion que Je me promet de vous mettre mon coeur en main, afin que vous en epuisiez toutes ses veritez. Vous qui estes le plus honneste et le plus genereux de tous les hommes que j'ay jamais connu ne pouvois pas, sans faire tort à vostre grand merite et à mon peu de jugement, vous méfier que Je sois sans aucune reserve, Monsieur, etc.

Source: H-1, pp. 226–228; *LB*, pp. 310–312.

[1] Undated in H-1 and BM, but presumably the same day as the preceding letter.

[2] The incident which led Etherege to admire the Marquis du Héron is described in a letter of August 1, 1686, to Middleton.

Ratisbon January 15, 1688
To Mr. Wynne with a Copie of the letter from Cologne about the Election.
Source: H-1, p. 228.

To The Earl of Middleton January 19, 1688
Ratisbon

My Lord.

This day we expect to hear that the Emperor is come to Vienna. The setling the affaires of Hungarie is put off to an other Diette. The season of the year and the absence of the Count de Windisgratz makes the Ministers here think of nothing but sliding and Feasting. The Comte left a paper to be made publique when he went for Presbourg which is a satyr on some of the Electoralls, who are preparing an answer to wellcome him at his returne. This quarrell among our Major ministers will not prove so fatal as that which has been betweene your Minor Poets.[1] I am glad to hear our Abott has got something. I want him here extreamely and wou'd not have my Lord Melford[2] debauch him. I hope he is so continent that nothing can tempt him to leave his old wife and go a whoring into Scotland.

All is in blood and confusion at Constantinople, the Rebells wanting mony to satisfie the Army after the deposing of the Sultan. This and the height the difference is grown to betweene his Christian Majestie and his Holyness fills all the politick mouths of this Town. I am, My Lord, Your Lordships most faithfull and most humble Servant

Geo Etherege

Source: M-2, ff. 128–129; H-1, pp. 228–229; *LB*, pp. 312–313.

[1] A reference to the death of William Wharton after a duel with Robert Wolseley. See above, p. 168, n. 4.
[2] John Drummond, Earl of Melfort (1649–1714), was converted to Roman Catholicism in 1686. He followed James II to St. Germain and became leader of the Non-Compounders at the Court in exile.

To George Bradbury January 19, 1688
Dito

Mr. Bradbury.

It is so long, Sir, since I have hop'd to hear from you that I begin to despair of the favour. I shou'd have consider'd better how I might be able to deserve your friendship before I reley'd so firmly on it. More good nature than is usuall is requir'd to be mindfull of the concerns of a poor man who is at so great a distance.

You gave me long since an Imperfect account of what Mr. Smithsby had receiv'd of my pension. I remember I excepted against the interest which you reckon'd to be due on the Bond to which you have not yet made me any answer. Pray adjust the accounts with Mr. Richards and lett him send it me. I referr'd wholely to you the determining of the suite depending with West and Barbone.[1] It is now 5 or 6 Moneths since, and you have not yet acquainted me with so much as your opinion of it. I desir'd you to employ some body to search the Records about Maynard's business. My Cousin Middleton's Will[2] wo'd have given some light as to the time, but I know the world too well to be surpris'd that nothing is done on my behalf. Tho' you are unmindfull of me now, the trouble I have given you formerly will allways make me remember the obligation I have to be, Sir, Your most humble Servant

G.E.

Source: H-1, p. 229; *LB,* p. 313.

[1] An attempt to recover, from Dr. Nicholas Barbone and John West, two strips of land in Westminster given to Mary Arnold (later Lady Etherege) as security for a loan. The suit is described in detail by Dorothy Foster, *N&Q,* 153 (1927), 456–458.
[2] Sir George was legal heir to a two-thirds interest in the Manor of Hartford, Huntingdonshire, formerly owned by his grandfather's cousin William Middleton. But the property was taken over by Sir John Cotton and Robert Pulleyn, who had obtained judgments against Elizabeth Middleton's husband, Sir Thomas Bateman. Etherege was unable to produce Middleton's will and was kept out of his inheritance. See Foster, *N&Q,* 153 (1927), 472–474.

Omitted: January 19, 1688. To Wynne explaining why he sends so little news.
Source: H-1, p. 230; *LB,* pp. 313–314.

To The Earl of Sunderland   January 19, 1688
                                                                  Dito
My Lord.
I am told from England that all things are now agreed on and that my Lady Anne Spencer is suddainly to be married to my Lord Arran.[1] I cannot but congratulate with your Lordship the choice you have made of so good a son in Law. Not to mention his other eminent vertues, you know he is an industrious Courtier, and if I may take any measures from the confidences he has often made me, I can assure you he is an able Lover. I wish all manner of happiness to the

174

deserving Couple, and to your Lordship and my Lady Sonderland all the joy which your indulgence will make you capable of in seeing the young Lady well dispos'd of.

[A summary of the political situation in Europe.]

Source: H-1, pp. 231–232; *LB*, pp. 314–316.

1 James Douglas, styled Earl of Arran, later Duke of Hamilton, who was killed in a famous duel with Lord Mohun.

[January 19, 1688]

Mr. Montstephens
and Mr. Geo: Etherege.
with the news to Brother Wynne.
Source: H-1, p. 232.

To The Earl of Middleton   January 26, 1688
                                                                               Ratisbon
My Lord.

[Nothing done at the Diet.]

How to entertain you in this vacation I know not. There are changes in men as in other matters. The passion which was chief Minister and dispos'd of all things may now be in disgrace, and an other taken into favour. I know you are Mr. Secretary still, but I know not whether you are still the same Lord Middleton I left you. You may be grown as temperate as Sir Charles Sydlie and as uxurious as my Lord Dorset. 'T wou'd be a fine way then to make my Court to you to talke of wine and women. No, till you are pleas'd to instruct me better, I shall keep myself upon my guard and be as foppish as any one you have in your province. To shew you I am in earnest, I will begin from this moment, protesting I am with all respect and Duty, My very good Lord.
Source: H-1, p. 233; *LB*, pp. 316–317.

Dito

To Mr. Corbet and
Sir Peter Wyche
Source: H-1, p. 233.

Ratisbon January 29, 1688
To Sir William Trumbull about Mr. Schmettau's rememb'ring him.
With a paper of news.
To Mr. Wynne. About the Earl of Carlingford's[1] being nam'd Envoyé
Extraordinaire for the Emperor's Court.

Ratisbon February 2, 1688
To Mr. Manlove.
To Sir Peter Wyche.
    Source: H-1, p. 234.

[1] Nicholas Taaffe, 2nd Earl of Carlingford and elder brother to Francis,
Viscount Taaffe.

Omitted: February 2, 1688. A letter of miscellaneous diplomatic news
to Middleton.
    Source: M-2, ff. 130–131; H-1, pp. 234–235; *LB,* pp. 317–319.

Omitted: February 2, 1688. To Wynne, about difficulties of com-
munication with his office.
    Source: H-1, pp. 235–236; *LB,* pp. 319–320.

To The Earl of Carlingford   February 2, 1688
                                                              Dito
My Lord.
    I learnt by my last letters from England that his Majestie has been
pleas'd to name you his Envoyé Extraordinarie for Vienna, and cannot but congratulate with your Lordship your coming to a Court
where you will have so many advantages both in your affaires and in
your pleasures. The memory it yet retains of your father and the great
merit and interest of your Brother will unlock the hearts of the Ministers and engage the Civility and respect of the Courtiers to you.
    I wish your Lordship cou'd find out some way to make me service-
able to you in the post I am in. At least for old acquaintance sake I
must beg you not to rob me of the happiness of seeing you. Make
this your road, that I may have the pleasure of talking with you and
of knowing how our friends pass their time in England and whether
the poor dog and Patridge[1] is not alltogether neglected. A day or two
with you will help me to forget what I have suffer'd since I left them.

176

I have not had any correspondence with my Lord Taaff since he has been in Tyrol. News etc. I am, etc.

Source: H-1, p. 236; LB, pp. 320–321.

[1] The Dog and Partridge was a tavern on Fleet Street frequented by Etherege's friends.

Omitted: February 5, 1688. To d'Albeville, with news of the Diet and a request for news from Holland.

Source: H-1, pp. 236–237; *LB*, pp. 321–322.

Dito [February 5, 1688]

To Mr. Wynne. Of the apprehension of finding an answer to Laverdins protestation[1] in the Gazet and of inviting Monsieur d'Albeville to write.

Source: H-1, p. 237; *LB*, p. 322.

[1] The Marquis of Lavardin, French ambassador at Rome, had strongly protested the Pope's limiting of extraterritorial rights to ambassadors and their families (*LB*, p. 315).

To Owen Wynne   February 5, 1688
                                                        Ratisbon
Sir.

I am sorry to find by many Letters from Holland which are communicated to me by my friends that that ungratefull people comply no better with his Majesty's amicable intentions. The Swarms of Lyes which fly about the Empire to blacken his Majestie's just and reasonable designs at home come for the most part from that Hive where Ferguson[1] by connivance and Burnet[2] by allowance unload the poison they are swell'd with. I have expos'd the calumny and knavery of many reports and printed papers which were design'd to make evill impressions in the Protestants. Had I the advantage of being better inform'd, it may be I might do better service.

[Treaty between Denmark and Holland broken off.]

The Elector of Bavaria is set forward for Venice and like a good Husband has taken his wife with him, but intends to ease himself of her by the way and leave her with the Queen of Poland at Insprug 'till he returns. Most think it is onely a journey of pleasure. Never the less it is given out he goes to have an opportunity to conferr

177

personally with the Prince of Tuscany about a marriage with Mademoiselle de Baviere.

[News from Rome of an answer to Lavardin's protestation.]

Pray remember my most humble duty to my Lord and communicate to him what you think fit of this letter and of the news which is enclos'd. I am, Sir, your very faithfull humble servant.

Geo: Etherege

Tho' the Marquis d'Albeville has given me no notice of his arrivall in Holland, I have ventur'd a letter to invite him to a correspondence, judging it necessary for his Majestie's service.

Source: M-2, ff. 132–133. In Hughes' hand, but signed by Etherege.

1 Robert Ferguson (1637–1714), involved in both the Rye House Plot and Monmouth's Rebellion, fled to Holland in 1685 and worked in behalf of William of Orange.

2 Gilbert Burnet (1643–1715), outlawed by James II for supporting William of Orange, had become a naturalized Dutch citizen. He returned to England with the Invasion Fleet and was made Royal Chaplain and Bishop of Salisbury.

Omitted: February 9, 1688. To Middleton with news of the entertainment for the Elector of Bavaria and of libels from Holland.

Source: M-2, ff. 134–135; H-1, pp. 238–239; *LB*, pp. 323–324.

[February 9, 1688]

To Mr. Wynne with a touch about Postscripts and the Conspiracy in Transylvania.

Ratisbon February 12, 1688

To Mr. Richards with the State of the accounts with Mr. Bradbury.
To Mrs. Merry and two lines.
To Mr. Wynne with the news.
To my Lady.

Source: H-1, p. 239.

Omitted: February 12, 1688. A short note to Middleton enclosing news from Vienna.

Source: M-2, f. 136.

Expressions in a letter to Mr. Richards of the 2/12 Feb. 87/8. It is well known when play or women are in the case I am no Sleeper. I am asham'd to have given you so much trouble, but over shoes, over bootes. Pray continue your care. Remember me to all my friends at the Rose,[1] and do not forget the lilly at the Bar. I am sorry for the bright Nymph who you write me word is under a cloud. I made hay with her, I confess, while the sun shin'd, and have run the risque with many more who were nothing near so handsome of having a sad occasion to mark a black day in my Almanach. You may venture to send me the Scandall you mention. Now I am growing grave, I would not loose anything which may make me laugh.

Source: BM, f. 163; *LB*, pp. 324–325.

[1] A tavern on Russell Street, Covent Garden. It had been a meeting place for the Wits, but by 1688 it was famous as headquarters for the Rose Tavern Club, a group of supporters of William of Orange, "the so-called Treason Club" (John Carswell, *The Old Cause*, 1954, p. 68 fn.). Oddly enough, some of Etherege's friends, including Charles Godfrey, William Jephson, and probably Will Richards, were members.

To OWEN WYNNE   February 16, 1688
                                       Ratisbon
Sir.

While we have no principall Comissioner here, we have so little news stirring that I wonder how I am able to hold any reasonable correspondence with you.

[News from Denmark.]

The Elector of Bavaria's voyage, which has made so much noise, was broke the Day he shou'd have sett forwards. The Austrian Ministers ascribe the reason of it to severall affaires of State, but some letters which I have seen from that Court ascribe it to what men at his years are very subject to, a new passion for Mademoiselle Vehlin, one of the Electrice's Maids of honor, who 'tis believ'd has sacrific'd herself for her Mistresse's interest; for she may go a considerable snack while he stays at Munich, whereas had he gone to Venise, the Poor Princesse had never been call'd to twelve.

Long before I receiv'd your news paper of the 20th of the last moneth, I knew the answer the Dutch had made to Monsieur d'Albevilles' Memoriall concerning Burnet, and tho' I had no advise from England that the letter printed under Fagels[1] name was a Libell, my own reason told it me, and I have been industrious to hinder the reprinting of it here, which Valkenier had not fail'd to do in case I had not spoken to him rondly about it.

[Report of troops available for the next campaign.]

I enclose the News which comes by this Post and am, Sir, Your very humble and obedient servant.

Geo: Etherege

Source: M-2, ff. 138–139; H-1, pp. 239–240; *LB*, pp. 325–326.

In Hughes' hand but signed by Etherege.

1 Caspar Fagel (1634–1688), Grand Pensionary of Holland, had written a statement explaining why William of Orange could not approve James's Declaration of Indulgence, which suspended the laws against both Roman Catholics and Dissenters (*LB*, p. 324).

Dito [February 16, 1688]

To Mr. Bridgeman of the Duke of Lorrains Letter.
To Mr. Manlove with a note on Mr. Will Richards for 10 or 15 £.

Dito

To the Count de Thun.

Ratisbon February 19, 1688

To Mr. Wynne with the news.

Ratisbon February 23, 1688

To Mr. Manlove, about making an end of the suite.
To Mr. Wynne about the Hoods. Of an Envoyé from Tuscany expected at Munick. About his Majestie's letter to recall the Troopes from Holland.1 Of the Count de Windisgratz's being on his journey hither.

Source: H-1, pp. 240–241.

1 British soldiers, in the pay of the States General, had been in Holland since the days of Sir Philip Sidney. After a dispute with William of Orange about the appointment of a commander, James ordered the soldiers, individually, to return to England. Roman Catholics and their sympathizers did, but a good many British subjects remained in Holland, in support of William and Protestantism.

My Lord.

It is one of the boldest actions of a man's life to marry. Who ever passes that Rubicon has need of the fortune of Caesar to make him happy, but you have made so prudent a choice that you have secur'd to yourself all the joy I can wish you. The charms my Lady Anne has in her own person are sufficient for this work were they not join'd with that of being so nearly related to my Lord President. In this alliance you seem to have had an equall regard to your Love and your ambition. The daughter is the most beautifull object that you can sigh for, and the father is the best appuy this can desire.

But to be less serious with your Lordship, I have had the Honor of your confidance, and you have told me of mighty deeds you have perform'd. I shou'd be glad to be satisfy'd whether you are as great a Heroe now you fight in a good cause as when you drew your Sword in a *querelle d'Aleman*. The truth is that sorte of courrage is a little too violent for the present purpose. The business you have now on your hands is to be spun out in length, and not to be ended at once. Now the crowd of Complements is over, I hope your Lordship will pardon my presuming to write to you and to felicitate you on this occasion, since the most devoted of your clan is not with more passion than I am etc.

Source: H-1, p. 241; *LB*, p. 327.

My Lord. (Middleton)[1]

Shou'd I stay till the Dyet gives me occasion of writing to you I know not how long I shou'd wait. Those who are unacquainted with the proceedings of this assemblie wou'd wonder that where so many Ministers are met and maintain'd at so great a charge by their Masters, so little business is done and the little that is so slowly. All the news we have now is from other parts, and you have it as soon as we, if not before us. I send you what comes from Vienna, but that at this season is very inconsiderable.

All my acquaintance in London are either so busy or so lazie that I have very seldom the favour of hearing from any of them. This makes me a perfect stranger to the Town, and I know not whether there be any such thing as Love or good fellowship stirring. I was thinking of inviting Mr. Julian[2] to a correspondence, that I might at least know how scandale goes, but Monsieur Valkenier saves me that labour. You have never a Libell fix'd up in Whitehall or dispers'd elsewhere that he has not an account of in his Circular letter from Holland.

I shou'd enlarge this if I durst make bold, but I think it better to forbear till I know whether your Lordship is not grown too grave for raillerie. Be what you please, you can never be more happy than you were in Mrs. Fox's[3] days. Alas! against my will in this hard-hearted place there is not a maid of honor about Court [no not my Lady Etherege][4] who leads a more vertuous life than I do. Not to affect to be *Le Chevalier à bonne fortune*, the best adventure I have had here has been with a Comedian no less handsome and no less kind in Dutchland then Mrs. Johnson was in England. Our Ladys are ill natur'd for want of good examples; those of Vienna (as Fame says, and you ought to know whether she be a Lyar) have souls as great and sensible as either of the Coots[5] ever had, or the more Heroique Clambrasil.[6] You see, my Lord, what idlness produces. Had I had any businesse, your Modestie wou'd not have been offended with these loose lines by etc.

Source: H-1, pp. 242–243; *LB*, pp. 327–329.

[1] Hughes wrote in H-1 "My Lord (President)." Etherege deleted "(President)" and added "Middleton" in his own hand.

[2] Robert Julian, called "Secretary to the Muses," published and sold satires and libels on men and women of the Court (Brice Harris, "Captain Robert Julian, Secretary to the Muses," *ELH*, 10 [1943], 294).

[3] A Mrs. Fox is included in a list of "Irish whores" in Rochester's satire, "On the Women about Town" (*Complete Poems*, ed. David M. Vieth, 1968, p. 46).

[4] The phrase in brackets was added above the line in Etherege's hand and then deleted.

[5] "The Coots black and white," also mentioned in Rochester's list, were probably female relatives of Charles Coote, 2nd Earl of Mountrath.

[6] Lady Alice, wife of the Earl of Clanbrassil, who in 1671 was brought from Ireland in the hope that, if she could become mistress to the King, she might further Irish interests at Court, may have been the person referred to by Rochester and Etherege. Another possibility, however, is Ann, Dowager Countess of Clanbrassil, who was libeled by the Earl of Dorset (Brice Harris, *Charles Sackville*, p. 235) and by Fleetwood Shepherd (Wilson, *Court Wits*, p. 124) for her desperate eagerness to make conquests despite her age.

To Mr. Richard Etherege.
To my Lady
To Madame Neusted and
To Mr. George Etherege
Source: H-1, p. 243.

Omitted: March 1, 1688. To Middleton reporting news of Sweden and Denmark.
Source: M-2, ff. 141–142; H-1, pp. 243–245; *LB,* pp. 329–330.

Omitted: March 1, 1688. To d'Albeville: news of Dutch libels and of the Lavardin affair.
Source: H-1, pp. 245–247; *LB,* pp. 330–332.

To Sir Peter Wyche   March 1, 1688
                                       Dito

Sir.

I am in possession of your favour of the 4th of February, and tho' according to the Altena Treaty I ought to offer you nothing less than an Equivalent, yet you must be content (at least for the present) to construe this as an act of the Sincerity, Justice, and inclination I ow you, tho' you receive nothing proportionable to what your kind letters justly claim.

Our Catt the Count de Windisgratz being absent, here is nothing but playing. We maurice dance it all the night till the day peepes in upon us and sends us home to season us for an other meeting. Tho' you see we do nothing, yet I shou'd be glad to hear you at Altena do something, especially since you have nothing to excuse you as to want of matter to work upon. To speake plainer I do not mean yourself, who as I am inform'd is to appear at the Conference by his Majestie's instructions. I wish you all the sucess which your Zeal for his Majesties service and your own satisfaction can propose to you. I am etc.

                                       G.E.

Source: BM, f. 168; *LB,* p. 335.

Omitted: March 4, 1688. To Wynne, commenting on the refusal of British troops to return from Holland.
Source: M-2, ff. 143–144; H-1, p. 247; *LB,* pp. 332–333 (misdated). In Hughes' hand but signed by Etherege.

Sir.

Tho I have nothing worth the acquainting you with by this post, I cou'd not Omitt the acknowledging the obligation I have to you for your favour of the 24 of the last Moneth. The answer the States have made to his Majestie's demand of his Regiments in their service makes the greater part of the entertainment of the Ministers here. For my part I wonder not so much that those high and mighty Lords[1] shou'd want the justice to comply with his Majestie's desire as I do that our Countrey men shou'd want that loyalty for their King and that love for their countrey which every true English heart uses to be touch'd with. This makes me asham'd and angry.

I knew many of the officers when I was at the Hague and found them then so well inclin'd that I cou'd not have imagin'd in so little time to see that noble ardour extinguish'd which they had for his Majestie's Service. I doubt not but much pains and address has been employ'd to debauch them. There are who pretend to excuse them on the score of a tender conscience, which for the most part is a bad understanding which suckes in the jealous bait that cunning Knaves Fish with. I know not what Religion they can pretend to be of; the Christian Religion carefully teaches obedience to their Soveraigne. All who are not willingly blind see that His Majestie's word is sacred and unviolable. Never Prince was so firme to his promise. What pitty 'tis so many brave well meaning men shou'd be mislead by factious spirits who make them suspicious of the designs of so good and so righteous a King. All their arguments are grounded meerly on presumption. I wish his ungratefull subjects did not give him evident cause to be Jealouse of them. Dos not his Majesty equally employ according to his promise his subjects of different Religions, and no man wants his favour who is not wanting in his duty. Besides what Prince is more mercifull, more bountifull, or takes such particular care to advance all those who have any merrit?

I beg your pardon for saying so much on a matter which you are better able to discourse of than I am, but the inclination which I have had for many of these Officers has made me give way to the Transports of my present passion. I hope in a little time they will be sensible of their error, for I cannot but believe that most of them are, without malice, mistaken honest men. You cannot send any news which will be more welcome to, Sir, Your m. h. & m. o. servant.

Source: H-1, pp. 248–249; *LB*, pp. 333–334.

1 Probably Etherege's scornful translation of the Dutch *Hoogmogendheiden* (literally, "High Mightinesses"), the actual title of the States-General of Holland. Cf. *Hogen mogen* in the *OED*.

Omitted: March 8, 1688. To Middleton with news from Denmark.
Source: H-1, pp. 249–250; *LB*, pp. 335–336.

Omitted: March 8, 1688. To Wynne, a long report on the Lavardin affair.
Source: M-2, ff. 145–146. In Hughes' hand, signed by Etherege.

To WILLIAM JEPHSON   March 8, 1688
                                                       Dito

(Mr. Jephson)

Yesterday, Sir, I received your favour of the 25th of January. I doubt whether you have ever been so unhappy to be so long absent from what you love as to be perfectly sensible of the joy it gave me. Nature, you know, intended me for an idle fellow and gave me passions and qualities fitt for that blessed calling, but fortune has made a changling of me, and necessity now forces me to sett up for a fop of business. Ned Russell [1] has been more the object of my envy than the ablest Minister I know is. How pleasanter it is to jolt about in poor hackney Coaches to find out the harmless lust of the Town than to spend the time in a Roome of State in whispers to discover the ambitious designs of Princes. A letter from you so fires me with the thought of the life I have lead that I can hardly forbear railing at that I am condemn'd to. There is but one I like worse which is that of a Clergyman. The mischief they dayly do in the world makes me have no better an opinion of them than Lucian had of the ancient Philosophers.[2] Their pride, their passion, and their covetousness makes them endeavor to destroy the government they were instituted to Support, and instead of taking care of the quietness of our Souls they are industrious to make us cutt one an others throats.

I am beholden to you for leading me behind the Scenes. You put me in minde of the time I have well employ'd there. Sarah Cooke[3] was always fitter for a player than a Mistresse, and it is properer her lungs shou'd be wasted on the Stage than that she shou'd die of a disease

185

too gallant for her. Mrs. Percivall [4] had onely her youth and a maiden-head to recommend her, which makes me think you do not take it to heart that Mrs. Mumford is so discreet. Mrs. Barry[5] bears up as well as I myself have done. My poor Lord Rochester[6] cou'd not weather the Cape and live under the line fatal to puling constitutions.

Tho' I have given over writing plays, I shou'd be glad to read a good one, wherefore pray lett Will: Richards send me Mr. Shadwells[7] when it is printed, that I may know what follies are in fashion. The fops I know are grown stale, and he is likely to pick up the best collection of new ones. I expect to see my Lord Carlingford in his way to Vienna. Then you may be sure all the remains of the Dog and partridge will be remember'd. To make him more wellcome, I intend to have a Minister or two of my acquaintance who can swallow as well and are no less solid that his Lordship.

Our Carnival ends to morrow, and I am just now going to a Ball where there will be a great many and some pretty young women, tho' to tell you the truth I have of late liv'd as chast as my Lady Etherege. The best fortune I have had here has been a player something handsomer, and as much a jilt, as Mrs. Barry. Never the less this is a Countrey to satisfy Sir Robert Parkers[8] vanity, for few foul their fingers with touching of a Cunt that dos not belong to a Countess. Do me all the good offices you can to keep me in the memory of my friends, and never lett me have the displeasure of suspecting you have forgot, Sir, etc.

Source: H-1, pp. 250–252; *LB*, pp. 336–339.

[1] Probably Edward, son of William Russell, 5th Earl and 1st Duke of Bedford, rather than his more famous cousin, Admiral Edward Russell, who was one of the seven principal conspirators in behalf of William of Orange.

[2] At the end of *Hermotimus,* after a Socratic analysis of the disputing sects by Lycinus [Lucian], the disciple Hermotimus concludes, "Henceforth, if I meet a philosopher on my walks . . . , I shall turn aside and avoid him as I would a mad dog."

[3] An actress in the King's Company.

[4] Susanna Perceval, an actress in the King's Company, married the actor-dramatist William Mountford. The name is often spelled Mumford.

[5] Elizabeth Barry, star of the Duke's Company, was thought by some to have been Etherege's mistress.

[6] John Wilmot, Earl of Rochester, died July 26, 1680, at the age of 33.

[7] Probably *The Squire of Alsatia,* produced in May 1688.

[8] A Robert Parker of Ratton, Willington, Sussex, paid £1,095 for a baronetcy in 1674 (*CTB,* 4, p. 534).

To Mr. Will. Richards.
Source: H-1, p. 252.

Omitted: March 11, 1688. To d'Albeville, about his Memorials and the recalcitrant British troops.
Source: H-2, p. 1; *LB,* p. 339.

Omitted: March 11, 1688. To Middleton, reporting a conversation with the Swedish envoy about Denmark.
Source: H-2, pp. 2–3; *LB,* pp. 339–341. This is the last letter copied into BM and hence the last in *LB,* except for those printed in the Appendix.

Dito [March 11, 1688]
To Mr. Robson about Extraordinaries.
Source: H-2, p. 3.

To The Earl of Middleton   March 15, 1688
                                                             Ratisbon

My Lord.

On the 8th instant the Elector of Bavaria goeing a hunting had the misfortune to have his Horse fall with him. It was fear'd at first he had broak his knee pan, which wou'd have been of dangerous consequence, but by a Letter yesterday from Munick I am told there is no more apprehension of it and that all the mischiffe is it will oblige him to keep his bed 3 weeks or a month.

When we shall have any work here I know not, we having yet no news of the Marquis of Baden's return from the winter campaign he is gon to make at Raab. If Alba-Regalis be not in very great necessity, it will hardly surrender on the aproach of so dreadfull an Enemy as the unwieldy Marquis, the Comte de Ricardi, and the Emperors cheife Druggerman. Caraffa had a better game to play at Mungatz.[1] Instead of the Emperors giving the Marquis satisfaction against him, I have seen in a Letter from a good hand in Vienna that Caraffa[2] now in his turne demands satisfaction against the other for the injurious words he has spoaken of him, and that the Spanish Ambassador manages this affaire for him during his absence in Transilvania. I am, My Lord, Your Lordships most faithfull and most Obedient Servant

Geo: Etherege

Source: M-2, ff. 147–148; H-2, p. 3.

[1] The fortress of Munkács, under siege by the Austrians since 1685, had surrendered in January to Count Caraffa.
[2] Count Caraffa's charges against Prince Hermann of Baden (cf. p. 165) led to a protracted dispute, which was finally settled without bloodshed. See Etherege's letter of April 19, 1688.

Omitted: March 15, 1688. To d'Albeville about the English officers who refused to return from Holland.
Source: H-2, p. 4.

Dito [March 15, 1688]

To my Lady Etherege and to Sir Peter Wyche—about knif blades.
Source: H-2, p. 4.

Omitted: March 18, 1688. To Middleton about the actions of the Brandenburg minister at the Diet.
Source: M-2, ff. 149–150; H-2, p. 5.

Omitted: March 22, 1688. To d'Albeville about the election of a Bishop Coadjutor at Passau.
Source: H-2, pp. 5–6.

Dito [March 22, 1688]

To Mr. Wynne. Of the Elector of Bavaria's recovery and about spurring Mr. Robson.
Source: H-2, p. 6.

Omitted: March 22, 1688. To Owen Wynne, as above.
Source: M-2, f. 151. In Hughes' hand but signed by Etherege.

To The Earl of Middleton   March 25, 1688
Ratisbon

My Lord.

I have allways had (as well as your Lordship) such an Alacrity in Laziness that I cannot in my heart but approve of the Wisdom of the

Diette in proceeding so slowly in the affaires they have to deliberat on. We have had a severe winter, and the spring hardly yet begins to smile uppon us. No insect is seen hetherto crawling out of his warme hole, but the Marquis of Baden is to be here before Easter, and it is said that then the Ministers will leave their Stoubens, fly to the Towne house, and begin to buzz again. Till when you must expect nothing from hence but the little news I receave from Vienna.

I am beholden to your Lordship for recommending some Books to our Abbot. He promises me I shall have my share of pleasure in the enjoyment of them. Reading is the most constant and best entertainement I have now. The conversation I find is as tedious to me as Books were when I had the advantage of good Companie, and I am yet so far from forgetting the relish of it that I wou'd consent to be condem'd to heare the most impertinent Fop this firtill place affords talk a wholle Month togeather to have the satisfaction of being with you and some of your Friends one night in London. The hopes of that happiness one day makes all the cheerfullness of, My Lord, Your Lordships most faithfull and most humble Servant

Geo: Etherege.

Source: M-2, ff. 153–154; H-2, pp. 6–7.

Ratisbon March 29, 1688

To Mr. Manlove to make an end of the Suite
To Mr. Wynne of a good correspondence with the Marquis d'Albyville and of my Lady Etherege's health.

Source: H-2, p. 7.

To Owen Wynne   March 29, 1688
Ratisbon

Sir.

I receiv'd yesterday the favour of two packets from you, one of the 24th of February and an other of the 2d Instant. I have now a constant correspondence with the Marquis d'Albyville, which gives me the advantage of knowing almost as soon as you what passes in Holland and helpes me better to undeceive those here whom the malicious faction that oppose his Majestie's desseins endeavours to corrupt by sham news and sham letters.

[Military news from Hungary.]

I hear my wife has been ill of an aguish distemper, wherefore I pray (when you go that way) deliver the letter I enclose for her with

189

your own hands and do me the kindness to say all that is necessary to shew the concern I have for her health, and be sure you own that it was you who gave me notice of her illness.

Your Brother will send you the news for my Lord. I am, Sir, very faithfully your most humble Servant.

Geo: Etherege.

Source: M-2, ff. 155–156.

In Hughes' handwriting but signed by Etherege.

To THE MARQUIS D'ALBEVILLE   March 29, 1688
                                                              Dito
Sir.

I have from England the substance of the Capitulation which is found Sign'd by the Prince of Orange and my late Lord of Ossery concerning the 6 Regiments. I had the answer to fagells letter before I receiv'd it in your favour of the 18 Instant. I hear there are remarks made on the answer, which I expect by the next post from Berlin. The answer is writt with so much moderation, Soundness of Reasoning, and so much Judgement in all particulars that I am curious to see what exceptions a zealous reformed Critick can find to it. I wish the Bishop of Oxford had made two Treaties of one, that he had onely urg'd his 4 reasons for abolishing the Test, which are good ones, in the first and had cleard the point of transubstantiation and Idolatry in the second. By it self, in my weak opinion, it wou'd have done better.

I must confess the sham letter from P. Peters to P. de la C.[1] is very well writt. I am sure it was no Dutch man pen'd it: their ingenuity seldom goes higher than an Emblem, and they make their best flights with a pencil. Burnet may have had a finger in the pye. He has witt and malice enough. I wish he and all the rest of his Majestie's disloyall Subjects had as little witt as they have honesty for the good of our Countrey.

The letters which came from Rome yesterday say matters are still on the same foot and have made no advance since the taking of the Interdict from the Church of St. Louis.

I cannot yet tell you what will be the operations of the next Campagne against the Turk. Things are kept so secret that even the Emperors Ministers know not yet the design. Therefore I shall not trouble you with the vain visions of those who think they can see

190

farther into a Milstone than their Neighbours. Do me Justice in be-
lieving that in all occasions you will find me, Sir.

Source: H-2, p. 7–8.

[1] Father Edward Petre (1631–1699), James II's Jesuit confessor, and Père la Chaise, Louis XIV's confessor.

Dito [March 29, 1688]

To my Lady—of her recovery.
To Mrs. Merry.
Mr. Bradbury. and
Mr. Richards.

Ratisbon April 1, 1688

To Mr. Wynne of the Change of the french Ministers at Berlin, Spaine and Cologne.

Source: H-2, p. 8.

To Owen Wynne   April 1, 1688
                                                     Ratisbon

Sir.

I have nothing this post worth the giving you the trouble of comuni-
cating to my Lord unless you think fitt, when you give him the little
news we have from Vienna, to tell him that upon the death of Monsieur de Fuquieres,[1] Monsieur de Rebenac, his second son, who is his
Christian Majestie's Envoyé at Berlin, is to go Ambassador into Spaine.
Monsieur de Gravel is remov'd from Cologne to Berlin, and Monsieur
du Heron, an acquaintance of mine whom I formerly have mention'd
in my letters to my Lord, is nam'd to succeed Monsieur Gravel at
Cologne.

I hope you will not fail to do what I desir'd you in my Last letter,
since it concerns my interest at Doctors Commons. As soon as Mr.
Robson letts me know how my affaires stand in the Treasury, I intend
to write to my friends there. Continue to do me all the kind offices
you can, and be confident I am as sensible as you can desire me to be.
Sir, Your most humble and obedient Servant

Geo: Etherege

Source: M-2, f. 157. In Hughes' hand, but signed by Etherege.

[1] Isaac de Pas, Marquis de Feuquières, was the French envoy to Madrid (HMC *Downshire*, 1, p. 946).

191

Omitted: April 5, 1688. To Middleton, with diplomatic news from Denmark, Munich, and the Diet.
Source: H-2, pp. 9–10.

Omitted: April 5, 1688. To d'Albeville with news as in the preceding letter.
Source: H-2, p. 10.

Dito [April 5, 1688]

To Sir Peter Wyche.
Source: H-2, p. 10.

Omitted: April 8, 1688. To Wynne, briefly reporting no news.
Source: M-2, f. 158.

Omitted: April 12, 1688. To Middleton reporting miscellaneous diplomatic and military news.
Source: M-2, ff. 159–160.

Omitted: April 12, 1688. To d'Albeville arguing that the Dutch are obligated to return the British soldiers.
Source: H-2, p. 12.

To The Earl of Middleton   April 19, 1688
                                                    Ratisbon
My Lord.

On Friday early in the morning the Comte de Windisgratz arriv'd here from Vienna. The Marquis of Baden is suddainly expected to follow him. He has sometime since obtain'd of the Emperor a Comission in which certaine persons are nam'd to examin the difference between him and Caraffa and to make a report of the matter.

[Rumors of the activities of Count Caraffa.]

You may judge, my Lord, by these idle conjectures I entertain you with there is nothing of moment to be expected from hence as yet.

I gave Mr. Wynne notice the 15th instant of Monsieur Puffendorfs[1] arrival here that day. I find he has been in England and was knighted by his late Majestie. We have seen one an other allready twice or thrice, and I have endeavor'd to lay a foundation to that good understanding which is necessarie for me to have with him towards the informing myselfe better in some affaires which may make me more

192

capable of discharging my Duty. I am, My Lord, Your Lordships most faithfull and most Obedient Servant

Geo: Etherege

Source: M-2, ff. 161–162; H-2, pp. 12–13.

[1] Esaias Puffendorf, a diplomat who, according to Etherege, had served the King of Sweden for thirty years before becoming the Danish minister at Ratisbon.

Dito [April 19, 1688]

To Mrs. Merry.
Mr. Richards and
Brother Wynne about entertainment and Extraordinaries

Ratisbon April 22, 1688

To Mr. Wynne with the news.
   Source: H-2, p. 13.

Omitted: April 26, 1688. To Middleton, reporting news of Prince Louis of Baden, Prince Herman of Baden, and Count Caraffa.
   Source: M-2, ff. 163–164; H-2 (in part), p. 14.

Omitted: April 26, 1688. To d'Albeville, commenting on Fagel's letter in reply to James Stewart, Danish affairs, and plans for the coming campaign.
   Source: H-2, pp. 14–16.

Ratisbon April 29, 1688

To Mr. Wynne with the news.

Ratisbon May 3, 1688

To Mr. Wynne with the news
   Source: H-2, p. 17.

To The Earl of Middleton

May 6, 1688
Ratisbon

My Lord.
   We are not like to have any great matter done here yet a while.

[No action on Crécy's memorial. Conference at Altona and Danish affairs.]

I accompanyed my Lord Carlingford and my Lord Abergaveny as far as Passau, where his Brother had given him a meeting, on purpose to be acquainted with my Lord Taaffe and to endeavour to remove by his means some malicious impressions which the Count de Windisgratz had made of me in several persons when he was last at Vienna. I had notice given me of this ill office by one of the Emperor's Ministers, who advis'd me to this journey. We parted on Sunday last, and my Lord Taaffe goes with his Brother as far as Lintz and from thence returns to Insprug.

The Duke of Lorraine is now arriv'd at Vienna, and till the Councill of War has been assembled and he has had some private discourse with the Emperor, no body knows otherwise than by the publique news what will be the operations of this Campagne. But certainly they may do whatever they please if all be true that we hear from Constantinople.

Today arriv'd here 12 hundred men, which tomorrow are to be embarqu'd for Hungary, belonging to the Marquis of Bareit.[1] I am with all Duty, My Lord, Your Lordships most faithfull and most humble Servant

Geo: Etherege

Source: M-2, ff. 165–166; H-2, pp. 17–18. In Hughes' handwriting but signed by Etherege.

[1] Bayreuth, the capital of Upper Franconia.

[May 6, 1688]

To Mr. Richards about the Debt from the Marq. W.[1]
To Mr. Wynne
Source: H-2, p. 18.

[1] The Marquis of Winchester is the only peer of that rank whose name begins with W in K. H. D. Haley's "A List of the English Peers, c. May, 1687," *English Historical Review*, 69 (1954), 302–306. Charles Paulet, or Powlett, 6th Marquis of Winchester (1630–1699) was created Duke of Bolton in 1689 (Cokayne, 12, p. 769).

TO THE EARL OF MIDDLETON   May 10, 1688
Ratisbon

My Lord.

We have so little to do here that all the discourses of our Ministers are of what is done elsewhere, and not much more to the purpos then the reasonings in the Holland Gazets. The most judicious are of Opinion that, notwithstanding many surmises and Jealosies, the quiet of Christendom will not be interrupted this Sommer.

My Lord Carlingford told me he was afraid his Majestie knew of the Advocats[1] writing to the pensioner, which has allways been contrarie to what I thought of the matter, and I shall not change my mind till I conceave it may be for the Kings service.

When I was at Passau My Lord Taaf told me his Brother Carlingford, besides the Complement which he was to make to the King of Hungarie, had a Letter for him from his Majestie, that the outside was very good which wou'd make it be receiv'd, but that he thought the inside wou'd not be approv'd of by the Council, meaning the Regia Serenitas, tho' as I take it the Emperor treats our Master with no more, and ask'd me what was best to be done in this case. I told him if he was sure it wou'd not be receiv'd nor answer'd as it ought to be, the best way in my mind was to make the Complement and not deliver the Letter.

One reason why I gave this advise is that uppon My Lord Carlingfords being nam'd to come to Vienna the Count de Lamberg ask'd me if his Majestie wou'd not write to the King of Hungarie. I beg'd leave to answer him with an other question, which was whether the King of Hungarie had writ to his Majestie to give him notice of his Coronation. He told me the King of Hungarie was to young. I answer'd if he was to young to write a Letter, I thought it cou'd not be expected he shou'd have one writ to him, and Monsieur de Coloberat being than at Munick in his Journy to Spaine, I ask'd him if the King of Hungarie had not writ to that Court. He answer'd that was an other matter. I replyd I knew no difference in the case without he wou'd explain himselfe and make me conceive it, and so the conversation ended. I am with all Duty, My Lord, Your Lordships most faithfull and most Obedient servant

Geo: Etherege.

Source: M-2, ff. 169–170; H-2, pp. 19–20.

[1] A reference to the letters written by James Stewart, a refugee at the Hague, to Fagel, urging him to persuade William to accept King James's religious policy. William took the opportunity, through Fagel, to define in reply his own position on religious questions in England (F. C. Turner, *James II*, p. 355). Etherege refused to accept the widely-held view that Stewart was acting as an agent of James II.

[May 10, 1688]

To My Lady.
Mr. Wynne and
Mrs. Merry.
Sir Peter Wyche.
Source: H-2, p. 20.

To Owen Wynne   May 10, 1688
                                                    Ratisbon
Sir.

Whatever surmises you may have in England of Alliances and Fleets,
I have no opinion that any thing will be undertaken this summer
which may interrupt the quiett of Christendome. I had notice before
the date of your letter of Mr. Cutts's[1] ingratitude and disloyalty to his
Majesty, and told my Lord Taaffe of it in order to ruine the reputation which he had got with him and the Duke of Lorraine.

I am this day removing to an other house,[2] which with the little
news we have now stirring here will, I hope, excuse the shortness of
this letter. I am, Sir, Your most humble and obedient servant.

                                              Geo: Etherege
Source: M-2, f. 167. In Hughes' handwriting, but signed by Etherege.

[1] John Cutts, later Baron Cutts of Gowran (1661–1707), was Lieutenant-
colonel of one of the English regiments in Holland. He refused to return
when the troops were recalled by James and went over to William of
Orange. For his distinguished service under Marlborough he won the nickname "The Salamander."

[2] This is the house "situated in the great place of St. James" in which
Etherege held his three-day feast in honor of the birth of the Prince of
Wales. It was identified in 1838 by C. Gumpelzhaimer (*Regensburg's
Geschichte*, 3, p. 1418) as the former Wilde house, and this is confirmed
by Oberarchivrat Hable from documents in the Stadtarchiv at Regensburg.
It is also confirmed by a drawing of the Wilde house in the possession of
Walter Zacharias of Regensburg, which shows the front illuminated for
the "Englischen Festin" with "flambeaux of white wax, which were held by
artificial arms," as Etherege described it in his account of the Feast.

The present address is #4 Arnulfsplatz, but in Etherege's day this square,
known as "unteren Jakobsplatz," was really part of the Jakobsplatz (St.
James Place), since the connecting space had not yet been reduced to a
narrow street by the present buildings on Neuhausstrasse. The Jakobsplatz
is now called the Bismarckplatz. The ground floor of Etherege's old house
is occupied by the Capitol cinema and a branch office of a washing-machine
company. Sic transit. . . .

To Robert Corbet   May 13, 1688
                                                    Ratisbon
(Mr. Corbet)

I am apt to believe, Sir, that my friends in London think the employment I am in gives me more time to be idle than it really dos. I
must confess if I cou'd content my self with observing and giving an
account onely of what passes in the Dyet and what is done in Hungary,

                            196

I shou'd not have much to do, but that is not the way to serve his Majesty faithfully and wou'd be an ungratefull return for his bounty.

In this place all publique affaires that are transacted in Christendom are known and carefully examin'd; and a man makes a very ill figure who is not industrious to informe himself of the desseins and interests of Princes, where he has dayly occasion to reason about them with wise and experienced Ministers. I am sure he will never be able to acquit himself of his duty, which is to promote those of his Master. But business has its charmes as well as other things, as you will easyly imagin when I own they have been able to engage me a little. Nor is it so hard to understand as many suppose. Good sense and good intelligence make it no more a misterie. The Number of accidents which attend human matters make the ablest often fail in the judgements they make of events. Nevertheless it is a great pleasure not to be deceiv'd by the wrong reasoning of fools, nor to have the Doctor put upon one[1] by the Swans in Politicks.

But to talk of a profession which is much more Laborious and which I thought not long since much more pleasant, I mean that of a Gamster, he is never well but when he is tugging at the Oar. If he happens to be at liberty, he runs about the Town impatient to find a Gally where he may put on his Chaine again. I cannot deny but this man has less leisure than I have. He can scarse afford himself time to eat, is as watchfull as a Generall when the ennemy is so near that he expects every moment they will attack him, and is heartily angry nature stands in need of sleep to repair her fraylty. He often neglects his Mistress too, tho' the love of her at that very instant makes up a great part of his Torment. He seldom can find in his heart to give an hour to his friends now and then. He avoids them, and sometimes if they catch him and press him to go with them, tho' he hates a lye in his nature, he cannot forbear making a false excuse to get from them, being asham'd to own the Truth. When he happens to be among them, if it be after a loss he is more thoughtfull and worse company than an ambitious Courtier who has miscarried in some desseins. Neither Love nor envy can tear the minde with sharper passions than the variety of fortune plagues him with. I cou'd say a Thousand things more on this subject, but this is enough to lett you see I am yet sensible of the pangs I have suffer'd.

I wish you had a minde to see the Empire. I have a house where you shou'd be Master, and I wou'd endeavour to entertain you with pleasures less violent than those you follow in London. I find I have the less business of the two and therefore ought not to expect to be

197

pay'd letter for letter, yet I love you so well that I am jealous of your friendship and coud wish you woud force yourself a little to oblige your etc.

Source: H-2, pp. 20–22.

[1] To "put the doctor on" a person meant to cheat him (Albert Barrère and Charles G. Leland, *A Dictionary of Slang, Jargon, and Cant,* 1889, p. 315).

To OWEN WYNNE

May 13, 1688
Ratisbon

Sir.

We are here still in expectation of the Principal Comissioner. The Duke of Lorrain on his coming to Vienna gave notice of his arrival to Prince Herman, who has thereuppon made him a visite. I tell you this because there has been a long pique between them. Monsieur Zeiler,[1] who is nam'd to come hither as Con-Comissarie, pass'd through this place 2 or 3 days since and is gon to Vienna to receave his instructions and power. When we have him, I will give My Lord his Character which, as I hear, is extraordinary. I have nothing more at present but the News enclos'd from Hungarie. I cannot but take it a little ill of Mr. Robson that he is so sparing of his paines in giving me an account how my affaires stand in the Treasury. It is now near 5 moneths since I have had a letter from him. I am, Sir, Your most humble and obedient Servant

Geo: Etherege.

Source: M-2, f. 171.

[1] Johann Friederich von Seiler, Co-Commissioner from July 25, 1688 to 1702 (*Repertorium,* 1, p. 137).

Omitted: May 17, 1688. To the Marquis d'Albeville, reporting the death of the Elector of Brandenburg.

Source: H-2, p. 22.

[May 17, 1688]

To Mr. Wynne of the Surrender of Alba Regalis.

Source: H-2, p. 22.

198

To Owen Wynne   May 20, 1688
                                             Ratisbon
Sir.

We have nothing since my last but some particulars writ by Monsieur Mindas of the Death of the Elector of Brandenbourg.[1] He dy'd about 9 in the morning the 29th of April Old Style in the 49th year of his Electorship. On the fryday before, he made himself be carried into his Council, where he made a long discourse of the present state of his affaires and told them in the conclusion it was the last time he shou'd sit in Council with them. He had afterwards a long conference with the Prince, who is now Elector, telling what he thought was his true interest, and after having given him many advises he gave him his blessing, which the Prince receiv'd kneeling. After this all the rest of the Princes and Princesses of that Court were admitted into his Chamber, and he tooke a solemn leave of them. I observ'd in this letter which was communicated to me that there is no other mention made of the Electrice Dowager saving that she was inconsolable. I doubt not never the less but the Elector before his death prudently labour'd to reconcile all Domestick differences.

I heare the Elector of Bavaria has sent a Courrier to Vienna to be satisfy'd in something he insists upon before he sets forward to make the Campagne. I know not what may be this difficulty, but it cannot be long a secret, the Courier being expected back this weeke.

Prince Herman of Baden has taken leave of all the Court and onely stays at Vienna to speak with his Nephew, Prince Lewis, when he returns thither. I am etc.

Source: H-2, p. 23.

[1] Frederick William (1620–1688), the Great Elector.

To Henry Guy   May 20, 1688
                                             Ratisbon
Sir.

I have often drawn my pen upon you in jeast, but never had an occasion before to doe it in earnest. You will find by the difference of the stile I am much more inclin'd to be merry than serious. I never beg'd a favour in my life but I did it with so ill a grace that I deserved not to succeed. You see how I bungle before I come to the Point, but I have some hope you will excuse my bashfullness since it is no common vice after fifty.

Mr. Robson has severall times made me believe he was in a fair way of getting some of my extraordinaries allow'd which are due to me since I left England, but by his last letter he tells me the best thing I can doe is to intreat you to represent my case favourably to the Lords Commissioners. I am not the richest man (you know) that his Majestie employs abroad, and my post has been as chargeable as any, considering the war in Hungary. My Bills will make it appear I am not unreasonable.

If this trouble be ungratefull to you, blame the evil Council that has been given me and excuse me who, after all I have sayd in this matter, leave you to doe what you shall think convenient in it. Modest men naturally withdraw after proposing a thing which puts them out of Countenance, wherefore you will not wonder I make such haste now to tell you.

Source: H-2, p. 24.

Dito [May 20, 1688]

To Mr. Robson with that for Mr. Guy enclos'd, and desiring to have an answer about Extraordinaries.

Source: H-2, p. 24.

Omitted: May 24, 1688. To Middleton with news of the campaign.

Source: M-2, ff. 173–174; H-2, p. 25 (in part).

To WILLIAM JEPHSON   May 24, 1688
                                                          Dito

Mr. Jeph[son]

Yours, Sir, of the 3d of April came to me but by the last post. I know not by what misfortune the pleasure I have in hearing from you was so long suspended. I have many things to husband in England, but there is nothing I shall be more carefull to improve than the kindness which you assure me you have for me. No man can love his Countrey better than I do, who know the true value of England by comparing it with the other parts of the world which I have seen. Yet I patiently bear with the loss of it, considering how much I have been beholden to my friends in hope of being in a Condition one day to acquit my self of those debts honestly. Methinks I am a little too confident. It is harder to repay a favour than a some of money. Never the less you cannot blame my good intentions, who am willing to work till I may be able to satisfy these obligations of the most generous kind.

I am sorry to hear you complain of an Ebb at your years. It makes me open my Eyes, and trust me it is a sad prospect a man has after fifty. No more Spring tydes of Love are to be expected. Yet I will endeavour to be as wise in this point as Anacreon[1] was and cherish the spark that remains, now I can blaze no longer.

How happy shou'd I be cou'd I love the rusling of papers so well as I have done the rusling of Petty-coats, cou'd I with as much pleasure harken to the Ministers, when they talk of alliances and changes in affaires of State, as I us'd to do to the women when they have tatled of who is well with who and who is false to such a one. What a change is it for me who was restless in London and still hurrying about to seeke some fresh adventure to sitt Ev'ry day two or three houres bound to the good behavior in a chair with armes to know the Capitulation a Town was surrender'd upon and to learn the desseins of an approaching Campagne. This may reclaime me and make me grave enough by that time I return to play a game at Backgamon with my Lord Dorset and Sir Charles Sydly, but it will hardly make me fop enough to be of a politick club. I leave that to Spicer and Mr. Vandibendy.

They are to be pittied that fall under Mr. Shadwells lash.[2] He lays on heavyly. His fools want mettle, and his witty men will scarce pass muster among the last recruits our General made for the Dog and Partridge. The Comedian I mention'd in my Last is married to the Lee[3] of that Troop, who watches her narrowly, yet she has made a 'scape and swears I render'd the first honour to Mr. Harlequin, her husband. You cannot expect to be very well entertain'd from a place where those who live in it have few occasions to be merry, wherefore you must excuse the ill returns which are made you by etc.

To Mr. Will: Richards.

Source: H-2, pp. 25–26.

[1] *Anacreontea*, 14 (Cowley's translation): " 'Tis time to live if I grow old . . . /Of little life the best to make,/And manage wisely the last stake."

[2] Etherege had received *The Squire of Alsatia* in a packet from England. See p. 96.

[3] Probably a reference to the famous English harlequin and comedian, Anthony Leigh, or Lee, who had played the part of Belfond, Sr. in *The Squire of Alsatia*.

To The Earl of Sunderland   May 27, 1688
                                                      Ratisbon

My Lord.

Since the Emperors Ministers have taken other Measures and seem resolv'd to observe the Truce and make no more noise about the

French fortifications, nothing is done in the Diet worth acquainting you with. All the discourse has been of what might be the issue of the conference at Altena and what was likely to be the consequence of the chicanes the States of Holland have made on his Majestie's recalling his subjects who are in their service. Many have been in apprehension of war, but every body now seemes confident the peace in Christendome will not be disturb'd this Summer.

What furnishes us with talk at present is the changes which may happen on the Death of the Elector of Brandenbourg. Most are of opinion it is this Electors interest to follow his fathers example and govern by the plan he has left him; yet it is sayd Monsieur Schomberg[1] and Monsieur D'Espence[2] are already discharg'd of the Commands they had and that Schoning commands in chief and old Durfling is recall'd to Court again.

You will have formal notice of the Death given you in England. When his Majestie thinks fit to send a Complement to the present Elector, your Lordship may be pleas'd to think of me, if you shall judge it proper and for my advantage to make that journey.

[News of the Empire.]

I am etc.
Source: H-2, pp. 27–28.

[1] Frederick Herman, Count Schomberg (c. 1609–90), "esteemed the greatest living master of the art of war" (Macaulay, 1, p. 410), had resigned the rank of Marshal of France after the revocation of the Edict of Nantes and entered the service of Brandenburg. He joined William of Orange in the invasion of England, led an army to Ireland, and was killed at the Battle of the Boyne.
[2] Louis de Beauveau, Count d'Espance, who in November, 1688, was sent to England as envoy from Brandenburg (*Repertorium*, 1, p. 575).

[May 27, 1688]
To my Lord Middleton, all the same news
To the Marquis D'Albyville the same
And to Sir Richard Bulstrode likewise.
To Mr. Wynne, about the men that were drownded and Muddimans news.
The news about Monsieur Schomberg and Monsieur D'Espences being put out, was contradicted by this post.
Source: H-2, p. 28.

Omitted: May 27, 1688. A letter to Middleton, calendared above.
　Source: M-2, f. 175.

Ratisbon May 31, 1688

To Mr. Wynne all news
To Mr. Richard Etherege and
To Mr. George Etherege.
　Source: H-2, p. 28.

To Owen Wynne   May 31, 1688
                                                      Ratisbon
Sir.
　My last to my Lord was of the 17th, since when I know of nothing
that has happen'd in the Empire worth troubling him with.

[News of the campaign. Prince Herman of Baden expected.]

It cannot be long before we have him here, and then we shall suddainly
have the displeasure of loosing the Count de Windisgratz. Had they
been to have stay'd together, we shou'd not have fail'd of seeing some
scenes more diverting than any you have in your new Comedies, if
all be true I hear of them. After having been tormented with a long
cold winter, without a kind Spring to prepare us for it, we are lep't
into a violent hot summer which makes us suffer no less from the
other extream, and I begin to be sensible of the unwholesome effects
of it already for finding myself indispos'd last night, I was forc'd to
be lett blood this morning by way of prevention. I received your packet
of the 4th of May Yesterday and am, Sir, your most humble and
obedient Servant.
                                           Geo: Etherege
P.S. The news here has been this weeke that the Marquis d'Albyville
is to be recall'd, and the Earl of Danby to go into Holland, and it is
talk'd too as if my Lord Godolphin were to be sent into France.
　By a Letter this day from Vienna of the 27th of May, New Style,
I learn that the Duke of Lorrains indisposition has caus'd his march
to the Army to be putt off till the middle of June; his Highness was
lett blood in his foot two days before, but was rather worse than better
after it, so that the rendevous is like to be late this Year.
　Source: M-2, ff. 177–178. In Hughes' handwriting, signed by Etherege.

To The Earl of Carlingford   June 2, 1688
                                              Ratisbon

My Lord.

To shew you my good nature, I was sorry to hear you were tormented with a fitt of the gout at Vienna, tho' I suffer'd some thing after my return hither by the journey I made with you to Passau. I have order'd Mr. Hughes to send you the news paper I receive from the office. It may be you are better inform'd, which is more than I can pretend to, at least from England. You will find, shou'd you not [three words illegible] again, your acquaintances there have but little time to spare in writing.

I have not known any thing done in Holland worth taking notice of since I saw you, till Yesterday a friend of mine here received a letter from an Eminent Minister at the Hague, which I have read. It says there is a pamphlet printed which is not sold underhand, like a libelle, but is publickly expos'd to sale in the Booksellers shops; which pamphlet impudently and Lyingly insinuates that his Majestie has forfeited his right by being a Roman Catholique and that the Princess and Prince of Orange have a just title to take possession and govern the kingdoms. This paper, which I shall have sent me, is pen'd in such a manner that it is Evident those who are privy to it have a violent desire that Prince shou'd raign, without waiting till it may come to his Turn.

Burnet is suppos'd by some to be the Author, but methinks it lookes more like a project of the desperate remains of Monmouth's party who, seeing the world will not be cozen'd with a false one, begin to play an other Game. Villaines never want the favour of the ambitious when they may be serviceable to them, and I believe Ferguson is not in disgrace with every body. I have had a letter from London which says all your acquaintance are well. etc. News, of no moment.

Source: H-2, pp. 28–29.

Omitted: June 3, 1688. To Middleton with news of the campaign and of the Dutch pamphlet.

Source: M-2, ff. 179–180; H-2, pp. 29–30.

                                              [June 3, 1688]

To Mr. Manlove about Mr. Middleton's will.
To Mr. Richards with a Compliment to my Lord Dorset.

To Mr. Watkins.
   Source: H-2, p. 30.

To The Earl of Middleton   June 7, 1688
                                            Ratisbon
My Lord.

The day before Yesterday the Marquis of Baden arriv'd at a Convent about an English Mile from this place, where he intends to stay till his Equipage is compleated before he comes to the Abby of St. Emerans,[1] where he is to reside. The Count of Windisgratz before he leaves us insists uppon having the Diet make him a farewell Complement by a deputation. This intrigue is the onely business which employs the Ministers at present, and I beleive the Count will miscarry in it for severall reasons which it wou'd be impertinent to entertain you with.

[News from Munich and Berlin.]

When the Baron de Swerin[2] has given notice of the late Electors death in England and his Majestie thinks of sending to that Court, I beg your Lordships favor in case I shou'd be thought of. I shou'd be fonder of the Journy if there be any thing to Nogociate, that I may try my fortune now I have a little experience in affaires. I am with all Duty, My Lord, Your Lordships most faithfull and most Obedient Servant

                                            Geo: Etherege
   Source: M-2, ff. 181–182; H-2, pp. 31–32.

[1] St. Emmeran's Abbey, founded in the Seventh century, has been converted into a palace for the Prince of Thurn and Taxis.
[2] Otto, Freiherr von Schwerin, the Prussian envoy to England (*Repertorium*, 1, p. 331).

To Sir Peter Wyche.
   Source: H-2, p. 32.

                                  Ratisbon June 10, 1688
To Marquis d'Albyville, being a little matter of news.
To Mr. Wynne of the Elector of Cologne's Death
   Source: H-2, p. 33.

June 14, 1688
                                                                    Ratisbon

My Lord.

It is a pleasure to worke for those who pay us well for it. The obliging returns you have made me for the impertinent letters I have sent you make me now more chearfully take pen in hand than when I write to those I never have the honor to hear from.

I am sorry his Majestie findes so much difficulty to perswade his Subjects to a thing they have (not many years since) so violently desir'd and which wou'd certainly be a great benefit to the Nation. I wish they were sensible how ill-grounded their Jealousies are and how much it is the interest of their malicious neighbours to augment them.

That which makes me say this to your Lordship is the advise I have lately receiv'd that the Bishops of the Church of England have made a scruple about reading his Majestie's last declaration for liberty of conscience in their Churches. How can they ever after confidently accuse another Clergy of following their interest rather than the Doctrine preach'd by Christ and his Apostles? They have still boasted their obedience to their Soveraign, and will they now renounce their claim to that universal Christian vertue? Never people had a Prince whose word they might so firmly rely on. His true desyre is to raise the reputation of our Country, and he is bless'd with those Heroick qualities which wou'd do it to a higher degree than it has been in the time of any of his predecessors, were not many among us enemys to their own happyness and to the glory of the Kingdome. I do all I can in these parts to give a true impression of his Majestie's just and reasonable intentions to such as are likely to be corrupted by the lies and Libells which come in swarms hither from Holland.

Pardon me this fit of gravity. I find it begins to wear off already. I hope ere long I may drink a health to the Prince of Wales, and then we shall see the scene chang'd. I shall take care to celebrate that good news as it ought to be, and tho' I have receiv'd none of my Extraordinaries since I have been abroad, I doubt not but you will see that article payd.

This is a little confident in a man who can no wayes be serviceable to you. Had I spent my time as wisely as Dick Brett,[1] Sir Patrick Trant,[2] and many others, I might discover misteries which wou'd deserve your favour, but I need not tell you I have preferr'd my pleasure to my profit and have followed what was likelier to ruin a fortune already made than make one: play and women. Of the two the Sex

206

is my strongest passion. I am wean'd from the very thought of play, but my minde dayly travells to a place where there was a famous Basset in Morin's[3] time. There I have envy'd a Sitter-by more than the deepest player at the table, and tooke a picture which I find suffers as little from time as the original.

Poor Mr. Waller has left a place empty,[4] but I am not yet duely qualify'd to succeed him. A few years more and there will be nothing to object against me, wherefore I pray use your interest to get the Survivance of what the old Philosopher enjoys for me. It may fall seasonably when I am recall'd and will be a pleasing expectation since a tender heart is a vanity which can never leave, My Lord, etc.

Source: H-2, pp. 33–35.

[1] Captain Richard Brett, a small importer of logwood in 1661 (*CSPD 1660–61*, p. 304), became an Excise Commissioner and by 1677 was rich enough to loan £2,000 to the King (*CTB*, 5, ii, p. 740).

[2] A wealthy Irish tax-farmer, whose handling of the Hearthmoney duties was thought to be irregular (*CTB*, 6, pp. 422, 431, 700).

[3] A French gambler named Morin is said to have introduced basset into England about 1677. He dealt the game at the Duchess Mazarin's house, where Etherege customarily played (Thorpe, *Poems*, pp. 85–87).

[4] Edmund Waller died October 21, 1687.

To The Earl of Middleton   June 14, 1688
                                             Ratisbon
My Lord.

The Marquis of Baden is still at the Chartreux, where he intends to stay Eight or Ten days longer. Monsieur de Puffendorfe has been to see him on the score of an old acquaintance. He tells me he finds him dejected and fallen away and that it is a misserable sight to see that vaste body with an Apron of Skin hanging downe to the midle of his Leggs. His Commission here, he says, is but for Six Moneths, and then he is to returne to Vienna to execute his charge of President of the Counseil of War. If he be of that Minde, very few are of his minde. A discourse was started touching the designes of this Campagne. He seem'd to laugh at one in the Companie who talk'd of beseiging Belgrade, and many are of opinion, the Operations beginning so late, that nothing will be endeavor'd but the taking of Illock and Lippa and blocking up of Canisa.

The Elector of Bavaria is perfectly recover'd of his Ague.

We hear not yet what has pass'd at Cologne since the Death of the Elector, nor what opposition the Coadjutor[1] is like to meet with. I

207

am with all duty, My Lord, Your Lordship's most faithfull and most
humble Servant

Geo: Etherege

Source: M-2, ff. 183–184; H-2, pp. 35–36.

₁ Cardinal Fürstenberg, coadjutor-archbishop of Cologne, was the French
candidate for the Electorship. See the following letter.

To The Earl of Middleton   June 17, 1688
Ratisbon

My Lord.

Upon the death of the Elector of Cologne, every body here expected
the Cardinal of Fürstemberg wou'd have sent a Minister to the Dyet
to have desir'd to be receiv'd into the College of Electors; and I am
confident, by what I know of the inclinations of that College, he
wou'd have succeeded in it. But he has rather chosen to submit himself
to a new Election (as our letters say from Cologne), having assurances
the Canons will not go from their word but remain firme in his favour.

Some wise Ministers here blame him for not insisting on his right,
the first Election being Canonical according to the Concordat of the
Empire. It is not good to put any thing to hazard when we may avoyd
it, much less a Principality having powerfull Rivalls. Those who know
him well say he has a very working head, which furnishes him with
Severall vewes in all affaires and that these make him often irresolute
and now and then take the worse way. It was unlucky that neither he
nor the Count Ferdinand (his Nephew) was at Bonne when the Elector
dy'd. By this fault the Will was chang'd, and he lost the being Executor,
which wou'd have putt it more in his power to have engag'd the Elector
of Bavaria in his interest. It is say'd the Count de Caunitz is gone from
Munich without taking leave of the Court. I am with all duty, etc.

Source: H-2, pp. 36–37.

To The Earl of Middleton   June 21, 1688
Ratisbon

My Lord.

By the letters I receiv'd yesterday I was acquainted that your Lordship had been ill of a fever, but that you were pretty well recover'd
and gon into the Country to take the aire. The latter part of this news
was very well come to me, for I cannot be in good health when my
Patron is attack'd with sickness, by whose favor I have onely a prospect
of Living. I shall be glad to learne any way you are grown so lusty
again as to be fit for all exercises in good Company, but if I had it

under your own hand it wou'd make the Joy the greater. It is a wonderfull thing to me you shou'd be so lazie in writing when I consider how active you are on all occasions to do what you can to oblige your Friends, and what is more even me, your poor creature. The little news that is here I have sent to Doctor Wynne. I am, My Lord, Your Lordships most faithfull and most humble Servant

Geo: Etherege.

Source: M-2, ff. 185–186; H-2, pp. 37–38.

Dito [June 21, 1688]

To Mr. Wynne about Prince Herman's disgrace, about the Coadjutorship of Cologne and about the Elector of Bavarias illness.

To My Lady Etherege, promising to order the payment of 30 £ of Mr. Richards and 30 The next quarter after.

To Mr. Richards ordering my Lady 30 £ out of the pension. with a note on Robson for 300.

To Mr. Robson ordering to pay Mr. Richards 300 £ and Mr. Martins[1] 150 £ to be return'd

Source: H-2, p. 38.

[1] Apparently a clerk in the Treasury Office.

Omitted: June 24, 1688. To Middleton about the Marquis of Baden's status at the Diet and a libel from Holland.

Source: M-2, ff. 187–188; H-2, pp. 38–39.

To The Earl of Middleton June 28, 1688
Ratisbon

My Lord.

The day before yesterday Monsieur Zeiler arriv'd here who comes in the place of Con-commissary, so that now the whole Equipage of the Imperial Commission is compleat, tho' nothing is likely to be don yet a while in the Diet. The Marquis of Baden has given me an howr at Fower a Clock this afternoone at the Chartreux, which will be the first time I have had the honor to see him.

[News of Prince Louis of Baden and Caraffa and of Count Kaunitz.]

Since the Bishops have made a Scruple about reading his Majesties declaration, not onely the Holland Gazettes but the States Ministers, especially Bielderbeck, their Resident at Collogne, endeavour to make it be beleiv'd in the Empire that great Revolutions will suddainly be seen in England and that no less than civill war is uppon the point of breaking out, but all prudent men look on this onely as the wishes and lyeing insinuations of hellish and Malignant Spirits. I am with all Duty, My Lord, Your Lordships most faithfull and most Obedient Servant

Geo: Etherege

[A postscript, in Hughes' hand, about a false report of the death of the Duke of Lorraine.]

Source: M-2, ff. 189–190; H-2, pp. 39–40.

Dito [June 28, 1688]

To the Marquis d'Albyville with the foregoing news.

Ratisbon June 30, 1688

To Mr. Wynne with the news. and a Complement to Mr. Cooke.
Source: H-2, p. 41.

Omitted: July 5, 1688. To Middleton, with news from Munich and Hungary, requesting verification of a report of the birth of a Prince of Wales.
Source: M-2, ff. 191–192; H-2, p. 41.

Dito [July 5, 1688]

To the Marquis d'Albyville.
To Sir Peter Wyche
To Mr. Wynne reproaching his bad correspondence with an item about Muddimans news 2 a week.
Source: H-2, p. 42.

To The Earl of Sunderland
July 8, 1688
Ratisbon

My Lord.

I cannot but rejoice with your Lordship on the happy news I have receiv'd of her Majestie's being safely brought to bed of a Prince. Tho the joy be universall among all honest men, you must needs have the greater share of all his Majesties faithfull Subjects; the great Zeal you shew and the great paines you take to serve his Majesty in what concernes the peace and Prosperity of his Kingdomes is a sufficient proof your passions are more lively touch'd with a blessing which will in-

210

faillibly make you succeed in that glorious design. I shall not at present trouble your Lordship with any thing from hence, knowing my Lord Middleton will communicate to you what is of moment. I wish I may have often occasion to congratulate your Lordship on what is capable of giving you the highest Satisfaction. I am sure of part of the pleasure, my inclinations more than all you have done to oblige me, making me
Source: H-2, p. 42.

Omitted: July 8, 1688. To Middleton reporting intrigues about the selection of an Elector of Cologne.
Source: M-2, ff. 193–194; H-2, pp. 42–44.

Dito [July 8, 1688]

To Mr. Richards with an acquittance for 40 Guineas to be received from the Lord Marquis of W[inchester]
To Mr. Wynne of the Civilities of the Ministers upon notice given by his Honour of the birth of the Prince of Wales; and of the Marquis of Baden's ill humor in his verbis—
All the rest either came or sent their compliments except the Marquis, who did not so much as send a gentleman but like the Count de Windisgratz thinks it is below him to be civill. I had been before to waite upon him, and upon the request of his man of business, made by a third person, lent him my Cellars and severall Roomes in my house to lay his goods in and inconvenienc'd myself a moneth at least till his appartments were ready, of which he tooke no notice when I saw him, nor has ever sent any servant to thank me. This is onely to let you see how well bred the great men are in Dutchland. etc.
To the Marquis D'Albyville.
Source: H-2, p. 44.

Ratisbon July 12, 1688

Sent a note by Monsieur Osterlin for 150 £ more to be return'd by Mr. Robson.
Source: H-2, p. 45.

To The Earl of Middleton   July 12, 1688
                                                             Ratisbon
My Lord.
It has pleas'd the Lords of the Treasury to Order me 550 £ for two yeares and 3 quarters Extraordinaries due in May last, but Mr. Robson writes me word that he cannot receive it all by reason I have not sent

Bills for the wholle time, wherefore I have sent one[1] which comprehends all which will be presented to you by Mr. Wynne, and I humbly beg your Lordship to allow it, the rest of the mony lyeing ready in the Exchequer.

The Abbot of St. James's and I have pitch'd on Sunday the 25th New Style of this instant, being St. James's Day, for singing the Te Deum for the birth of the Prince. This place being the Center of Europe and where there is a confluence of Ministers belonging to most of the Christian Princes, it is expected (and indeed necessarie) the rejoyceings on so blessed an occasion shou'd be distinguish'd by something Extraordinary. I shall take care (being Nevertheless as good a husband as I can) that what is done shall be answerable to the greatness of his Majestie and the reputation of the Nation. I have allready reconcil'd all Religions for that day, and none will make difficulty of coming to the Masses and te Deum, but what is harder to bring about, the removing Scruples touching Ceremonialls, tho' I have made some progress in it, I am still troubl'd in finding out expedients.

The Comte de Lobcowitz[2] in his Journy from France arriv'd here yesterday and lay at the Comte de Lambergs. This day he sets forward, with an odder belly then ever had any Polichinello, for Vienna to give his master a character of the present state of the Court he has left.

[Reports from Munich.]

The Prince of Baden has been a great while in making the last mile hither, and God knowes when he will arrive, but I will not trouble your Lordship with the impertinent blocks which ly in his way. I am with all Duty, my Lord, Your Lordships most faithfull and most humble servant

Geo: Etherege.

Source: M-2, ff. 195–196; H-2, pp. 45–46.

[1] Reproduced on pp. 290–291.
[2] Wenzel Ferdinand, Graf Poppel von Lobkowitz, was Imperial envoy to France until June 1688 (*Repertorium*, 1, p. 141).

Dito [July 12, 1688]

To Mr. Richards with orders to receive 150 £ when Mr. Robson Receives the full of 550 £ due for 2 years and 3 quarters Extraordinaries and 150 £ more out of the first Entertainment mony.

To Mr. Robson with orders to receive the 550 £ whereof 150 £ to be return'd fourthwith. in all 300 £.

Source: H-2, p. 46.

To Mr. Wynne. desiring him to have My Lord Middleton allow the Bill of Extraordinaries of 550 £ for 2 years and 3 quarters beginning from the 30 of Aug. 85, and ending the 20 of May. 1688.

To Mr. Manlove. ordering a search to be made for Mr. Middletons will and Mr. Manlove desir'd to give his judgement there-upon.

To Mrs. Merry.

Source: H-2, p. 47.

Omitted: July 15, 1688. To Middleton with news from Berlin and of the reception at the Diet of the news of the birth of the Prince of Wales.

Source: M-2, ff. 197–198; H-2, pp. 47–48.

To HENRY GUY   July 15, 1688
                                                          Dito

Sir.

Your favour of the 19th of June, tho' it be short, is so very sweet that were I not full allready with joy on the happy news of the birth of the Prince, it wou'd not have left a Corner of my heart Empty. I now begin to think myself a rich man and wou'd not change my fortune with any Banquer in London, but their is a difference in our way of reckoning, they by thousand pounds and to me, as the old saying is, the kindness is a Million.

I am preparing to rejoice with the whole dyet and therefore must beg your pardon for not making merry with you at present. I have a provision of good wine, which shall not be spar'd on the blessed prospect we have now of Concord and Prosperity.

> Antehac nefas depromere Caecubum
> Cellis avitis.[1]

In my next I shall have more leisure to express my gratitude for the substantiall obligations I have to be.

[1] Horace, *Odes,* I, 37, ll. 5–6. "Before this time it had been sinful to pour out Caecuban wine from the ancestral cellar."

                                                Dito [July 15, 1688]

To the Marquis D'Albyville.

Source: H-2, pp. 48–49.

To Mr. Wynne concerning what the Emperor sayd on the birth of the Prince of Wales

of the Duke of St. Albans[1] arrivall

of preparation for feasting. of Illock and P.W.[2] abandon'd by the Turks.

Source: H-2, pp. 48–49.

[1] Charles Beauclerk, Duke of St. Albans (1670–1726), son of Charles II and Nell Gwyn.

[2] Peterwardein (now Petrovaradin, Jugoslavia), a famous fortress town on the Danube.

Omitted: July 22, 1688. To Middleton, reporting military news.

Source: M-2, ff. 199–200; H-2, pp. 49–50.

To The Earl of Middleton   July 29, 1688
Ratisbon

My Lord.

I am very glad I am able to tell you I am alive and a livelike after the fatigue of above a fortnights care to set my house in order and to prepare things necessaire for so great a Solemnity as a publique rejoycing for the happy birth of the Prince.[1] On Sunday after the *te deum* I treated the Diet and the forraigne Ministers here. On Monday I gave a Ball to the Ladys and Cavaliers of the place and neighbourhood round about. On Tuesday I entertain'd all the Principal Magistrats of the Towne to thank them for their readiness and civillity in lending me their Canon and a Company of Souldiers to make the Feast more magnificent and to hinder any disorders which might happen by reason of the great concourse of people of all Sorts, some to be Spectators, the mobile to scramble for an Ox which was rosted whole, for bread and mony which was throwne among them, and wine which run out of artificial Fountains, the discription of which I shall not trouble your Lordship with. All past without any other mischiffe then fingers cut, many broken heads, not a few bloody noses, and an universall bloody Drunkenes.

There was the first day at Church and at the Table Two hundred Canons shot off and the last day Thirty to conclude the Feast, which ended with his Majestie's, the Queene's, and Princes's health. In this conjuncture the Count de Windisgratz and I were reconcil'd by the mediation of the Comte de Lamberg and Monsieur de Neiuforge, the Deputy for Bourgondy. The Counte made the first advance, he having been the cause of the difference. I invited him afterwards to the te Deum and Feast with the Marcgrave of Baden.

This reconcilliation has a little vex'd the Counte de Crecy, who did what he cou'd to disswade me from it, but I thought it better to follow the instructions you gave me, which was to live well with all the Ministers. Many Civillitys have pass'd betweene the Count de Windisgratz and me, and the Counte de Crecy and I live on the same foot of Friendship wee did, tho' he refus'd to come to the Feast because the Imperiall Commission was invited and he told me he cou'd not because of their disputes about place. I answer'd I was not oblig'd to take notice of that, uppon which, he growing a little warme, I bid him consider whether his Majestie sent me to him or to the Diet.

The Marquis and the Count de Windisgratz had really come but that they had a scruple, I having invited Monsieur Holsemius, the deputy for Cologne, who by a Courrier the day before was continued by A Letter under the Seale of the Chapter in the same power he had, which was no other then that of their Minister, but they gave him notice of the Election and postulation of the Cardinal of Furstemberg, of which he had signified to many Ministers. I declar'd I cou'd not avoid inviting him, being own'd by the Electorall Colledge as Envoyé of the Chapter, and that when his Masters healths came in order I wou'd onely drink to the Archbishoprick and Electorship of Cologne. The Comission had a mind to deturne him from coming, and this was negociated in the Cloister after the te deum by Monsieur de Schmettau, the Brandenbourg Minister, but he continu'd firme in his resolution to come, and I perceiving if he had yeilded he wou'd have gon neare to loose his right of sitting in the Colledge, which was intended to be disputed on that ground the next day, medled no more in the business.

The Marquis and the Count went to consult with the new Concomissarie Zeiler, and in little more then halfe an howr sent each of them a Complement, which was that they were infinitely sorry that they cou'd not, for some reasons which they wou'd acquaint me with when I saw them, come to show their respects to his Majestie and according to their Duty give open testimonies of the Joy they had for so great a blessing to all Europe. Since I cou'd not have them, I was glad I had not the Count de Crecy, for it had not fail'd to have made a great Noise if he had presided at a Feast made in the heart of the Empire on this occasion.

The Director of the Diet held the upper most place, and all the Electorats came, as well Roman Catholicks as reform'd, except the

215

Elector Palatins Minister, who I beleive had Comands to the Contrary. The King of Swedens Minister came and a great part of the Colledge of Princes, both Eclesiasticks and Seculars. Those who did not come the first day came en cavaliers and waited on the Ladys the Second. My Lord Abbott of St. James's came and brought with him the Count de Wartenberg, the Suffragan Bisshop of the Towne, who had sung high Mass.

[Dispute over the choice of Elector of Cologne.]

I am, My Lord, Your Lordships most humble and most obedient faithfull Servant

Geo: Etherege.

Source: M-2, ff. 201–209; H-2, pp. 50–55.

1 Etherege's *Relation of the Great Feast* is on pp. 279–285, below.

Omitted: August 2, 1688. To Middleton, reporting the conflict between supporters of Cardinal Fürstenberg and Prince Clement for the Electorship of Cologne.

Source: M-2, ff. 210–213; H-2, pp. 55–57.

Ratisbon August 5, 1688

To Mr. Wynne with the Elector of Bavaria's Minister's Protestation and the Relation [of the great Feast.]
To Mr. Richards.

Ratisbon August 9, 1688

To the Marquis d'Albyville with a Relation of the Feast.
To Mr. Wynne with a Bill of Extraordinaries.
To Sir Peter Wyche.
To the Earl of Sunderland in his verbis
Source: H-2, p. 57.

TO THE EARL OF SUNDERLAND   August 9, 1688

Many here doubt whether his Holyness will make such haste to confirm Prince Clement as the Emperor's Ministers wou'd make the world believe; it is a thing which deserves to be deliberated on, by reason of the consequences it may have. If a man may judge of your neighbours by their conduct, they not onely wish but seem confident things will come to an extremity, but I hope the Contrary and that expedients will be found to preserve the publick tranquillity of Chris-

216

tendom and disappoint the Designes of all who long to be fishing in troubl'd water.

[Political maneuvering at Munich and Vienna.]

The Imperialists are run away with the foregame, but the french have a good aftergame to play, and the way they have taken for some years, to do their business without a war, makes me think we shall have none on this occasion. When you us'd to laugh at me for other Matters, your Lordship little thought to have laugh'd at my politicks. With a Relation of the Feast.

Source: H-2, pp. 57–58.

Dito August 9, 1688

P.S. to Mr. Wynne of the Count de Windisgratz being recall'd, and of the surrender of Candia.

Source: H-2, p. 58.

Ratisbon August 11, 1688

To my Lord Carlinford.

Source: H-2, p. 59.

TO THE EARL OF CARLINGFORD   August 11, 1688

My Lord.

Had I not known you were of the number of those wise men who love not to have their quiet disturb'd with unnecessary and impertinent letters, I had not spar'd you so long. The reason I trouble you now is to lett you know I shall never be wanting in writing to you when it may be for your own interest or his Majestie's Service. The Rejouissance I made here for the birth of the Prince has been an occasion of making the Count de Windisgratz and I good friends, so that I am now well with all his Imperiall Majestie's Ministers here, in case they deal as sincerely as I do.

[Speculation about the Pope's decision "in the business of Cologne."]

The news we daily receive from Hollande strikes all wise and honest men here with horror and amazement. Things are push'd so far that I cannot see how a war will be prevented. No examples can make the ambitious take warning. The late Duke of Monmouths ill success is so far from keeping others from playing the fool like him that they seem to lett themselves be guided by the remaining part of those desperate villains who were the Cause of his ruin. I am.

Source: H-2, p. 66. Marginal note: "This was to be entered 8 pages before." [I.e., on p. 59, where it is calendared.]

To The Earl of Middleton   August 12, 1688
                                                                 Ratisbon

My Lord.

I am inform'd by a person of credit that Monsieur Benting[1] has been so well receiv'd at the Court of Hess and Cassell that the Landgrave sent Monsieur Goërtz (the President of his Council) to Vienna, where he has been so far listen'd to that instructions are sent to the Comte de Caunitz that in case the States of Holland shou'd cause any more propositions to be made, he may proceed to treat *cum spe rati*, as the terme is. The Landgrave himselfe has made a Journy to Berlin, where he and Benting have had severall conferences with that Elector, who no doubt uppon reasonable conditions will be brought to doe what the Prince of Orange desires. This looks like a project of old Waldeck,[2] who since the alliance of Ausbourg came to nothing, hopes by this meanes to see an Army able to mate the French on the banks of the Rhein.

People are every day more and more amaz'd here at the conduct of some in Holland as to what concernes his Majestie, and tho' there is scarce now any roome left for doubt, the horror of the thing makes many modest in their beleife. I am allmost perswaded the business of Cologne will end in a negociation, which if it dos, it will breake the measures of those Godly men who wou'd faine be shedding of Christian blood. It may happen that those who encourage this irregular ambition may satisfie it themselves at last; and the Soveraignty, which is so impatiently desir'd, being miss'd abroad, may be got at home. Those are not hardly dealt with who pay for their own folly; thus tho' the Crusibles are broke, and Epicure Mamon[3] disappointed of the gold he counted on, these dreggs may serve to cure the itch he is so abominably tormented with. I am, My Lord, Your Lordships most faithfull and most Obedient Servant

                                                              Geo: Etherege

Source: M-2, ff. 218–219; H-2, p. 59.

[1] William Bentinck (1649–1709), the Dutch statesman who had negotiated the marriage of William of Orange to James's daughter Mary, came to England with William in 1688 and was made the 1st Earl of Portland.
[2] George Frederick, Count Waldeck (1620–1692), who had served under

218

the Elector of Brandenburg, was enlisted by William of Orange to reorganize the Dutch army and became second in command to William in 1673.

3 Sir Epicure Mammon is the avaricious and lustful Puritan in Jonson's *The Alchemist*.

Omitted: August 12, 1688. To d'Albeville, reporting the news as in the preceding letter.
Source: H-2, pp. 60–61.

To The Earl of Middleton August 16, 1688
Ratisbon

My Lord.

The day before yesterday I made a visit to the Comte de Windis-gratz, in which among other things he ask'd me if it was true that the Prince of Wales was no more prayd for in her Royall Highness the Princess of Orange's Chapell, as it had been said in the Gazet. I told him the Marquis Dalbyville had confirm'd it to me in two Letters which I had lately receiv'd from him. He own'd he had been sur-pris'd at what Monsieur Cramprich[1] inform'd him happen'd at the Feast, but that this surpris'd him very much more, desiring to know of me what this cou'd meane?

I answer'd he was better vers'd then I in misteries of State and did not stand in need of my explaining the thing to him; but since we were uppon that Subject, I did not think it for his Majestie's service to mince the matter at a time when Benting was making Alliances for his Master in the Empire; That a Minister whom he knew to be one of the discreetest men here shew'd me in the written news he receiv'd the last week from Holland that the Prince of Orange re-pented his having sent Monsieur Zulestin[2] into England with the Complement, all which seem'd to make it plain to me that he begins to make use of all the shifts he can, that he may have it to say he never own'd a Prince which stands betweene him and the Crown he is impatient for. Nay, that this extraordinary Conduct made many wise and sober men begin to think that those most horrid and in-famous Libells which were publiquely sold in Holland were conniv'd at, if not countenanc'd, by some who in honor (to say no more) ought to have been diligent in suppressing them.

The Comte replyd it was hard to imagin any one cou'd be so foolish to hope to succeed in a business of this nature and that it was a folly beyond that of the late Duke of Monmoth's. I answer'd that by many examples it was manifest no measures cou'd be taken of a mans actions

219

who was deluded with the Visions of a Crown and that an Eminent Minister here some time since had told me the Prince had layd a designe to feigne a Journy of pleasure into Zealand and to take the Princess with him and to Embarque with her and a body of men which were to be drawn out of the Garisons and to invade England, depending on a party who had engag'd to rise at the time her Majestie sho'd be brought to bed, which was disappointed by her Majesties coming a Moneth sooner then they expected; that I gave little credit to this tho' I had it from good hands; that I never spoke of it till the prayeing for the Prince was forbidden, which made me think nothing was impossible.

The Count cry'd it was strange and wonderfull and at the same time ask'd me if I had not heard what progress Benting had made in the Alliances he was soliciting. I said I had and that the Landgrave of Hess and Cassell and he were then at Berlin, endeavoring to bring the Elector of Brandenbourg into the Alliance, and that from thence Benting was to go to the Court of Saxony and so to Hannover and that these Princes were to be perswaded it was for the Common interest of the Reform'd Religion, but that I had reason to suspect it was to bring an Army on the Rhine in case the Election at Cologne came to be disputed by the Sword which sho'd so engage the French that his Majestie sho'd have no succors in case of a Rebellion at home, a thing his Enemys flatter'd themselves with; That I heard also that Monsieur Goertz, the President of the Landgraves Council, had been at Vienna and had obtain'd an Order to be sent to the Comte de Caunitz to harken in case the Holland Ministers shou'd make any farther propositions and to begin a Treaty with hopes of it's being confirm'd.

He pretended to be ignorant of this, but Goertz has been since at Berlin, as I have intelligence, to confer with the Landgrave his Master, the Elector, and Benting and is since return'd to Vienna again. I told the Count he knew I had no instructions to Negociate any thing, and all this being but a discourse between him and me, I desir'd him not to speake of it to anybody; that as to what concern'd his Imperial Majestie I knew it was his interest to make Alliances in case the difference about Cologne cou'd not be Amicablie compos'd, yet I question'd not but his piety and the good intelligence betweene the King and him wou'd keep him from engaging in what may be to the prejudice of his Majesties Kingdomes.

As I left him, the Swedish Minister, famous for title tatle and lyeing, came in, to whom contrary to his promise I find the Comte told part

220

of our discourse, which has been the occasion of the inclos'd which I had this morning from Valkenier. I send your Lordship the answer I made him, which is short, thinking it not fit to enter into a detail with him nor to justifie myselfe towards any body else till I am satisfied they behave themselves as they sho'd towards his Majestie. Pray, My Lord, shew his Majestie these Letters, and if I have done amiss excuse me the best you can by layeing the fault on the Zeale I have for his Majesties service. I am, My Lord, Your Lordships most faithfull and most Obedient Servant

Geo: Etherege

Source: M-2, ff. 220–221; H-2, pp. 61–63.

[1] Daniel Johannes Kramprich von Kronenfeld was envoy from the Empire to Holland (*Repertorium*, 1, p. 653).
[2] William of Orange sent William Frederick Zuylestein (1645–1709) as special envoy to England, ostensibly to congratulate Queen Mary on the birth of the Prince of Wales, but also to observe and to report on the temper of the British people.

August 16, 1688
Ratisbon

Copie [Valkenier to Etherege]
Monsieur.

Il y a plus de huit jours que l'on me vint dire des grandes alarmes que vous faites presque par tout ou vous venez sur les conduites de son Altesse Serenissime Monseigneur le Prince d'Orange, comme s'il formoit des desseins et des alliances qui en vouloient à la Couronne de sa Majesté de la grande Bretagne, avec des reflexions la dessus et des circonstances qui ne sont seulement de la derniere consequence, mais qui touchent aussi sa Majesté Imperiale et quelques uns des premiers Estats de l'Empire. Du commencement je ne l'ay consideré que comme une raillerie, mais veu que depuis ce temps la, quelques Ministres des plus considerables de la Dïete m'ont donné de nouvelles asseurances que vous continuez de plus en plus les mêmes alarmes, et que vous y mélez mêmes leurs Hautes Puissances Messeigneurs mes Maistres, je me trouve obligé en vertu de mon devoir de vous avertir que je traiteray dorenavant ces sortes des discours des calomnies, contre un Prince si juste et si equitable comme celuy d'Orange, qui a l'honneur d'estre le plus proche parent du Roy, et que j'en rendray conte à son Altesse Serenissime par la poste d'aujourd'huy. Cependant je vous prie de vouloir desister de tels discours injurieux, qui n'ont point d'autre fondement que des suggestions d'autres et que des presumptions tirées de conséquences[1] sans source, et de m'en vouloir donner vostre eclaircissement en reponce de celle-cy, en quoy faisant vous m'obligerez comme, Monsieur, Vostre tres humble Serviteur

Pierre Valkenier

Source: M-2, ff. 222–223.

[1] MS: *conseiances*. The correct word appears when Etherege repeats the sentence, M-2, f. 230[r].

To Pierre Valkenier   August 16, 1688
                                                                Ratisbon

Monsieur.

Je ne suis point du tout surpris de La Lettre que vous venez de m'envoyer. Il n'y a rien de si ordinaire que de voir des gens qui aiment a rire aux depens des autres, et qui ne peuvent pas souffrir la moindre raillerie. Je suis bien aise de vous trouver si sensible aux Calomnies; il est a souhaiter que tous les gens de votre pais craignent tant la medisance, qu'ils n'osent plus médire de personne. Vous pouvez mander tout ce qu'il vous plaise a son Altesse le Prince d'Orange; mais prenez garde que le mensonge ne soit trop melé avec la verité. Pour eviter cela songez bien au caractere de ceux qui vous ont donné le detail des affaires dont vous faites mention. Les ombrages donnent lieu aux jalousies, et le monde raisonnera toujours selon les apparences. Je suis, Monsieur, Vostre tres humble serviteur

G: E:

Source: M-2, f. 224. A copy in an unknown hand but dated and initialed by Etherege.

To Owen Wynne   August 19, 1688
                                                                Ratisbon

Sir.

I writ you a letter of the 6/16 of February which begins: "while we have no Principall Commissioner here, etc.", and in the following part there is this Paragraphe: "tho' I had no advise from England that the letter printed under Fagell's name was a Libell, my own reason told it me, and I have been industrious to hinder the reprinting of it here, which Valkenier had not fail'd to do in case I had not spoke to him roundly about it."

I was very much surpris'd to see this Paragraphe turn'd into french in the Elector of Brandenbourg's Minister's hand, and in stead of [speaking to him roundly] there was *si je ne l'avois fortement menacé.*

Valkenier chicanes about the word threatning, and appeales to two Ministers which were by whether he lett himself be threatned by me. These Ministers do not remember that I threatned him, but that I spoke to him very freely about it. From this the worthy Burgomaster, now we have an other dispute, wou'd imply that I write things into England which are not true.

This is a business of no consequence. Nevertheless I must be so free to tell you that it lookes a little strange, not to me onely, but to most of the Ministers here, that the Hollanders shou'd have intelligence in our Secretary of State's office and be able to take out Copies of whatever concernes them. I write this to you that you may take care whom you trust your letters to and that you may be the better able to find out the man who betrays you.[1] This dos me no harm here, since what I said was sharper than a down right threatning, but it is a little reproach on them who shou'd take care what is communicated out of the office, and if any thing of this kind shou'd happen once more I must be so plain as to tell you I shall be oblig'd to take notice of it to my Lord.

[News from Cologne.]

I have been attack'd here by a very impertinent letter, which Valkenier writ to me on munday last. In my next I intend to give my Lord a farther account of that business. In the mean time you may give him the inclosed news from Vienna. I am, etc.

The letter inclos'd, which comes from the Abbot of Kempten, who is a Prince of the Empire, was given me by his Minister here to be sent his Majesty. It is a congratulation on the birth of the Prince.

Source: H-2, pp. 64–65.

[1] Samuel De Paz, a clerk in the Secretary of State's office, was dismissed in early March 1688 for "discovering the secrets of the council into Holland" (George H. Jones, *Charles Middleton*, Chicago, 1967, p. 122.) De Paz may have collaborated with Etherege's secretary Hugo Hughes, whose private copy of the Letterbook was available to Valkenier (*HLB*, pp. 332–333). Hughes discontinued his private copying of Etherege's letters in early March 1688, just about the time of De Paz's dismissal.

Dito [August 19, 1688]

To Mr. Robson about Extraordinaries
To Mr. Richards.

Source: H-2, p. 65.

My Lord.

During the time you were at Vienna you cou'd not but have experience of the great virtues of the Austricians, wherefore I shall not trouble you with the praises of their humility and sincerity. In my last of the 6th instant your Lordship sees the obligations I have to the Count de Windisgratz; tho' I am not ingratefull, I doe not think it convenient yet a while to acknowledge his favour.

I have writ a Letter to the Swedish Minister here on the occasion of that which was sent me from Monsieur Valkenier. You have a Copy enclos'd to entertain you: pray let it not be made publique, since I have thought fit to suppress it till I see the effect of what is writ to the Prince of Orange. My intentions were not at first to make a Noise, and it shall not be my fault if the thing dos not dye, now the Prince of Wales is prayd for. In case it dos not, when there is occasion I shall give you an account of all that was communicated to me by Ministers of the greatest credit in this place and of what was writ to me myselfe, which I hope will justifie me in the discourse I held in confidance with one of the Emperor's Principal Commissioners.

[News from Belgrade.]

You will have heard from Berlin of the Electrice's being brought to bed of a prince, and that the Princess of Ratzville (the Marcgrave's widdow),[1] not being able to hold out till the Prince of Poland arriv'd (who is contracted to her and was on his way with a splendid Equipage), surrender'd herselfe to Prince Charles of Neubourg, who presently went to bed and took possession of the Castle before the Elector (who was gon a hunting that day with all the publique Ministers) cou'd come back to prevent it, tho' he had speedy notice given him of it. This may make some bussle, her Estate lyeing in Lithuania. I am, My Lord, Your Lordships most faithfull and most humble Servant

                                                            Geo: Etherege

Source: M-2, ff. 226–227; H-2, pp. 67–68.

---

[1] Louis, Margrave of Brandenburg, the second son of the Elector, died in the spring of 1687. His widow was the daughter and heiress of Prince Radziwill of Poland (*LB*, p. 185). Etherege described her, in a letter of April 17, 1687, as "the richest and the handsomest widow in the Empire."

To Mr. Manlove about the mannour of Herford.[1]
   Source: H-2, p. 68.

[1] The disputed property in Huntingdonshire which Etherege claimed to
have inherited from William Middleton. See above, p. 76, n. 3.

To Georg Fredrik von Snoilsky   [undated, but enclosed with
                                        letter of August 23, 1688]

Monsieur [Schnolsky]

Scachant combien vous aimez à rire, je vous serois bien ingrat, ayant
en souvent le bonheur de gognarder avec vous dans plusieurs occasions, si je vous en cachois une du dernier ridicule. Vous connoissez
mieux que moy Monsieur pierre Valkenier, ou vous le devez pour le
moins, par les grandes habitudes que vous avez avec luy: il s'est mis en
tête de m'envoyer une Lettre sur le sujet d'un discour que je devois
avoir tenu avec Monsieur le Comte de Vindisgratz, touchant plusieurs
nouvelles qui ont depuis peu parcouru cette ville.

Il m'ecrit qu'il y a plus de huict jours que l'on luy vint dire des
grandes alarmes que je faisois presque partout ou je venois sur les
conduites de son Altesse Serenissime Monseigneur Le Prince D'Orange,
comme sil formoit des desseins et des alliances qui en voulussent à la
couronne de sa Majesté de La Grande Bretagne, avec des refflexions
la dessus et des Circonstances qui ne sont seulement de la derniere
Consequence, mais qui touchent aussi sa Majesté Imperiale et quelques
uns des premiers Estats de L'Empire. Il me semble qu'il veut faire
accroire que quelques Ministres d'icy sont fort assidu a luy faire leur
Cour, ayant couru plus de huict jours de suite pour luy donner de
L'intelligence. Si les nouvelles de La Haye, qui disent qu'on ne prie
pas pour le Prince de Galle dans la Chappelle de son Altesse Royalle,
la Princesse D'Orange, donnent des alarmes, est-ce moy qui fait ces
alarmes, en faisant purement mon devoir envers le Roy mon Maistre?

Je m'etonne qu'il se met en peine de ce qui pouvoit toucher sa
Majesté Imperiale et quelques uns des premiers Estats de L'Empire.
Ils ont tous des Ministres icy, qui sont (sans faire tort a Monsieur
Valkenier) pour le moins aussi habiles que luy, lesquels n'auroient pas
manqué de prendre soin en cas que leur Maitres eussent esté aucune-
ment offencé. Il dit que du Commencement il ne consideroit ces refflexions et ces Circonstances, qui sont de la derniere Consequence,
que Comme une raillerie. N'est-ce pas là bien entendre la raillerie?

Mais vû que depuis ce temps quelques Ministres des plus Considerables de La Diette luy avoient donné des nouvelles assurances que je continuois de plus en plus les mémes alarmes, et que j'y melois méme leurs hautes Puissances ses Seigneurs ses Maistres, il se trouvoit obligé, en vertu de son devoir, de m'avertir qu'il traitteroit dorenavant ces sortes de discours de Calomnies contre un Prince si juste et si equitable comme celuy D'Orange, qui a L'honneur d'estre le plus proche parent du Roy, et qu'il en rendroit conte par la poste de ce jour là a son Altesse Serenissime. Il veut traitter de Calomnies des discours que j'ay raison de Croire qu'il en est aussy mal informé que d'ordinaire il l'est de tout ce qui se passe icy.

Quoyqu'il dit que ses Maistres y estoient melez, il ne se trouve obligé, en vertu de son devoir, que de traitter seulement de Calomnies les Discours contre le Prince D'Orange, et seulement de luy rendre conte de ce qu'il avoit entendu dire: est-ce la faire son devoir envers leurs hautes Puissances ses Seigneurs ses Maistres? Merite-il d'avoir tant de Caractere en poche qu'il pretend d'en avoir, quand * il parle

---

* [Marginal note] Il me fit dire par Monsieur de Suede qu'il pouvoit prendre quel caractere il luy plairoit en arrivant dernierement d'hollande, et L'ayant rencontré chez Monsieur de Suede je luy demanda quel caractere il avoit. Il me dit qu'il n'en avoit point et me tournant vers Monsieur de Suede je luy demanday s'il ne m'avoit pas dit que Monsieur Valkenier n'avoit qu'à choisir son Caractere. Il me repondit qu'il estoit vray, mais qu'alors son ami avoit seulement parlé en Ministre.

---

en Ministre? Si j'avois parlé de quelque Chose de la derniere Consequence, ne devoit-il pas en avoir averti les Estats Generaux, et ne pas s'avoir amusé a m'ecrire tant d'impertinences? Il y a fort peu de secretaire a la Diette qui n'auroient pas mieux pris leurs mesures: Cependant aprez ces terribles menaces, tout d'un coup il file doux, et me prie de me vouloir desister de tels discours injurieux, qui n'ont point d'autre fondement que des suggestions des autres et des presomptions tirées des consequences sans source. Il est icy si joli, que j'ay eu de la peine a m'empecher de m'y rendre; la Caution bourgeoise* ne seroit pas une bagatelle, si on ne la donnoit point dans de

---

* [Marginal note] Il est bourgeois d'Amsterdam.

---

la Creme foüettée.

En achevant, il demande que je luy veüille donner mon eclaircissement en reponce de sa lettre: belle demande! Comme si le Roy mon

Maistre m'envoyoit icy pour m'eclaircir avec Monsieur pierre Valkenier sur des affaires qui le peuvent toucher; mais quoyque je n'aÿe
point d'instruction là dessus, il peut bien estre qu'il en a, et que dans
cette fripperie de Caractere qu'il a apporté avec luy a son dernier
retour d'hollande, il en pourra trouver un pour se couvrir avec, digne
d'une telle negociation.

Mais pour nous egayer un peu sur ce sujet, supposez que j'avois
fais des refflexions sur la conduite de son Altesse le Prince D'Orange,
est-ce a un hollandois à crier tout haut la dessus, quand Chaque
miserable gazettier chez luy fait des sots raisonnements et tient des
discours injurieux sur la conduite de toutes les têtes Couronneés de
L'Europe? Si j'ay parlé sur des nouvelles qui courent,* je ne les ay pas

* [Marginal note] Comme il fit les fausses nouvelles d'une défaite
que le feu Duc de Monmouth avoit remportée sur les troupes de
sa Majesté dans L'Oest.

envoyeés de Ministre en Ministre, et je ne les ay pas fait imprimer.
Mais je ne veux pas m'embourber dans son pais, ou il y a de certaines
gens qui font metier de mentir, et ou nonobstant le grand negoce qui
s'y fait, il se debite plus de mensonges que de toutes autres sortes de
Marchandises.

Aprez tout je crois veritablement que Monsieur Valkenier est bon
homme, et qu'il n'y entre pas beaucoup de malice dans les écoles,
qu'il fait en la politique. Si j'estois aussy bien avec luy que vous, bien
loin de prendre plaisir a l'exposer, je tacherois de luy faire comprendre
combien il est dangereux, a un Ministre grave et serieux, de donner
prise aux railleurs. Quand vous aurez les pipes en bouche radoucissez
vous un peu envers votre ami. C'est la veritable heure du berger. Si
vous ne le faites pas, que ce tendre moment vous manque, faites le
quand vous le souhaiterez auprez de quelque belle dans vôtre jardin.
Je suis, Monsieur

Source: M-2, ff. 228–231. An unsigned copy, not in Etherege's hand,
but inscribed on f. 231v "For my Lord. from Sir G Etherege. Rx 25
Aug. 88. Sir George Ethereges Letter to the Swedish Minister about
Monsieur Valkenier. Rx 25 Aug. 88"

To WILLIAM JEPHSON   August 26, 1688
                                                     Ratisbon
(Mr. Jephson)

I have had, Sir, a letter of yours by me more than a fortnight without answering it. This wou'd be no reproach to a man taken up with

the pleasures of London, but it ought to be a shame to me, who am dozing here. How can I employ my time better than in sending my thoughts to my friends, who inspire me with all of them which are agreeable? I might say something in Justification of my negligence, but it wou'd be to no purpose, knowing you have goodness enough to forgive me were it onely the effect of Lazyness.

You write me word the now prevailing passions are hope and fear; I have been so happy in that condition heretofore that I can scarce pitty those who make it a Torment to themselves. Certainly no wise man but esteemes it a misfortune to have an employment that engages him in the politicks. What miserable Fops are they, then, who break their brains in drawing consequences from affaires they are not call'd to. The greatest curse on mankind is that we are generally industrious and ingenuous to make ourselves unhappy.

Can any thing be more ridiculous than that the same oysterwife who not many years since lock'd her Fish up to run and cry no Bishop[1] shou'd now be ready to open her pouch and contribute to a bonefire for joy that the Right Reverend and Reverend[2] did narrowly escape a scouring? Who can forbear laughing to see an honorable clergy make such advances of civility to John Calvin, who has taken them by the ears and lugg'd them out of the pulpit?

I know you are so perfect a Philosopher that these matters can never disturb the quietness of your minde, which is onely active in the pursuite of pleasure. I wish all our friends may leave the rest to providence. Do not quarrel with that word, I beseech you. I never had a very good opinion of the morals of Johanne and shall never forgive him the ingratitude you mention.

I have an inclination here I shou'd not be asham'd to own in England. Never the lesse the handsome young thing newly come upon the stage[3] makes me impatient to see the scene of my past Triumphs and my Loves. Tho' there is such a deal of underwood grown up, an old oak seldom failes to strike the eye with some respect. Nymphs have shelter'd themselves in that hollow Trunk, your neighbour in Bowstreet, but the truth is, pinch'd at home with want and stragling abroad, they allways became the prey of a brawny Ravisher.

You may hear something of the rejoycing I made for the birth of the Prince of Wales, but you will miss one thing in the relation which shews more than any thing else the greatness of it. For eight days together my house was open to all who were young and handsome, and at least 5 or 600 of the sex were constantly coming and going. Some of my acquaintance wholely employ'd themselves in laying springes for Maidenheads, and I believe there was as many gotten, and cuckolds made, as there were omes of wine drunk, which cou'd not be fewer than threescore. But as the master of the feast always fares the worse by reason of the little leisure he has to eat, I had the least share. Had all the Dog and Patridge men been here, and as great gluttons as I have known them, they might have had their bellyfulls of *cher'entiere*.[4]

I am extream glad to find Colonel Godfry has not forgot me, and as for what Will Richards has of mine in his hands, you cannot do me a greater favour than to take it all at what rate you please. I am etc.

Dito [August 26, 1688]

To Mr. Wynne.
Source: H-2, pp. 68–70.

[1] Cf. *Hudibras,* I, ii, ll. 539–540:
   The Oyster-women lock'd their fish up,
   And trudg'd away, to cry No Bishop.
[2] A reference to the acquittal, on June 30, of the Seven Bishops, charged with seditious libel for protesting James's order that his second Declaration of Indulgence be read in churches.
[3] Identified by Sybil Rosenfeld ("The Second Letterbook of Sir George Etherege," *RES,* n.s. 3 [1952], 21) as "Mrs. Bracegirdle who had appeared in *The Squire of Alsatia* at Drury Lane a few months previously."
[4] *Chère entière:* food and entertainment.

To The Earl of Dover

August 30, 1688
Ratisbon

My Lord.
Who ever thought, when you gave the fashion to the men and was the onely man in fashion with the women, to see so fine a Courtier on the suddain become an honest Countrey Gentleman, marry and gain the hearts of your neighbours by your hospitality, and pursue hawking and hunting as eagerly as you had done play and galantrie? Your acting these two differing parts so well shewes you are universall; and therefore I am not surpris'd, now greatness has call'd you back to the element you were bred in, to find you a man of business.

One of the chiefest vertues in that is a facility in dispatching matters, and it is plain to me by your letter of the 10th of the last moneth you can say more in a few lines than an other can express in a whole sheet of paper. You still increase a debt I have been long unable to pay you, but I bear an honest minde and am willing, according to an ancient Roman Law, to be your slave since I am unsolvable. You have often lost your liberty, but you never lost it more agreeably than I do mine on this occasion.

I desir'd Mr. Wynne to give your Lordship a Copy of the account I sent of the rejoycing here for the birth of the Prince of Wales; it may be I have a little out run the Constable. Their passions are weak who can think of managing in an extasie of joy. I have so little of that in my nature, that I wou'd freely part with all the little I have to see a good Parlement comply with his Majestie's desire. The hopes of this makes all my happyness, etc.

Source: H-2, pp. 70–71.

To The Earl of Middleton   August 30, 1688
                                              Ratisbon
My Lord.

I send your Lordship the Copys of two Decrees of Commission which have been lately dictated here. One is concerning Fort Louis; the other is to stir up the Diet to dispatch publique affaires. They have often been spur'd before, yet they have never mended their pace, which makes people think they will still keep to their Dull Trot.

The Count de Windisgratz has sent away most part of his Equipage and go's himselfe as soon as the Diet has given him their blessing, a Complement at parting. This business is now negociating, and the Colledge of Electors, who have oppos'd it, are inclining to it rather than be troubl'd with him any longer, so that it is said he will have his hearts desire when the next Conclusion is deliver'd to the Margrave.

I have nothing more at present without I shou'd trouble you with a tedious discourse of Ceremonies uppon the pretentions of the new Con-Commisary, Monsieur Zeiler,[1] but I hope your Lordship will not take it ill I am Lazie on this occasion. Leti[2] and Wickford[3] can divert you as agreeably. I am, My Lord, Your Lordships most faithfull and most humble Servant

                                              Geo: Etherege.
Source: M-2, ff. 232–233; H-2, p. 71.

[1] This episode is typical of the endless disputes at the Diet over protocol, and of Etherege's handling of them. It is described, with amused disapproval, by the Count de Crécy in an official dispatch to the French Foreign Office (Correspondence Politique, Allemagne, Vol. 322, ff. 211–212). I owe this reference to Dr. Ludwig Hammermeyer.

Etherege's first official visit to Seiler was not returned. Hearing that the new Co-Commissioner was boasting of having treated him with patronizing haughtiness, Etherege requested a second appointment, and when he arrived at the proper hour, without descending from his coach he sent to inquire where the Co-Commissioner might be. Being told that M. Seiler awaited him above, Sir George sent back word that he awaited M. Seiler below and wanted to speak to him. The Co-Commissioner, whose pretensions, according to De Crécy, were "ridicules et insoutenables," sat tight in his apartment. Etherege then sent him word that he had come to M. Seiler's house the first time to see his horses, not the Co-Commissioner, and that when M. Seiler should return the visit by calling on Etherege's horses, Sir George would consider what he ought to do regarding the Co-Commissioner and how they might get along together.

2 Gregorio Leti (1630–1701), a prolific Italian historian, lived in London from 1680 to 1682 as Historiographer Royal. His *Teatro Britannico*, an indiscreet history of England, was suppressed in December 1682, and Leti was ordered to leave the kingdom.

3 According to the list compiled by his secretary (Appendix III), Etherege owned a copy of the well-known treatise on diplomacy, *L'Ambassadeur et Ses Fonctions*, by Abraham van Wicquefort. As a former Envoy Extraordinary to Vienna, Middleton probably knew the book. No one would be apt to read it for diversion.

Dito [August 30, 1688]

To Mr. Richards.
   Source: H-2, p. 71.

To ROBERT CORBET September 2, 1688
Ratisbon

Sir.

My Letters from England tell me that this summer my Lord Chamberlain[1] has wonn the money at bowls, and my Lord Devonshire[2] at dice. I hope neither of them has been lucky at your cost. Before you receive this, I reckon you will be in Your Winter quarters, where you may have leisure to give me an account of what Pass'd in the Campagne at Tunbridge.

I cannot but remember Mr. Maule, tho' he seemes to have quite forgott me; he is a very extraordinary person, and I find he had rather lend a friend a hundred pounds than take the pains to write him. I am sensible his many employments afford him little leisure, and I shou'd pitty his Mistress but that I am perswaded his providence has made him chose her in the family.

The women here are not generally handsome, yet there is a file of Young ladys in this Town whose arms would glitter were they drawn up against the maids of Honor; but the Devill's in't, marriage is so much their buisness that they cannot satisfy a Lover who has desires more fervent than Franck Villars.[3] 'Tis a fine thing for a man who has been nurrish'd so many years with good substantiall flesh and blood to be reduc'd to sighs and wishes and all those airy courses which are serv'd up to entertaine a *belle passion*, but to comfort myself in my misfortune, I have learn'd to ogle and languish in publick like any Walcop[4] and to content my self in private with a piece of houshold bread as well as Whitaker.

However unkind fortune has been to you, do not revenge yourself on me; force the sulleness of your temper, and lett me hear from you. It is not reasonable I shou'd loose a friend because you have lost your money.

Source: H-2, pp. 72–73. Printed in *Familiar Letters* (1697), Vol. II and in *LB*, p. 422.

[1] The Earl of Mulgrave.

[2] William Cavendish, 4th Earl of Devonshire (1640–1707), was "addicted to sport, especially horse-racing and cock-fighting" (*DNB*).

[3] Francis Villiers, son of George Villiers, 4th Viscount Grandison and a cousin of Barbara Villiers, Duchess of Cleveland, was appointed one of the four Tellers of the Exchequer in 1671 (*CTB*, III, part 2, p. 1142). He was ridiculed in the satires of the time for his extended and fruitless courting of Lady Cartwright and for his impotence. In "The Lovers Sessions 1687" (Danvers Miscellany, BM Add. MS. 34362, f. 158), the "Exchequer Clerks" attribute his spotless virginity not to virtue but to "want of desire."

[4] Possibly the Captain Warcup described (V&A, Dyce MS 43, p. 495) as the "Second Scandall Carrier" of Tunbridge Wells and ridiculed for his "Trapstic Legs and foolish Puny Face."

Dito [September 2, 1688]

To Mr. Wynne about Belgrade, my Lord Kingstons being suddainly expected, Mr. Robsons slowness, and of Gradeska and Jatzonovitz, with Prince Lowes of Baden's expedition against the Bassa of Bosnea, but that this news brought by Baron Beck wants confirmation.

Source: H-2, p. 73.

Omitted: September 6, 1688. A long letter of diplomatic news to Middleton.

Source: M-2, ff. 234–235; H-2, pp. 73–75.

Ratisbon September 9, 1688

To my Lady. with a word to Mr. Wynne.

Source: H-2, p. 75.

Omitted: September 13, 1688. To Middleton, reporting troop movements toward Cologne and the capture of Belgrade.
Source: M-2, ff. 236–238; H-2, pp. 75–76.

[September 13, 1688]

To Mrs. Merry.

Dito

To Mr. Skelton of the taking of Belgrade

Ratisbon September 14, 1688

To Sir William Trumbull

Ratisbon September 16, 1688

To Mr. Wynne
Source: H-2, p. 76.

To Owen Wynne   September 20, 1688
                                                                    Ratisbon

Sir.

By your letter of the 27 of August I find you are a little angry that I tooke the freedome to tell you in one of mine[1] that you wou'd doe well to take care to whom you trusted the perusal of your papers. You do me wrong if you imagin I ever had the least suspicion of your self. You make an unkind interpretation of my meaning. You needed not have bid me use all my skill. I am a plain dealing man, and without artifice, and therefore cannot but tell you, whatever you suppose, I never writ or spoke of that business to any body but yourself. I shall say no more than that I am sorry I have given you the Trouble of writing on a matter of so little moment, my first intention being not to reproach you but to intimate kindly to you that some body might not deserve the confidence you put in him.

I had the news of his Majestie's declaring he wou'd have a parlament meet in November before I receiv'd your bundle of Gazzetts. I am etc.
Source: H-2, p. 77.

[1] See above, pp. 222–223.

Dito [September 20, 1688.]

To Sir Peter Wyche.
Source: H-2, p. 77.

Omitted: September 20, 1688. To Middleton reporting a conference between the Elector of Brandenburg and the Prince of Orange at Minden.

Source: M-2, ff. 239–240; H-2, pp. 77–78.

To The Earl of Carlingford   September 22, 1688
                                                              Ratisbon

My Lord. (Carlinford)

. . . to acquaint you that no body doubts but the Prince of Orange has a designe against England. So great an armement was never made by sea and Land in Holland since they were a state; their fleet consists of about three score and ten of their biggest ships, upon which are imbarqu'd the 9000 mariners which have been levied, divided into compagnies, and ready disciplin'd to serve in a descent; besides, the 21 of this moneth (which was yesterday) 6000 saddles, 6000 broad swords, and 6000 pair of Pistolls were to be ready to be ship'd. They have rais'd 12000 foot and 6000 horse, which are join'd to their old Troopes. The protestant Princes of the Empire furnish them with many thousand Auxiliaries; the Prince of Orange hir'd them after the manner of the State of Venice and paies no subsidies after the ancient manner. All these are to be ready to march the last day of this moneth.

Towards the expence of these levies it is sayd four millions of livers have been remitted to Amsterdam by a faction in England, who have chosen the Prince of Orange for the Protector of their Religion, and has made bold with four millions more, which the States intended for the fortifications. I shou'd not say so much of the greatness of this power to an other; but I think it necessary to write the truth of things to you, that you may the better take your measures in what concerns his Majestie's interest.

Upon the delivery of these Memorialls the States immediately sent Monsieur van Citters[1] back into England, on the same Yacht which brought over the Marquis d'Albyville, and dispatch'd a Courier to recall the Prince of Orange, who was come to Minden (as I suppose you have heard) to conferr with the Elector of Brandenbourg, the Princes of Lunenbourg, and the Landgrave of Hesse and Cassel. His Partisans are allarm'd with these Memorialls, this business being carried on by them without the knowledge of the greatest number of the Members of the State, contrary to the Union of Utrecht; they were drawn in to give way to this by being made believe that a thing of so much moment as the preservation of their Religion and

234

their Trade requir'd Secrecy, which cou'd not be hop'd in case it were communicated to many.

The French by their evill Policy have given the Prince of Orange a great advantage against his Majesty, their vigorous persecution of the Hugonots and their provoaking the Hollanders in prohibiting the vent of some Commodities, but that is not the thing to be consider'd at present. That Prince is in a manner Master of the States, who have putt their Fleet and Army into his hands. If there be any good Patriots left, I question whether they have courage enough to oppose him, and I fear (now things are gone on so far) it will be hard to hinder him from attempting to invade our Countrey.

Things are no more whisper'd at the Hague, but the public talke is the Prince of Wales is suppos'd, and the booke which has been so often mention'd in private letters is now come forth in English, latin, Dutch, and French, under the title of The Crown usurp'd and the Prince suppos'd: by which under 4 heads it is pretended to be proved that the Prince of Orange has an immediate right to the Kingdome.

His Majestie's fleet consists of 40 frigats, and 20 french ships I believe by this time have join'd them. The King of France has sent 15000 men under the Command of the Marshall d'Humieres on the Coast near Callis to be embarqu'd if his Majesty wants them, and the Hollanders have order'd a part of their Fleet to sail that way to hinder their transportation. The unhappy difference about the Election at Cologne gives the Prince of Orange an occasion of putting his wicked design in Execution. The Emperor is glad to have an army on the Rhein to employ the French, till the Emperor has made a peace with the Turk and put himself in a condition to regain what is lost. The Prince of Orange is glad of an occasion of hindring the French from assisting his Majestie. He seemes confident of finding a considerable party in our Countrey. Shou'd he be deceiv'd in this, we have not much to fear, but shou'd he not, we run great hazard, if we have no pow'rfull neighbour to assist us.

His Majesty and the King of France have sent expresses to Rome to inform his Holyness of the truth of these matters, who has been far from suspecting the Prince of Orange's intentions, and I think you will not do amiss to entertain the Nuntio at Vienna on the same subject, but your own judgement will tell you what is best to be done. The Emperor's Ministers here talk of these conferences between the Reformed Princes as if it were purely an interest of Religion, but they have their own ends in it, or else they wou'd not be so calm, and I am affraid however zealous they seem, the growth of the Roman Catholique Religion is less consider'd by them than the pulling down the greatness of France. But it may be when the Prince of Orange and the Confederate Princes have made themselves considerable, they may have the same exception to the Emperor which they have to the King our Master. You may sound some of the Emperor's Ministers whom you are acquaint'd with, to see what they think of the Prince of Orange's proceedings.

It is to be wish'd his Holyness wou'd not decide of this Election till this storm is blown over, which threatnes not onely our Countrey but the Peace and happiness of Christendom. I send your Lordship a letter which came on Sunday last in my packet, and am with much respect. etc. With 2 Memorialls given in at the Hague.

Source: H-2, pp. 79–82.

[1] Arnold van Citters, Dutch Ambassador to England.

Omitted: September 23, 1688. To Middleton: of the Pope's confirmation of Prince Clement, of the Prince of Orange's conference with Protestant princes, and of a Dutch book, *The Crown Usurped.*
Source: M-2, ff. 241–243; H-2, pp. 82–84.

To The Earl of Carlingford   September 26, 1688
                                                                                           Ratisbon

P.S. to my Lord Carlinford.

I am sorry to hear since my writing this letter that his Holyness by an Express from Rome has promis'd to confirm Prince Clement. It is onely delay'd till the 50 days are elaps'd which the Law allows for producing what the 2 parties have to say for themselves. Notwithstanding, I cannot forbear desiring you to insinuate to Cardinal Bonvisi the dangerous consequence of this affaire, in case he thinks fit to write of it to his Holyness. An advise from his own Minister may weigh more with him than all that my Lord Howard [1] or the Cardinal d'Estre [2] can say. Many consultations have been held by the Emperor and his Ministers, what way is best to be taken to putt the Prince in possession of the Electorate. I doubt not but since the Elector of Bavaria's arrivall att that Court many more have been held on the same purpose and that something has been resolv'd on before he went for Munich.

[Diplomatic rumors at the Diet.]

By this time it is generally believ'd the Prince of Orange is at sea. I know not how kindly they deal with you out of England; I have nothing sent me but Muddiman's newspaper, which is wonderfull now affaires of so much consequence are on foot. Were it not for the expence I am at for Intelligence and the favour some Ministers do me of communicating their letters to me, I shou'd not be able to contradict the many malicious lies which come hither with every Post from Holland. My Letter of the 12/22 to you miss'd the opportunity of the last post.

I send your Lordship the contents of a Memoriall given to the Dyet by the French Plenipotentiary here, which is to be dictated tomorrow. The French King has rais'd 36000 men to be added to the Troops which are already on foot, and some Ministers here, who pretend to have very good intelligence from France, say they are to be encreas'd to 50000.

Source: H-2, pp. 85–86.

1 Cardinal Philip Thomas Howard, known as the Cardinal of Norfolk, was the unofficial representative at Rome of the English Roman Catholics.
2 Cardinal César d'Estrées (1628–1714) was Louis XIV's special emissary to Rome.

Ratisbon September 27, 1688

To Mr. Robson ordering him to return 300 £ if received out of the Treasury; if not, to demande it of Mr. Richards.
To Mr. Richards desiring him to pay 300 £ to Mr. Robson or what part of it he shall want to make good the Bill.
A Bill by Osterlin for 300 £ on Mr. Robson.

Source: H-2, p. 86.

To OWEN WYNNE   September 27, 1688
                                                                   Dito
Sir.

By the little I receive from you I find you are very busy or else very quiett in England. In the mean time I and all who wish well to our Countrey here are in some paine, we receiving more and more particulars of the great armament in Holland which is to back the Prince of Orange's design and not hearing what preparations are made towards the Entertaining of so worthy a Knight Errant. I hope you will take care, in case there be any action, to lett us know the truth of things, that I may be able to contradict the malicious lyes which our impudent enemys will be very industrious to make fly about the Empire. This I suppose may be necessary for his Majestie's service and the Reputation of the nation. I am, etc.

Source: H-2, pp. 86–87.

To The Earl of Middleton   September 27, 1688
Ratisbon

My Lord.

In my Letter of the 13/23 instant I told you that Monsieur Kanitz, the Elector of Brandenbourg's Envoyé at Vienna, had writ word hither that the confirmation of Prince Clement was arriv'd the 19th, New Style, but he was deceiv'd. It was onely a promise of sending it. Yesterday I saw a Letter from the Cardinal D'Estre which says his Holyness was very much surpris'd and alarm'd when he gave him an account of the Prince of Oranges designe against England, it having been kept altogeather from his knowledge and he being perswaded that all the forces that Prince has rais'd were onely to oppose the French, who wou'd maintain the Cardinal in possession of the Electorat of Cologne.

[Imperial preparations for war with France.]

Those who have a great Opinion of the Wisdome of the States of Holland are most surpris'd with the designe of the Prince of Orange. It is beleiv'd here he is allready at Sea. May this 88 be as fatal to the fleet of this ungratefull Snake as the last 88 was to the invisible Armado of their Auncient Master. I am, My Lord, Your Lordships most faithfull and most humble servant

Geo: Etherege

Source: M-2, ff. 244–245; H-2, pp. 87–88.

Ratisbon September 28, 1688

To Sir William Trumbull.

Source: H-2, p. 88.

Omitted: September 30, 1688. To Middleton, reporting the confirmation of Prince Clement by the Pope.

Source: M-2, ff. 246–247; H-2, pp. 89.

My Lord.

On Fryday last in the Evening a Staffeta brought the news of Philipsbourgs being besieg'd and of Kaiserslautren's being taken to the Margrave of Baden, and on Saturday a Staffeta dispatch'd by the Elector Palatin to his Minister arriv'd here. The Minister reports Neustat is likewise taken and that the Elector his Master apprehends being beseig'd in Manheim.

[Reactions in the Diet.]

This beginning makes a great noise in the Empire, and many say it is done with designe to hinder the peace which is treating of with the Turk, or to oblige the Emperor to accept of one less advantagious. These are the reasonings of such who think a man dos them an injustice, when they have a mind to come to blows, if he dos not let them strike first.

I cannot but be unquiet, whatever Monsieur van Citers may say in London or Monsieur Fagel at the Hague. It dos not seem probable to me that the great Fleet which the Hollanders have, on which so many men are ship'd besides so many thousand sadles and armes for Horses, shou'd be onely design'd against France, when I see letters which I cannot but give credit to which say the Town of Amsterdam will not consent to the prohibiting of their [i.e., French] commoditys, which wou'd be nonsense shou'd the Fleet be design'd against them [i.e., France]. It is strange to me in the same Letters to see it possitively affirm'd that vast sommes of mony have been remitted by a party in England to be employ'd in this Armament. In a word, that which perswades me something is intended against his Majestie is the States deferring so long their answer to the Marquis D'Albyvills last memorial, the continuance of the same conduct by some who influence them, and the dayly increase of the Doze of Venome which is mingled in all their Pamphlets.

I find by what I hear his Majestie has very much disappointed the malice of his Enemys by refusing the aide the French King offer'd him. I hope the report of the Swedes being embarqu'd to assist in the descent will animate our country men in their Duty, the robberies and violence they are guilty of in their invasions being notoriously known.

I am, My Lord, Your Lordships most faithfull and most humble Servant

Geo: Etherege

Source: M-2, ff. 248–250; H-2, pp. 89–92.

[No date, but H-2 labels this a
P.S. to the preceding letter.]

I find by the Letters which we have this day from Vienna that the 30th of September, the day the post set out from thence, they knew nothing of the progress the French have made, in so much that the Emperor had nam'd an Envoyé which was to be dispatch'd to his Christian Majesty to know the reason of the marching so many Troops towards Cologne.

The Holland Minister Valkenier in a discourse he had with an other Minister here the last week maintain'd nothing cou'd make the designe fail against England, there being no other power able to assist us. The other nam'd France. He answer'd the French would have enough to doe to defend themselves. He nam'd Denmark. He answer'd they durst not, there being 18 thousand Swedes ready who watch'd such an Opportunity to fall in to their Country.

Source: M-2, f. 251; H-2, pp. 91–92.

Dito [October 4, 1688]

To Mr. Guy of my Lord Spencer's[1] Death.

Source: H-2, p. 92.

[1] Robert, Lord Spencer, eldest son of the Earl of Sunderland, died in Paris on September 5, 1688, at the age of 22.

Omitted: October 7, 1688. To Middleton, reporting that Berlin supports the Prince of Orange, hoping thus to protect the Protestant religion.

Source: M-2, ff. 252–253; H-2, pp. 92–93.

Omitted: October 11, 1688. To Sunderland, apologizing if his reports on the invasion seem exaggerated, reporting on Brandenburg's support of William of Orange, and asking for instructions.

Source: H-2, pp. 93–95.

My Lord.

I receiv'd Yesterday in a paquet from Mr. Wynne his Majesties Declaration of the 21th of September. I wish it had come out much sooner, in order to informe all those (who are poison'd with the malice of his Enemys) of the justice and Sincerity of his intentions. I shall presume forthwith (I hope with your good liking) to cause it to be printed in French and Dutch that it may be spread about the Empire.

The Prince of Orange covers his designe here with the specious pretence of obliging the King to call a free Parlament in order to confirme the fundamentall Laws of the Kingdom. This cheat is old and obvious, yet on the other side it is true that mankind, tho' the subtilest of all Animalls, is most easely deceiv'd.

That which gives me the greatest apprehention are the vast sommes of mony which I find by publique Ministers Letters have been return'd out of England. It is enough to confound the ablest man in the world to consider how the States of Holland and so many Princes have been drawn in, allmost all to engage against their own interest. The Germains call on God for justice against the French and curse them bell, book, and candle. The Imperial Commission has receiv'd no instructions from Vienna since they have broak into the Empire, unless any are brought by this post. That which makes the surprise greater is the confidence they had (on the false account their Ministers have given of the Court of France) that this thing cou'd not happen.

When the time is proper I shall, according to the best observations I have been able to make, acquaint your Lordship what his Majestie is to expect from the Friendship of the Princes of the Empire, as well Roman Catholicks as reform'd. God preserve his Majestie and bless him with Victorie. As for Mevius

Mala soluta navis exit alite.[1]

I have much adoe to forbeare prayeing all the Ode over. I am, My Lord, Your Lordships most faithfull and most humble Servant

                                                        Geo: Etherege

Source: M-2, ff. 254–255; H-2, pp. 95–96.

[1] Horace, *Epode* X, 1. William of Orange is here identified with Maevius, Horace's enemy. "With evil omen the ship [bringing Maevius] sets sail."

Dito [October 14, 1688]

To Mr. Robson desiring him to sollicite my Lord Dover and Mr. Guy for near 3 quarters Entertainment money.

To Mr. Wynne to spur Mr. Robson.

Source: H-2, p. 97.

Omitted: October 18, 1688. To Middleton, reporting that Valkenier's chaplain has publicly prayed for the success of the Prince of Orange. Source: M-2, ff. 256–257.

Dito [October 18, 1688]

To Sir Peter Wyche

Source: H-2, p. 97.

To The Earl of Middleton   October 21, 1688
                                                                         Ratisbon

My Lord.

As affaires now stand I have nothing to write you from hence which may be for his Majestie's service. I am not surpris'd to hear Monsieur Schomberg is embarqu'd with the Prince of Orange, and you need not wonder that the Elector Palatin's Minister here assists at the prayers which are made at Valkenier's for a blessing on that Prince's designe, false zealots ever wanting gratitude and common honesty. Some Roman Catholick Ministers allow the enterprise is unjust, but at the same time they say some publique good may come by it. I know not which of the two are most wicked, they who act on a false principle of Religion or they who give way to their proceedings thro' a politick interest.

I cannot think his Majestie will be so abandon'd by his people as is generally beleiv'd here by the reports which come from Holland; the maine building is founded on lyes, and that is a foundation which is never lasting. I hope suddainly to have the News that all those who endeavor his Majestie's and our Country's ruin have contributed to their greater Glory and happyness. Then his Majestie, reflecting on the conduct of others in this conjuncture, will see what is the best interest he can follow. I am, My Lord, Your Lordships most faithfull and most humble Servant

                                                                 Geo: Etherege

    Source: M-2, ff. 258–259; H-2, p. 98.

242

Dito [October 21, 1688]
To Mr. Manlove about commencing a suite.
  Source: H-2, p. 98.

To The Earl of Middleton   October 25, 1688
                                                        Ratisbon
My Lord.

The incursions the French make into Franconia and Swabia frighten many even in Neuremberg and Ausbourg, and dayly Wagons loaded with goods and writings come to be in safety here. There is no appearance yet of any force to oppose this Torrent. I do all I can to make the Germains sensible of the trick the Prince of Orange has playd them in employeing the Troops he has drawn out of the Empire to carry on his own designe and not in their defence, as was generally expected, but they are so transported against the French that their impatience will not let them reflect on any injustice done by others. Tho' they cry out and are not at present able to help themselves, they cannot endure to hear of a peace on the same foot of the Truce. They had rather suffer the worst that can come till they are in a condition to doe themselves justice.

This resolution makes some more firme in the Opinion they have that the Empire wou'd have broke with the French on some pretence or other when the time had been proper, and the French are still urging this in their justification. It is allways good to be before hand. We cannot be too jealous of our Enemys, tho they speak us faire. I have not heard from England since the 21th of September. I hope in God the next News I receive will be good. I am, My Lord, Your Lordships most faithfull and most humble Servant.

                                                    Geo: Etherege
  Source: M-2, ff. 260–261; H-2, pp. 98–99.

To The Earl of Sunderland   October 28, 1688
                                                        Ratisbon
My Lord.

I have sent you a Duplicate of the letter I writt this day to my Lord Middleton. I inform'd the Emperor's Ministers of what Valkenier had sayd reflecting on their Masters, which I mention'd in my Last to your Lordship, but the Elector of Bavaria's Deputy urging he had it not immediately from him [Valkenier] and being unwilling to name the man who told it him, Valkenier was quit for denying he sayd it, tho'

                            243

it is certain the thing had been publickly discours'd of in the house where the Diete meet.

The preparations in Holland are so vast that I find I must not expect, 'till it appears his Majesty is able to contest the business with them, to stand in competition of favour here with the States Minister. God preserve his Majestie and give him a glorious victory over his ennemys. 'Tis near 3 moneths since I have been perswaded of this design and have cry'd out sufficiently. I wish you had taken the allarm as soon in England. I am with all duty, etc.

Source: H-2, p. 99.

To The Earl of Middleton   October 28, 1688
                                                      Ratisbon

My Lord.

The French have made incursions so far into Franconia that they have order to put the Town of Nurenberg (within 12 miles[1] of this place) under contribution, and they demand 50000 Crowns. In the meane time the Emperor and his Council do nothing to stop the progress of their Armes. It is certain they waite at Vienna to see the event of the horrid designe against our King and Country that they may take their measures accordingly.

All the Roman Catholicks here who wish and pray for the safety and prosperity of his Majestie are glad to hear of the changes made in England. They beleive he follows his true interest, and the Joy amongst all honest men is as universall as it can be in London. They look on the face of things as chang'd and begin to hope well of what they dispair'd (in a manner) before.

On Tuesday last I receiv'd a Copie of the States answer to the Marquis D'Albyvill's last Memorial, with which I was not at all surpris'd. They have gon to far to abate of their insolence. Did I not look uppon it as a manefest of the Great man who commands his Masters, I shou'd think all those High and Mighty Lords are run mad for the loss of the publique Liberty, as Van buning[2] is for his private Estate. Cou'd they take more uppon them were England a province depending on their Seaven? They take his Majesties subjects into their protection and invade his Kingdoms under the same pretext the Rebell Parlament in 41 made war to remove evill Counsellors etc., and without question to make him as glorious a king as those Traytors did his Royall Father. How carefully they couple all along the king and the Nation. This arrogant nonsense will remain a Record of the Shameless wickedness of their Governement.

I have sent this admirable piece to my Lord Carlinford, that he may communicate it to the Emperor and Cardinal Bonvisi that his Holiness may be thoroughly inform'd of the merrits of the Champion who was to see his Bulls executed. I am, my Lord, Your Lordships most faithfull and most humble Servant

Geo: Etherege

Source: M-2, ff. 262–263; H-2, pp. 100–101. This is the last of the holograph letters in the Middleton Papers.

1 Etherege has in mind the German "Meile," which is equal to 4.6 English miles.

2 Conrad van Beuningen was Ambassador Extraordinary to England from 1681 to 1683. His madness is said to have been caused by the murder of Johan de Witt and by losses in the stock of the Dutch East India Company (*Biographisch Woordenboek*, 2, p. 473).

To Owen Wynne   November 1, 1688
Ratisbon

Sir.

The last news we receiv'd from England makes many who gave our King and Countrey for lost a little doubtful of the success of the preparations which are made in Holland to invade us. If we do not hear to morrow that their Fleet have sett sail, it will be believ'd that the great design (as tis call'd) is given over. This has occasion'd already many reasonings here how they who have this great power in hand will employ it afterwards. The Empire wish it may be turn'd against The French, but they fear it will not, there being a report that the Prince, that he may be no looser by the game, will endeavour to execute a design his Father had, and laying hold on so favourable an opportunity possess himself of Amsterdam, seize on the Bank their, and declare himself Soveraign of the Seaven Provinces.

> [The Protestant Princes dissatisfied with the Emperor's wait-and-see policy toward the French.]

The letters yesterday from Munich confirm the report of the Electrice of Bavaria's being with Child. Pray communicate this letter to my Lord. I am etc.

Source: H-2, pp. 101–102.

Dito [November 1, 1688]

To the Marquis d'Albyville with the same news.
To my Lord Carlinford.

Source: H-2, p. 102.

To The Earl of Middleton   November 4, 1688
                                                 Ratisbon
My Lord.

The Emperor has been so press'd by the Protestant Princes that he cou'd no longer delay the giving of a Commission's Decree against the French. It is long and in Dutch, so that I cannot send it you translated before the next post. The inclosed answer to the French Manifest was annex'd to it.

By the last letters from Holland the Prince of Orange himself was to imbark on the 16/26 Instant, and the next day a publick fast and prayers were to be all over the 7 Provinces. A Copy of the prayer was sent to a friend of mine here, which we have endeavour'd to gett printed in this Town, that the blasphemies of these villains may be made publick in the Empire, but this morning it was stopp'd. I shall learn out the authors today, being in doubt whether it proceeds from the Magistrates of the Town or the Emperors Ministers or from both jointly, they having the whole power in these matters.

If the Emperors Ministers are concern'd, I intend to send a Copy of it by the next post to my Lord Carlinford, that he may shew it the Emperor and the Nuncio and complain of the partiality. I question not but it is spread all over England, that all who are truely devoute may see the execrable impiety of his Majestie's enemys.

I do not fear the force which invades us, but I fear very much there may be some treason at home. I hope God has discover'd the bottom of it to his Majesty and will grant him a Victory as glorious as his cause is just.

It is sayd the French, to make the contributions come in, have burnt some villages about Wirtzbourg, and this night a Staffeta came to give the Deputy of Nuremberg Notice that they began to ruin the Countrey by parties of 500 and 1000 men within two miles of that Town. I am etc.

Source: H-2, pp. 102–103.

                                   Ratisbon November 7, 1688

To my Lord Carlinford
Source: H-2, p. 103.

To The Earl of Middleton   November 8, 1688
                                                 Ratisbon
My Lord.

I send your Lordship the Decree of Commission I promis'd in my last.

246

The Count de Lamberg, to whom I apply'd myself to get the prayer which was made in Hollande for the Prince of Orange printed, made such difficulties about it that I lett it fall for fear of receiving an affront in the businesse, and I shall ever hereafter for his sake suspect the moralls of one who is half a man of honour and half a churchman. I have sent Copies of it to my Lord Carlinford for the Emperor and the Cardinals Bonvisi and Colonitz.

On fryday last Valkenier receiv'd the Declaration his Masters made the 18/28 Instant of what mov'd them to assist the Prince with ships, etc. After such swarms of Lybells in that Countrey, to crown the work the Government it self has made one more infamous than all the rest, borrowing the heads of it from the remonstrances of the most notorious Rebells that ever tooke up arms against their Lawfull Soveraign.

Methinks all the Princes in Europe sh'd be allarm'd to see this Senate of Cheesemongers arrogate to themselves the being Moderators of the actions of so great a King. The Deputy of Ostfrise was the Herald who read it publickly in the hall where the diette meets to all the members, and yesterday it came out in print. I wou'd go on purpose this day to complain of the partiality to the Imperiall Commission, did I not know their Sentiments too well, wherefore I shall forbear till (without exposing his Majestie's honour and prostituting myself to their pride) I have an opportunity to make them asham'd of their Conduct. I am etc.

Source: H-2, pp. 104–105.

Dito [November 8, 1688]

To Mr. Richards with order to pay Mr. Martins 300 £ to be return'd. To Mr. Robson desiring his accounts.

Ratisbon November 10, 1688

To my Lord Carlinford with the contents of the Marquis d'Albyville's letter of the Prince of Oranges return.

Source: H-2, p. 105.

To The Marquis d'Albeville   November 11, 1688
                                                  Ratisbon
Sir.

You may imagin how wellcome your last letter, which gave an account of the Fleet's being return'd to Hellevoet sluce,[1] was to a man who, Roman-like, is ready to vow himself for the service of his King and Countrey. It came so seasonably that I believe it spoil'd the tast of the good Cheer which Schnolsky, the Deputy of Sweden, had prepard to rejoice with all the Ministers here who are well wishers to the Prince of Orange's design, the number of which are so great (the high Dutch having as great a faculty to believe lies as the Low Dutch have to write them) that I know not above four who have either the good will or courage to be honest. However the Imperialists flatter themselves, it is evident to all who reason well on affaires that the Empire cannot find what they expect shou'd the Captain of our Rebells bring his ends about.

I have seen the Resolution of the States of the 18/28 of October in which they borrow the pretext of lending their Forces against his Majesty from the infamous Remonstrances of our Rebellious Parliament, which begun in 41. I hear the popular Dr. Burnet has drawn up and presented to the Prince an address in the name of all the Protestants of England. Their tender consciences cannot be put into better hands. A Socinian and a Traytor must necessarily employ them for the publick Christian good. The Prince, I am inform'd, upon this has founded his Remonstrance. Having a particular knowledge of the Piety and great Estate of Harbert[2] in my minde, they cou'd not choose a properer man to carry the Flagg of Religion and Liberty.

I reckon by the Damage they receiv'd it will take up some days before they are in a Condition to sett sail again. Besides their being baffled in their first attempt, the Extraordinary expence they are at, and his Majestie's gaining time to be better able to receive them are things very considerable. By their Gazette they seem to apprehend assassinats from the Jesuits, but that Notorious Jesuit John Ketch[3] ought to be fear'd by most of them more than the whole Society. I am etc.

A Copy of this the same day to Mr. Wynne.

Source: H-2, pp. 105–106.

[1] On October 31, the invasion fleet, which had sailed the day before, was scattered by a storm. All but one ship made it back to Hellevoetsluys, and there were no casualties except among the horses on board.

[2] William Harbord, a wealthy Whig refugee who had joined William of Orange's staff. See above, p. 48, n.

[3] Jack Ketch is the traditional nickname for the public hangman. The original John Ketch, who bungled the execution of Lord Russell in 1683 and of the Duke of Monmouth in 1685, had died in 1686.

To The Earl of Middleton   November 15, 1688
                                                   Ratisbon
My Lord.

On fryday last the Baron of Neuhaus, the Elector of Bavaria's Deputy, came with the Officers of the Town back'd with the authority of the Imperiall Comission to the house of Monsieur Holsemius, Deputy for the Chapter of Cologne, and seis'd on and carried away all his papers. Prince Clement having yet made no application to the Dyett and this being done without a Decree of Commission, it is look'd upon as an injustice, tho' so inconsiderable a one it is scarce worth mentioning as things now go in Europe. That which is urg'd to justify this is the ill treatment that the Elector's Minister receiv'd at Cologne. Besides, the Elector as heir and his Brother as successor to the late Arch Bishop of that place pretend a right to these papers, but I believe the true reason of seizing them was to gett into their hands a Protestation which the Chapter had sent to be made against Prince Clement when his admission into the College of Electors shou'd be propos'd.

By the last ordinary from Holland, Valkenier receiv'd a Copy of that false and infamous Memoriall pretended to be made by the Protestants in England to the Prince of Orange. I have been with the Magistrats of the Town, who at my request have sent for their Printers and forbid them the printing of it here unless it be by the allowance of the Imperiall Commission, and they have promis'd me nothing shall be printed for Valkenier here in which his Majesty is concern'd before I have had a sight of it. I have, ever since no body cou'd pretend to be ignorant of the Prince of Orange's dessein, endeavour'd to convince the Emperors Ministers that it is not their Masters interest he shou'd succeed in it, and that they will find to their cost, when it may be too late, that he and his Confederates have a prospect, beyond what they dream of, that all reasonable men cannot but imagin.

These Protestant Princes expect to find their account in some thing more solid than the pretext of promoting their Religion, and I am confident their are private pacts between them all, especially between the Prince of Orange and his kinsman the Elector of Brandenbourg, such as were they known wou'd strangely allarm not onely the States General but the Spaniard and possibly the Emperor himself. But they are so enrag'd against the French that I think they wou'd sacrifice all in hope of being reveng'd on them. They still continue in the opinion the Prince of Orange's enterprise cannot fail, and like good solid Germans they give intire credit to all the fullsom lyes that come

249

from Holland. They are so poor spirited, they avoid seeing me for fear of offending the Hollander. All this cannot abate any thing of that boldness with which I ought to act for his Majestie's Service.

This being St. Leopolds day the Margrave[1] treats all the Ministers. I have taken care to be inform'd whether Valkenier is invited and whether his Masters and the Prince of Orange's health is drunk. In my minde he shou'd look on the Prince as his Master, after the complaisant answer which the President of the States Generall made to the speech he spoke in taking leave of them.

On Saturday last the Imperial Commission gave in an other Decree of Commission to the Diett to animate them unanimously to engage in a warre against the French. Your Lordship shall have it translated into French by the next post.

The Princesse of Baden arriv'd here the last weeke and lives with her Brother.

The Young Prince of Wirtemberg is come from Stuttgart and has taken a house in this Town.

With a Duplicate to the Earl of Sunderland.

Source: H-2, pp. 107–109.

1 Prince Hermann of Baden, the Principal Commissioner at the Diet, honoring the Emperor, Leopold I.

Dito [November 15, 1688]

To Mr. Wynne About Mr. Richards and Mr. Robsons silence.

Source: H-2, p. 109.

To The Earl of Sunderland   November 15, 1688
Dito

My Lord.

Since I writ the Inclosed letter to my Lord Middleton, I have learn'd the Hollander was invited by the Margrave with the other Ministers here, tho' he is without a Character as I am. This may confirm you what an opinion they have of his Majestie's affaires. Is it not wonderfull to see men who shou'd have some degrees of prudence act against their conscences, their Religion, and their Masters interest?

I shall hereafter give you the reasons which make me suspect the Emperor's Ministers, or at least the chief of them (tho it has been kept, it may be, from his knowledge), have been privy to the dessein against his Majesty. I know not how my Lord Carlinford finds them at Vienna or whether ever he puts them to the touche, having seldom a line from him in answer of what I write to him. At such a time as this a man is not to waite for instructions but to hazard all to save his King and Countrey. I should be glad of a word now and then to encourage me, but the want of that shall never coole the passion I have to perform my duty. I am etc.

Source: H-2, p. 109.

Source: H-2, p. 109.

To The Earl of Carlingford   November 17, 1688
                                                              Ratisbon
My Lord.

I have seen severall letters from Vienna, since Monsieur Hop's[1] arrivall there. He has been long at the Court of Brandenbourg, where the mistery of iniquity is carried on by the same hellish spirit of Calvinisme which works against the King our Master in Holland. His business is to solicite the Emperor (as I doubt not you already know) to enter into an Alliance with the Prince of Orange and his Confederates against the French, to which end he has presented him a letter from the Prince wherein he acquaints his Imperiall Majesty that he has already sett forward for England, where his intention is, not to dethrone the King but to oblige him to call a free Parlament to settle the fundamentall Laws and Religion of the Countrey, assuring the Emperor that he has no intention neither to persecute the Roman Catholics but to give them the Liberty of Exercising their Religion in their own houses, and farther to oblige our Master to break with France.

It is easy for us to see the cheat and imposture of all this, but it is not so easy to us to undeceive those who are strangers to the affaires of England, especially when they are flatter'd it makes for their interest. This is a time, my Lord, when those who are in his Majestie's Service and really Love Him and their Countrey shou'd be very industrious in their duty. In these extraordinary occasions we ought to act boldly and not wait for instructions, which may come too late. I doubt not but you are of my minde, which makes me write so freely to you.

I shou'd be glad to hear you have on this demanded audience of the Emperor and pull'd off the Mask of the Prince's design, that the villainy of it may be apparent, which is no less than to cut his Majestie's throat and conquer his Kingdomes. In order to this they have blackn'd the most just and righteous king that ever reign'd with all the infamous crimes imaginable, vizt., with overthrowing the fundamentall Laws of the Kingdome, with breaking of his Coronation-Oath, with introducing Arbitrary power and Papisme into the Countrey,

251

with murders, and what more nearly yet touches his honor with supposing of a son to disinherit his daughter, as is apparent by the Memoriall Burnet has had drawn up under the name of all the Protestants in England, which was lett loose the day the Prince sett sail from the Brill and now flyes about the Empire.

Upon this Devillish foundation the Prince has built his Remonstrance, of which he has carried a great number with him in order to disperse them when he Lands in England. This dessein was engender'd, brôt forth, and is now nurs'd by the spirit of Calvinisme and is no other than a concatenation of horrid and malicious lyes, as by the progress of it is clear to all those who will not be willfully blind. You wou'd do well, as I have done, to examine it from the begining and in a short narration shew the Emperor and his Ministers how it is concerted, one forgery having still a rapport to the other.

> [A long account of what Carlingford should say to the Emperor to refute and counteract William of Oranges' Remonstrance.]

> Source: H-2, pp. 110–114.

[1] Cornelis Hop (1620–1704), a diplomat in the service of William of Orange.

To The Earl of Middleton   November 18, 1688
                                                    Ratisbon
My Lord.

Knowing that Monsieur Hop is arrived at Vienna and that he has presented a very obliging letter (as the Dutch are pleased to terme it) to the Emperor from the Prince of Orange, I made bold yesterday, thinking my Lord Carlinford dos not much delight in businesse, to write to him to stirr him up to oppose the falsehoods which Hop has order to insinuate at that Court; and I have thought it not a miss to send your Lordship a Copy of my Letter, since it contains some of those arguments which I have us'd to undeceive the Emperor's Ministers here. Our Traytors help the Hollanders to sham, and they impose grossly on these wise gentlemen what can scarce pass on a Schoolboy in England.

On St. Leopold's day the Imperiall Commission thought fit to neglect me and to invite Peter Valkenier to a high Mass at St. Emeran's, tho' he is without a Caracter as well as myself. A friend of mine who was present told me that that impertinent noisie Fool during the service had the insolence to preach Burnets false Doctrine that the Prince

252

of Wales is suppos'd, appuying it with Texts out of his late Memorial forg'd under the name of the Protestants of England.

This you may imagin warmed me extreamly, and I had almost resolved the next time I mett him to have us'd him as the Rascall deserves, but considering I am look'd on as a publique Minister, I was unwilling to expose his Majesty's honor by using violent means in a Countrey which is not favourable to us. I therefore chose rather to seem not to know it, especially since it would deprive me of seeing and reasoning with the greatest part of the Ministers here and put me out of the capacity of doing his Majesty any manner of service. Besides this Citizen of Amsterdam is fitter for the businesse of a shop than those of the State, and so poor a Spirited wretch it would be a dishonor to beat him. Nevertheless I have desir'd one whom I can trust to advise him as from himself to keep within bounds and not to meddle with affaires which do not imediately concern his Masters, the consequence being dangerous, and I hope his fear hereafter will make him constrain his Impudence. I am etc. with a Commission Decree against the French.

Source: H-2, pp. 114–115.

Omitted: November 22, 1688. To Owen Wynne, complaining of a lack of authentic news from England to correct the rumors coming through "that stinking channel" of Holland.

Source: H-2, pp. 115–116.

To Mr. Lane[1]   November 24, 1688
                                                         Ratisbon

Sir.

I suppose you have heard that the Prince of Orange imbark'd again the 11th Instant, and the next day, the wind being favorable, he sailed towards the South of England. Herbert[2] and his Squadron, being seperated by the former storm, came in but three days before, and it is not doubted but some considerable ships are lost.

[A long and detailed refutation of the Prince of Orange's Remonstrance and a prophecy that the Empire will make an alliance with the States of Holland against France.]

I shall be very glad to hear my Lord is return'd to his post that we may do what we can to hinder his Majesty from having the chagrin of seeing even the Roman Catholick Princes, whom he has never disoblig'd, wish well to those notorious scelerates,[3] his enemys. I am very glad to find by yours of the 14th of November that you have been so industrious. Pray continue to be so and you will most certainly be rewarded both here and hereafter. I am etc.

Source: H-2, pp. 117–120.

[1] Secretary to Lord Carlingford at Vienna.
[2] Arthur Herbert commanded the Invasion Fleet. See above, p. 109, n. 2.
[3] "An atrociously wicked person" (OED).

To Viscount Preston[1]   November 29, 1688
                                                         Ratisbon

My Lord.

Yesterday I received Mr. Muddiman's news paper of the 2d Instant, but it coming onely wrap'd up with a Gazette, I know not whom I am oblig'd to for the favour. I have the pleasure to learn by it that, on my Lord Sunderlands being out of affaires, it has pleased his Majesty to make your Lordship Secretary of State. The present conjuncture requires a person so eminent for his abilities and loyalty, and I must congratulate my Country as well as your Lordship on this occasion since that receives the most considerable advantage by it.

The Zele you have for his Majestie's Service I know will incline you to encourage those in your Province who are expert and industrious in performing their Duty, but the greatest pretence I can have to your favour is the faithfullness with which I serve his Majesty. Tho' I have been but a little while in business and want the help of experience, nevertheless ever since I had the first light (which was early) of the design to envade our Countrey, I have ventured to act vigorously even without instructions in the discovery of the forgeries and hellish intentions of those notorious scelerates, who complot the ruin of his Majesty and of all his loyall Subjects, and by an assiduous and earnest representation of things to the Ministers here I have convinc'd many of the Truth who were deluded by the specious pretexts of the Hollanders.

[Arguments used with the Emperor's ministers.]

I am impatient to hear some good news out of England. Nothing has been done here worth troubling you with this ordinary. God preserve his Majesty and bless him with a glorious victory. I am etc.

Source: H-2, pp. 120–122.

[1] Richard Graham, Viscount Preston (1648–1695), became Secretary of State for the Northern department when Sunderland was dismissed from office, and Middleton became Principal Secretary.

To Mr. Lane.
Source: H-2, p. 122.

To VISCOUNT PRESTON

December 2, 1688
Ratisbon

My Lord.

The day before yesterday I received your Lordships letter of the 30th of October, but having had advice before of your being Secretary of State, I presum'd to write to you on munday last, and to beget in you a good opinion of my care, I believe I forgot to date my letter.

I canot but with displeasure hear the Emperors Ministers roar against the injustice of the French and at the same time talk of the Prince of Oranges invasion as if it were scarce a Crime. Nevertheless I dissemble my resentment, thinking it for his Majestie's Service at present to see them as often as I can and by good reason convince them that it is their Masters interest the King should with glory repell his enemys.

Having an intimation that Valkenier, the Holland Minister, intended to gett the Prince of Orange's Manifest printed here, I have by my applications prevented it. Yesterday I visited the Margrave of Baden about this business. I told him what his Majesty had been graciously pleas'd to do to satisfy such of his subjects as might be poison'd by the Forgeries in Holland concerning the birth of the Prince of Wales. He seem'd curious to see the Depositions[1] and told me I would do well to spred them in the Empire to undeceive people, there being many who were cheated.

I had advis'd before with Monsieur Puffendorff, the King of Denmark's Envoyé (who is not onely the ablest but the honestest man here and has given more proofs of his zeal for the prosperity of his Majesty than all the Diet Together). He was of opinion it wou'd do good service in case it were translated into Dutch and printed, which made me forth with give order about it, and I hope it will be approv'd of by your Lordship.

[Argument with Prince Hermann about the foreign policy of the Empire. Rumor of troops from Sweden and Brandenburg on the Invasion Fleet.]

Source: H-2, pp. 122–124.

[1] After taking evidence from a large group of Privy Councillors and other notables, James made public a formal Declaration of the genuineness of the birth of the Prince of Wales.

To Mr. Griffith. for Correspondence

To Mr. Wynne about the names in the other office.
To Mrs. Merry.
To Mr. Griffith of their being no news.
Source: H-2, pp. 124–125.

Omitted: December 8, 1688. Part of a letter to Mr. Lane about the conversation with Count Lamberg reported in the following letter.
Source: H-2, p. 125.

To VISCOUNT PRESTON   December 9, 1688
                                                         Ratisbon
My Lord.

I question not but my Lord Carlinford takes care to inform you of what is done at Vienna, wherefore I shall not trouble your Lordship with any thing concerning the Treaty with the Turkish Envoyé or Monsieur Hopp's negotiation to forward it.

[Movements of Imperial and Protestant troops.]

Monsieur d'Ankelman,[1] who is lately come hither as chief Deputy for the Elector of Brandenbourg, sent me a complement and gave me notice of his arrivall. Yesterday I saw him and made him an obliging return. He made me no advances from his Master relating to his Majestie, and I never mention'd the Elector. His discourse was chiefly, being bred a Civilian, about the Laws and Institutions of England, to which I found him altogether a Stranger. I shew'd him how they were divided into common Law and Statute Lawes, what were his Majestie's prerogatives, and what were the privileges of his Subjects, and what Laws might properly be called Fundamentall Laws of the Government, and did all I cou'd to make him sensible of the Knavery and falshood of the many Libells which have been printed in Holland.

He told me at parting he was verily perswaded the difference between his Majesty and the Prince of Orange wou'd be amicably ended by expedients which wou'd be found out. I told him I was sorry that Prince's conduct and his manifest wou'd not lett me be of his opinion. He sayd he was confident the Prince had no ill design against his Majesties person or his Crown. I answer'd he must pardon me if I had

256

not complaisance enough to renounce the little common sense God has given me.

I still continue my visits to the Emperor's Ministers here, tho' they make me not the least return of Civility, but I shou'd not be concern'd at that did they not give me dayly proofs of their want of Sincerity. It is so much against my nature to dissemble an injury that the necessity of doing it at this time is no small mortification to me.

The Count de Lamberg (who before the Prince of Oranges conspiracy made a publick profession of being my friend) the last weeke tooke me into a private Chamber where he summ'd up all the Prince of Orange objects against his Majestie in his Manifest under the name of evill Counsellors to see what I woud answer to it. After I had reply'd what I thought fitt, I desir'd him to answer in his turn some just exceptions which the people of England might make against their receiving that Prince for their Master and made a short History of what he had done in Holland, where he was but the State's Servant. He betray'd me the next day in the Dyet, where it was publickly sayd I had blasphem'd the Prince of Orange.

In this conversation we talk'd of the Strict allyance between his Majesty and France, which was forg'd in Holland. I urg'd many circumstances which made the imposture plain, which was never doubted of by any man who was not byass'd, since his Majesty had order'd the Marquis d'Albyville to give the States his Royall word he had no alliances with France but what were then in print and which the Emperor cou'd not take amiss, he not being in a condition to assist his Majesty in case of need. He told me I was mistaken, smilingly. I answer'd I knew not how, unless he meant he had it in his power to prevent what has happened, whereupon he cry'd *Well* and laughed out right.

I have had reason allways to believe that pious Prince's Ministers have been privy to the design against his Majesty, which will stain all the honor he has gain'd by his many victories against the Turk. They begin to be much dissatisfy'd with his Holyness, who seemes to be sensible he has been missinform'd. I hope he will give them more reason to be so, since all they do shews they will think it their interest the Prince of Orange's unnaturall and unchristian enterprise shou'd succeed.

When Valkenier received the Prince of Orange's Manifest, I spoke to the Magistrats about it, and they promis'd me it shou'd not be printed in this Town unless it were by command from the imperiall comission, whereupon I went to the Margrave of Baden, who gave me his word he would not consent to it. Yesterday I was surpris'd to have one brôt me wett from the Press and to learn that there were five hundred Copies printed. Upon examining the business I find the Magistrats (tho' Reformed) are men of Honor and that the good Roman Catholick (the Margrave), having refus'd Valkenier the first time he desir'd his consent, was not proof against a second charge but has shamefully broken his word. I am with all duty etc.

Source: H-2, pp. 126–130.

1 Eberhard von Danckelman (1643–1722).

Dito

To the Marquis d'Albyville
Source: H-2, p. 130.

To The Earl of Middleton   December 13, 1688
                                        Ratisbon
My Lord.

Tho' I am now out of your Province[1] I hope you will give me leave allways to depend on your favour. As things stand at present you will easily excuse me for not entertaining you with the impertinances of this place. You know I am a wellwisher to Laziness, yet I assure you I have never been unactive when his Majestie's Service required it, and I preferr the reputation of being an honest man to all the other advantages of this world. I know this is enough to prevail with you constantly to do me all the good offices you can. The many obligations I have already to your Lordship need not this addition to make me all my life Long rejoice at your prosperity and be etc.

Source: H-2, p. 130.

1 Middleton took over the Southern department and became Principal Secretary when Sunderland was dismissed.

Dito [December 13, 1688]

To Mr. Griffith
Sir Peter Wyche
Source: H-2, p. 130.

To THE EARL OF SUNDERLAND   December 13, 1688
                                                        Dito
My Lord.

All my hopes being founded on your favour, I cannot express how much I am afflicted to hear you are out of affaires. I owe my being in this post to your goodness, and I question not but the faithfullness with which I serve his Majesty will be so far from making you repent it that it will help to preserve me in your good opinion and incline you to make me what friends you can. Tho' this world is full of changes, my gratitude will make me constantly, My Lord, etc.

Source: H-2, pp. 130–131.

To VISCOUNT PRESTON   December 16, 1688
                                                      Ratisbon
My Lord.

On Saturday last Prince Clement of Bavaria was receiv'd by his Deputy into the College of Electors with a Protestation that it shou'd not be an example to the prejudice of the golden Bull [1] nor of any other institution of the Empire, his nonage being dispens'd with in consideration of the greatness and meritts of his family and of the instances the Emperor has been pleas'd to make in his behalf.

Yesterday an Imperiall Decree was dictated which prohibites the Dyet the receiving any more acts from the French Plenipotentiary, enjoining him to leave this Town in three days, and to be out of the Emperor's Territories in 15. This was afterwards sent to him by an Officer from the Imperiall Commission, with a Passport from the Emperor annexed to it. The Emperors Troops which are to march towards the Rhin will (it is sayd) in the Spring be made up ii Regiments.

These proceedings take away the hope which many had of things coming to a Treaty, so that I am in a post where in all likelihood there will be little to doe. This is a great affliction to me in a time when all true men shou'd be active in his Majestie's Service.

My Lord Cornbury's [2] base dissertion dos not give so ill an opinion of his Majestie's affaires to some judicious Ministers here as the unseasonable petition which was deliver'd him to call a Parlement, whose freedome is impracticable in this conjuncture, and it cannot be consistent either with his Safety or his Honor. I wou'd write the severall reasons they alledge but that I know they have been obvious

259

to you, who have made serious reflections on this matter. All Loyall men will think his royall word a sufficient Security that his Majesty will assemble his Parlement as soon as it is possible, and no modest man can desire his Majesty to lett the Law be given him by inveterate enemys, Traytors, and Rebells. It is an ill mark for men to draw petitions on their King when they shou'd draw their swords in defense of him and their Countrey. I hope to hear that they who were engag'd in this business repent themselves of it, I having reason to believe most of them mistaken honest men. I am etc.

Source: H-2, pp. 131–133.

[1] The Golden Bull issued by Emperor Charles IV in 1356 named the seven Electors, gave them sovereign rights, and prescribed rules for the inheritance of their rights.

[2] Viscount Cornbury, eldest son of Henry Hyde, 2nd Earl of Clarendon, had joined William of Orange on November 14.

Dito [December 16, 1688]

To Mr. Richards, to return 130 £ by Mr. Martins.

Source: H-2, p. 133.

To Mr. Tempest[1]   December 20, 1688
                                                 Ratisbon

To Mr. Tempest, wherein it follow'd thus:

I send you a Copy of the Imperiall Decree which was deliver'd to the French Plenipotentiary the last week, with a Copy of a Decree of Commission which was dictated thereupon in the Dyette. The Plenipotentiary left this place yesterday; I believe the jealousie they had at Vienna of his delivering some act upon the receiving Prince Clement into the Electorall College hasten'd this business. Besides it is certain that the Emperor, shou'd he have a minde to treat with the French, will for many reasons never consent it shall be here again. . . .[2]

Here are some Ministers who pretend to have letters from England of the 6th of December New Style which mention so horrid a Conspiracy even against his Majestie's person[3] that I am in the greatest paine imaginable 'till I receive some of the same date. I cannot think heaven will abandon the best of Kings and permitt unnaturall and ungratefull Traytors to succeed in the fowlest enterprise that was ever known. Shou'd they, there needs no more to make me curse my

Countrey, which has been the scene of too many villainys allready. I am, etc.

Source: H-2, pp. 133–134.

1 Secretary to Viscount Preston (*Ellis Correspondence*, 2, p. 287).

2 The ellipsis marks are in the MS.

3 James himself said he believed that Lord Churchill was planning to kidnap him while he was inspecting his troops at Warminster and to take him a prisoner to William (Maurice Ashley, *The Glorious Revolution*, London 1966, p. 168).

To HENRY GUY   December 20, 1688
                                                    Dito
Sir.

In the hurry and confusion that everybody now must needs be in at Court, it is a confident thing in me to give you the least trouble. My modesty has long kept me silent, and I shou'd not yet speake had I not spent 500 £ of my own money, which has been remitted me by a friend out of England and which is to a penny all I can command. I am in a Countrey which is not favourable to his Majestie's interest and where, as our affaires stand, Creditors are very importunate.

I intend to sollicite my recall, since now the war is broke out here, I do not see how I can be any way serviceable to his Majesty in this post. In the mean time, I will be carefull his Majestie's honor shall not suffer in the least. Mr. Wynne in delivering you this will lett you know what is due to me out of the Treasury, and I am so confident of your favour that I do not doubt but you will use what means you can with the Lords who wish me well to gett me so much of it as is possible, towards the supporting me 'till things are settled. I am asham'd of the freedom I have taken; yet when I call to minde your goodness towards me, I cannot but hope, if you can do nothing else for me, at least you will excuse the boldness of, Sir, etc.

Source: H-2, pp. 134–135.

                                        Dito [December 20, 1688]
To Mr. Wynne of our want of money, with orders to tell Mr. Guy that in February next there will be a whole year's entertainment due to his honor, that Mr. Robson has two hundred pounds yet to receive of the last Extraordinaries allow'd him. That his Honor is out 350 £ on the birth of the Prince of Wales, besides other Extraor-

dinaries which are due since May last. About a Bill of Credit and the 500 £ mention'd in Mr. Guy's. . . .
Source: H-2, pp. 134–135.

Ratisbon December 23, 1688
To Mr. Tempest.
Source: H-2, p. 135.

To Viscount Preston   December 27, 1688
                                                             Ratisbon
My Lord.

On Saturday last a certain paper came to my hands which I find was read a day or two before in the Hall of Re- et Correlatione to most of the members of the Dyet by Dankleman, the Elector of Brandenburg's Deputy. I send it to your Lordship translated into french. I believe you will be very much surpris'd at the insolence of this Deputy, who durst publish in so auguste an assembly so infamous a Libell against his Majesty. To vex me the more I cannot prudently at this time take so much notice of it as I shou'd, but must waite for a more favourable conjuncture. In the mean time all I can do is to expose the weakness and deceitfullness of his arguments in such places as are proper.

The States of Holland and the Protestant Princes who are engag'd in the Prince of Orange's dessein, recollecting themselves that a war begun by them on the account of Religion may be of dangerous consequence shou'd it be taken notice of by the Roman Catholick Princes before they have proceeded so far as to fix the foundation of that vast building which seems to be projected by them, have order'd their Ministers, especially those who are employ'd in the Empire, to insinuate and declare that the invasion of our Countrey by the Prince of Orange is not so much to establish the affaires of the Church as to regulate the affaires of State in order to lessen the greatness of France and is purely grounded on a politick interest. They hope with this to amuse the Roman Catholicks while they carry on their own business, but to make this sham take, the Prince of Orange shou'd have made an other manifest. I wish all our Countreymen who are misled by an apprehension that their Religion is in danger were well inform'd of these practices that they may be no longer cheated by any tincell pretexts.

The foolish and impudent author of the inclosed is so confident of the success of his party that he already places the Prince of Orange on the Throne regulating the affaires of England. The house of Austria can do nothing without the help of this almanzor.[1] He will do them justice against the French and fight for all the Princes who will favour his Ambition. No wonder, since it is to make way for so generall a blessing, that his Majesty is unjustly attack'd under the name of evill Counsellors, and the Prince of Wales presum'd to be suppos'd. Notwithstanding the pains he takes to dissemble, he is not able to hold out to the end of the Chapter. His praising a notable pamphlet called L'Europe Esclave, si l'Angleterre ne rompt ses fers, which was written by the same foolish Zealot who made Le Croisade des Protestants, ou projet sur l'institution des Chevaliers de St. Paul, discovers what his principles are at bottom. I am etc.

Source: H-2, pp. 135–137. Printed in *LB*, pp. 433–434, with incorrect date.

[1] The hero of Dryden's *The Conquest of Granada*.

Ratisbon December 29, 1688

To my Lord Carlinford to press the Emperor by Cardinal Bonvisi to listen to an Accommodation with France, and to acquaint him with the dessein on foot against the Roman Catholick Church. With the Libell of Danckelman.

Ratisbon December 30, 1688

To Mr. Tempest with the News.
Source: H-2, p. 137.

[UNADDRESSED]   December 31, 1688
                                                        Ratisbon

Ayant examiné les Contes de Monsieur Österlin, je trouve que je luy suis redevable de cent huit florins et quarante cinq creutzers, que je promets de luy payer.

[The following note is written on the same page. Like the first entry, it appears to be in Hughes' handwriting. It refers to the 130 £ requested in a letter of December 16, 1688, to Mr. Richards.]

For the 130 £ which is to be received the Merchand is to give 945 gülders and 45 x [kreutzers] at the rate of 4 Rxds [Reichsdollars] and 76 x $\frac{1}{2}$ per pound.
Source: H-2, unnumbered page preceding page 1.

January 3, 1689
Ratisbon

My Lord.

The Prince Lewis of Baden has been here three days with the Margrave his unckle and this morning is gone post for Munick, from whence he goes to the Elector of Saxony and other chief Princes of the Empire to execute a Secret Commission which he has from the Emperor. I believe it is nothing else than to assure them that he will jointly with them make a vigorous war against the French the next spring and to take such measures with them as are necessary for the begining of the Campagne. The French have so enrag'd the Germans with the many outrages they have committed in the Countrey that the severall States were never so united and animated to revenge them. This makes me hope but little success from any endeavours which may be us'd to prevent the bloody war which is threatned.

His Majesty has been so shamefully betray'd at home that our Nation has justly lost the little reputation it had recover'd. Honour and honesty are look'd upon by forreigners to be no more of the growth of our unhappy Island. A Parlament is call'd (I hear). I wish it cou'd be such a one as wou'd sincerely labour to establish a healing peace among us by having a due regard to his Majestie's Prerogative as well as to the Priviledge of the Subject. I must confess the greatest good I expect from it is that it will Open the eys of many well meaning men who have been grossly impos'd upon.

God preserve his Majesty from the hands of his enemies. While his person is not in their power, it will mark the place where all his faithfull subjects may rally, whose number cannot but be considerable tho' the perfidious and ungratefull have seduc'd many with them. The most considerable thing in this conjuncture is to gain time. Impostures cannot be long conceal'd. Mankind is unconstant, especially the humor of a whole Nation. The face of affaires cannot be long the same in Christendom, so that a powerfull assistance may be had in case it be requisite.

I hope your Lordship will pardon me the confidence I have taken in communicating to you a few of my Sentiments on this Matter. The Zeal I have to serve his Majesty makes me very uneasy in a place where I cannot shew it as I wou'd do, wherefore I think of coming into England. Pray, my Lord, if this shou'd happen, prepare his Majesty to forgive me my not waiting till I was recall'd. I am so useless here that I hope you will think it a Lawfull ambition to desire to be where I may venture my Life in performing my Duty. My allegiance and my gratitude tell me it is base to be unactive when my King and my Masters Crown and person are in danger. I am.

Source: H-2, pp. 137–139.

Dito [January 3, 1689]

To Mr. Tempest and
To Mr. Richards to return the 130 £.
Source: H-2, p. 139; *LB*, pp. 432–433.

To Mr. Tempest   January 3, 1689
                                                Ratisbon
Sir.

While things go so ill in England, I imagin you are not very curious to know what passes in the Empire; wherefore I shall not trouble you with an account of what farther contributions are demanded, what Towns have been plunder'd, and what Villages have been lately burnt by the French. I have receiv'd your Letter of the 4th of this instant, which is so obliging that I am impatient to be personally acquainted with you. When I see my wicked Country again, I shall take care to give you reall proofs of my being, Sir, Your most humble and Obedient Servant

Geo: Etherege

Source: Holograph letter owned by Sir Fergus Graham, Netherby, Longtown, Cumberland.

To The Earl of Carlingford   January 12, 1689
                                                Ratisbon
My Lord.

I am sorry I received Mr. Lane's letter no sooner, that I might have sent you the Greyhounds you desir'd. Things going so ill in England, I dispose of all I have here in order to go and find the Queen in France. I wish I may be serviceable to his Majesty in some other Countrey; I find I cannot be so here any Longer.

The French have left Swabia and Franconia, and the Germans ascribe it to the success the Prince of Orange has had. I do not doubt but there will be desseins on foot in the Empire ere long which may make them repent it. The Prince Louis of Baden has been return'd these three days from Munich, and Yesterday went from hence in order to find the Elector of Saxony at Schwinfurt. I saw him often during his stay here with the Margrave, his Uncle. He told me the

265

Emperor thought it not his interest to miss an opportunity to drive the French from the banks of the Rhin, in order to which nothing was able to hinder a bloody war between the Empire and his Most Christian Majesty, and that his Imperiall Majesty cou'd not conceive how the affaires of Religion in England concern'd him. After this you may think what you please of the Piety of the Court of Vienna.

I intend to go from hence in few days, but where ever I am You will learn I cannot follow the Example of my perfidious Countreymen, and you shall never want testimonies of my being   I am, etc.

I have sold my saddle horses to the Duke of Wirtemberg, and have given my dogs to the Prince of Hohenzoleren.

Source: H-2, p. 140.

To The Earl of Carlingford   January 19, 1689
                                                              Ratisbon

My Lord.

I received yesterday a letter of the 8th Instant from Paris which confirms his Majestie's Safe arrivall there, the best news I cou'd expect in this unhappy conjuncture. The posts have been for some time stopp'd in England, so that I have not yet received a Bill of Exchange which I order'd to be return'd me from thence. This has kept me here longer than I thought. Nevertheless I will find a way of disengaging myself and intend very suddainly to be with his Majesty, being resolv'd to live and dy in serving him faithfully.

I have seen a letter which came by the last post from Vienna which gives an account of a Memoriall you gave, together with the Prince of Orange's 3d Declaration to the Emperor. I desire you to lett Mr. Laine send me a Copy of it. If it come not time enough to find me in this place, I have given order it shall be sent after me. I hear the Prince of Orange has writ an other letter to the Emperor, in which he endeavours to excuse the Cruelties and outrages which are acted against the Roman Catholiques by laying them on the rage of the people. I would fain know whether that rage penn'd his Declaration. It is certain the madness and rebellious spirit of our Nation call'd him in and maintains him in his usurpation, and when that is spent I hope our Countreymen will recover their right senses again.

Monsieur Hop is an active and a dangerous Minister. You can hardly be carefull enough in countermining his false suggestions and artificiall insinuations in the Court you reside at. I shall think myself happy if you have so good an opinion of me as to honor me with any commands. I shall not fail when I am in France to continue my correspondence with you and give you constantly a true account of his Majestie's affaires to the best of my knowledge, being with all the faithfullness imaginable, My Lord, etc.

Pray assure my Lord Taaffe that I have that real honor and esteem for him which he deserves.

Source: H-2, p. 141.

Paris le 20 fevrier 1689
    Monsieur L'Abbé Flemming,
    Monsieur Poffendorf
Paris le 3me Mars—89
    Monsieur L Abbé Flemming
Paris le 9me Mars Monsieur Richards
    Dito Madame Merry
    Dito Monsieur Jephson
Paris le 29me Mars Monsieur Martins
    Dito Monsieur Richards
Paris Monsieur Jephson le 2me avril
Paris le 6me avril Monsieur Robson
    dito Madame Merry
    dito Monsieur Merttins
Paris le 9me avril Monsieur Wynn
    Dito Madame Etherege
    Dito Monsieur Richards
Paris le 13e avril Monsieur Mertins
Paris le 15me dito Monsieur Flemming
Paris le 7me May Monsieur Merttins
    dito Madame Merry
Paris le premier Juin Mr Merttins
    Dito Madame Etherege
Paris le 4me Juin Monsieur Wynn
    Dito Monsieur Flemming
    dito Monsieur Österlin
    dito Madame Etherege
Paris le 22e Juin Madame Merry
    Dito Madame Etherege
Paris le 28e Septembre Madame Merry
    Dito Mr Österlin
    Source: H-2, p. 142.

APPENDIX I
Letters Received

FROM THE EARL OF MIDDLETON   December 7, 1685.
                                                 Whitehall.

Sir.

I was very glad to hear of your safe arrivall at Ratisbonne. I thanke you for your letters, by which you approve yourself a very pretty proficient: I hope in a little time we may hear something of your diversions, as well as your businesse, which wou'd be much pleasanter and perhaps as instructive. I can tell you for comfort that this place is as dull as your Dyett. The young fellows you left hear are so unlike you that they have not had vigour enough to afford Scandall, nor witt enough to invent any. For the little we have had, we have been beholding to a Dutch Tapster,[1] which onely begot a Ballad below Humphrey Bell, to the tune of four pence half-penny Farthing.

Every weeke there are plays at Court. The last time, Sir Fopling appear'd with the usuall applause, and the King was pleas'd to tell me that he expected you shou'd put on your socks, which putts me in minde of Denham on Killigrew.

> He has plotted and penn'd
> Six plays, to attend
> The Farce of his negotiation.[2]

This you are to consider as an Instruction, and as for advice Iagos[3] is the best that can be given you by, Sir, Your most faithfull Servant.
                                                      Middleton.

Source: BM, f. 173.

[1] The scandal referred to was probably the affair between Lady Mary Mordaunt, Duchess of Norfolk, and John Germain, which was discovered in the summer of 1685 and led to a separation in the fall. Germain, according to Evelyn (*Diary*, April 1700) was "a Dutch gamester of mean extraction." Lucas (*Lives of the Gamesters*, p. 212) is more specific: "His parents kept an

ordinary at Delft in Holland, where he was born." Germain eventually was knighted, bought a baronetcy, and married Lady Mary in 1701.

2 Quoted from Denham's "On Mr. Killigrew's Return from Venice. . . ." During his unsuccessful negotiation at Venice in behalf of Charles II in 1649, Killigrew wrote six plays (Alfred Harbage, *Thomas Killigrew*, 1930, p. 87).

3 Presumably the advice is, "Put money in thy purse."

FROM AMBASSADOR BARRILLON   January 22, 1686
                                                              London

Monsieur.

J'ay reçeu la lettre que vous m'avez fait la faveur de m'écrire; elle a esté leüe en bonne compagnie, et a esté fort aprouveé de quantité de Milford[s], qui ne donnent pas legerement leur aprobation. Vôtre description de traisneaux nous a fait regreter d'estre icy dans un climat si temperé, que nous ne pouvons pas esperer des semblables divertissemens.

J'ay, Monsieur, une grand joye d'avoir pû contribuer a la liaison qui me paroist estre entre Monsieur de Crecy et vous. Je suis assuré qu'elle augmentera a proportion que vous vous cognoistrez d'avantage. Croyez je vous prie, Monsieur, que Je suis avec beaucoup d'estime et de verite, Monsieur, Vostre tres humble et tres obeissant serviteur.

                                                              Barrillon

À Londres ce 22.ᵉ Janvier 1686.
    Source: BM, f. 173.

FROM JOHN DRYDEN   [Undated] 1
    To you who live in chill degree
    (As map informs) of fifty three
    And do not much for cold attone
    By bringing thether fifty one,
    Methinks all Climes should be alike
    From Tropique ev'n to pole artique,
    Since you have such a constitution
    As no where suffers diminution.
    You can be old in grave debate
    And young in Love's affaires of State,
    And both to wives and Husbands show
    The vigour of a Plenipo.
    Like mighty Missioner you come
    Ad partes Infidelium,
    A work of wondrous merit sure

270

So farr to go, so much endure,
And all to preach to German Dame
Where sound of Cupid never came.
Less had you done had you been sent
As far as Drake or Pinto² went
For Cloves and Nutmegs to the Line á
Or ev'n for Oranges to China.
That had indeed been Charity ⎤
Where lovesick Ladys helpless ly ⎬
Chopt, and for want of liquor dry. ⎦
But you have made your zeal appear
Within the Circle of the Bear.
What region of the Earth so dull
That is not of your labours full?
Triptolemus³ (so sing the nine)
Strew'd plenty from his Cart divine,
But spight of all those fable makers
He never sow'd on Almain Acres.
No, that was left by fate's Decree
To be perform'd and sung by thee.
Thou breakst through formes with as much ease
As the French King through articles.
In grand affaires thy days are spent ⎤
Of waging weighty compliment ⎬
With such as Monarchs represent. ⎦
They who such vast fatigues attend
Want some soft minutes to unbend,
To shew the world now and then
Great Ministers are mortall men.
Then Renish Rummers walk the round;
In bumpers every King is Crown'd
Besides three holy miter'd Hectors
And the whole College of Electors.
No health of Potentate is sunk
That pays to make his Envoy drunk.
These dutch delights I mention'd last
Suit not, I know, your English tast;
For wine, to leave a whore or play
Was ne're your Excellencies way.
Nor need the title give offence
For here you were his Excellence

271

For gaming, writing, speaking, keeping:
His excellence for all but sleeping.
Now if you tope in form and treat ⎤
'Tis the sowr sawce to your sweet meat, ⎬
The fine you pay for being great. ⎦
Nay, there is a harder imposition
Which is indeed the Courts petition
That setting worldly pomp aside
(Which Poet has at Font defy'd)
You wou'd be pleas'd in humble way
To write a Trifle call'd a play.
This Truly is a Degradation ⎤
But wou'd oblige the Crown and Nation ⎬
Next to your wise Negotiation. ⎦
If you pretend (as well you may) ⎤
Your high Degree, your friends will say ⎬
That Duke St. Aignan[4] made a Play. ⎦
If Gallique Poet convince you scarce
His Grace of Bucks has writ a Farce,[5]
And you whose Comique wit is ters all
Can hardly fall below rehersall.
Then finish what you here began
But Scribble faster, if you can,
For yet noe George, to our discerning,
Has writ without a ten years warning.[6]

Source: BM, ff. 174–175. At the end of the poem Hughes has written "Thought to be writen by Mr. Dryden and sent to Sir G by my Lord Middleton."

[1] If these verses were written at Middleton's suggestion as an answer to Etherege's Second Verse Letter, as internal evidence suggests, they probably date from the summer of 1686.

[2] Fernão Mendes Pinto (1509–1583), a Portuguese traveller whose description of his voyages in the Far East was translated into English in 1614.

[3] In Greek myth Triptolemus was the inventor of the plow. In a chariot given him by Demeter he took seeds, and the art of growing them, to all parts of the earth.

[4] The tragicomedy *Bradamante*, by François de Beauvillier, Duc de Saint-Aignan (Thorpe, *Poems*, p. 121).

[5] *The Rehearsal*, in which Dryden was ridiculed.

[6] In March 1686 it would have been just ten years since the first production of *The Man of Mode*. Dryden is complaining that Etherege, like the Duke of Buckingham, takes a long time between plays. For Buckingham's slowness, see Thorpe, *Poems*, p. 121.

Sir.

His Majesty having thought it necessary for his Service to regulate the Extraordinary allowances of his Ministers employ'd abroad, and having thereupon pass'd an order under his Royall Signet and Signe Manuall the 7th of this instant February, He hath been pleas'd thereby to declare that if your accounts of Extraordinaries exceed the summe of Fifty pounds every quarter of a yeare during your Residence at Ratisbon in his Majesties Service, his Majesty will allow no more than Fifty pounds a Quarter, & that no other Extraordinaries shall be allow'd you from time to time upon any occasion, except for such extraordinary Expences as shall be made by you in pursuance of his Majesties particular Order to be signify'd by one of his Principall Secretaries of State or for such expences as shall appear absolutely necessary for his Majesties Service in case there be not time to send or receive his Majesties directions in the matter. And his Majesty hath commanded me to signify this his pleasure unto you, that you may govern yourself accordingly. I am, Sir, Your most humble servant

Middleton.

Source: BM, f. 175.

FROM CAPTAIN SOLOMON SLATER[1]   December 28, 1686
                                                      Paris

Sir.

Mr. Skelton being come to this place in Quality of his Majestie's Envoyé Extraordinary and being as yet in such a hurry upon his first arrivall, that he has not time to write to you himself, has done me the honor to desire me to do it for him, and make you a tender of the services of this Station, which I am sure he will with a great deal of sincerity most readily give you.

Sir, I have had formerly thoughts of troubling you with a letter out of the esteem I have for you, to give you an account of Reports which we had in Holland that in your discourses, where you are, you frequently made Reflections upon the conduct of Mr. Skelton in his negotiations abroad, and particularly that you have of late much condemn'd the seizing of Sir Robert Peyton at Roterdam and vindicated him from being a Rebell. I am concern'd for this for your sake, for as for Mr. Skelton he knew the grounds he went upon, and the King has very well approv'd of what he did, and you are under a great mistake if you do not think him as guilty as any man.

And I have also heard that you accuse Mr. Skelton with breach of faith for endeavouring to seize a man with whom he was in treaty for the obtaining his pardon. This is a great mistake too, for tho' he receiv'd letters from Peyton entreating his sollicitations in his behalf to which he made no other returns than that he wou'd send over his Letters to the King, as he did those he ever receiv'd from any other Rebells and made known to his Majesty all the offers that were made to him by this man or others, yet he never did or cou'd make any promises of safty to him, and coming in his way, was as lyable to be apprehended as Ferguson himself. You will excuse me for endeavouring the rectifying your mistakes in this matter. I am sure I aime onely at your Service in it, and continue to be with great esteem, Sir, Your most faithfull humble servant.

Sol. Slater

Source: BM, ff. 177–178.

[1] See Etherege's letter to Slater, February 13, 1687.

FROM THOMAS MAULE February 4, 1687
London

Sir.

Yours inclosed in one to Mr. Corbet I have receiv'd, and sorry I cannot say so much of an other you mention to have sent me formerly. I hope my not answering of it, in all this time, is a sufficient demonstration to you that I never receiv'd it, for you cannot think I understand my advantage so little as not embrace the first opportunity of holding so good a Correspondence with one whose friendship I ever valu'd at too high a Rate to venture the loosing of it by so unpardonable a neglect, and to tell you the Truth I have bin very often out of countenance and somewhat out of humor not to be able to give an account of Sir George Etherege, when inquir'd for amongst his friends, & have not drunk his health with that gusto I us'd to do, but have either spilt my wine or putt on a sullen grave face, thinking by that foolish means to be reveng'd on you; but now we are fully reconcil'd (and that is a word at this time of no small importance) I will confesse to you that I am not so fond of my Court-Employment as you imagine, because that either I grow old, or the sett of maids do so, and consequently have not many Charmes to make any one sigh but poor Robin Sayers, who has blown (not in Sunderlands Cant) Mrs. Yarburgh[1] into the North, there to lead Apes in hell, for she has left the Court, and her court Portion is payd without any obligation of marrying.

Her place is not ill supply'd by Mrs. Fairefax, who was once married (and I doubt not as good a maide as any of the whole Sett) to Lord Abergavenny, who releas'd her for a thousand pound. The widdow Swan,[2] they say, is disposing of her person, whose place will not be ill fill'd by Mrs. Fragmorton, who has made Packes[3] eyes water a hundred times even when Lady Dorset[4] sat governess of his unruly passion. Mrs. Frazier[5] will not declare herself 'till she knows whether Scarborogh's[6] passion will keep alive a year and a day at Lisbon. As for the Pr[incess Anne's] maides I suppose you are not very sollicitous to know what is become of them, since Mrs. Notts face was spoil'd with the small Pox. However I cannot forbear telling of you that Harry Wharton[7] is no more the Constant (and that gives great allarms to Ginee Deer least the disease shou'd run in a blood, and infect poor Tom) for he has forsaken Mrs. Mary, and makes violent love to Mrs. Drumar, by the help of his friend Lord Scarsdale,[8] who is contented at present with an amusement with Mrs. Ogle.[9]

The Lord [10] you desire to be inform'd of deceives nobodys expectations, for ever since the first moneth of their marriage, 'tis Cross and Pile[11] but that before night they part, and nothing hinders of his side but the two thousand per annum seperate maintenance; but now the quarrells are so loud that Bitch and Rogue are words of very civil respect. So that very soon you will hear of an Elopement, which they say she did very lately for 2 or 3 days, and he, being very unwilling to part with any ready mony, submitted and made Peace, but it is no more expected to be kept than betwixt the Turks and Christians.

I will now fill up my sheet & tell you that the King has taken away my Lord Shrewsburys and Lord Lumleys Regiments for reasons best known to himself, tho' the Town will have it because of their refusall to comply with the Kings desires in taking off the Test.[12] But of these matters of state I know you have a much better account, therefore will not further trouble you but to assure you I am Your most obedient and humble servant

T Maule

Source: BM, ff. 178–179.

[1] Probably Henrietta Yarburgh, a Maid of Honour who was granted a marriage portion of £2,000 on December 9, 1686 (*LB*, p. 353). According to the proverb, girls who die unmarried will lead apes in Hell. See *The Taming of the Shrew*, II, i, 33.

[2] "A New Satire, 1681" (V&A, Dyce MS 43, p. 564) mentions, among the Court ladies, "Widow Swan/(For such she is, since Ossory is gone)." Thomas Butler, eldest son of the Duke of Ormonde and known as the Earl of Ossory, died in 1680.

³ Apparently the Captain Packe referred to on p. 101, above.

⁴ Mary Bagot, Countess of Falmouth and first wife of the Earl of Dorset.

⁵ Cary Frazier, daughter of the King's physician and a Maid of Honour to the Queen, was a frequent target of satire (Wilson, *Court Wits*, p. 120). Secretly married to Charles, Viscount Mordaunt, in 1675, she was still referred to in the 1680s as "Fair Frazer" (V&A, Dyce MS 43, p. 412).

⁶ Sir Charles Scarborough went as envoy to Portugal in March 1686 (*LB*, p. 353).

⁷ Henry Wharton and his older brother Thomas, 1st Marquis of Wharton, were famous rakes of the time. "Harry" Wharton was constantly linked in the satires of the period with Mary (Mall) Howard; Jenny Dering, or Deering, was evidently the mistress of Thomas Wharton. Mrs. Drumar was a Maid of Honour to Princess Anne. I owe these identifications to John Harold Wilson.

⁸ Robert Leke, Earl of Scarsdale (1654–1707).

⁹ Probably the sister of John ("Mad Jack") Ogle, the gamester. She was a gentlewoman to the Countess of Inchiquin and later mistress to the Duke of York, according to the *DNB*.

¹⁰ Probably the Earl of Mulgrave. Etherege commented on his marriage in letters to Middleton on March 14 and 21, 1686.

¹¹ "A tossup," referring to the two sides of a coin (*OED*).

¹² James claimed the right to dispense with the Test Act in particular cases, especially when Catholic army officers were involved.

FROM JOHN DRYDEN   February 16, 1687
                                                      London

A guilty man, you know Sir, naturally avoids one who can convince him of his faults, and I acknowledge myself to be of that number, for which reason I have not dared in three weeks time since your last letter lay by me, yet to open it. For my conscience tells me that tho' you may express yourself with all imaginable civility, and I believe kindness too, yet there must be somewhat of upbraiding me for my neglect, which I will not go about to excuse, because I cannot. 'Tis a blott, and you may enter, if you will not forgive an oversight, which you may safely do and win the game afterwards in good writing. For I will never enter the lists in Prose with the undoubted best author of it which our nation has produced.

Therefore, O thou immortall source of Idleness (you see I am ready to make prayers to you and invoke you by your darling attribute), pardon a poor creature who is your image, and whom no gratitude, no consideration of friendship, no letters tho' never so elegantly written can oblige to take up the penn, tho' it be but to manage it half an hour. For while I am writing this, I have layd it down and almost concluded with an imperfect sentence. I am almost lazy enough to get a Stamp for my name like the King of France, which indeed wou'd be to be great in idleness.

I have made my Court to the King once in Seaven moneths, have seen my Lord Chamberlain full as often. I believe, if they think of me at all, they imagine I am very proud, but I am gloriously lazy. I have a sonn, whom I love intirely, with my Lord Middleton, but I never thank him for his kindness for fear of opening my mouth. I might probably get something at Court, but my Lord Sunderland, I imagine, thinks me dead while I am silently wishing him all prosperity, for wishes cost me no more than thinking. In short without Apoplexy, Wycherleys long sickness, I forget every thing to enjoy nothing that is myself. Can you expect news out of Covent Garden from such a man?

The Coffeehouse[1] stands certainly where it did, and angry men meet in the Square sometimes, as Abercomy and Goodman[2] lately did, where they say Alexander the great was wounded in the arme, by which you may note he had better have been idle. I cannot help hearing that white sticks change their Masters[3] and that officers of the Army are not immortall in their places,[4] because the King finds they will not vote for him in the next Sessions. Oh that our Monarch wou'd encourage noble idleness by his own example, as he of blessed memory did before him, for my minde misgives me that he will not much advance his affaires by stirring.

I was going on but am glad to be admonishd by the paper. Ask me not of Love, for every man hates every man perfectly, and women are still the same Bitches. But after all I will contradict myself and come off with an exception as to my own particular, who am as much as idleness will dispence with me, Sir, Your most faithfull servant

John Dryden.

Source: BM, ff. 179–180.

[1] Will's Coffeehouse, Dryden's favorite, was at the corner of Russell and Bow streets, just off the Square.

[2] Cardell Goodman of the King's Company, known as Alexander the Great from his role in Lee's *The Rival Queens*, fought with Duncan Abercromy, "a profane, roistering fellow" and a captain in the Duke of Grafton's first regiment of footguards (J. H. Wilson, *Mr. Goodman the Player*, Pittsburgh, 1964, p. 104).

[3] Laurence Hyde, Earl of Rochester, had recently been dismissed from his post as Treasury Commissioner.

[4] The Earl of Shrewsbury and Richard, Baron Lumley, gave up their commissions because of dissatisfaction with the King's policies. Both later signed the invitation to William of Orange.

  Whitehall

I saw t'other day by chance a letter of yours to Mr. Dryden, which put me in mind of one I received from you a good while ago, as well as of the Lady in the Garret. For the last memorandum I thank you with all my heart, the remembrance of her being very sweet, both as a pleasure enjoy'd and a danger escap'd, and I am not so young now but that I can chew the Cud of Lechery with some sorte of Satisfaction. You who are so amorous and vigorous may have your minde wholely taken up with the present, but we grave, decayd people, alas, are glad to steal a thought some times towards the passt and then are to ask God forgiveness for it too. This is a little revenge for your suspicion of my being alter'd, as well as a vindication of my innocency in that particular. But to speak more seriously you shall never find me chang'd, whenever there is any occasion of employing Your humble servant

                                                                      Mulgrave

Source: BM, ff. 180–181.

Note: I have omitted here five letters from Sir Edward Vaudrey regarding the siege of Buda and a short note from Bevil Skelton. These may be found in *LB*, pp. 358–365.

APPENDIX II
Etherege's Account of the Feast Honoring the Birth of the Prince of Wales

Sent away. 26. July./5. Aug. 1688.

A Relation of the great Feast
Kept at Ratisbon the 15th/25 July
being St. James's day, 1688.

On tuesday the 6th of July, new style, I received the happy news of her Majestie's being safely brought to bed of a Prince, which was long wish'd for and impatiently expected by all pious and honest people here, as being the onely thing wanting to compleate the felicity of his Majesty and to secure the peace and glory of his Kingdoms. The great marks of satisfaction which appear'd in me in reading of the letter made those who were by me conclude there was some thing extraordinary in it; and I had not the power to conceal it one minute from them. This in a moment was spread all over the House, and the Servants, transported as well as the Master, open'd the Cellar before I had time to give them order, and every one abandon'd himself to joy and good drinking.

After a little recollection, I sent my Secretary to notify this blessing to the Imperiall Commission and to most of the Ministers, but in the first place to those I knew it wou'd be most wellcome to, who all return'd me their complements by their Principall Domesticks, and many of them came themselves to testify the great part they tooke in what is for the common good of all Europe. In a word never news was received here with so universall a concurrence of applaus, and tho' the Ministers which compose this body are divided by severall interests, they all agreed to rejoice in this conjuncture. The Abbot of St. James, an ancient Monastry founded in this Town in the time of

279

Charles-maign by William, Brother to Achaius King of the Scots, came running hither, fill'd with joy proportionable to the Zeal he has always had for the glory and prosperity of his Majesty. He and I, after we had given way to the first motions of our passion, consulted together what was fit to be done by us in this place, on so great an occasion.

We consider'd we were at the generall Dyet of the Empire, which is held in a manner in the heart of all Christendom, where feasts and publick divertisments have been made for the Coronation of Emperors and for the choice of Kings of the Romans; where there is a greater confluence of Ministers than at the courts of the greatest monarchs who hold intelligence the whole world over, and that the Plenipotentiary of France had but a few years since splendidly treated them and all the Town on the birth of the Duke of Burgundy, wherefore we concluded it was necessary to do something which was answerable to his Majestie's greatness and the honor of the nation. Having taken this resolution, I desir'd the abbot to charge himself with what was convenient to be done in the church, thanksgivings and praises to God being the first things by which all good Christians shou'd acknowledge his mercies. He willingly accepted of that care, and I myself undertook to order and cause to be got ready all which might make the feasting part delightfull and surprising.

We pitch'd on Sunday the 25th of the same moneth, being St. James's day, to begin the celebration of the feast at the Monastry aforesaid. The abbot having prepar'd and beautify'd his Church invited the Imperiall Commission to a *Te Deum Laudamus* in consideration of the holy day, and I invited the Margrave of Baden, the Count de Windisgratz, the french Plenipotentiary, all the members of the Dyet, and what other Ministers are here, thither to celebrate the young Prince's birth, and after the *Te Deum* to a dinner at my house.

The Magistrates of the Town were very civill and obliging to me. They lent me their Canon, which is not very usuall, and in a greater number than ever they had done before. They sent me a Company of foot to keep good order and to hinder the rable from Crowding into my house,[1] which is the most convenient in Ratisbon by reason of the largeness and number of appartments and it's being scituated in the great place of St. Jame's, which will hold many thousands of people.

The day being come, the first signal of the feast was given about 4 a clock in the morning by the discharge of 24 great pieces of Canon, immediately after which the great Bells of the Monastry rang and prayers began, which lasted till 12 a clock. At eight a sermon was

[1] This is the so-called Wildsche house. See above, p. 196, n.

280

preach'd by the Reverend Father Laurence Beer of the Society of Iesus suitable to the occasion, with generall applaus. That ended, the high Mass was sung by the Count of Wartemberg of [the] house of Bavaria, suffragan Bishop of this place and Bishop of Laodicea in partibus. I having been with the Abbot to visit him and to invite him to do us this favour, he seem'd overjoy'd at our request, and after having given the young Prince a thousand blessings, sayd nothing cou'd be propos'd to him so conformable to his wishes.

After Mass the Te Deum was sung, and during the whole service diverse Masses were sayd by all the orders of Religious here for their Majesties' and the Prince's conservation, for the preservation of the peace of their Realmes, and victory over their enemies; The Margrave of Baden, the Count de Windisgratz, The French Plenipotentiary, the Director, and all the members of the Dyet, as well Roman Catholic as Reformed being present. The Margrave and the Count sent their Trumpetts and Tymballs, and the Abbot had taken care to have all the best concerts the Town cou'd afford of Instrumentall and vocall musick. Above 80 pieces of Canon were shott off while the high Mass and the *Te Deum* were singing. The reports the day before in what manner this was to be perform'd made many Ladies and Cavaliers of different Religions meet there. The Church was throng'd, and all the places without were fill'd with crowds of people, who were curious to see what pass'd at so great a solemnity.

In the place before my house was erected two large substantiall buildings; the one a kitchin where an ox was roasted whole, a thing which is usuall here on the coronation of an Emperor and never otherwise. The other was a triumphall Pyramide built Triangular, the Top being cover'd with an Imperiall Crown. Beneath was an arbour wrought artificially with branches of trees in which a concert of hautbois play'd. Below that was a rock out of which three fountains of wine sprang; in the hollow of this were plac'd the men which were to play the engins and direct the pipes. In the Frontise piece were his Majestie's arms, on the side next the house the Prince's, and on the other side the four banners of England, Scotland, France and Ireland. In the 3 corners were erected in carved work two Lyons and an unicorn, as big as the life, as they are in the Supporters of the arms; the wine pouring from the Lyons mouths and the unicorn's horn.

The Lower part was a representation of an antick pallace, the Pillars of the Dorick order, with cornishes and festons; on the Front was painted a Bacchus presiding at the celebration of a Bacchanal with this inscription

Nunc est bibendum nunc pede libero
Pulsanda tellus.[2]

On another side a Cornucopia was drawn, with beds below on which
the guests lay extended as in the feasts of the ancients, they and their
gobletts crown'd with red and white roses mixt, handsome youths waiting on them, and bringing in Jarrs of wine with this writ:

Antehac nefas depromere Caecubum
Cellis avitis.[3]

On the third side Mars appear'd above, and the drunken combat between the Centaurs and Lapithes was describ'd with these words
likewise out of Horace:

Natis in usum Laetitiae Scyphis
Pugnare Thracum est.[4]

The Ministers coming, I receiv'd them (as the Ceremony is) at their
Coaches, with the sound of Trumpetts and Kettle-drums, and conducted them into an upper appartment where a band of violins were
playing. The Table had 45 covers, and as soon as the meat was serv'd
up, the Signal was given by the discharge of 6 pieces of Canon. The
dinner consisted of 3 severall Services each of 52 dishes loaded with
venison and all manner of fowl which the Countrey cou'd yield for
above 30 English miles in Circumference. The shouts and acclamations
of joy among the people made them rise from the Table to be Spectators. The wine run, and it was a pleasant sight to see the contests that
arose and the strifes the rable made, who shou'd get the greatest share.
Severall workmen who were appointed for that purpose broke down
the sides of the Kitchin, and the ox and all the Materialls expos'd to
be their Spoile. While this was doing 20 dozen of bread was thrown out
among them.

The Ministers turning from the window, they saw the Table cover'd
anew with a banquett of sweatmeats and all manner of fruits in season.
A large dish in the middle held three Pyramides, on each of which a

2 Horace, *Odes*, I, 37, 1–2. "Now is the time for drinking and dancing."

3 Horace, *Odes*, I, 37, 5–6. "Before this time it had been sinful to pour
out Caecuban wine from the ancestral cellar."

4 Horace, *Odes*, I, 27, 1–2. "It is a Thracian trick to fight with wine
cups intended for pleasure."

flag was display'd: the first was his Majesty represented by Neptun with this writ above:

Summus moderator aquarum.[5]

Beneath, her Majesty represented by a Sea-Goddess bearing a Royall infant in her arms environ'd with Nereides with this verse out of Virgil:[6]

Felix et Nato, felix et conjuge Peleus

And at the bottom

Halcyonei Dies.[7]

The second was the Prince's arms. On the Top was writ

Spes Britanniae[8]

And below

Deodatus tribus regnis Die Sanctissimae Trinitatis 1688.[9]

The third was the Prince represented by an Infant Neptun sleeping in a shell on a bed of Moss, and rock'd by the waves. The Inscription above was[10]

Ingens Pacis Europaeae pignus.

Beneath were severall River-Gods with their urns from which severall Streams discharg'd themselves into the sea, and under that these words:

Ad me confluunt omnes.[11]

---

[5] "Most noble ruler of the seas."
[6] In BM, f. 190ᵛ, Hughes added here, "(devis'd by Mr. H. H.)." Since I am unable to find the quotation in Virgil, I assume that Etherege was mistaken in his attribution. "Happy both in the child and as the wife of Peleus."
[7] "Halcyon day."
[8] "The hope of Britain."
[9] The word *deodatus* does not appear in *Thesaurus Linguae Latinae* nor in the standard dictionaries of Medieval Latin. Presumably it is Hughes's coinage: "God-given (?) to the three Kingdoms on Trinity Sunday, 1688."
[10] In BM, f. 190ᵛ, Hughes added here, "(by Mr. H. H.)." The inscription may be translated, "Illustrious pledge of the peace of Europe."
[11] "All things flow together toward me."

The entertainment lasted from two a clock till between 9 and 10, during which time above 100 pieces of Canon were shott off for the severall healths that were drunk, and to conclude the day, after 9 omers[12] of wine were run out, I caus'd two more to be given to the people with the ends knock'd out, bidding them drink the Prince of Wales his health, and at the same time I call'd for the biggest glass on the buffet and drank it to the Ministers (it having been drunk in form before), who all pleadg'd it, 12 Canon being discharg'd and the Trumpetts and Tymballs sounding all the while.

On the second day I entertain'd all the Ladys and Cavaliers of the Town and Neighbourhood. When the Company were all assembled, I took 400 pieces of Silver each about the value of a shilling, and having first flung two or three handfulls myself out of the window among the poore people, I gave a handfull to every Lady, begining with them of the greatest quality, and desir'd them to follow my example. While the crowd was scrambling and fighting for the money, footmen who were plac'd in the windows by, for that purpose, flung 3 or 400 Squibs to part them who were most mutinous. This had an admirable effect and caus'd much laughter. As soon as this was over, all the house from Top to bottom was illuminated without with a great number of flambeaux of white wax, which were held by artificiall arms; and all the Lustres and Sconces within were lighted.

This day I having a great many more guests, two large tables were prepar'd in two adjoyning rooms with between 80 and 100 Covers. The Ladys sat at one, and such Ministers who were galant enough to come again for their sakes and the Cavaliers sat at the other. The Supper was an ambigue,[13] very handsomely serv'd by the helps of Cookes and other officers which were appointed by my friends to serve me. The first day I had all sorts of good wines which can be had here, with great plenty of Ice, but this day I had, over and above, all sorts of waters, cream, and fruits frozen. The Trumpets sounded and the Kettledrums beat while the supper lasted, after which the Ladys were led into an other appartment, where they were invited to begin the Ball by a Concert of Violins and flutes.

About 2 a Clock in the morning I invited them into an other room, where they were surpris'd with an other scene: being a banquett consisting of 9 Pyramides of dry sweetmeats. The Spaces were fill'd with Liquids, Chocolades, Confits, and an abundance of China Oranges

[12] Estimates as to the equivalent of an omer, or homer, vary from 80 to 40 gallons. In this context, the latter seems more likely.

[13] An assortment of varied dishes.

and Lemons, which were all given up to be plunder'd. The Citizens wives, their daughters, and all the Chambermaids were admitted to be Spectators and to partake of the remainder of the Spoile, so that I think no less than 400 people eat and drank in my house this day.

The third day I entertain'd the Chief Magistrates and the whole Senate with so good a dinner that they own'd they never saw the like. They had good wine, and they spar'd it not. I gave them likewise the Diversion of seeing 3 barrels of wine run among the people, and while they were entertaining themselves with that, a banquett of Sweet-meats was set on the Table, and I propos'd to them to send for their wives to carry that away, as the Ladys had done the other The day before: and the violins being there, they might dance if they thought fit. Some were for it and others, who preferr'd drinking, excus'd them-selves by pretending their wives cou'd not be dress'd in time, so the confitures were given them in basons, which they like good husbands sent home to their dear halfs, and Gamons of Bacon, neats-tongues, Bellonia-Sauciges, and cheese being set on the table in their stead, the glasses went round; and when I saw every one had his load, I desir'd the Canon Might be drawn out of the arsenall, which is near my house (and was the reason I cou'd have no fireworks), to conclude the Feast.

While this was a doing I caus'd a vessel of five Omers to be brought out of my Cellar, which was imediately done by wine Coopers, and souldiers having kept off the Croud till the Top was beat out, the people were told they were to drink their Majestie's and the Prince's health. At the same time I call'd for three of the biggest glasses and drank them to the chief Magistrate, and thirty pieces of Canon were shot off. The Senate was so pleas'd with their Entertainment that they refus'd to take money for the powder I had putt them to the expense of, and I had much ado after a long contest of Civilities to oblige them to accept of it.

Finis.

Source: H-2, ff. 120–117 (numbering from the back). When a note-book was not completely filled, it was common practice to turn it upside down and begin, or continue, numbering the unused pages from what had been the last page in the book.

APPENDIX III
A Catalogue of Sir George's Bookes

English Bookes:

    The History of the Council of Trent
    Cowleys Works
    The Hinde and Panther
    Shakespear's Plays
    The State of the Empire
    Rymer's Tragedy of the last age
    An English Common Prayer Book
    Lovell's Indicus universalis
    Reflections on Aristotle's Treatise of Poesy
    Procopius Secret History
    Mazerine's Memoires
    Plato Redivivus
    The Ladys new-years gift

French Books:

    Dictionaire de l'Abbé d'Anet
    Histoire de la reformation. Burn[et]
    Dictionaire en 3 langue[s], Es[pagnole], Fr[ancaise], It[alienne]
    Les Ouvres de Voiture
    L'Ambassadeur par Wickfordt
    Lucrece par Morralles
    Juvenal and Perse par M.D.M.
    Properse
    Catulle
    Tibulle
    Tite-Live. 14 t. par Frenchems [Freinshemius]
    Critiques sur Horace. 5 tomes
    Quinte-Curse. par Vaugelas and Ryer
    Tacite 3 t. par d'Ablancourt

Lucien 2 t. par D'Ablancourt
Commentaires de Caesar
Com[mentaires] de Terence par Sibour
Polybe et ses frag[ments] par du Ryer
Erasme cum notis varior[um]
Hist[oire] de Francois I, en 2 t. par Varillas
    "   de Henry 2, par Varillas
    "   de Charles 9 par Varillas
    "   de l'Empire 2 t. par Heiss
Decamaron de Bocace. 2 tomes
La vie du vicomte de Turenne
La vie de Gust. Adolphe par de Prade
Recherche de la verité
Ouvres de Moliere 2 tomes
Ouvres de Sarazin, 1 t.
Memoires Gallans
Histoires de Medicis par Varillas
Histoire de M. de la Roche
L'Homme de Cour
Nouveaux Dialogues des morts
La Princesse de Monferrat
Le Parlement Pacifique
Les Comparaisons de Grands Hommes
Memoires de La Morée
Voyage de Chardin en Perse
5 Dialogues par Oratius Tubero
Boilau :/: L'Alcoran
Histoire des Oracles. Duc de Monm.
Education des Princes
Histoire abregé de l'Europe
Histoire de la paix. nouv: Inter. de Princes
Maximes des Princes
Le Triomphe de l'Amour
Lettres d'Ossat
La vie de Coligni

Italian Bookes:

Oudins Dictionario
Machiavello. 4 Tomes

Source: BM, f. 192

287

APPENDIX IV
Etherege's Accounts for Extraordinary Expenses

Etherege's difficulties in getting the Treasury to pay the extraordinary expenses to which he was entitled are well documented in the letters. The first four bills he sent, at intervals between February 11, 1686, and September 11, 1687 (printed in *LB*, pp. 365–367), are deleted in the manuscript letterbooks. Presumably they were ignored by the Treasury, and Etherege sent, sometime after May 20, 1688, a composite bill for "Extraordinaries layd out by him" from August 30, 1685 to May 20, 1688. Individual items are not specified, but the total is £ 550.

On July 12, 1688, Etherege writes Middleton that the Lords of the Treasury have approved this amount but that Mr. Robson cannot get it to send to Etherege because Robson does not have individual bills for the whole period. Two bills had been "sent by the Packet of the 3/13 Octob., 87;" they cover Etherege's first two years in Ratisbon and total £ 368. To these, Etherege now adds the bill ("Sent the 30. July. O.S. 1688") for £ 181, which covers the period from August 30, 1687 to May 30, 1688, and brings the total to £ 549.

Of this amount, Etherege seems to have received only £ 350,[1] most of which he already owed to the money-lender Oesterlin. On December 20, 1688, he begs Henry Guy to try to get him the £ 200 remaining, plus a whole year's entertainment money, amount not specified. He adds that he has already spent £ 500 of his own money, "which is to a penny all I can command," and that "creditors are very importunate." The only other record of money received is Hughes' mention (p. 310) of the 500 thalers[2] which arrived after Etherege "had left his post and was retired to France." Will Richards, who sent the money, insisted that it was from Sir George's friends and not an official pay-

---

[1] Eleanore Boswell, *RES*, 7 (1931), 209.
[2] According to Etherege (p. 148, above), a "dollar" was worth "just four shillings English."

ment, but Hughes nevertheless "laid an arrest upon it," claiming it was due him as back salary. That Etherege's financial difficulties continued after his arrival in France is indicated by the list of letters from Paris: 13 of the 29 letters are addressed to Treasury officials or money lenders.

1

Sir George Etherege Employ'd by his Majestie at Ratisbon humbly desires allowance for Extraordinaries layd out by him from the 30th of August 1685 to the 20th of May 1688, being two Yeares and three Quarters.

For passing a privy seal	
For money layd out in Holland for his Majestie's Service	
For Travelling Charges from London to Ratisbon	
For mourning for the Empress Dowager and for the Dutchesse of Modena	
For Postage of letters and Stationer's ware	
For procuring Copies of Memorialls Recesses and getting them translated	
For Intelligence	
For Fees in the Treasury and the Charges of receiving money out of the Exchequer	
The Severall Bills I have sent being reduc'd into one make	£ 550 00

This bill was not allow'd
Geo: Etherege.
Source: H-2, f. 121 (numbering from the back).

2

Sir George Etherege employ'd by his Majestie at Ratisbon humbly desires allowance for these Extraordinaries following layd out by him from the 30th of August, 1685, to the 11th of February 1686/7, being year and a half.

	£	s.	
For Charges of passing a Privy Seal and receiving money out of the Exchequer	29	00	00
For Severall journies in Holland, and money layd out upon Mr. Dowglass in order to his Majesties Service	10	00	00
For mourning for the Empress Dowager	20	00	00
For Postage, Stationer's ware, Copies and Translates of Memorialls, Recesses etc.	37	00	00
For Intelligence	44	00	00
For Fees in the Treasury and the charges of receiving more money out of the Exchequer	140	00.	

Geo: Etherege

3

These 2 Bills were sent by the Packet of the 3/13 Octob. 87

Sir George Etherege etc. from the 11th of February 86/7 to the 30th of Aug. 87

	£	s.	
For Postage and Stationer's ware	7	13	00
For Intelligence	20	00	00
For mourning for the Dutchesse of Modena by his Majestie's Command for myself, my secretary, my family, and Coach	80	00	00
	107	13	00
	140		

Geo. Etherege

	247	13	0

The Extraordinaries for 2 years ending the 30th of August, 1687 come to 368 £.

Source: H-2, f. 136 (numbering from the back).

4

Sent the 30. July. O.S. 1688.

Sir George Etherege, employ'd by his Majesty at Ratisbon, humbly desires allowance for these Extraordinaries following, which being added to Bills he has formerly sent make up two years 3 quarters Extraordinaries from the 30 of August, 85, to the 30 of May, 88.

	£	s.
For Postage	18	
For Intelligence from Vienna, Munick, and other places	} 60	
For procuring all the Acts of the Dyet and to a man for translating them out of Dutch into french.	} 20	
For Stationers ware	9	
More for mourning for the Dutchess of Modena (which was omitted in my Last Bill)	} 25	
For the relief of severall poore English, Scotch, and Irish, in their passage to and from the Army during the three Campaigns I have been here.	} 27	
Payd for one Clarke who had got his Majestie's recommendation, being Brother to the parson who was kill'd in the West for giving notice of the Duke of Monmouth's Landing, to keep him out of Goal, being pursued by his Creditors from Vienna hither, and to carry him into England that he might no longer remain in this Countrey a shame to our nation.	} 22	
For fees in the Treasury and charges of receiving money out of the Exchequer.	}	

Geo. Etherege.

Source: H-2, f. 121 (numbering from the back).

APPENDIX V

An account[1] of Sir G's life and manner of Living, writt in Severall Letters from Ratisbonne

I

Sir.[2]

I suppose you have been already inform'd (and therefore there is no need I shou'd tell you) of what past at the Hague: either as to his loosing 250 £ by play, his haunting pittifull and mean houses contrary to Mr. Skelton's advice, or as to his making Love for which he was Sufficiently laugh'd at.

And not to mention his caressing every dirty Drab that came in his way from Holland to this place, I shall onely begin with the manner of his life and conversation after his arrivall. He had two letters of Recomendation he brought with him from London, the one from Monsieur Barillon to the french Plenipotentiary, the other from the Spanish Ambassadour to Monsieur de Neuforge, the Burgundian Minister. As for the first, the letter was deliver'd him in 2 or 3 days, and thereupon S.G. [Sir George Etherege] made him 2 or 3 visits (as he fancy'd) incognito. But as for the other, S.G. was here 5 months before he made him a visit, or gave him any account of the letter sent by him. It is not to be known whether the french were more glad or The

---

[1] By Hugo Hughes, Etherege's secretary. The date must be the last week in November 1686. "Honoured Sir," to whom the four letters are addressed, left Ratisbon on November 23, 1686 (*HLB*, 339–340). The attack on Etherege's house by Baron Sensheim occurred on "munday the 15 of November" (p. 300, below), but this must be an Old Style date, since Etherege's insulting note to Sensheim is dated November 26. Hughes certainly wrote after November 25, and probably soon after.

[2] The identity of Hughes's correspondent can only be guessed. My guess (*HLB*, pp. 339–340) is Hughes's friend and Etherege's enemy, William Harbord.

Burgundian more dissatisfy'd with this way of proceeding. This writ back to complain of it; the other return'd thanks for so hopefull an acquaintance, and Sir G. himself writ to Monsieur Barillon complaining of the formality and gravity of the Ministers, and letting him know how much he was oblig'd to him, for that (as he said) there was not a house in all the Town, besides the Count de Crecy's, where he cou'd go when he pleas'd without standing upon Ceremonys and idle Punctillos.

And now having Layd the foundation of his future acquaintance at the french ambassadour's, the next thing he judg'd necessary was to find out gamesters, as such as wou'd help him (as he call'd it) to pass away the time. Thus instead of making his visits and getting acquaintance with the Ministers, he presently fell to gameing, for there were in Town at that time Severall french sharpers, who hearing of his laudable desseins, were not a little glad of such a Guest, nor in the least wanting (you may be sure) to make the best use and advantage they cou'd of so fair an opportunity. So then as soon as some of them were brought into acquaintance with him by the french Ambassadour's people, they never ceas'd to introduce one an other, till the whole gang of them begun to resort and haunt his house.

They manag'd him so dexterously, and play'd their Cards so well, that he cou'd not either eat or drink without some of them, but not being content with living upon him (his house day and night being full of them) nor with winning his money at a slow rate, they found him out or (as others say) sent on purpose to Vienna for an other gamster, who went by the name of Count Purpurat.[3] The frenchmen were known to go partner with this Rooke, who play'd with him constantly night and day till he had won upwards of 10,000 florins, and thereupon wou'd have left off playing till the money was pay'd, but Sir George, quarrelling with him upon it, forced him to play till it came onely to 1500 florins in part whereof Sir G pay'd 800 florins and towards the other Seaven, gave him a pair of Pistolls and a fusil, which he had caus'd to be made just before he came from London. The Spark finding there was no more money to be had and that Sir G. wou'd not play with him any longer (having heard that they had bragg'd of their winnings and that they said to others of their friends: *nous le deplumerons*) return'd to Vienna, whence it was written afterwards in the publik news papers that he had shew'd the Pistolls and fusil at the Emperours Court: boasting that he had won them at play,

[3] Etherege wrote to a Monsieur Purpurat on February 27, 1686.

and making it appear where he had had them by Sir G's Coat of Arms which remain'd upon them.

The next pickpocket they recommended to him was a shabby Count fled from justice att Augsbourg for severall tricks and for stealing away his Landlords maid. This person was so notoriously scandalous that some of the Ministers sent to Sir G. to disswade him from having any thing to do with him, but instead of taking advise, he became so fond of his compagny that he thought every minute lost when the time call'd him from his presence. It was not above 5 or 6 in 24 hours that they used to be asunder, for either he came to Sir G or Sir G went to him at his Lodgings in a paultry Common Alehouse, and tho' all the Town wonder'd he was not asham'd of such a Camarade, yet he was so far from it that out of familiarity (and I know not what) he lent him a hundred florins, with which he won from Sir G. 600 florins more, and (as it was thought) wou'd have cheated him of his Coach and horses if the Magistrats of the Town had not prevented it by threating to clap him up in prison for former cheats, which made him sneak with his 700 florins out of Town.

Tho' Sir G. found at Last that he had been practis'd upon, yet he had not the power to leave off embracing his french acquaintance; however finding his money grown short, he resolv'd to look after their play a little more narrowly than hitherto he had done. But as their cheats and tricks became apparent, so they did not fail to produce their known effects of constant quarelling and wrangling, till the whole Town began to ring of it. One while they shou'd seem as fond as children of each other, and an other time they wou'd be at Daggers-drawing, calling names and challenging: but still all this ended amicably, Sir G. not being able to live without them, nor they much less without him.

All the fine they us'd to impose upon themselves was onely to forbear playing for 2 or 3 days, and in the mean time their Trade was to drink till 2 or 3 a clock in the morning, and (if they were able) to go and walk about the Streets with clubs in their hands to guard themselves and their Musick. You will easily imagin, Sir, how famous he must needs make himself by such an extravagant course of life; for one night they wou'd make themselves so drunk that endeavouring to go home they shou'd be found next morning to lie sleeping in the Streets, an other night they wou'd break windows, and a third attack indifferently all such persons (whether men or women) as had the misfortune to come in their way, tho' sometimes they return'd all

294

cover'd with blows and bruses, the true recompence of such Knight-Errantry. et sic de caeteris.

Thus past the winter: and the Campagne[4] drawing on, these Sparks began to retire, which gave him leisure to bethink himself of making his first visits; wherein he went so slowly to work, that he has not made them all to this day. The Elector of Bavaria's Envoye absolutely refus'd to admitt him to the first visit, and all the other Ministers have either refus'd to receive him to a second visit or have not repay'd it after they had accepted it, so that it is now near seaven months since he Receiv'd the last from any one what-soever.

About the begining of summer one Monsieur le Febure,[5] forced to flye from Vienna for severall extravagances, was kindly entertain'd and receiv'd by Sir G. This persone had lately belong'd to a compagnie of foot in the quality of a player on the Hautbois, which prov'd such an effectuall recommendation that no person or profession cou'd have been more wellcome. The frenchman, perceiving that his Countrey men here were resolv'd to take no notice of him, had found a conveniency of sending his bundle by the Augsbourg Messenger, in order to return for france, and was just ready to march after it when Sir G., hearing of it, sent to invite him to his house, and having gently prevail'd with him to stay, a footman was dispatch'd away on horsback for Augsbourg to fetch back his tromperie, and he presently finding whom he had to deal with, became so predominant in a short time that the whole house was at his command.

He seldom went abroad but in Sir G's Coach, who wou'd never stirr without him, when it was generally observ'd and laugh'd at by all that he likewise gave him the hand. Le Febure, to requite these civilities, brought him acquainted with all the Cracks of the Town, with whom they wou'd pass whole nights at one scandalous Alehouse or another. When this trade fail'd, their manner was to torment the whole Town with Coaching, fidling, piping, and dancing till 2, 3, and 4 a clock in the morning. The whole Town complain'd of the noise and stirr they made night after night. Of all others the Countesse de Windischgratz was most angry with them, for by her jealous Husband's instigation, she threatned them publickly and laid an ambuscade of stout fellows to watch for them, whose clutches they escap'd narrowly one night and so saved drubbing. Therefore they durst not

---

[4] The siege and capture of Buda.
[5] Etherege wrote to "Monsieur Le Febure" on September 20, 1686.

venture there any more, tho' the rest of the Town cou'd never be rid of them till cold weather began to keep them at home.

What they did upon St. Louis's day was more famous than all the rest; for Sir G. not thinking it enough to have had two sisters in his chamber that night, where they all danced Stark naked, went afterwards about the streets with Le Febure, having nothing on but their shirts. One of these sisters was a wench that Sir G. at his first coming hither had taken from drawing beer at a poor miserable alehouse to make her his Mistress. By his often going abroad, he brought home a distemper with him at last, which infected both his Maid and his Valet de Chamber, and neither of them escaped much better than himself who lay six weekes under a Chyrurgeon's hand. This was known over all the Town, for the Land Lord, having quarrell'd with Sir G. about the disorders he committed in his house, was not wanting to complain both in publick and in private: That they had spoil'd him 3 of his featherbeds.

After he had kept this second sister about half a year, he turn'd her away for her insolent behaviour and for bragging of his favours. As soon as she was gone, her sister from an other Alehouse was taken in her stead. And I suppose she will ever repent it, for an other disaster having befallen Sir George about two months ago (of which he is not as yet well recover'd), she likewise shared in it, which made her be sent out of the house about a fortnight since. The Chyrurgeon made a great deal of noise before he promised to take her to cure, having never receiv'd any money for his pains nor for any Physick he administred. Here it may be seen what a paymaster he is to others, who is not willing to pay his Physitian.

He seldom rises out of bed before 2 or 3 a clock in the afternoon, dines most commonly at 5 or 6, and then goes to the french ambassador's for 3 or 4 hours every night in the weeke. This gave one of the Austrians an occasion to say: On voudroit bien savoir si c'est par l'ordre du Roy qu'il donne tant d'ombrage à tous les Ministres de l'Empire. He is so intirely for the french Interest that, meeting the Swedish Envoye at his going from hence to the congress at Augsbourg, he made him a Complement and wish'd his fine coach might break on the way,[6] because he went to make an alliance against France.

To justify his siding with the french, he has allways given it out for certain truth that His Majestie had made an alliance offensive and defensive with the french King. His reporting of this allarm'd

[6] Hughes is here maliciously reporting the gossip in Ratisbon. Cf. Etherege's account of the incident in his letter of February 26, 1687.

all the Ministers and gave them a worse opinion of him than before. When first he heard the news of the taking of Buda, he sayd he neither believ'd it nor hop'd it to be true, and some 2 or 3 days after, the Jesuits Students happen'd to have a Comedy, where every Minister but himself was particularly invited. However he went thither and heard his very words repeated on the Stage, neq credo neq spero. The Austrians upon this news sent to give notice of it to all the Ministers, Sir Geo. onely excepted, who was in the like manner neglected when they made their feasts: he was very much offended to see himself not taken notice of, and therefore he began to exclaim heavily against the Bishop of Passau. In the next place he told the french Ambassadour that he had heard the Count de Windischgrätz say that the Emperor did not intend to treat in earnst of the Execution of the Armistice, and onely made the french believe it till the end of an other Campagne. Altho' this may be suppos'd to be their dessein, yet it is something hard to believe that the Count de Windischgrätz shou'd tell it to Sir G., whom he knew to be so much a friend to the French as wou'd be sure to tell them whatever he heard, tho' it shou'd prove the cause of an immediate war, and the want of treating of the Execution of the peace is the likeliest thing I know to be the occasion of.

The Compliment he sent the Count de Lamberg was That tho' he had heard nothing of the Taking of Buda either himself, or from any of the Imperiall Ministers, yet he cou'd not but lett Him know that he had heard it as a common report, and therefore desir'd an opportunity to make him a visit and to congratulate with him upon that occasion. Count Lamberg sent his steward before night to carry this message, that the Count had strangers to sup with him that night and if Sir George wou'd bring his dancing Master along with him he shou'd be wellcome. Spesso vengono rebuttate le personne mordenti con morsi più fieri.[7]

Whatever Ministers come hither or goe away, they allways forgett to give him notice of it, tho' they are very punctuall with every body but himself. And tho' the Count de Crecy tells him to his face all his loose life and conversation, yet he is far from speaking well of him even behind his back, for one night that S.G. happen'd not to go to his house, his expressions the next day at dinner were: Je m'etonne ou estoit Monsieur d'Etheridge hier au soir; peut estre qu'il a resté au logis pour jouer comme il fait quelque fois pour des liards avec son valet de Chambre et son Maitre d'Hotel. Il ne sort jamais

[7] "A biter is often thwarted by a more severe bite."

d'icy sans gagner quelques ecus de Madame la Comtesse parce qu'
autrement il n'auroit rien pour maintenir sa famille. Ce que je trouve
de plus pire en luy que toutes ses debauches est qu'il est profane, et
voudroit persuader tout le monde d'estre de son sentiment. He has
disoblig'd the Magistrats in calling them all rascalls for turning the
whores out of Town, and saying that if he were Elector of Bavaria
he wou'd raze the walls of the Town and build an Hospitall for de-
cayed whores in the place where the Councill-house stands. I must not
forget to give you an account of what past on monday the 2^d day
after your departure, but before I come to the story, it is necessary
I shou'd tell you something by way of Introduction.

Before it was known what distemper Sir G. was sick of, the Countesse of Crecy was pleas'd to tell one of her women, J'entens que Monsieur d'Etherige est malade pour l'amour de moy. S'il l'est qu'il meurt.
It seems he pretended some such thing, but when he had heard what
she sayd, it turn'd his Love into dispaire, as you will see by the verses
inclosed. This I can assure you caus'd a great deal of Laughter amongst
all the Ministers, who hate him as well as the french, and are glad to
hear of any ridiculous thing.

About ten dayes ago, one of the Ministers happen'd to give a Collation to 20 or 30 persons, where S.G. was present (it being the first time
of his appearing again in publick), but of all the whole compagny, he
was the onely person that satt by himself, without being taken notice
of or asked to come to the table. On Thursday last a great company
of gentlemen and Ladys met to take their pleasure of riding thro'
the Town in Trenaux according to the fashion of this Country, and
because S.G. wou'd be of the number, they contriv'd it so that he was
the 19th and the last of all the gang, which the meanest Minister
but himself wou'd have been asham'd of. Being come to the house
where they were to make merry, he offer'd to salute the Countesse of
Schalemberg, who gave him this reprimande in the hearing of all,
Monsieur, je vous prie ne faites pas tant de familiarité avec moy,
parceque je suis la Contesse de Schalemberg et non pas une Comé-
dienne.

This was nothing to what follow'd, which seems to have been done
by complot on purpose to affront him. One person being left to keep
S.G. in discourse, the rest of the company sat down at Table and
reserved onely a place for one. S.G. approaching and thinking to sit
down, the other without ceremony prepossessed the place, leaving
S.G. a noun Substantive. To expose him the more the Anhalt-Minister,
whom he had formerly abused, ask'd him faintly to sitt down, but

without any farther care of him, they fell to it, all strutting and stretching to keep him out, when otherwise they cou'd have made place enough for half a dozen more. S.G. seeing himself thus abandon'd immediately sent for his Coach and told them uppbraidingly that he cou'd find a supper at home.

Some few nights ago one of his footmen was carried to prison for making noise in the streets, and an other night the Dancing Master, whom he admires for his debauches, being pursued by the watch was forced to flie to the french Ambassadour's, and having got within the gate, he took up a stone and knock'd down the formost, but the rest wou'd have paid him for it had not the Ambassadour ran down in his night gown with his Sword in hand to save him, as being come within his Liberties.

Amongst a Company of Strawlers lately come hither from Nurenberg (under the name of Comedians) there happen'd to be one woman who seem'd to have something of grace in her face, tho none in her manners. She had not been here many days before His Excellence S.G.E., intending to forestall the rest of the Ministers in paying the honour due to her Character (of an errant whore), was civily pleas'd to send his Steward to make her a complement and to desire audience (which is the onely kind he has hitherto had). It is not to be doubted but so forward a zeal was well accepted, especially in such a place as this, where people stand so much upon the punctillos of honour that none, certainly, but himself wou'd have done it. Having seen her Credentialls and finding her plein pouvoir conformable to his own, tho not according to the stile of the Empire, he gently propos'd that without any cavil or contestation, they shou'd presently proceed to name a place ad designandos Limites[8] (as France and the Empire had done some days before). The Whalefish[9] (a Paltry little Alehouse) where she lodg'd was pitch'd upon for one, and his Excellence's house for an other.

They lost no time in their negociation: for either he sent his Coach to fetch her, or went himself to her lodgings, where he wou'd make his Coach wait on him for whole nights and most part of the Day, for fear (as it were) that the Town shou'd not come to the knowledge of the Scandall. She was so bare in Cloaths as His Excellence was of money and Credit at that time, which made him pawn his watch to buy her a new Suit. The Jew who had it was affraid of his bargain

[8] "For designating the limits"—that is, agreeing on the time, place, and conditions of the Truce.

[9] The Gasthaus "Zum Walfisch" still stands on the Schwiboggenstrasse.

and therefore shew'd it in so many places, till at last the whole Town came to ring of it; but he was so far from being concern'd at what any one said that sometimes after the play was ended, he has putt her into his coach before all the Company notwithstanding all the giggling and hishing of the Austrian Ladys and of the Ministers wives and Daughters, himself humbly walking home on foot. These and other Civilityes made the Damsell report at last that S.G. had a design to marry her, if the Magistrats had not hinder'd the match by turning her out of Town.

II

Honoured Sir.[10]

On munday the 15 of november about 3 a clock his Excellence S.G.E. sent his coach for the Commedian to come and dine with him in private according to his Custome. Severall young fellows, hearing of this entertainment (tho' it was no news to them), resolv'd to shew some feats for the honor of their Countrey; and like so many London prentices (that now and then use to shew their displeasure against Whetsones Parke)[11] they muster'd up a good handsome Company. About 7 a clock severall parties of them appear'd in sight and posted themselves in severall places about the house and garden according to their orders. By eight a clock they had form'd the siege; and within less than half an hour after they began to make their regular approaches, advancing within 5 or 6 yeards of the very doore. They continued to carry on their works with silence till nine. Then they loudly proclaim'd an open warr, and threatned if this Helena was not deliver'd into their hands, they wou'd presently let Paris see the dire effects of his obstinacy. In expectation of an answer, they lost no time in wheting their swords in the stonewalls and pavements, in fixing their fire-arms etc.

A little before ten his Excellence began to parley with them out at the window, and desired they wou'd grant him an hour's time to consider of their proposition. Having obtain'd it with some difficulty, he

[10] This letter must have been written early in December 1686—that is, long enough after Sensheim's attack (November 25) for the comedienne to have returned to Nuremberg and been imprisoned there, and for the news to have reached Sir George.

[11] Whetstone Park, a street between Holborn and Lincoln's Inn Fields, was notorious for its prostitutes.

resolv'd to make the best use he cou'd of it to prepare for his defence. This shews Mahomet was no true Lover, who brought out his fair Irene and sacrificed her with his own hand to the rage of the multitude; and In spite of all his murmuring Soldiers, Titus Vespatian had never banish'd Berenice out of Rome, if he had had but half the courage of this truely heroiq and valiant Knight.

Much about 11 his Excellence with a detatchment of his three footmen, two french Laquays, his fencing, Dancing, and Hoffmasters (the Secretary not thinking fit to concern himself at all with their broils) sallied out upon 7 or 8 persons who were left to keep the Trenches, and being seconded by his french Vice-Bassa, who commanded the reserve (the Cook, Coachman, and Kitching wench), wou'd have totally routed them but that his second thoughts proved better than his first. However some blows happen'd, for a Luteplayer having clap'd his Excellence two or three times on the back (pretending likely to take him prisoner) was answer'd with a slap on the face, and the Dancing Master, more accustom'd to a Capriole than the use of the Sabre, gave an other of the enemies a slight cutt in the neck, for which the vice-Bassa knock'd him down for fear of farther mischief. The Ring-leader seem'd to be the Baron de Sensheim disguis'd in a footmans habit; his Janizaries were his valet de Chambre, his two footmen, two or three Laquays belonging to the Count de Lamberg, etc.

As soon as they saw his Excellence retreat, they took it for sign of victory and began again to play the Rabshakehs,[12] so that their Language was so opprobrious and scurrilous as none but those who have been at Billingsgate ever hard the like. Notwithstanding all their outrages, her Ladyship resolv'd rather to venture home, with a good convoy, than to suffer things to come to extremity and runn the risk of a generall assault. The order of the procession was as follows: Two footmen marching before with Pistols ready cocked in one hand, and flambaux in the other, the Damsel with a man and a musketoon follow'd after in the Coach, which was garded on each side by two persons and behind by three more, all well furnished with swords and pistolls.

Baron de Sensheim and his company pursued them closely, but fearing by their appearance they might make too great an opposition, they were forced to content themselves with hooting and hollowing,

[12] Rab-shakeh, sent by Sennacherib against Jerusalem, used violent and profane language in demanding the surrender of the city (2 *Kings*, 18, 27).

except onely one action that happen'd on this manner: the fencing master, perceiving that some of the enemy were like to fall in upon them in the flank by the favour of a defilée where they annoy'd them with stones, betook himself to pursue them with all his might, till by running he happen'd to stumble over a turn-stile, which was like to cost him his neck, but having escap'd this ambuscade, he return'd to the main body and so they continued on, some crying one thing and some an other; but all with one voice agreed in this: *that great was the Diana of the English Envoye.*

Thus attended she arrived at her Lodgings, having passt along three of the principall streets and two of the most public places of the Town. It is not known which was greater, the shew and the musik that went along with it or the noise it made in the Town the next morning. The Fame of this expedition was not a little increas'd by a letter which his Excellence writ to Baron de Sensheim, en termes piquants, wherof a Copie goes herewith.

The Comedian, being privately warn'd by the Magistrates to leave the Town, troop'd immediately away for Nurnberg, where as soon as ever she arrived, the Councill gave order to take her into custody and carry her to the Zuchthause, or Bridewell, where Sir G.s fine cloathes are like to maintain her for some years on bread and water. Count Lamberg Casheer'd one of his footmen, and the Chamberlain of this Town made the Luteplayer be putt in prison for 2 or 3 dayes upon a promise S.G. gave him of living more regular for the future. Very many doubt of it, since he designes already to visit Nurenberg and to plague that Town, as well as this, if his Mistress be not released. No body knows where the business between him and Monsieur Sensheim is like to end, but for fear of the worse S.G. carries a Musketoon in his Coach, and each footman has allways since a pair of pocket pistolls ready Charged.

The Letter above mention'd

Monsieur.

J'estois surpris d'apprendre que ce jolli gentilhomme travesti en Italian hier au soir estoit le Baron de Sensheim. Je ne savois pas que les honnêtes gens se mêloient avec des Laquays ramassés pour faire les fanfarons et les batteurs des pavés. Si vous avez quelque chose à me dire, faites la moy Scavoir comme vous devez, et ne vous amusez plus à venir insulter mes Domestiques ni ma maison. Soyez content que vous l'avez echappé belle, et ne retournez plus chercher les recompenses des telles follies. Pour vos beaux Compagnions, j'ay des autres mesures à garder avec eux.

Geo: Etheridge.

III

Honoured Sir.

How fast soever we thought the Commedian, it is now but too apparent we all lay under a mistake, for if ever Hannibal and Alaricus made the Roman Senators tremble, the Patricians of Nurenberg (as they say) were no less freightned when they hear'd that S.G. design'd them a visit. It shews how much they were allarm'd at the report of his coming, when for fear of drawing Judgement on their own heads they were glad to turn loose his attoning Mistress for a Scape-goat. And rather than not be able to stop his journey, his approach (we may safely conclud) might have been sufficient to procure a generall Goal-delivery. But why I shou'd trouble you with probabilitys I know not, since matter of fact is more than I can tell you.

As soon as she had got her Liberty she gave notice of it by a letter, and within few days after arriv'd in person in the suburbs of Bayrischenhoff,[13] where she took a lodging at a famous Alehouse call'd the Golden Lyon. It is true some few visits were made her, but they were look'd upon to be merely out of formality and for fashions sake, Since Sir George wou'd neither procure her leave to enter within the gates, nor vindicate his own honor and authority so far as to coach her into the Town Triumphantly in spite of all the Magistrates (as he wou'd often propose to himself.) One wou'd think it somewhat strange that a person of her publick note and Character shou'd pretend to gett into the Town incognito, when the guards were doubled on purpose to keep her out. However as we are most likely and subject to be deceiv'd by our own selves, so she made use of a souldiers habit, and by that means got in, tho' she finds after all that Sir George is run out of all his money, and therefore trading is like to be broke.

You see, Sir, I cannot forbear to write to you for fear of neglecting my promise, which you may call duty; for tho' I be but one of the meanest of his Sacred Majestie's subjects, yet I can frame to myself such an Idea of his Honor as will not suffer me without grief and shame to see it abused.][14]

[13] The present Stadt-am-Hof, just across the Danube.
[14] The lines in brackets are deleted in the MS.

Ratisbon February 6, 1687

Honoured Sir.

According to the Liberty you were pleased to grant me, I made bold
to send you by the last post what I cou'd not well resolve upon before
I heard of your safe arrivall in England, the news whereof did very
much alleviate my heart, for otherwise I shou'd scarce have been able
to write of such things as wou'd infallibly be taken for fabulous Knight-
Errantrys if all that live in this Town did not know them to be real
truths.

S.G., who has not as yet ten words of Dutch,[15] being forc'd not
onely to make use of a Trucheman[16] but also to intrust one or an
other of his Laquays with all his intrigues, was discover'd in every
thing as soon as it was done; for whatever any one has a mind to
publish, he need not but lett a Dutch servant know it for a Secret and
he shall be sure to tell it wherever he goes. And whereas one wou'd
think that S.G. in particular shou'd be kind to his servants, as the onely
means to engage them to silence, yet it has allways been observ'd on
the contrary that his footmen of all others have the hardest service
and the worst usage, for when others sup, they dine; when it is time
to be abed and asleep, they are forced to wander up and down the
streets, etc., which has been the Cause that S.G. has had about 22
different Dutch servants within this twelvemonth, and never above 5
or 6 at a time, as a Cook and Kitching wench, a Coachman, and two
or three Laquays.

Although S.Gs own servants had been never so Silent, yet the
Straglers that constantly live upon him, and generally such as have
the name of Idle fellows, were enough to disclose all his concerns. I
believe there has past great many things which I have not heard, for
at his first coming hither, I thought I cou'd do no less than inform
him of such stories as I had heard reported of him, but finding he
was far from taking it in good part, by asking how I was concerned,
If I was sent with him for his governour, etc., I resolv'd to say nothing,
and being left to follow his own Course, he did all his endeavours to
keep things from my hearing, least It shou'd be told him again that
such a night he had been visiting all the alehouses of the Town accompanied with his servants, his valets de Chambre, his hoffmaster,

[15] I.e., German.
[16] Dragoman, an interpreter.

and his Dancing and fighting Master, all with their Coats turn'd inside outward's.

Sir George, having promised me in England threescore pound a year, with my own and my man's Diet, wou'd have flincht from his bargain when he came to Ratisbon, but money being sent him to Ratisbon after he had left his post and was retired to france, I laid an arrest upon it till I sho'd be paid what he owed me by his note in writing. After all my fair proposalls to be satisfy'd, he wou'd have shuffled me off and writ to the Magistrats against me, calling me his Domestick, with other harsh terms, which gave occasion to the following letter, sent him to Paris.

Nobilissimis, amplissimis, Prudentissimis, Sacri Romani Imperii Liberae Civitatis Ratisbonensis Dominis Camerariis ut et reliquis Senatoribus Spectatissimis Dominis meis maxime Devenerandis:

Sub initio Literarum suarum Dominus Etherege judicium suum fert de actionibus ignominiosis; omnibus agnoscendum, et vero verius est, quod ille optimo jure de his possit decernere, cum sit homo vulgatae nequitiae, et ad usum omnium facinorum peritissimus. Impii mores et vitae ipsius vitia satis superque omnibus sunt nota. Et hinc aliis persuasum habere vellet, quod Labe contagionis (uti pestis proprium est) me inquinaverit: sed Deum Ter optimum maximum qui intactum me hucusque conservavit pro bonitate sua divinâ spero me semper conservatarum! Videtur quod sit Dominus Etheregius qui maximam prorsus infamiam subiit eo magis quod propter Lenocinia et effusas in omni intemperantia libidines, illi non suppeditebat unde mihi aliisque Creditoribus satisfaceret, quando hinc abiit ad asylum apud Gallos quaerendum. Hisce literis suis singulatim ennarrare simulat res omnes quae mihi cum illo intercessêre. Sed non satis possum admirari, quod ille audeat dicere se cum fratre me pactum fecisse. Nemone cui meliori debeamus jure fidem adhibere quam Domino Etheregio? Quid! illumne latet, quod male audit, et quod omnes qui plane boni sunt et cum primis honesti, hominem illum ducunt sine existimatione necnon honoris et virtutis expertem? Putatne titulum illum Equitis aurati sufficere, quo minus de fide[17] et probitate suâ dubitandum sit? Audetne sub hoc titulo veritati facere injuriam? Et speratne Legationem suam Ratisbonnensem unquam efficere, ut probra quaeque, et dedecorosae ipsius vitae actiones in oblivionem veniant? Paucis dicam, si tantillum honoris vel honestatis Domino Etheregio

[17] MS: *fine.*

305

reliquum est, set non denegaret veritatem rei quam cum illo habui; bene ac pro certo scit, quod fratri meo promisit, antequem cum illo unquam alloquutus sum, se mihi sexagintas libras angliae quotannis daturum si illi negotiis suis Ratisbonae exequendis adesse vellem. Ibi me frater enixe petiit, ut dictum Dominum Etheregium viserem, et cum illum invenerim apud Chyrurgum quendam gallum nomine Fucadium, ipse Etheregius jamtum mihimet ipsi etiam atque etiam non solum 60 libras sed et pedissequum meum victu pascere pollicitus est, uti antea fratri meo promiserat. Ad haec responsum dedi mihi deliberatum esse una cum illo Ratisbonam petere, ita ut ad iter me paratum esse monuit. Tantum abfuit quando huc venissem ut *Liberalitate* et *beneficiis* me prosequeretur ut contra justitiam et honestos mores ne promissis ipsis stare voluit: subjiciendo non plus habuisse secretarium Domini Polei quam 40 Libras per annum, ex quo evenit ut mihi opus fuit cum illo contendere atque ante oculos ponere quanto dedecoris sensu illum afficere deberet me viginti Libris defraudare. His verbis commotus de novo se pactione devinxit has mihi 20 libras e sumptibus extraordinariis daturum; et id responsum a me tulit, quod non multum curarem ex quo argento mihi persolveret, dummodo summa rationum in 60 Libras quadraret, uti prius promiserat, si Regem rationibus suis in fraudem inducere illi potius fuit, quam ut ex proprio mihi numeraret argento. Queritur in literis quod viginti fere millia florenorum illi debentur ex aerario publico sed quod hoc ad me? Ullamne cum illo pactionem feci, me pro libitu suo stipendium accepturum? Ullamne inter se proportionem habent trecenti Thaleri, et quinque millia Thalerorum quos quotannis habuit Dominus Etheregius praeter sumptos extraordinarios? Legationis suae munus per tres annos et sex menses administravit, et nulla ratio est quod ego ducentos et quinquaginta Thaleros illi condonarem quia viginta millia florenos ex aerario regio non accepit, quorum fere dimidium falso et graeca fide rationibus suis addidit, contra juramentum et sub praetextu sumptuum Extraordinariorum; uti manifestum faciam, si opus fuerit Porro literis suis addit, illum non plus extraordinariorum accepisse quam ad annum unum et novem menses nihilominus fatetur, quod ex his quidem debitum 40 Librarum mihi numeravit pro duobus annis. Nonne restat ergo, ut mihi altero sesquianno satisfaceret? Et quando quidem mihi trimestris spatii stipendium absolvit etsi non accepisset, satis constat, illum pecunias mihi debitas non dedisse secundum quantitatem acceptam, sed secundum suam nummositatem aut nummariam difficultatem. Mentionem facit de scripto quodam cui Chirographum meum est appositum, persuadere vellet me illi acceptilationem dedisse; hinc insignem se deceptorem praebet. Nonne ille ipse scit bene aeque ac omnes ejus domestici, quam magnam cum illo controversiam et altercationem mihi habere necesse fuit antequam ab illo hoc scriptum extorquere potui, quod nihil aliud est quam apographum scripti, quod mihi coactus fuit dare, quasi per vim et post multas minas praesentibus et audientibus suis Domesticis cum nonnullis aliis, quia animadvertebam illum mihi debitum solvere non curare et abeundi solummodo occasionem quaerere, ut me aeque ac famulum suum Cubicularem defraudaret. Haeccine ergo in me Domini Etheregii liberalitas? qui cum vidisset se non abiturum nisi prius mihi solvendi promissum faceret (quod et propria manu se attestatus est facturum quamprimum illi pecuniam acciperet) autoramentum seu obligationem hanc mihi aegre tradidit et necesse illi fuit me obtestari patienter ferre, praetendendo pecuniam illi ad iter faciendum non suppeditare. Forte fortuito Procurator Domini Etheregii post ipsius decessum huc ex Anglia quingentos misit thaleros sed ut mihi fucum faciat pro solutione debiti, falso persuadere vellet quod sunt ex amicis suis intimis, qui praeter expectationem hunc illi pecuniam misêre. Bene notum est quod Dominus Etheregius ne minimum habet redditum annualem nec vitae nec cultus subsidia praeter pensionem quam Rex illi quottannis pendebat. Erat Dominus Robsonius et postea Dominus Richardus qui pensionem hanc ex aerario regio cepêre. Eratque etiam dictus Richardus qui hos quingentos thaleros huc misit more solito et per litera Cambii Domino Martino datas. Praeterea cum Domino Etheregio et non cum Rege pactionem hanc feci; est ergo dictus Etheregius qui mihi conditiones et promissa praestare debet: et ad hoc jure tenetur. Magistratus haud dubio justitiam colunt et spero quod id re comprobaturi sunt, adjudicando mihi debitum, et Dominum Etheregium ad solutionem condemnando. Magnis quidem laudibus et encomiis rationem suam vivendi celebrat, et valde apud illos se gratiosum esse ambitiose sibi pollicetur. Sed de his penitus inquirendi alia mihi vice occasionem expecto. Quod quidem pensum in me libenter accipiam. Caeteroquin quomodo possumus magni id estimare, quod per Deum et per honorem asserit, quandoquidem omnibus bene notum est, quod laudem affectat et gloriatur de eo, quod non credit esse Deum; quoad honorem attinet, nemo certe omnino non scit, quod ille nunquam honoris famam sibi conciliavit, sed e contra susque deque semper habuit. Jam vestrum, viri praestantissimi, judicium appello, si sua in me liberalitas et quam jactat Largitio non jure potiori fraudis et mali doli titulum mercantur. Quod ita res se habet Dei hominumque fidem imploro, et pro justitia et virtute qua omnes ad recte agendum inclinantur senatum vestrum, Egregii viri, quam primum de hac se decreturum spero etc.

Source: BM, ff. 192–202; *LB,* pp. 378–400.

Translation of Hugo Hughes' Latin Letter

To the most noble, powerful, and wise Magistrates of the Free City of Ratisbon of the Holy Roman Empire and to the remaining Senators, my most distinguished and venerable Lords:

At the beginning of his letter, Sir George Etherege sets himself up as a judge of dishonorable behavior; certainly everyone knows that he is best qualified to decide such matters since he is notoriously an evil man and most expert in the practice of all villainy. He is a hardened sinner, and his vices are more than well enough known to all. And hence he would like to persuade others that he has defiled me with the stain of infection (as is characteristic of the disease); but I hope that the thrice-best and greatest God, who has preserved me unharmed up till now by his divine goodness, will ever preserve me!

It seems that it is Sir George Etherege who has incurred the greatest infamy, especially because, through foppishness of dress and squandering in all kinds of intemperate lust, he was not able to satisfy me and his other creditors when he left here to seek refuge with the French. In his letter he pretends to narrate one by one all the transactions that have taken place between us. But I cannot wonder enough that he should dare to say that he made a compact with my brother-in-law. Is there no one better entitled to be believed than Sir George Etherege? What? doesn't he know that he has a bad reputation and that all really good and honest men consider him devoid of character and lacking in both honor and virtue? Does he think that the title of gilded knight is enough to remove all doubt of his good faith and integrity? Does he dare, on the strength of this title, to do injury to the truth? Does he hope that his embassy to Ratisbon will ever wipe out all the shameful and dishonorable actions of his life?

I assert, in short, that if Sir George Etherege has even a trace of honor or honesty left, he will not deny the truth of the business between us. He certainly knows that even before I spoke with him, he promised my brother-in-law that he would pay me 60 pounds English per year if I would travel to Ratisbon to carry out his business. Then my brother-in-law earnestly asked me to talk to the said Sir George Etherege, and when I found him at the house of a French surgeon named Fucadius,[18] Etherege himself again and again prom-

---

[18] Florent Fourcade. See above, p. 47.

308

ised me personally not only 60 pounds but also to provide for my footman, as he had promised my brother-in-law before. To this I answered that I had decided to go to Ratisbon with him, and he warned me to be ready for the journey.

But when I arrived here, he was so far from treating me with liberality and kindness that, contrary to justice and decency, he would not even stand by what he had promised, arguing that Mr. Poley's secretary had no more than 40 pounds a year. I had to struggle with him to make him see that cheating me of 20 pounds ought to be a disgrace to him. Moved by these words, he bound himself with a new compact to pay me the 20 pounds from his Extraordinary expenses, and I told him that it didn't much matter to me what fund he paid me from—so long as the total squared with the 60 pounds he had promised me earlier—if it was preferable to cheat the King than to pay me out of his own money.

He complains in his letter that the public treasury owes him almost 20,000 florins, but what is that to me? Did I make any agreement with him that I would accept payment at his convenience? Is there any proportion between 300 thalers and the 5,000 thalers that Sir George Etherege had annually besides his Extraordinary expenses? He administered the duties of his legation for three years and six months, and there is no reason that I should forgive him 250 thalers just because he has not received 20,000 florins from the Royal Treasury, more than half of which he added to his accounts by false and Greek faith, contrary to his oath, and under the pretext that they were Extraordinary expenses. Moreover, further in his letter he reveals that he has received nothing more of his Extraordinaries than for one year and nine months and that he has paid me from this fund a debt of 40 pounds for two years. Doesn't it follow, then, that he ought to pay me for the other year and a half? And since for three months he paid me the stipend even though he had not received it, it is evident that he did not give me the money due me according to the amount that he had received but according to his wealth or his financial difficulties.

He mentions a certain document bearing my signature and would like to have it believed to be a bill of discharge from me for the debt. Here he shows himself to be an outstanding deceiver. Doesn't he know, as well as his servants do, how great a controversy and dispute it took before I was able to extort that paper from him, which is nothing else than a copy of a note that he was compelled to give me, by force and after many threats, with his servants and many others present and listening, because I saw that he didn't want to pay me that debt and was only looking for an opportunity to leave Ratisbon in order to cheat me and his chamberlain? Is this then the liberality of Sir George Etherege toward me?—who when he saw that he could not leave without keeping his promise to pay me (which in his own handwriting he was sworn to do as soon as he received the money) reluctantly gave me this contract or bond, and he had to beg me to endure patiently, pretending that he did not have enough money to make the journey.

By chance, the agent of Sir George Etherege, after his departure, sent hither from England 500 thalers, but in order to make excuse to me for payment of the debt, tried to persuade me falsely that the money came from his intimate friends, who contrary to expectation had sent him this money. It is well known that Sir George Etherege has not the smallest annual income nor means of support beyond the pension which the King paid him annually. It was Mr. Robson, and afterwards Mr. Richards, who received this pension from the Royal Treasury. It was the said Richards, too, who sent the 500 thalers here in the usual way and by a letter of exchange given to Mr. Martins. Moreover, I made this pact with Sir George Etherege and not with the King; therefore the said Etherege ought to be responsible for the conditions and promises to me, and he is bound by law to do this.

The magistrates no doubt have regard for justice, and I hope that they are going to prove the fact by adjudging the debt to me and condemning Sir George to paying it. He celebrates his own way of life by a great deal of self-praise and vaingloriously promises himself that he is in great favor with those gentlemen [the magistrates]. But I hope for the opportunity of inquiring into these matters in depth on another occasion, although I will gladly accept what is awarded me. For the rest, how can we consider it of great significance that he has sworn by God and on his honor, especially when it is well known that he seeks praise for, and takes pride in, the fact that he does not believe in God. As far as honor is concerned, nobody at all is ignorant that he has never acquired a reputation for honor, but has always on the contrary considered honor as neither here nor there. Now, illustrious gentlemen, I call on you to judge whether his liberality and the largesse of which he boasts do not more rightly earn the title of fraud and wicked deceit. I call on God and men to witness that that is how things are, and for the sake of that sense of justice and virtue by which all men are moved to right action, I hope that your senate, gentlemen, will come to a decision on this matter as soon as possible.

INDEX

E indicates Sir George Etherege. "Letter(s) omitted" indicates existing letters not included in this edition. "Letter(s) listed" indicates letters noted in the Harvard Letterbooks but not known to have survived.

311

Countess of Kaunitz, 40; goes to Carnival at Venice, 76, 77; wounded at Buda, 140, 141; has a new mistress, 179; mentioned, 107, 124, 171, 177, 187, 188, 199, 207, 208, 209, 216, 236

Beck, Baron, 232

Beer, Rev. Father Laurence, 281

Belgrade, capture of, 233

Bellamy, Mr., companion to Lord George Savile, 49

Belque, General, 44

Benedictine Monastery, Ratisbon, xxiii; E leaves books to, xxn

Bentinck, William, 218, 219, 220

Bermuda, Captain George Etherege in, xiv

Berwick, Duke of: new title of Mr. Fitzjames, 112; leaves Ratisbon for Hungary, 123; arrives at Ratisbon, 154; needs to be pushed for advancement, 159; must have Order of the Garter, 160; mentioned, 114, 128, 137, 144, 145, 148, 151, 158. *See also* Fitzjames, Mr.

Betterton, Mary Saunderson: wife of Thomas, 120n

Betterton, Thomas: Letter to, 119–120; played lead in *The Man of Mode,* 120n

Beuningen, Coenrad van, 245

Beyreuth, Marquis of, 194

Bilderbeck: Dutch resident at Cologne, 209

Birmingham, University of: copy of Etherege Letterbook, xiin

Bonvisi, Cardinal, 236, 245, 247, 263

Books, in E's library, 286–287

Bow Street, E resident in, 228

Boyle, Charles, 59n, 101; Letter to, 118; Letter listed, 62

Boyne, Battle of, xxiii

Bracegirdle, Mrs., 229n

Bradbury, George: reports E's death, xxiii; in Green Ribbon Club, 76n; Letter to, 173–174; Letters listed, 29, 43, 90, 142, 147, 149, 191; mentioned, 178

Brandenburg, Frederick, Elector of:

confers with Prince of Orange, 234; private pact with Prince of Orange, 249; mentioned, 220

Brandenburg, Frederick William, Elector of (The Great Elector): death of, 198, 199, 202; mentioned, 10, 26, 39, 111

Brandenburg, Louis, Marquis of, 224n

Bray Church: records destroyed, xiv

Brett, Richard, 206

Brett-Smith, H.F.B.: biographical sketch of E, xiv; comments on E's correspondence, xxiv

Bridgeman, William, 47n; Letters to, 127, 139; Letters listed, 47, 52, 53, 159, 162, 180; E pays debt to, 127

Brown, Capt., 128

Buckhurst, Lord (later Earl of Dorset), xix

Buckingham, George Villiers, Duke of: attends opening of *She Wou'd if She Cou'd,* xvi; retirement to Yorkshire, 66; death of, 116; *The Rehearsal,* 138, 272; Letters to, 66–70, 92–97; mentioned, 135

Buda, capture of, xxii, 56, 58; news of the siege, 47–56 *passim*

Bulkeley, Henry, xvii

Bulstrode, Sir Richard, xiin, 14n; Letter omitted, 20; Letter listed, 202

Burch, Mr., 49

Burgundy, Duke of, 280

Burnet, Gilbert, 178n; wit and malice of, 190; claims Prince of Wales is supposititious, 252; reputed author of a libel, 204; mentioned, 179, 248, 252

Calvin, John, 228

Candia, surrender of, 217

Caprara, Aenius Sylvius, Count of, 16n; besieging Princess Rákóczy, 19; mentioned, 24, 30

Caraffa, Antonio, Count: accuses Prince Hermann of Baden, 165n; mentioned, 187, 193, 209

Carlingford, Nicholas Taaffe, Earl of: named envoy to Vienna, 176; to stop

312

at Ratisbon, 186; E accompanies to Passau, 193; seldom answers E's letters, 250; does not delight in business, 252; Letters to, 176–177, 204, 217–218, 234–236, 236–237, 251–252, 265–266, 266–267; Letters listed, 245, 246, 247, 263; mentioned, xxii, 195, 245, 246, 247, 256

Carnival, time of, 25, 26

Carossio, Monsieur, 46

Carr, Mr., 49

Castlemaine, Lady Barbara, 171n

Castlemaine, Roger Palmer, Earl of: Ambassador to the Pope, 98

Charles II, 171n, 214n

Cheke, Capt. Thomas, 31n

Chimacam of Constantinople, Ibraham Pasha, 5

Chimacam (Kaimakam) of the Porte, 3, 6n

Churchill, Arabella, 122n

Clanbrassil, Dowager Countess of, 182n

Clanbrassil, Lady Alice, Countess of, 182n

Clark, Mr.: writes from Buda, 49; refugee from Vienna, 291; mentioned, 75, 81, 106

Clement, Prince of Bavaria, 109; candidate for Electorship of Cologne, 171; confirmed as Elector of Cologne, 236, 238; received into College of Electors, 259; mentioned, 216, 249

Colbert, Jean-Baptiste, Marquis de Torcy, 21n

Coloberat, Monsieur de, 195

Cologne, Elector of, 205, 211, 216

Colonitz, Cardinal, 247

Comedienne from Nuremberg, xix; handsome but cruel, 78; E writes French song for, 80; as much a jilt as Mrs. Barry, 186; has married an actor, 201; lodged at the Whalefish ale house, 299; attacked by Baron Sensheim, 300–302; released from prison in Nuremberg, 303; slips into Ratisbon disguised as a soldier, 303; mentioned, 72, 182

Comedy, by players from Nuremberg, 71

Commercy, Prince of, 140, 141

Congreve, William, xi

Conquest, Dr. Richard, 101n

Constantinople, xvi

Conway, Lady Ursula, 28

Cooke, John, chief clerk, 28n; Letter to, 163; Letters listed, 29, 63, 149; mentioned, 59n, 210

Cooke, Mr., of Constantinople, 71

Cooke, Sarah, 185

Coots, black and white, the, 182n

Copt Hall, 136

Corbet, Robert: gentleman gambler, 58n; E's correspondent on basset, 73; Letters to, 100–101, 113, 133, 152–153, 196–198, 231–232; Letters listed, 58, 75, 79, 99, 157, 169, 175; mentioned, 274

Cornbury, Viscount Edward: deserts James II, 259

Cotton, Sir John, 174n

Covent Garden, news from, 277

Crafts, Mr., 98

Cramprich, Monsieur, 219. See also Kramprich

Crécy, Countess of: plays six-penny ombre, xix; rejects E's love, 298; mentioned, 134, 147, 155, 171

Crécy, Louis Verjus, Comte de: French plenipotentiary, xix; E's first meeting with, 8; entertains without ceremony, 18, 125; requests leave in France, 20; goes to France, 122; returns to Ratisbon, 155; a *bel esprit*, but hard to please, 161; refuses to attend Great Feast, 215; ordered to leave Ratisbon, 259; said to slander E behind his back, 297; rescues E's footman, 299; Letter to, 133–134; mentioned, xx, 16, 27, 60, 61n, 73, 82, 83, 99, 102, 151, 171, 193, 231n, 260, 270, 281, 293

Créqui, Marquis de, 151, 152

Croissy, Monsieur de, 143

Crown Usurped and the Prince Supposed, The, 235, 236

Crowne, John, 113

Etherege, George: grandfather of Sir George, xiv, xv, xvi, 163

Etherege, Sir George
—Letters of: manuscript sources, xi–xiii; punctuation and spelling in, xxiv; principles of selection, xxiv; dating of, xxv; calendared from Paris (1689), xxiii
—Life: birth and childhood, xiv–xv; education, xv; articled clerk to an attorney, xvi; goes to London, xvi; Gentleman of the Privy Chamber in Ordinary, xvi; secretary to ambassador to Turkey, xvii; in Paris (1671), xvii; in service of the Duchess of York, xvi; marriage and knighthood, xvii; suit against Barbone and West, xviii, 43n, 174n; his "noble laziness of the mind," 85, 103, 185; loyalty to James II, 139; illness in harsh climate, xix, 17, 31, 73, 75, 151, 152, 155, 156, 189, 203; venereal disease, 47n, 147, 296; death, xxiii
—Ratisbon: post as Resident, xi, 259; arrival at Ratisbon, 7; Hughes' account of E's way of life; 292–305; entertained without ceremony at de Crécy's xix, 125, 296; domestic arrangements, 9, 11, 196n, 280; library, 286–287; "my damnation in Germany," 113; "a very odd surfeit of Danube water," 150; amusements and recreations, xix, 101, 119, 120, 163, 167, 189, 232, 271; discovers a relish for business, xxi, 116, 131, 197; stirs up Carlingford, 251–252; deplores drinking in, 68, 92; asks Middleton to aid Abbot Fleming, 109; hostility of German ministers, xx, 17, 83, 88, 115, 124, 250, 253, 297–298; failure of security in Wynne's office, 222–223; deflates Co-Commissioner Seiler, 231n; takes revenge on Countess Windischgrätz, 130; explains English law, 256; the Great Feast, 214–216, 279–285; love affairs, xix, 92, 94–96, 113, 155, 167, 201, 299–300, 303; financial problems, 54, 230, 261;

income and expenses, 65, 86, 97, 127, 209, 211, 273, 288–291; abandons post at, xxii, 261, 264, 265, 266
—Writings: *The Comical Revenge,* xvi; *She Wou'd if She Cou'd,* xvi; *The Man of Mode,* xi, xvi, xvii, 120n, 269, 272n; *A Relation of the Great Feast,* 279–285
—Personal traits: admits being a fop at heart, 170; said to rise after noon, 296; justifies his nickname, Easy Etherege, xxi; cultivates young people, 157; a plain dealing man without artifice, 233; banishes age from his thoughts, 111; said to break windows and beat passers-by, 294; loves the rustling of petticoats, 200–201; preferred his pleasure to his profit, 206; views on religion, 147, 168, 185, 228; report of conversion to Catholicism, xxiii; fondness for gambling, xviii, 86, 101, 197, 293, 294; has given up gambling, 12, 153, 207

Etherege, Lady Mary: Sir George's wife, xvii; E dissipates her fortune, xviii; calls E "rogue" by letter, 100; estate administered, xxiv; Letter to, 100; Letters listed, 4, 30, 36, 43, 62, 70, 82, 99, 114, 131, 142, 159, 170, 178, 183, 188, 191, 195, 209, 232, 267; mentioned, 174n, 182

Etherege, Mary (later Mrs. Newstead): E's mother, xiv

Etherege, Richard (E's brother): Letters listed, 66, 164, 183, 203

Evelyn, John, 136n

Fagel, Caspar, 180n, 190, 222, 239

Fairefax, Mrs., 275

Falstaff, 157

Feast honoring the Prince of Wales, 279–285

Ferguson, Robert, 177, 204, 274

Feuquières, Isaac de Pas, Marquis of, 191n

Fitzjames, James, 42n (*See also* Berwick, Duke of): unharmed at Buda,

315

51; sends courier to King James, 57; arrives in Ratisbon, 73; leaves for Buda, 83; Letters to, 107–108, 112; Letter listed, 48; mentioned, 44, 63, 72, 88, 105, 108

Fleming, Placid: Abbot of Benedictines at Ratisbon, xxn; E requests favor for, 115; in England, 152; to share new books with E, 189; celebrating Prince of Wales' birth, 212, 279; Letters listed, 170, 267; mentioned, 8, 98, 109, 123, 173, 216

Forbes, Mr., 49, 53, 56

Forde, Lord Grey of Wark, 7

Fort, French on the Moselle, 150

Fourcade, Florent, 47n, 308n; Letter listed, 47

Fox, Mrs., 182

Fox, Sir Stephen, 85

Fragmorton, Mrs., 275

France, King of: offers military aid, 235

Frazier, Mrs. Cary, 275

French song, 80

Fucadius. *See* Fourcade, Florent

Fuchs, Monsieur, 161

Fünfkirchen, surrender of, 65

Fürstenberg, Cardinal William Egon von: candidate for Electorship of Cologne, 171; chooses to stand for election to College, 208; mentioned, 215, 216

Fürstenberg, Count Ferdinand: nephew of the Cardinal, 208

Gennes, Monsieur de: Letters to, 129–130, 146–147

Germain, John: Letter to, 10; affair with Duchess of Norfolk, 11n, 269n

Godfrey, Captain Charles, 122n, 179n, 229

Godolphin, Sidney, Earl of: Commissioner of the Treasury, 85n; Letter to, 84–85; Letter listed, 142; mentioned, 102, 107, 120, 203

Goertz, Monsieur, 218, 220

Gombo, Monsieur de: French diplomat, 143

Goodman, Cardell, 277n

Gosnold, George, attorney: E clerk to, xvi

Grafton, Duke of, 171n

Grafton, Lady Isabella, 170

Graham, Sir Fergus, 265

Graham, James, Privy Purse: Letters listed, 76, 164

Grand Signor (Sultan of Turkey), 3, 4, 171

Grand Vizier, 152, 154

Gravel, Monsieur, 191

Green Ribbon Club, 76n, 122n

Griffith, Mr.: Letters listed, 256, 258

Guy, Henry: Secretary to Lords of the Treasury, 45n; contributes to chapel at Tunbridge Wells, 59n; Letters to, 80–81, 106–107, 120, 138–139, 157, 166–167, 199–200, 213; Letters listed, 45, 62, 65, 86, 240, 261; mentioned, 121, 200, 242, 288

Gwyn, Nell, 25, 214n

Gwynne, Sir Roland: Letter listed, 131

Hamilton, Lord Charles: Letter listed, 131; mentioned, 123, 151

Hammermeyer, Dr. Ludwig, xixn, xx

Harbord, William: fanatical enemy of Catholicism, 48n, 49, 248; Letters listed, 41, 48

Hartford, Manor of: suit for, 76n

Harvard letterbooks, xii, 13

Harvey, Sir Daniel: Ambassador to Turkey, xvi, 3, 5

Hellevoetsluys, Holland, 247

Henrietta Maria, Queen of England, xiv

Herbert, Arthur, admiral, 108; commands invasion fleet, 253

Herbert, William, 31n

Hesse and Cassell, Landgrave of, 218, 220, 234

Heywood, John: *The Fair Maid of the West,* 72n

Hind and the Panther Transversed, The, 138n

Hoffman, Madame, story of, 93–96

Hoffman, Monsieur: wine merchant of Ratisbon, 93

Hohenzollern, Prince of, xix, 266

Holsemius, Monsieur: deputy for Cologne, 215, 249

Holstein-Gottorp, Christian Albert, Duke of, xxi, 46n

Holy Roman Empire: Diet of, at Ratisbon, xi, xxi

Hop, Cornelis, 252n, 256, 266

Horace: odes and epodes quoted, 120, 164, 213, 241, 282n

Howard, Mary (Moll), 276n

Howard, Philip, Cardinal of Norfolk, 110, 236

Howard, Lord Thomas, 108

Hughes, Hugo: E's secretary, xii; a Puritan Whig, in league against E, xiii, 44n, 223n; accuses E of drunken brawls, xx; first meeting with E, 47n, 308; Dr. Wynne's "brother," 117; devised Latin quotations, 283n; sequesters E's money from England, 284, 305; *An account of Sir G's life and manner of living*, 292–305, Latin letter to the Magistrates, 305–308; mentioned, 42n, 48n, 84n, 162, 178, 180, 188, 190, 191, 194, 203, 204, 272, 292n

Hughes, Margaret: mistress to Prince Rupert, 118, 162

Humières, Marshall d', 235

Hungary, King of, 195

Hunsdon, Robert Carey, Baron, 108

Huygens, Constantin, 122n

Iago, 269

Ibrahim Pasha, Kaimakam of Constantinople, 5

James II, King of England: Whig threat against, xxii; E's loyalty to, xxii; 139, 244, 247, 251, 260, 264, 266; takes refuge in France, xxii; invasion of Ireland, xxiii; court in exile, 173; orders return of British soldiers in Holland, 180n; Declaration of Indulgence, 206, 241; conspiracy to kidnap, 261n; safe arrival in Paris, 266; mentioned, 87, 144, 204, 235, 255

Jephson, William: Whig friend of E, 122n; Rose Tavern Club, 179n; Letters to, 185–186, 200–201, 227–229; Letters listed, 267; mentioned, 45n, 76n

Jermyn, Henry. *See* Dover, Earl of

Johnson, Mrs., actress, 72, 182

Jonson, Ben: *Epicoene*, 107n; *The Alchemist*, 219n

Joseph, Archduke: coronation of, 145, 159, 164

Julian, Robert, 182

Kaimakam (Chimacam), 6n

Kaiserslautern, captured by French, 239

Kaunitz, Domenic Andrew, Count of, 40n; envoy to England, 60, 76; reports malicious letters about E, 114; member of Emperor's secret council, 154; Order of the Golden Fleece, 158; mentioned, 102, 106, 116, 133, 171, 208, 209, 218, 220, 238

Kaunitz, Countess of: affair in Munich, 40, 78n

Kempten, Abbot of, 223

Ketch, Jack, 248n

Killigrew, Thomas, 269

Kingston, Lord, 232

Kinnoul, George Hay, Earl of, 128; death at Mohács, 145, 148

Kramprich von Kronenfeld, Daniel, 221n

La Chaise, Père, 190

La Haye, Monsieur de, 151

Lady in the Garret, 278

Lamberg, Leopold Joseph, Count of, 35n; E cultivates, 84; civilities from, 108; requests a good English gelding, 114; refuses to help E, 247; snubs E, 297; mentioned, 44, 87, 97, 115, 116, 195, 214, 257, 301, 302

Lane, Mr. (Lord Carlingford's secretary): letter to, 253–254; Letter omitted, 256; Letter listed, 255; mentioned, 265, 266

Lavardin, Marquis of, 177, 183, 185

League of Augsburg, War of the, xxi, 61n

Lee, Anthony, 201

Lee, Edward Henry, Earl of Lichfield, 118

Lee, F. H., xv

Lee, Nathaniel, 135, 277n

Le Febure, Monsieur: Letter to, 61; scandalous life at E's house, 295–296

Leigh, Anthony, harlequin, 201

Leill, Count de, 37

Lengenberg, Mr.: Letter listed, 43

Leopold I, Emperor of the Holy Roman Empire, 8 and *passim;* does nothing to check the French, 243

Leslie, Count Jacob, 30n; Letter listed, 30; mentioned, 35, 37

Leslie, William, 30n

Leti, Gregorio, 231n

L'Eveque, Mr., 130

Lichfield, Edward Henry Lee, Earl of, 119n

Limerick, Earl of, 125n

Lobkowitz, Count Wenzel, 212

Longinus, 166

Lord William's Grammar School, Thame, xv

Lorraine, Charles, Duke of, 21; Letter omitted, 162; at siege of Buda, 49; demands surrender of Buda, 50; tries to destroy bridge at Esseck, 59; mentioned, 31, 37, 41, 142n, 143, 156, 180, 194, 196, 198, 203, 210

Louis XI, King of France: surgery on, 77, 139n

Lucian: *Hermotimus,* 185

Lucullus, Lucius, 85, 86n

Lumley, Richard Baron: E owes ten guineas to, 121; mentioned, 275, 277n

Lunenberg, Prince of, 234

Luttrell, Narcissus: reports E's death, xxiii

Mackarel, Betty, 61n

Maevius: enemy of Horace, 241n

Maidenhead: seat of Etherege family, xiv

Mainz, Deputy of, 12, 13

Mammon, Sir Epicure, 218

Manlove, Mr., Etherege's attorney: Letters listed, 43, 59, 82, 147, 149, 162, 169, 176, 180, 189, 204, 213, 225, 243

Mantua, Duke of, 143

Marlowe, *Dr. Faustus,* 100n

Martin, Geoffrey, xiv

Martins, Mr. (Treasury Office): Letters listed, 209, 247, 260, 267, 310

Marvell, Andrew, xvii

Mary of Modena, Duchess of York: Etherege in service of, xvi; at Bath, 145 and *passim*

Mary of Modena, Queen, xxiii, 210, 265, 283

Mary, Princess of Orange, 204, 219, 225

Marylebone Gardens, 113n

Maule, Thomas, friend of Etherege, 40n; fortune smiles on, 153; Gentleman of the Prince's Bedchamber, 169; seems to have forgotten E, 231; Letters to, 99–100, 169–170; Letters listed, 40, 79, 98, 142; Letter from, 274–275; mentioned, 58n, 100, 113, 133

Mazarin, Duchess: presides over gambling salon, xviii, xix, 73n, 207n

McHattie, James, xx

Mecklenburg, Duke of, 29, 148

Meggs, Mrs. Mary, 25

Melfort, John Drummond, Earl of, 173n

Mercy, Count Peter, 36n, 56

Merry, Elizabeth (Etherege's sister), 38n; Letters listed, 38, 59, 64, 76, 87, 111, 112, 137, 142, 147, 158, 164, 178, 191, 193, 195, 213, 233, 256, 267

Merry, Squire Thomas, 76n

Middleton, Charles, 2nd Earl of, xiin; former envoy to Vienna, 231n; made Principal Secretary of State, 254n; replaces Sunderland, 258n;

Nostitz, Countess of, 17
Nott, Mrs., 275
Numps (The Earl of Mulgrave), 28
Nuremberg: company of players from, 70; put under contribution by the French, 244; E frightens the Council into freeing the comedienne, 302, 303

Oesterlin, Monsieur: a moneylender, 162, 211, 237, 263, 267, 288
Ogle, Mrs., 275
Old stlyle in dates, xxv
Oldys, William: *Biographia Britannica*, xiv; conjecture on E's foreign travel, xv
Orleans, Duchess of, 28, 61n
Ossory, Thomas Butler, Earl of, 190, 275n
Ovid: dejected at Pontus, 163; Julia, mistaken for the comedienne, 164n
Oxford, Bishop of, 190

Pack, Captain, 101n, 275
Paisible, James, 118
Palatine, Elector, 216, 239
Pálffy, General Johann Karl, 48n; killed at Esseck, 134
Parenzie, Mr.: Letters listed, 62, 64
Paris: E's departure for (1689), xxii
Parker, Sir Robert, 186
Passau, Bishop of: nominally Principal Commissioner, xviii; described, 13, 61; to leave Ratisbon, 30; feast for capture of Buda, 64; incapacity of, 117, 121, 124; mentioned, 8, 12, 15, 20, 132, 297
Pepys, Samuel, xvi, 104n
Percival, Susanna, 186
Peterborough, Henry Mordaunt, 2nd Earl of, 60, 61n, 72n
Peterwaradin, Hungary, 152, 214n
Petit, Daniel, 54n, 98; causes misunderstanding with Skelton, 117; E reconciled to, 126; Letter listed, 54
Petre, Father (confessor to James II), 136n, 190

Petronius, 93
Peyton, Sir Robert, 89, 273; rescued by mob in Amsterdam, 90n
Philippsburg: besieged by the French, 239
Pinto, Fernão Mendes, 271
Poland, Prince of, 224
Poley, Edmund: former Resident at Ratisbon, 11, 91; Letter to, 170–171; Letter omitted, 146; Letter listed, 137
Pötting, Sebastian von (Bishop of Passau), 9n
Powis, William Herbert, Earl of, 31n, 109n
Powney, Mary: maiden name of E's mother, xiv. *See* Etherege, Mary Powney; Newstead, Mrs.
Powney, Richard, xiv
Preston, Richard Graham, Viscount: new Secretary of State, 254n; Letters to, 254, 255, 256–258, 259–260, 262–263, 264–265
Preston, Sir Thomas, 31n
Puffendorf, Esaias, 192, 207, 255; Letter listed, 267
Pulleyn, Robert, 174n
Purpurat, Monsieur: Letter to, 26; Letters listed, 30, 81; said to have cheated E, 293

Radziwill, Princess of, 224
Ragotzi. *See* Rákóczy
Rákóczy, Princess Helen of, 15; besieged in fortress at Munkács, 19; mentioned, 30
Ratisbon (Regensburg, Bavaria): Diet of the Holy Roman Empire at, xi; ministers always grave and formal, 18; heavy drinking in, 68; reservedness of the ladies, 69; mentioned, *passim*
Rebenac, François de Pas, Comte de, 191
Régale, Mlls., 105, 138
Revolter, The, 137, 138
Rhine, French fortifications on, 64, 76
Ricardi, Count di, 187

Richards, Jacob, 24, 36

Richards, Will, 64n, 179n; Letters to, 121–122, 179; Letters listed, 64, 90, 112, 134, 149, 159, 164, 169, 178, 187, 191, 193, 194, 201, 204, 209, 211, 212, 216, 223, 231, 237, 247, 260, 265, 267; mentioned, 167, 180, 186, 250, 263, 288, 310

Robson, Thomas: treasury clerk, 37n; E presses for expense money, 126; note for 12 guineas to, 127; thanks for £500, 146; neglectful of E's request for accounting, 198; needs individual bills of expense, 288; receives E's pension from Treasury, 310; Letter to, 127; Letters listed, 38, 52, 59, 64, 71, 77, 81, 91, 106, 112, 121, 132, 137, 142, 149, 162, 164, 187, 200, 209, 212, 223, 237, 242, 247, 267; mentioned, 76n, 90, 102, 121, 139, 145, 188, 191, 200, 209, 211, 232, 250, 261

Rochester, John Wilmot, Earl of: attack on the watch at Epsom, xvii, 122n; "On the Women about Town," 182; could not weather the Cape, 186; mentioned, xix, 119n

Rochester, Laurence Hyde, Earl of, 20n; Letters to, 19–20; 105–106, Letter omitted, 79; Letter listed, 46; mentioned, 106n, 277n

Roman months, 17n, 23, 28, 29, 113, 115, 125, 147

Rooth, Fr., Letter listed, 70

Rose Tavern, The: E and friends patronize, 65n, 179; The Treason Club, 179n

Rosenfeld, Sybil: edition of Etherege letters, xi, xii, xxiv

Rowley, John: borrows money from Mary Arnold, xviii

Roy, Count de, 151

Rupert, Prince, 119n, 162

Russell, Edward, 185

Russell, Admiral Edward, 186n

Russell, Lord William, 248n

Russell, William, 1st Duke of Bedford, 186n

Rycaut, Paul, 3

St. Aignan, Duke of, 272

St. Albans, Charles Beauclerk, Duke of, 214

Saint-Évremond, 93

St. Germain: exiled Court of James II, xii, xxiii

St. John, Captain, 42

Saunderson, Mary (Mrs. Betterton), 120n

Savile, Lord George, 30n, 49; Letter listed, 30

Savile, Henry, 30n, 81n, 139n

Savoy, Prince Eugene of, 140

Saxe-Lowenberg, Prince of, 156

Saxony, Elector of, 264

Sayers, Robin, 274

Scarsdale, Robert Leke, Earl of, 275

Schalemberg, Countess of, 298

Schärffenberg, Friedrich Sigmund, Graf von, 48n, 56, 57, 59

Schmettau, Wolfgang von: Minister from Brandenberg, 146; arrives in Ratisbon, 161; E likes him, 170; mentioned, 176, 215

Schnolsky. See Snoilsky

Schomberg, Frederick Herman, Count, 202n; embarked with William of Orange, 242

Schöning, Hans Adam von, 39n

Schwerin, Otto Freiherr von, 205

Scottish Catholic Archive, xxn

Sedley, Sir Charles: Bellamira, 96, 122n, 129; boast of amatory prowess, 103; witty in conversation, 121; turns to good hours and sobriety, 167, 175; mentioned, xvi, xix, 92, 201

Segedin, 24; capture of, 65

Seiler (or Seilern), Johann Friedrich von: named Co-Commissioner, 198; arrives in Ratisbon, 209; pretensions of, 230–231n; mentioned, 215

Sensheim, Baron de: Letter to, 74; attack on E's house, 292n; disguised as a footman, 301; E writes insulting letter to, 302

Sereni, Count Johann Karl, 40n

Sertorius, Quintus, 135

Seven Bishops, acquittal of, 229

cuses E of favoring the French, 124; has written letters against E, 125; tormented with kidney stone, 128; his "haughty and violent temper," 155; given Order of the Golden Fleece, 158; festivities in absence of, 183; makes scenes more diverting than new comedies, 203; betrays E's secret, 220; reconciled with E, 214; insists on farewell compliment from Diet, 205, 230; mentioned, 19, 20, 24, 35, 37, 45, 65, 83, 108, 116, 132, 146, 148, 149, 151, 171, 192, 194, 211, 217, 219, 224, 225, 280, 281, 297

Windischgrätz, Countess of, 60; cranes her neck to spy on E, 130; hires bullies to ambush E, 295

Windischgrätz, Mlle., 130

Wine, fountains of, 281, 284

Wolseley, Robert, 168

Wood, Anthony à, xv

Wood, Roger, 167

Wood, Thomas: *Juvenalis Redivivum*, xviii

Wright, Mrs., actress, 72

Württemberg, Count of, 216, 250, 266, 281

Wyche, Sir Peter, 14n; Letter to, 183; Letters listed, 40, 42, 44, 48, 56, 58, 63, 66, 77, 82, 90, 107, 116, 128, 131, 134, 142, 146, 157, 159, 165, 175, 176, 188, 192, 195, 205, 210, 216, 233, 242, 258

Wycherley, William, xi, 277

Wynne, Dr. Owen: Lord Middleton's secretary, 14n; related to Hughes, 42n; urges Hughes to become E's secretary, 308; Letters to, 36–37, 63–64, 73–74, 91, 98, 98–99, 114–115, 115–116, 117–118, 121, 126, 128, 137–138, 145–146, 148–149, 154–155, 156, 177–178, 179–180, 189–190, 191, 196, 198, 199, 211, 222–223, 233, 237–238, 245; Letters omitted, 110, 123, 128, 131, 136, 142, 159, 164, 174, 176, 183, 185, 192, 253; Letters listed, 29, 36, 40, 43, 48, 52, 54, 55, 62, 65, 66, 71, 75, 76, 77, 81, 82, 87, 90, 91, 102, 106, 108, 111, 112, 114, 119, 121, 122, 123, 131, 132, 134, 137, 140, 149, 150, 158, 159, 161, 162, 169, 171, 173, 176, 178, 180, 193, 194, 198, 202, 203, 205, 209, 210, 213, 214, 216, 229, 232, 233, 242, 250, 256, 261, 267; mentioned, 16, 24, 73, 129, 145, 209, 212, 217, 230, 232, 248

Yarburgh, Henrietta, 274, 275

Zell, Duke of, 26, 32, 37, 111

Zinzendorf, Countess of, 79, 130

Zuylestin, Monsieur, 219